Spotlight
on CAE

Francesca Mansfield and Carol Nuttall

Student's Book

HEINLE

Mexico • Singapore • Spain • United Kingdom • United States

HEINLE
CENGAGE Learning

Spotlight on CAE Student's Book
Francesca Mansfield and Carol Nuttall

Publisher: Jason Mann
Development Editor: Amanda Cole
Head of Marketing: Marcin Wojtynski
Content Project Editor: Amy Smith
Manufacturing Buyer: Maeve Healy
Art Director: Natasa Arsenidou
Cover Designer: Lisa Sjukur
Text Designer: Rouli Manias
Compositor: Rouli Manias &
Sofia Ioannidou
Audio: Martin Williamson, Prolingua
Productions

ISBN 978-1-4240-1676-1 [with pin code]
ISBN 978-1-4240-6075-7 [without pin code]

Heinle, Cengage Learning EMEA
Cheriton House
North Way
Andover
Hampshire
SP10 5BE
United Kingdom

Cengage Learning is a leading provider of customised learning solutions with office locations around the globe, including Singapore, the United Kingdom, Australia, Mexico, Brazil and Japan. Locate our local office at: **international.cengage.com/region**

Cengage Learning products are represented in Canada by Nelson Education, Ltd.

Visit Heinle online at **http://elt.heinle.com**
Visit our corporate website at **www.cengage.com**

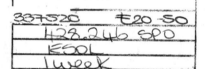
Authors' acknowledgements
Dedicated to Peter Francis Mansfield.

The authors would like to thank their families for their support and understanding.
The authors would also like to thank the Editorial team: Amanda Cole, Bryan Fletcher, Howard Middle, Heidi North, John Waterman, Karen Jamieson and Jennifer Nunan; the Production team: Amy Smith and Maeve Healy; the designer Rouli Manias; and the Recording team of Martin and Dave. Thanks are also extended to the reviewers, Sarah Jackson and Maggie Baigent; Panayiotis Ptohopoulos for his advice and comments; Kostas Kitsos for his photographic input; Nikos Magitsis, Vasilis Kapodistrias, Spiros Vampoulas, Nikolaos Dervenis, Nikos Kitsos and Miltos Kitsos for their contributions.

Printed in Singapore
1 2 3 4 5 6 7 8 9 10 – 12 11 10

Contents

	Vocabulary	Grammar	Use of English
Unit 1 **Beginnings**	• Origins and new experiences • Phrases with *starting again* • Key word: *make*	• Tenses review: past and present	• Paper 3, part 5: key word transformations
Unit 2 **A child's world**	• Childhood, education • 'Parts of the body' idioms • Phrasal verbs: *pick up* • Key word: *run*	• Passive and causative forms	• Paper 3, part 1: recognising option types in multiple-choice cloze
Unit 3 **Are you game?**	• Endurance sports • Phrases with *up and down* • Phrasal verbs with *take* • Key word: *game*	• Modal auxiliaries (1) in discussion; speculation and suggestion	• Paper 3, part 2: grammatical items
Unit 4 **Eureka!**	• Science and discovery, dinosaurs, robots, future lifestyles • Colourful language • Key word: *tell*	• Talking about the future; future time in subordinate clauses	• Paper 3, part 3: prefixes, word formation
Unit 5 **Safe and Sound?**	• Crime and punishment, DNA profiling, fire and safety precautions • Phrasal verbs with *turn* • Key word: *law*	• Verbs followed by particles; verbs followed by infinitive or *-ing*	• Paper 3, part 4: finding the right word in gapped sentences
Unit 6 **Hale and hearty**	• Healthy lifestyles, diet, nutrition, alternative medicine, expressions with food • Using idioms in speech • Key word: *life*	• Conditionals and conditional forms	• Paper 3, part 1: identifying collocations
Unit 7 **Wish you were there...**	• Travel and tourism, virtual worlds, describing places • Phrasal verbs and phrases with *look* • Key word: *road*	• Using and recognising inversion	• Paper 3, part 2: contrast and tone in the text
Unit 8 **Making our mark**	• Architecture, archaeology, adjectives for describing buildings and monuments • Phrases and phrasal verbs with *bring* • Key word: *that*	• Relative pronouns; defining and non-defining relative clauses; reduced relative clauses	• Paper 3, part 3: word building (noun groups)

Reading	Listening	Speaking	Writing
• Paper 1, part 1: reading for specific information	• Paper 4, part 3: short extracts; interpreting contexts from vocabulary	• Paper 5, part 1: talking about new experiences (social talk)	• Paper 2, part 2: planning a descriptive or narrative piece (letter)
• Paper 1, part 2: identifying connectors in gapped texts	• Paper 4, part 2: predicting information for incomplete sentences	• Paper 5, part 2: using visual prompts; expressing opinions	• Paper 2, part 2: a review, sentence development
• Paper 1, part 3: understanding attitude and tone; difficult words in a reading text	• Paper 4, part 3: understanding the speaker's attitude	• Paper 5, part 3: interaction in the Speaking Paper	• Paper 2, part 1: a formal letter; appropriate register and language
• Paper 1, part 4: scanning multiple texts for information	• Paper 4, part 4: getting the gist; doing simultaneous tasks	• Paper 5, part 4: developing discussion topics in a three-way activity	• Paper 2, part 1: a newspaper or magazine article; analysing or organising input material
• Paper 1, part 2: following a line of argument in a text	• Paper 4, part 2: sentence completion; distinguishing key information	• Paper 5, part 1: giving personal information	• Paper 2, part 2: a report
• Paper 1, part 1: text analysis; understanding written texts; analysing unknown words	• Paper 4, part 3: understanding a speaker's main points	• Paper 5, part 2: comparing pictures	• Paper 2, part 2: an essay; developing an argument; doing an essay plan
• Paper 1, part 4: interpreting the question	• Paper 4, part 4: interpreting context to identify the speaker in multiple extracts	• Paper 5, part 4: discussing possible future developments	• Paper 2, part 1: a proposal; using persuasive language
• Paper 1, part 3: understanding opinion	• Paper 4, part 1: interpreting context	• Paper 5, part 3: reaching a decision through negotiation	• Paper 2, part 2: a contribution to a larger piece; brainstorming vocabulary

	Vocabulary	Grammar	Use of English
Unit 9 **Brushstrokes and blueprints**	• Forms of art and craft, artistic opinions • Compound words • Key word: *pay*	• Changing structures for emphasis or a different meaning	• Paper 3, part 5: key word transformations
Unit 10 **The good life**	• Family life, ethical living, community • Fixed phrases • Key word: *pull*	• Direct and reported speech	• Paper 3, part 4: lexical context in gapped sentences
Unit 11 **Making ends meet**	• Credit card fraud, attitudes towards money • Idiomatic phrases with *out* and *penny* • Key word: *money*	• Modal auxiliaries (2): making plans and predictions, expressing criticism, annoyance and resignation	• Paper 3, part 1: words of similar meaning, different uses
Unit 12 **Behind the silver screen**	• Describing film and technique, Hollywood • Adverbs, intensifiers and modifiers • Key word: *quite*	• Present and past participle clauses; participles as adjectives	• Paper 3, part 2: identifying parts of speech
Unit 13 **Getting the message across**	• Sending messages, communicating ideas • Key word: *set*	• Text references *this, that, it, such, there, those*; *it/there* as introductory pronouns	• Paper 3, part 4: making educated guesses in gapped sentences
Unit 14 **Gaia's legacy**	• The Earth and its history, Gaia theory, nature, biodiversity, overpopulation • Adjectives followed by particles • Idioms from nature • Key word: *earth*	• Unreal past; the subjunctive	• Paper 3, part 3: word formation; suffixes
Unit 15 **Our global village**	• Cultures, customs, taboos, people, civilisation • Phrasal verbs and phrases with *pass* • Key word: *pass*	• Adverbial phrases; clauses of time, concession and result	• Paper 3, parts 2, 3, 5: open cloze; gapped sentences; key word transformations
Unit 16 **Endings – and new beginnings**	• Saying goodbye to a way of life, making changes, time travel • Word partners • Phrases with *end* • Key word: *end*	• Making and intensifying comparisons	• Paper 3, parts 1, 3, 5: gapped sentences, key word transformations; consolidation of things to look for in Paper 3

Reading	Listening	Speaking	Writing
• Paper 1, part 1: understanding tone and implication in a text	• Paper 4, part 3: understanding stated opinion	• Paper 5, part 3: suggesting solutions, justifying ideas	• Paper 2, part 2: competition entry; justifying choices
• Paper 1, part 2: text structure, paragraph cohesion and coherence; odd paragraphs	• Paper 4, part 4: identifying speakers; focusing on questions; note-taking	• Paper 5, part 2: organising a larger unit of discourse	• Paper 2, part 2: an information sheet; using register
• Paper 1, part 3: literary devices; interpreting literature	• Paper 4, part 2: listening for statistics, dates and figures	• Paper 5, part 4: responding to other people's ideas; disagreeing with someone else's opinion	• Paper 2, part 1: a report; being concise
• Paper 1, part 4: understanding humour, irony and sarcasm	• Paper 4, part 1: understanding purpose and function	• Paper 5, parts 3 and 4: exchanging ideas	• Paper 2, part 2: a film review; planning a review
• Paper 1, part 2: predicting information	• Paper 4, part 4: doing multiple tasks at once	• Paper 5, part 3: sustaining interaction	• Paper 2, part 2: a contribution to a longer piece
• Paper 1, part 3: matching gist to detail in multiple choice questions	• Paper 4, part 2: focused listening	• Paper 5, part 3: evaluating; making choices; thinking out loud	• Paper 2, part 1: an essay; discussing issues that surround a topic
• Paper 1, part 1: texts from different sources; purpose and main idea	• Paper 4, part 3: attitude and opinion; multiple speakers	• Paper 5, part 1: talking about your country, culture and background	• Paper 2, part 1: an article (2); using description and anecdote
• Paper 1, part 4: looking for specific information in multiple matching texts	• Paper 4, part 1: recognising agreement and disagreement in short extracts	• Paper 5, part 2: individual long turn	• Paper 2, part 2: letter of reference; checking your work

Spotlight on CAE: Introduction

Spotlight on CAE is a new preparation course for students intending to take the Cambridge ESOL Certificate in Advanced English examination. The course is based on the new Cambridge exam guidelines for December 2008 and onwards.

Approach of the book

Spotlight on CAE consists of sixteen stimulating units covering a wide range of themes that will take you from First Certificate through to an advanced level of English. For those hoping to continue with Proficiency of English it will act as an essential stepping stone. For others it is a valuable certificate in its own right.

Preparing for the exam

The student's book will help you to develop the skills you need to be successful in the exam. You will learn how to approach the exam and each paper with confidence, while building essential skills that will enable you to use the English language at an advanced level.

Exam spotlights feature

The Exam Spotlights and Spotlight on Skills boxes provide valuable information and advice on different parts of the exam, and they help you to focus on key skills and techniques that you will need to develop in order to pass the exam. Most Spotlights are 'active' which means that you are required to do something to consolidate the skills being focused on.

Language development

Each unit includes a Language Development section which focuses on important language areas such as phrasal verbs, idiomatic expressions, key words, vocabulary groups, collocations and word formation exercises.

'Key word' feature

Each unit includes a key word feature, which focuses on one common word or a word that has already appeared in the unit. This feature analyses the different uses that the specific word has, either grammatically, or lexically, or both.

Vocabulary organiser

At the end of each unit there is a Vocabulary organiser. This will help you to organise, develop and consolidate vocabulary as you learn it through the course of each unit. Ideally, each exercise should be completed alongside the tasks in the unit as you complete them.

'In other words' feature

This feature appears either in the Writing or the Speaking Papers and focuses on useful ways you can develop your vocabulary when using the English language actively (that is, when speaking or writing).

Phrasal verbs and expressions

Each unit focuses either on phrasal verbs or idiomatic expressions or both. In order to pass the CAE exam, you'll need to be aware of a wide range of idiomatic expressions and their correct usage.

Approach to grammar

If you're taking the CAE exam you will already be familiar with the main areas of English grammar covered up to FCE level. The CAE student's book revises and consolidates what you should already know, and develops certain areas to a more advanced level.

➡ Each grammar section is linked to the Grammar Reference section on pages 169–182, which should be consulted as you do each section.

Reading

There are a wide variety of reading texts from a number of sources such as you will find in the CAE exam. As well as giving you plenty of exam practice, the topics covered in the Reading sections should create plenty of opportunities for discussion and help you develop your vocabulary and language skills.

Writing

The writing sections cover each of the writing task types that may appear in the exam and give guidelines and practice at writing for both part one and part two of the Writing Paper. This section looks in detail at how to analyse a question, brainstorm ideas, use input material where required, draw up a detailed writing plan, improve vocabulary and paragraph structure, before attempting a similar task by yourself, either during the lesson or for homework.

➡ You can also refer to the Writing Guide on pages 183–192 to see samples of model pieces for each task type and guidelines of how to approach the task, as well as additional task questions for extra practice.

Use of English

Spotlight on CAE includes an in-depth section on the Use of English Paper, with detailed guidelines and tasks to help you approach each part of the paper with confidence. Each section will also help you improve your level of English and develop further skills for reading, writing and speaking.

Listening

The listening sections throughout the student's book cover all four parts of the Listening Paper and are designed to help you develop the necessary skills required for each part. Each section also includes useful advice and tips.

Speaking

Spotlight on CAE affords innumerable opportunities to discuss the subjects and topics raised in each unit. In addition to this, there is a focused speaking section in each unit that looks at a different part of the speaking paper so that all four parts are covered. The speaking sections present useful functions and expressions which you will use in real life but which are also practised in the context of an exam-type task.

➡ The Speaking Files on pages 193–201 contain extra practice and useful expressions.

Finally, don't forget to use the *Exam Booster* workbook which provides further practice in all these areas and includes a student's listening CD which can be used by you at home.

Have fun with your course, and good luck!

Francesca and Carol

Overview of the exam

The Certificate in Advanced English examination, just like the First Certificate examination, consists of five papers, each worth an equal 40 marks of the maximum 200 marks. Grades A, B and C represent a pass grade. Grades D and E are a fail. It is not necessary to achieve a satisfactory grade in all five papers in order to receive a final passing grade.

PAPER 1 (1 HOUR 15 MINUTES)

Reading
- Four parts testing a range of reading skills
- You must answer all four parts
- There are 34 questions in total
- You receive two marks for each correct answer in parts 1, 2 and 3 and one mark for each correct answer in part 4

Part 1: Multiple choice
You have to read three short themed texts from a range of sources. Each text is followed by two multiple choice questions with four options each. Emphasis is on the understanding of detail, tone, purpose, implication, attitude and also text organisation features.

Part 2: Gapped text
Six paragraphs have been removed from a longer text and placed in a jumbled order, together with an additional paragraph. You have to choose the missing paragraph for each gap. Emphasis is on understanding how texts are structured and following text development.

Part 3: Multiple choice
A longer text followed by seven four-option multiple choice questions. Emphasis is on the understanding of a long text, including detail, opinion, tone, purpose, main idea, implication, attitude, and organisation.

Part 4: Multiple matching
A text or several short texts is preceded by 15 multiple-matching questions. Emphasis is on locating specific information, detail, opinion and attitude in texts.

SPOTLIGHT ON CAE

PAPER 1
See the following pages for Spotlights on Reading: 2, 12, 22, 32, 44, 45, 54, 55, 64, 74, 86, 96, 97, 106, 116, 128, 138, 148 and 158.

PAPER 2 (1 HOUR 30 MINUTES)

Writing
- Two parts
- You must answer both parts (a compulsory one in part 1, one from a choice of five in part 2)

Part 1: One compulsory question
You may be asked to write any of the following: an article, a letter, a proposal, a report. You must use the input material and write 180–220 words.

Part 2: One from a choice of writing tasks
You can choose one task from a choice of five questions (including the set text options). You may be asked to write any of the following: an article, a contribution to a longer piece, an essay, an information sheet, a letter, a proposal, a report, a review or a competition entry. You must write 220–260 words.

SPOTLIGHT ON CAE

PAPER 2
See the following pages for Spotlights on Writing: 8, 18, 28, 38, 39, 50, 60, 71, 80, 91, 102, 113, 122, 123, 145, 154, 164 and 165.

SPOTLIGHT ON VOCABULARY
See the following pages for Spotlights on Vocabulary: 9, 10, 22, 37, 56, 59, 81, 88, 101, 102, 111, 118, 120, 140 and 156.

GRAMMAR SPOTLIGHT
See the following pages for Spotlights on Grammar: 25, 35, 47, 69, 78, 100, 110, 120, 131, 134, 141, 143, 152 and 161.

PAPER 3 (1 HOUR)

Use of English
- There are five parts with 50 questions in total
- Parts 1, 2 and 5 test both grammar and vocabulary. Parts 3 and 4 test vocabulary
- Parts 1, 2, and 3: each correct answer receives 1 mark. Part 4: each correct answer receives 2 marks. Part 5: each answer receives up to 2 marks

Part 1: Multiple-choice cloze
A modified cloze test containing 12 gaps and followed by 12 four-option multiple choice items. You must choose the option that correctly fills the gap.

Part 2: Open cloze
A modified open cloze test containing 15 gaps. You must write one word to fill each gap.

Part 3: Word formation
You must read a text containing 10 gaps. Each gap corresponds to a word. The stems of the missing words are given beside the text.

Part 4: Gapped sentences
There are five questions, each of which contains three separate sentences. Each sentence contains one gap, which must be completed with one appropriate word.

Part 5: Key word transformations
There are eight separate questions, each with a lead-in sentence and a gapped second sentence to be completed in three to six words, including a given 'key word'.

SPOTLIGHT ON CAE

PAPER 3
See the following pages for Spotlights on Use of English: 6, 7, 17, 27, 37, 49, 67, 79, 90, 121, 132 and 162.

PAPER 4 (APPROXIMATELY 40 MINUTES)

Listening

- Four parts
- Each part contains a recorded text or texts and corresponding comprehension tasks
- Each part is heard twice
- There are 30 questions in total.

Part 1: Multiple choice
Three short extracts, from exchanges between interacting speakers. There are two four-option multiple choice questions for each extract.

Part 2: Sentence completion
A monologue with a sentence completion task which has eight items. You must complete each sentence with a word that you hear in the recording.

Part 3: Multiple choice
A longer dialogue or conversation involving interacting speakers, with six multiple choice questions.

Part 4: Multiple matching
Five short themed monologues, with 10 multiple-matching questions. There are two tasks to complete.

SPOTLIGHT ON CAE

PAPER 4

See the following pages for Spotlights on Listening: 6, 16, 26, 36, 48, 58, 68, 77, 89, 99, 109, 119, 133, 142, 151, and 163.

PAPER 5 (15 MINUTES)

Speaking

- Four parts
- There will be one interlocutor and one invigilator
- There will be two or three candidates per group
- You will be expected to respond to questions and to interact in conversational English.

Part 1: Introductory questions
A conversation between the interlocutor and each candidate (spoken questions).

Part 2: Individual long turn
An individual 'long turn' for each candidate with a brief response from the second candidate (visual and written stimuli, with spoken instructions).

Part 3: Two way conversation
A two-way conversation between the candidates (visual and written stimuli, with spoken instructions).

Part 4: Extension of discussion topics
A discussion on topics related to part 3 (spoken questions).

SPOTLIGHT ON CAE

PAPER 5

See the following pages for Spotlights on Speaking: 7, 16, 27, 36, 58, 77, 101, 121, 132 and 142.

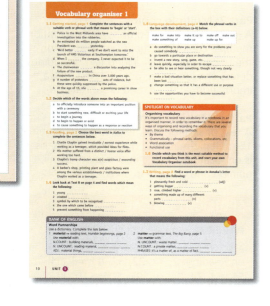

What are the differences between the old exam and the revised exam?

You're probably wondering what the differences between the old and revised exam are. There are still five papers, but overall time has been reduced in length by approximately one hour. It is now four hours and forty minutes. The new exam will also contain new and improved task types. and is designed to be more 'user-friendly'.

Revised exam	Differences
1 Paper 1: Reading 1 Themed texts (6 questions) **NEW** 2 Gapped text (6 questions) 3 Multiple choice (7 questions) 4 Multiple-matching (15 questions)	Introduction of three texts in part 1, each with two four-option multiple choice questions. A broader text range used (for example, fiction and reports are now introduced).
2 Paper 2: Writing 1 Input reduced to 150 words. (1 compulsory task) Answer reduced to 180–220 words 2 Answer to be 220–260 words (1 task from a choice of 5) Possible set texts option. **NEW**	Candidate is given less material as a writing prompt. Candidate's response is reduced from 250 words. Tasks added: 'Contributions to longer pieces', 'essays' and set texts.
3 Paper 3: Use of English 1 Multiple-choice cloze (12 questions) 2 Open cloze (15 questions) 3 Word formation (10 questions) 4 Gapped sentences (5 questions) **NEW** 5 Key word transformations (8 questions) **NEW**	In part 4, the candidate now needs to complete a gap in a set of three sentences with the same word removed. In part 5, the candidate needs to rewrite the first sentence into the second, using three to six words, including the 'key' word given. The old section, error correction, has been removed.
4 Paper 4: Listening 1 Short extracts (6 questions) **NEW** 2 Sentence completion (8 questions) 3 Multiple choice (6 questions) 4 Multiple matching (10 questions)	Introduction of three extracts of interacting speakers in part 1, each with two three-option questions. Candidates can now listen twice to all parts.
5 Paper 5: Speaking 1 Spoken questions between the interlocutor and each candidate (3 minutes) 2 Individual 'long turn' for each candidate and a brief response from the other candidate (1 minute + 30 seconds) 3 A two-way conversation between candidates with written and visual stimuli used in a decision-making task (4 minutes) **NEW** 4 A discussion on topics related to the collaborative task (4 minutes)	Candidate to candidate interaction removed from part 1 Written prompts with visuals now used in parts 2 and 3.

CAE Exam Glossary

Article: a piece of non-fictional writing, usually forming part of a magazine or newspaper. The reader is usually understood to have similar interests to the writer. The aim is to interest and connect with the reader, so there should be some opinion or comment.

Cloze test: A type of gap-filling task in which whole words have been removed from a text. Candidates must replace the missing word.

Coherence: language which is coherent is clear and planned well. All the parts and ideas should form a unified whole.

Competition entry: written for a judge or panel of judges. You're usually expected to nominate somebody for something or to put yourself forward for selection for something, such as a study grant. A competition entry will be fairly persuasive, giving reason(s) why your choice is best.

Contribution to a longer piece: written for someone who is in the middle of collecting information for use in a larger document, such as a guidebook or a piece of research. The aim is to supply information and opinion. The choice of register is likely to be influenced by the purpose of the longer document, as indicated in the exam instructions. A contribution should be clearly organised. It may also include headings.

Discourse: written or spoken communication.

Email: an electronic letter, usually less formal in language than a letter.

Essay: a structured piece of writing on a specific topic. An essay is often written for a teacher, or perhaps as a follow-up to a class activity. It should be clearly structured: with an introduction, organised development and a fitting conclusion. The main purpose of the task is to develop an argument and/or to discuss issues surrounding a certain topic. You're expected to give reasons for your opinions.

Gap-filling item: any type of item requiring the candidate to insert some written material into the spaces in the text. This material may include letters, numbers, single words, phrases, sentences or paragraphs. The response may be selected from a set of options, or supplied by the candidate.

Gist: the central theme/meaning of the text.

Information sheet: written for an audience who needs information, instruction or help in some area. You're expected to produce clear factual information, and/or advice on a topic. It needs to be clearly organised and may also include headings.

Interlocutor: the Speaking Paper examiner who conducts the test and makes an assessment of each candidate's performance.

Key word: the word which must be used in an answer to an item in Use of English Paper, part 5.

Letter: written in reply to the situation outlined in the exam question. Letters in the CAE Writing Paper need a response which is reliably suitable for the particular target reader. Exam candidates can expect to be asked to write letters to, for example, the editor of a magazine or newspaper, to the director of an international business, to a principal of a school, or to a friend.

Long turn: the section in the Speaking Paper allowing a candidate to talk uninterrupted for a period of time. They will produce an extended piece of discourse.

Multiple choice: a task where candidates are given several possible answers, with only one being correct.

Multiple matching: a task in which a number of questions or sentence completion items are set. They are generally based on a reading text. The responses are provided in the form of a word or phrase bank. Each of these responses can be used an unlimited number of times.

Options: the individual words in the set of possible answers for a multiple choice item.

Paraphrase: to use different words to convey the meaning of something.

Phrasal verb: a verb which takes on a new meaning when followed by a certain adverb or preposition.

Proposal: written for a superior work colleague or members of a committee. You're expected to make at least one suggestion, and to support this with some factual information, in order to persuade the reader of a course of action. A proposal should be clearly organised and may include headings.

Register: the tone of a piece of writing. It should be appropriate for the task and target reader.

Report: usually written for someone higher than you at work, such as a boss or a college principal. Sometimes it's also written for a peer group, like fellow members of a club. You're expected to give some factual information and make suggestions or recommendations. A report should be clearly organised and may include headings.

Review: generally written for an English-language magazine, newspaper or website. The main objective is to describe and articulate a personal opinion about something which the writer has experienced. It may, for example, be about a film, a holiday, or a product. The review needs to give the reader a clear idea about the item discussed. Description and explanation are key areas for this task. Usually, a review will include a recommendation to the reader as well.

Rubrics: the instructions to an examination question which tell the candidate what to do when answering the question.

Set text: a piece of literature chosen for study.

Short story: a piece of fiction dealing with only a few characters and incidents.

Stem word: the word at the end of each line in the Use of English Paper, part 3. This word should form the basis for the word that has to be formed.

1 Beginnings

MAIN MENU

Topics:	beginnings, new experiences, origins
Language development:	fixed phrases: *starting again;* key word: *make*
Grammar:	tenses

EXAM MENU

Reading:	specific information
Listening:	understanding contexts
Speaking:	introductions
Use of English:	transforming words
Writing:	planning a letter

Getting started

1 Work in pairs. These pictures all show the beginning of something. What do they show the beginning of? List other types of beginnings. Who can list the most in one minute?

2 **GENERAL KNOWLEDGE** Look at the quiz below and see if you can answer any of the questions.

QUIZ

1 Greenpeace was originally *established* to
 a protect Canada's wildlife.
 b protest against nuclear testing.
 c campaign for world peace.

2 The 2006 FIFA World Cup *kicked off* in
 a South Africa.
 b Japan.
 c Germany.

3 Christopher Columbus *set off* on his voyage of discovery to
 a discover a new continent.
 b find another trade.
 c prove that the world was flat.

4 SS Titanic, which sank on her maiden voyage, was *launched* in
 a 1911.
 b 1931.
 c 1951.

5 In 1994 Nelson Mandela was *inaugurated* as President of
 a South Africa.
 b Mexico.
 c India.

6 Democracy is said to have *originated* in
 a 18th century America.
 b medieval England.
 c ancient Greece.

➡ Information File 1.1, page 202

3 The following verbs and phrasal verbs can also have similar meanings but are used in different contexts. Match the words to the contexts (a–d) below the box.

activate	bring about	conceive	embark on	engender
found	generate	incite	initiate	inspire
instigate	launch into	produce	prompt	provoke
set up	set about	stimulate	spawn	trigger

a Cause something to begin or happen
b Create something
c Start doing something
d Establish something

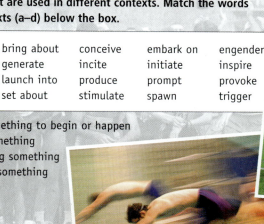

Reading: reading for specific information

1 **Discuss.** Do you know who the people in the photographs are? What do they have in common?

TEXT A

2 Read the passage and find out when Charlie Chaplin first performed on the stage and why he had to work so hard as a boy.

TEXT A

Humble Beginnings

Charlie Chaplin remains to this day one of the world's most famous and best loved comedians. However, Chaplin's background was somewhat less than auspicious. Born on April 15th, 1889, in London, to parents who were Music Hall performers, he was taught to sing and dance from the moment he could walk. He made his debut appearance on stage at the age of five when his mother became hoarse and was unable to perform. He was a resounding success, and from then on secured several engagements as a child actor. Disaster struck in 1901 when his father died of alcoholism, aged 37. Charlie's mother suffered a mental breakdown which led to her being placed in a psychiatric institution. He and his half-brother Sydney were sent to a home, and for a while, Charlie lived on the streets.

Between the ages of 12 and 14, Chaplin worked in various establishments to make ends meet, including a barbershop, a stationer's, a doctor's surgery, a glass factory and a printing plant. His experiences in these places no doubt provided him with invaluable material for the films he would eventually make. Charlie began performing in earnest, and after making a name for himself in Vaudeville, travelled to the United States, where his real career began.

SPOTLIGHT ON READING

Reading for specific information

You may be asked to find specific information in the texts you have been given in Paper 1. However, the language in the questions will probably be different from that used in the text, so it's important to be able to recognise ideas expressed in different ways.

3 **Look at the following pair of sentences about Charlie Chaplin, and decide whether they convey the same information [S] as that which appears in the text above, or different [D].**

a Charlie's first performance occurred when his mother was taken ill.   S / D

b Charlie made a living as a child actor between the ages of 12 and 14.   S / D

4 **Decide whether the following statements are true (T) or false (F).**

a Charlie Chaplin first went on stage as soon as he could walk.   T / F

b He was successful as a child actor.   T / F

c He ended up living on the streets after his mother became mentally ill.   T / F

d Charlie acted in a film about a barber shop when he was 12.   T / F

e The writer suggests that Charlie's films were inspired by the jobs he undertook as a teenager.   T / F

5 Quickly read through the text about a word that owes its very existence to the Internet. What does it have in common with Text A?

The 'birth' of a word?

Language is constantly developing in response to the changing world around us, yet when Larry Page and Sergey Brin hit upon the idea of calling their fledgling company 'Google', they could not have imagined they were also creating a new entry for the dictionary. 'Google' is a play on the word 'googol', in itself a relatively young word. Coined by Milton Sirotta in the mid-twentieth century, googol refers to the number one followed by 100 zeros. The company chose the term as its trademark to highlight its aim to organise information on the Internet.

The success of Page and Brin's search engine was so great that their form of the word, 'google', began to be used in a variety of ways. Now it has followed its predecessor into the dictionary, and the entries for it seem to be expanding fairly rapidly. Webster's *New Millennium Dictionary* gives two definitions of google as a transitive verb. *Wiktionary* goes a step further, including not only an entry for google as an intransitive verb, but also two definitions of google as a transitive verb, along with an impressive list of derived terms such as 'googledork' and 'googlicious'. 'Google', the company, has taken exception in some cases to what it calls 'inappropriate usage of its trademark', but can it really hope to curb the tide? The words are already listed, and the fair amount of 'googling' that went into researching this article proves the point!

6 Text C is about someone who decided to return to an activity she abandoned as a child. Read the text and find out why she gave it up originally.

Back to the drawing board

As a child, I loved creating pictures and would spend hour after blissful hour doodling, until some bright spark of a teacher started telling me what to draw and how to draw it. Although his intentions were honourable, he succeeded in destroying the creative fire burning within me. Frustrated by my inability to meet his demands, I did the only sensible thing a ten-year-old could do … quit.

Now, older and, I hope, less vulnerable to criticism, I've decided to make a fresh start. I'm not taking any chances, though, so I'm starting from scratch, in a Beginner's class. In the first lesson, our teacher gave each of us a blank sheet of paper and told us to look at a chair. Then she instructed us to begin at the edge of the paper and gradually shade in the space surrounding the chair. Rather than draw the object, we should focus on the space around it. The results were amazing! All of us managed to achieve a fairly distinct outline of the chair, simply by creating its 'space' on the paper! Telling us that the secret to improving one's drawing skills lay in changing the way we see things, she invited each of us to comment on what we'd just done. She refrained from commenting herself, thus dispelling any fears of rejection. I came away feeling elated. Roll on the next lesson!

7 Answer the following questions about the Text B.

a How did the founders of 'Google' feel when their name became officially accepted into the English language?

_____

_____

b Why did they call their company 'Google'?

_____

_____

c According to the text, how many different definitions have appeared in dictionaries so far? _____

8 Decide which of the following statements express the same points as Text B and underline the information that shows this.

a 'Google' is a trademark name that is derived from another word.

b 'Google' is a mathematical term that was invented by Milton Sirotta.

c The company is appalled that their trademark has entered the dictionary.

d The company disapproves of some of the ways in which their trademark is being used.

9 In the following multiple choice questions about Text C, you're given the three incorrect 'distractor' options. Decide what the correct answer should be, and write it, using your own words.

1 What reason does the writer give for abandoning art as a child?

A _____

B She felt her teacher's intention was to curb her individual style.

C Her teacher was strict and unpleasant towards her.

D She realised she could no longer draw well.

2 What was the purpose of the drawing task in the first lesson of the writer's new class?

A To learn to effectively create shadow on a page.

B _____

C To allow the students to express their feelings about their art.

D To enable the teacher to see what the students could do.

10 Discuss. What feelings do you experience when you start something new? How do these feelings differ when you return to an activity after having abandoned it?

Language development:
starting again

1 Discuss. The title of Text C in the Reading section, *Back to the drawing board*, has a double meaning. What is it? Find other phrases in the text which mean 'to start again'.

2 Complete the phrases below with the words in the box. There is one extra word.

fresh	leaf	scratch	slate	source	square

a To make a _____ start.

b To turn over a new _____.

c Back to _____ one.

d To start from _____.

e To wipe the _____ clean.

3 What similar meaning do you think the above expressions all convey?

4 **PAPER 3, PART 4** For questions 1–3 below, use one word only from the exercise above which can be used appropriately in all three sentences.

1 Gillian decided it was time to turn over a new _____ and forget her past mistakes.

Why don't you take a _____ out of Simon's book and start helping your mother?

Autumn came suddenly and the first _____ had fallen before August had even ended.

2 There was a deep red _____ on her arm, so I assumed they'd been fighting again.

The cake was a complete disaster so I decided to throw it in the bin and start from _____.

Paul's work hasn't been up to _____ lately, so we're thinking of asking him to leave.

3 Although it was a bit _____, it was a lovely day for a walk in the hills.

When Jenny moved to the city she was determined to make a _____ start.

There's nothing like the smell of _____ Brazilian coffee to wake you up in the morning.

5 The following phrases all appeared in the reading texts. Use them to complete the sentences below.

make (one's) debut	make ends meet
make a name for oneself	

1 Leonardo di Caprio _____ in the film *What's Eating Gilbert Grape* but didn't become famous until he appeared in *Romeo and Juliet*.

2 Although Roald Dahl wrote several books for adults, he _____ as a writer of children's books.

3 While she was writing her first novel, Helena worked as a waitress to _____.

Key word: *make*

6 Explain what the word *make* means in each of the sentences below.

a Everyone was yelling so much that I found it hard to make myself heard.

b 'I haven't got a clue what this question is asking us to do.' 'That makes two of us.'

c 'A small box of Nachos, please. No, make it a large one.'

d News of the flooding made the national papers.

e He made me stay in and do my homework even though I had been invited to a party.

7 Complete the following sentences using the correct form of one of the phrases in the box below.

make a go of	make do with	make it
make like	make-or-break	make the best of

1 He grabbed hold of the rock and pulled himself up. He was exhausted, but he'd finally _____!

2 She _____ she was searching for something on the ground, so the boy wouldn't notice she'd been staring at him.

3 David realised that he was in a _____ situation. Success would mean certain promotion, while failure would result in the loss of his job.

4 Jim and Sally have had their problems, but they've decided to _____ their marriage.

5 The rain spoiled their plans for a picnic, but they _____ it by playing games indoors.

6 I can't afford to buy a new car this year, so I'll have to _____ my old one.

Grammar: review of tenses (past and present)

1 Discuss. How did the universe begin or has it always existed? What do you think will happen to it in the future?

2 Read the text below. Find examples of the following tenses:

a Present simple _____
b Present perfect _____
c Past simple _____
d Present continuous _____
e Present perfect continuous _____

The ultimate beginning

Throughout history we have been searching for answers to explain how the universe began. While there have been countless theories, much of what we know is still only speculation, and most of the information we have collected is still being questioned and re-evaluated. However, through the revelations of modern science, we have been able to offer firm theories for some of the answers we once called hypotheses. True to the nature of science, a majority of these answers have only led to more intriguing and complex questions. It seems to be inherent in our search for knowledge that questions will continue to arise and maybe there will never be any definite answer.

3 Decide which of these tenses is used here to talk about ...?

a an activity that started in the past but has not yet ended
b a present state
c a finished past event
d an event that began in the past but relates to the present
e an activity happening in the present

4 Read the text at the top of the next column. Name the past tenses that have been underlined.

The expanding universe

Until Edwin Hubble (1) <u>proposed</u> that the universe (2) <u>was expanding</u>, it (3) <u>had been assumed</u> by the majority of scientists that the universe (4) <u>existed</u> in a constant state, that it (5) <u>had</u> no past or future and simply 'was'. Yet, although Hubble (6) <u>had not been trying</u> to explain the universe's beginning, his discovery would seriously challenge this notion. Hubble (7) <u>knew</u> that all the galaxies (8) <u>were moving</u> away from each other, but he (9) <u>noticed</u> that the speed they (10) <u>were travelling</u> was proportional to their distance from Earth. This could only mean one thing: the universe (11) <u>was expanding</u> and therefore in a state of flux. It clearly (12) <u>had</u> a past, a present, and it was logical to assume, a future.

➡ Grammar Reference 1.1, page 169

5 Rewrite the following sentences so that the tenses are used correctly.

a He had been looking at the stars but he wasn't finding any new planets.
b He realised that the universe was growing for 13 billion years.
c It all was starting with a big bang, according to some scientists.
d We searched for answers and we are still looking.
e The universe has been starting to expand a very long time ago.

6 What 'notion' would Hubble's discovery challenge? Why was this? Answer in your own words.

7 Read the text below. Complete each gap with the correct form of the verb in brackets. In some places more than one answer may be possible.

The Big Bang

Hubble's discovery that the universe (1) _____ (expand) lent weight to a hypothesis that (2) _____ (put forward) in 1927 by a Belgian priest Georges Lemaître. He (3) _____ (postulate) that all the matter in the universe (4) _____ (spring) from a single source, now called a 'singularity' – a point so small it (5) _____ (have no dimensions) – and that at some indefinably minuscule slither of time approximately 13.7 billion years ago, all this matter (6) _____ (explode) outwards from its source in a massive blast – so massive in fact that it (7) _____ (still/go on), and the universe (8) _____ (expand) ever since. The term 'The Big Bang' (9) _____ (coin) some time later by scientist Fred Hoyle, who, at the time (10) _____ (try) to criticise the hypothesis, but it (11) _____ (stick), and now this (12) _____ (be) the idea that most scientists seem to favour.

➡ Grammar Reference 1.1, page 169

8 In pairs. Student A: describe in your own words the process mentioned in *The Big Bang* above.
Student B: ask questions about anything you don't understand.

Listening: short extracts

1 Discuss. Do you like doing any of the activities shown in the pictures? Why or why not?

SPOTLIGHT ON LISTENING

Interpreting context from vocabulary
Certain words and phrases can be associated with specific subjects. By reading the questions carefully before you listen, you should be able to anticipate the context from the key words.

2 Look at the following list of words and expressions associated with books, cinema and the Internet and place them in the appropriate category.

animation	chapter	download	excerpt
extract	front cover	first edition	online
scene	special effects	surfing	paperback
soundtrack	print out	trailer	web page

3 You are going to hear someone reading out an advert. Before you listen, look at the questions below and underline the key words.

1 The advertisement is for
   a an arts and crafts book.
   b a design to make something.
   c a do-it-yourself kit.

2 The speaker is reading from
   a a magazine.
   b a mail order catalogue.
   c the Internet.

4 ∩ **1.1** Listen to the extract and answer the multiple choice questions above. Turn to the tapescript on page 204 and underline the key words that helped you find the answers.

5 Read the questions for the second extract below and complete the rubric in your own words.

You are going to hear _____ .
Read the questions below and then listen to the extract.
1 What is the couple's main reason for moving?
2 How does the main speaker feel about the move?

6 ∩ **1.2** Listen and see if you were correct. Now answer the questions in 5.

7 Listen again, and write down any words which describe how the main speaker feels. Turn to the tapescript on page 00 and underline these words.

8 Decide whether the following statements are true or false.

a The couple are moving to another country.   T / **F**
b The man is worried that the sheep farm may not work.   T / **F**
c The woman is used to a lot of noise.   **T** / F
d She thinks that the move will be good for them.   T / **F**

9 Read the rubric for the third extract below. Which of the words from exercise 2 in the Spotlight might you hear?

You are going to hear two people discussing plans to make a film based on a book.

10 ∩ **1.3** Listen to the extract and answer the question below.

The woman expresses concern about
a the proposed lack of special effects in the film.
b the complex nature of some of the drafted scenes.
c the film potentially being too superficial in its approach.

Use of English: key word transformations

EXAM SPOTLIGHT

PAPER 3, PART 5 **Similar meaning in transformed sentences**
In Paper 3, part 5 you have to complete the second sentence so that it has a similar meaning to the first sentence. It's important to check carefully that the meaning of the second sentence is similar to the first one.

1 Look at the two sentences below. How does the second sentence have a different meaning?
He learned to drive when he was seventeen.
been
He *has been learning to drive* since he was seventeen.

2 For each of the sentences below, decide which of the options that follows is closest in meaning. Explain why the other two don't mean the same thing.

1 I've had enough of teaching, and would like a change.
   a I've been doing quite a lot of teaching, and I need a holiday.
   b I'm tired of teaching, and would like to make a fresh start.
   c I've had a lot of experience teaching, and am looking for a new post.

2 He was doing well at work, but he suddenly decided to pack it all in and go to live on an island.
   a Although he was successful, he gave it all up and went to live on an island.
   b Due to his success, he decided to give it all up and live on an island.
   c Despite going to live on an island, he was successful.

3 PAPER 3, PART 5 For questions 1–8, complete the second sentence so that it has a similar meaning to the first sentence, using the word given. Do not change the word given. You must use between **three** and **six** words, including the word given.

1 She passed her driving test in 1995.
driving
She _____ 1995.

2 I urgently need to give Simon a message about where to meet Jane.
deliver
I have to _____ Simon about where to meet Jane.

3 Please hurry up and decide which film to watch.
mind
I wish you would _____ about which film to watch.

4 I found it quite hard to get this place at university.
easy
It has _____ get this place at university.

5 I'd been worrying about the test, but it was easy.
expected
I _____ be so easy.

6 The police suspect that he killed his wife.
of
He _____ his wife.

7 Now that he's retired, he likes to go fishing a lot.
taken
Since he retired he _____ a hobby.

8 She's taking karate lessons, and kickboxing as well.
is
Not only _____ she's also doing kickboxing.

4 Look at the checklist below and decide whether the points are true or false, based on exercise 3.

1 Both sentences should have the same meaning.　　T / F

2 Both sentences should be in the same tense.　　T / F

3 An idiom, phrasal verb or fixed phrase could replace a verb or noun.　　T / F

4 One or more words in the sentence may change form.　　T / F

5 The key word must be put into the appropriate form.　　T / F

6 Inverted sentences may not be used.　　T / F

7 An active sentence could be transformed into a passive sentence.　　T / F

8 A positive sentence cannot be transformed into a negative sentence.　　T / F

5 Match the sentences in exercise 3 to the checklist above.

Speaking: talking about new experiences

1 In pairs, describe the pictures. What do they all have in common?

2 A friend of yours has just told you the following about a new experience she has had:

> Guess what! I've taken up hang gliding! I had my first lesson this morning.

What questions would you ask her about this to gain more information?

3 Discuss. The following statements are answers to the question: 'Tell me about a new experience you have had recently'. What else could you say to expand on them?

> Last week I went to the Science Museum in London, and I found it very interesting.
> _____
> _____

> I took the First Certificate exam two months ago, and I was anxious about the Speaking Paper!
> _____
> _____

> I went to Spain on holiday this summer.
> _____
> _____

4 **PAPER 5, PART 1** Work in pairs.

Student A: You are the examiner. Ask student B to describe a significant experience that changed his/her life, and to say in what way it changed it.

Student B: Listen to the question carefully, and give a detailed answer. Use the 'In other words' box below to help you.

Student A: Make sure that student B answers your question fully.

Swap roles.

In other words

5 Match the sentences in column A below with the more detailed sentences in column B.

A
1   It was fun.
2   I felt scared.
3   I won't forget it.
4   I would do it differently.
5   It did me good.
6   I quit too easily.
7   I was given a chance.

B
a   I can still clearly remember every moment.
b   It was a long time ago but I still remember how terrified I felt.
c   If only I hadn't given up so easily.
d   If I could relive the experience, I would try to change the way I reacted.
e   Despite what happened to me I benefited in a number of ways.
f   I realised that I had been given a unique opportunity.
g   It was probably the most enjoyable experience I had ever had.

Writing: planning a descriptive or narrative piece of writing (letter)

SPOTLIGHT ON WRITING

Planning your work
Planning is always important and should take up a good part of your allotted writing time.

1 Use the five point plan below for any piece of writing you do.
Five Point Plan: Put each of the planning stages in the correct order: *writing, selecting vocabulary, brainstorming, checking, outlining.*

1 _____   2 _____   3 _____
4 _____   5 _____

2 Read the following announcement in a student magazine. What are you being asked to write? What two things are you being asked to include in it?

> We are offering readers a free holiday weekend for the best descriptive account of a new or unusual experience that you have had. Write a letter describing the experience and explaining what made it so memorable or significant.

EXAM SPOTLIGHT

PAPER 2 Descriptive or narrative writing
In Paper 2, you may be asked to write a piece that has descriptive or narrative elements, or outlines a personal experience. This could be in the form of a letter, an article, a review, a contribution to a longer piece or a competition entry. You therefore need to familiarise yourself with the structures and vocabulary relevant to describing, narrating, and explaining, and you should know how to express levels of formality. A letter to a newspaper or magazine may include a narrative element which details personal experience. If you haven't had any unusual experiences that you think are worth writing about, it doesn't mean you can't attempt the task.

3 Use your imagination to write down three ideas for an unusual experience. This is known as the 'brainstorming' stage.

 Spend no more than a few minutes on this stage.

4 ∩ **1.4** Listen to a class of students discussing their ideas. How many ideas did they think up in the brainstorming session?

5 ⌖ **1.5 Listen to the group outlining the paragraph structure. Complete the structure below that they agree on, then look at the tapescript to check your answers.**

Paragraph 1 _____

Paragraph 2 _____

Paragraph 3 _____

6 A friend of yours submitted the letter on the right to the magazine. Read it and decide what structural problems it has.

7 Write a suitable ending to Anneka's letter. Make sure you answer the second part of the question.

8 Look back at Anneka's letter and underline the words and phrases she uses to describe:

a the weather.

b the view from the air.

c the writer's feelings about the experience.

9 Don't waste time writing your letter out in rough and then copying it again neatly. But do remember to check your letter – it's your last chance to gain a few points by correcting mistakes.

Work in pairs. Look at your partner's ending to Anneka's letter and check it for mistakes.

Dear Editor,

I had always dreamed of going up in a hot-air balloon, so when I was offered the chance last year, I jumped at it. It was my mother's fiftieth birthday, and as a special treat, my dad decided to take the whole family up. I think it must have been quite expensive but it was well worth it. It was a beautiful summer's day with a fresh crisp wind blowing from the east - ideal weather for a balloon ride. Nevertheless, we wrapped up warm and equipped ourselves with hats, sunglasses, cameras and binoculars. I had expected to be frightened but as the balloon rose gently into the air I was amazed at how safe I felt. We could see the airfield getting smaller and the horizon expanding as we ascended over the nearby village. It was amazing to see how quickly it started to look like a toy town. Before long, everything below was just a patchwork of fields and roads. We were floating effortlessly in a blue sky with only the sound of the wind buffeting round the balloon itself. It was breathtaking. We each took turns regulating the amount of hot air needed to keep us at just the right height until it was time to begin our descent. Naturally, we were reluctant to return to earth.

Yours faithfully,

Anneka Johansson

---

10 Read the following writing question.

PAPER 2, PART 2

We are offering three months' free subscription to our magazine to the reader that sends in the best account of an important turning point in their life. This will be published in a special supplement entitled 'A Fresh Start'. Write a letter and tell us how you turned your life around and what made it happen.

Write your letter. Use between 220–260 words. Make sure you follow all the planning stages.

Vocabulary organiser 1

1.1 Getting started, page 1 Complete the sentences with a suitable verb or phrasal verb that means to 'begin' or 'start'.

a Police in the West Midlands area have _____ an official investigation into the robberies.

b An estimated six million people watched as the new President was _____ yesterday.

c 'We'd better _____ early if we don't want to miss the launch of HMS Victorious at Southampton tomorrow.'

d When I _____ the company, I never expected it to be so successful.

e The chairwoman _____ a discussion into analysing the failure of the new product.

f Acupuncture _____ in China over 3,000 years ago.

g A number of protestors _____ acts of violence, but these were quickly suppressed by the police.

h At the age of 15, she _____ a promising career in show business.

1.2 Decide which of the words above mean the following:

a to officially introduce someone into an important position with a ceremony

b to start something new, difficult or exciting your life

c to begin a journey

d to begin to happen or exist

e to cause something to happen as a response or reaction

1.3 Reading, page 2 Choose the best word in *italics* to complete the sentences below.

1 Charlie Chaplin gained *invaluable / earnest* experience while working as a teenager, which provided ideas for films.

2 His mother suffered from a *distinct / hoarse* voice after working too hard.

3 Chaplin's tramp character was a(n) *auspicious / resounding* success.

4 A barber's shop, printing plant and glass factory were among the various *establishments / institutions* where Chaplin worked as a teenager.

1.4 Look back at Text B on page 3 and find words which mean the following:

1 young _____

2 created _____

3 symbol by which to be recognised _____

4 the one which came before _____

5 prevent something from happening _____

1.5 Language development, page 4 Match the phrasal verbs in the box with their definitions (a–h) below.

make for	make into	make it up to	make off	make out
make something of		make up		make up for

a do something to show you are sorry for the problems you caused somebody _____

b go towards a particular place or destination _____

c invent a new story, song, game, etc. _____

d leave quickly, especially in order to escape _____

e be able to see or hear something, though not very clearly _____

f make a bad situation better, or replace something that has been lost _____

g change something so that it has a different use or purpose _____

h use the opportunities you have to become successful _____

SPOTLIGHT ON VOCABULARY

Organising vocabulary

It's important to record new vocabulary in a notebook in an organised manner, in order to remember it. There are several ways of organising and recording the vocabulary that you learn. Discuss the following methods:

- By theme
- Grammatically – phrasal verbs, idioms, collocations, etc.
- Word association
- Functional use

1.6 Decide which you think is the most suitable method to record vocabulary from this unit, and start your own Vocabulary organiser notebook.

1.7 Writing, page 8 Find a word or phrase in Anneka's letter that means the following:

1 pleasantly fresh and cold _____ (adj)

2 getting bigger _____ (v)

3 rose, climbed higher _____ (v)

4 something made up of many different parts _____ (n)

5 blowing _____ (v)

BANK OF ENGLISH

Word partnerships

Use a dictionary. Complete the lists below.

1 *material* → reading text, *Humble beginnings*, page 2
Use *material* with:
N.COUNT.: building materials, _____, _____, _____
N. UNCOUNT.: reading material, _____, _____, _____
ADJ.: material things, _____, _____, _____

2 *matter* → grammar text, *The Big Bang*, page 5
Use *matter* with:
N. UNCOUNT.: waste matter, _____, _____, _____
N.COUNT.: a private matter, _____, _____, _____
PHRASES: it's a matter of, as a matter of fact, _____, _____, _____

2 A child's world

MAIN MENU

Topics:	childhood, education
Language development:	parts of the body idioms; phrasal verbs: *pick up*; key word: *run*
Grammar:	passive and causative forms

EXAM MENU

Reading:	identifying connectors
Use of English:	multiple-choice cloze
Listening:	predicting information
Speaking:	using visual prompts; expressing opinions
Writing:	a review

Getting started

1 Work in pairs. Use some of the verbs below to describe what the children are doing in the pictures on this page and the next. Which of these activities did you most like to do when you were younger?

bound	clamber	climb	heave	hop	jump
leap	march	paddle	skip	slide	stride
stroll	swing	tiptoe	wade	wander	wrestle

2 🎧 2.1 Listen to a man describing a family outing during his childhood. Tick the words from the box above that he uses.

3 Discuss. Which of the following statements do you agree with?

> Forget toys. Let children go outside and play in the garden, with nothing but their imagination to guide them!

> Children are given too many toys that they never play with. Books are more important.

> Toys are important educational tools for the pre-school child.

> Carefully chosen toys can help a child develop.

Reading: gapped texts

1 Read the headline below and predict the subject of the text that follows.

> ### 'Pioneer nursery stays outdoors – in all weathers
> Enthusiastic parents see kindergarten as antidote to sedentary lifestyle.'

2 In pairs. Read the two paragraphs that follow. The middle paragraph is missing. What information would you expect it to contain?

> Freddie and Alastair clambered around their childminder's garden snugly dressed in their unofficial uniform: chest-high waterproof trousers, rainbow braces, thick jumpers and welly boots. Blond and ruddy, the pair, aged two and three, earnestly heaved stones about and wrestled with a wooden wheelbarrow before bounding off for their daily session on the open-air trampoline.

> Their childminder, Cathy Bache, is planning to open Britain's first outdoors nursery, a lottery-funded kindergarten where the children will be taught and entertained in a wood. All day, every day. Whatever the weather.

SPOTLIGHT ON READING

Identifying connectors
Look closely at the paragraphs both before and after the gap. There are several factors that could link them to the missing paragraph.

3 Find the following in the first paragraph:
  a the names of two boys
  b a noun that refers to them
  c another person

4 Find the following in the second paragraph:
  a the name of a person
  b a possessive pronoun referring to the boys
  c a plural noun referring to the boys
  d two synonymous words that refer to a place where the children are

5 Discuss. What common themes do the two paragraphs share?

6 Read the three paragraphs below and decide which would best fit between the two paragraphs in exercise 2. Explain your reasons.

Option A
Their unusual uniform was chosen by the local education authority for being the most practical solution in these circumstances. The boys seem to like it and so there are plans to market it and have it in the shops by the time school starts in September.

Option B
These two boys, wrapped up like seafarers against the squally autumn weather that often drenches their corner of north-east Fife, are about to be pioneers in a nursery education experiment. And it is a project that could make many urban parents fearful.

Option C
Both boys felt cold and irritable and had demonstrated a marked disinclination to get involved with any of the team projects, despite Cathy's intention to introduce them to the rigours of outdoor living.

7 Read the rest of the newspaper article on page 13. Six paragraphs have been removed and replaced with two headings. Choose the heading in each case (a or b) which you think would best summarise the content of the missing paragraph.

8 Decide if the questions below are true or false according to the newspaper article. Correct the false statements with reference to the text.

  a Children will go inside when the weather drops below freezing. T / F
  b Children enjoy playing outdoors all day in the rain. T / F
  c The new nursery will have much of the equipment found in an indoor nursery. T / F
  d The children will grow vegetables and look after animals. T / F
  e This kind of nursery has never existed before. T / F
  f The children will learn to identify poisonous plants. T / F
  g This kind of education may damage the children's confidence. T / F
  h It's not good for the children's health or development to stay outside all day. T / F
  i Several of the parents have expressed concern about the outdoor nursery. T / F
  j One aim of the nursery is to counter the rise in childhood obesity. T / F

Ms Bache, 46, has been given £10,000 by the lottery-based 'Awards for All' scheme to help create an open-air nursery for up to 24 children alongside Monimail Tower, a recently restored medieval tower that once formed part of a summer palace used by the ancient bishops of St Andrews.

1 a *Ms Bache wins the lottery*
   b *Monimail Tower*

When the Secret Garden nursery opens next autumn, the children will have none of the games and equipment seen in a normal suburban nursery: plastic see-saws, cushioned vinyl floors and sterilised building blocks. Their curriculum will be devoted to nature walks, rearing chickens, climbing trees, "mud play" and vegetable gardening. Their playground will be the forest, and their shelter a wattle and daub "cob" building with outdoor toilets. The children Ms Bache cares for are oblivious to the weather, she said, even sub-zero temperatures.

2 a *The children and the weather*
   b *The school curriculum*

'When it gets particularly cold we light a bonfire and play running around games. In February we were out all day in minus six and the children were perfectly happy. I thought: "If I can stay out in this, we can stay out in anything". It's us that imagine they're not going to like the weather. It's a cultural attitude, but if you're warm and dry, you don't notice.'

3 a *Scottish winters*
   b *What it is hoped the school will do for the children*

Ms Bache borrowed the idea for the Secret Garden, which will cost at least £100,000 to open, from Norway. 'It's embedded in their cultural life, being outdoors, in the same way it's embedded in ours to stay indoors,' she said. The Childcare Commission, Scotland's childcare regulator, 'think it's fantastic. They're 100% in support of what I'm doing.'

4 a *How Mrs Bache got started*
   b *Schools and attitudes in Norway*

After six months keeping the children indoors, with a few hours' play in the garden, she realised the kids thrived outdoors. So, like Alastair and Freddie, they stayed there. 'In a normal nursery you might have to learn about shapes, but these children know the difference between an oak tree and a birch tree, which is a lot more complex than a square and a circle,' she said.

5 a *A parent's view*
   b *The dangers of school illnesses*

'The risks can be exaggerated,' added Alastair's mother. 'With the best will in the world, all children will pick up things even when I'm watching them,' she said. 'But I do think they're probably too protected in a lot of environments. No one wants them to come to any harm, but they've got to learn – in as safe an environment as is possible.' The most important thing is that it is a real confidence builder. Strangely, it can be pouring with rain all day, but when they get home they don't even mention the weather.'

6 a *The children's reactions*
   b *After school activities*

9 Look again at the heading you chose for missing paragraph 1 in exercise 7. Find the paragraph from A–G below that matches it. Underline the key words in the paragraph.

10 PAPER 1, PART 2 Read the paragraphs A–G below and choose the one which fits each gap (2–6). There is one extra paragraph which you do not need to use.

A A primary school and drama teacher for 20 years, Ms Bache left teaching to run a small childminding business from her home on the edge of Letham, about 15 miles west of St Andrews.

B Katie Connolly, a graphic designer, said her sons, Freddie and Magnus, four, preferred it to their other nursery. 'There isn't much outdoor space there and they get frustrated. They talk about the things they do here a lot more, and they bring home bits of fungus or a rosehip necklace and tell me all about it.'

C When they graduate to primary school, alumni of the Secret Garden can expect to be expert in poisonous fungi and able to spot dangerous yew berries or foxgloves, the flowers that contain the toxin *digitalis*, at a hundred paces. 'They know what poisonous means, and they really do avoid it. They learn so quickly.'

D 'We've recently had two full days with seven hours of solid rain, and the kids don't bat an eyelid. As soon as it rains heavily here, there's a stream comes down the wee road outside – they build dams on it. They loved it.'

E Ms Bache looks after 17 children during the week. Their parents are enthusiastic about her approach. Kirsty Licence, 40, a doctor and Alastair's mother, believes the nursery will be an antidote to Britain's increasingly sedentary, over-protective culture. 'Childhood obesity is a big problem, and one of the things is that children spend too long inside.'

F Their sedentary lifestyle clearly was not helping with their academic progress. As the pounds went on, the marks began to decline and the children showed no enthusiasm about becoming involved in physical activities, preferring to stay in and battle it out with the TV games from the couch.

G Monimail, which sits in a sheltered dip in the hills just south of the Firth of Tay, was bought in ruins in 1985 by a group of Edinburgh psychotherapists as a therapeutic retreat. Now owned by a trust, it is home to environmentalists running a 'sustainable living' commune. Another donor, who has asked to remain anonymous, has pledged £20,000, the first big sum raised by the Secret Garden's well-connected local parents and supporters.

11 Discuss. What are your views about this kind of kindergarten? Do you think it would be successful in your country?

Language development:
'parts of the body' idioms

1 Discuss. In the first sentence of missing paragraph D in the text on page 13, there is the phrase 'the children don't bat an eyelid'. What does this phrase mean in the context?

2 Match the three 'parts of the body' idioms used in the captions below with an appropriate cartoon.

   a 'Jemma's just had a brainwave! Listen to her great idea.'

   b 'I saw Andrea in town. She really gave me the cold shoulder even though I said I was sorry!'

   c 'You look a bit down in the mouth. Have you had a bad day?'

3 Complete the sentences using idioms from the box below.

all fingers and thumbs	bat an eyelid
pain in the neck	see eye to eye
tongue in cheek	wet behind the ears

   a Bill doesn't like his new boss. They never
_____.

   b My Chemistry practical exam was a disaster! I was
_____ and spilled the liquid all
over the floor!

   c Nick's little brother is a real _____!
He wouldn't let us listen to music, and kept interrupting us
all the time!

   d I think the teacher's remark about punishing the whole class
was _____! She didn't mean it,
did she?

   e When I told William I was going to marry his sister, he
didn't _____.

   f James will make a great businessman one day but at the
moment he's completely _____.

Phrasal verbs: *pick up*

4 In the reading text on page 13, the phrasal verb 'pick up' was used. Which of the definitions below matches the context in which it was used?

   1 to get someone and go somewhere in your car

   2 to be arrested

   3 to learn a skill without much effort

   4 to catch an illness

   5 to receive or detect a signal

   6 to refer to a subject that has already been mentioned

   7 to increase or improve

   8 to get more interesting

5 Match the above definitions to the example sentences that follow.

   a They *picked* him *up* trying to leave the country. _____

   b You probably *picked* it *up* at school – there's something going round at the moment. _____

   c To begin with it was so boring I nearly fell asleep, but fortunately the second half *picked up* a bit. _____

   d I'll *pick* you *up* at seven. _____

   e Trade *picked up* slowly over the next six months. _____

   f Can I *pick up* on the point you raised earlier ... _____

   g Dogs can *pick up* sounds well beyond the range of our own hearing. _____

   h Even though Julia had only heard the song once, she managed to *pick* it *up* right away. _____

Key word: *run*

'Ms Bache left teaching to run a small childminding business.'

6 Which five things in the list below cannot 'run' or 'be run'?
Use a dictionary if necessary.

a bus	an idea	a risk
counter to someone	a business	a message
a road	for cover somewhere	a conversation
a party	a story in a newspaper	for office
the bath	an errand	a race
a temperature	politics	water

7 Match each definition below with one of the phrases above.

   a to do a task for someone

   b to go against or in opposition to something or someone

   c to publish an article / a s/

   d to become a political candidate

   e to do something that is dangerous or uncertain — a risk

Grammar: passive forms

1 The following sentences appeared in the reading text on pages 12–13. Underline the passive structures in each sentence.

'… Cathy Bache is planning to open Britain's first outdoors nursery, a lottery-funded kindergarten where the children will be taught and entertained in a wood.'

'Their curriculum will be devoted to nature walks, rearing chickens, climbing trees, "mud play" and vegetable gardening.'

2 Look at this sentence from the passage on page 13: *The risks can be exaggerated.*
Which of these sentences best represents its meaning in the context of the passage?

a People are able to exaggerate the risks.
b It is possible the risks have been exaggerated.
c The risks are sometimes exaggerated.

3 Look at the following sentences (1–4). Match them with the corresponding active sentence (a–d).

1 The outdoor curriculum will be regarded with suspicion.
2 The outdoor curriculum may/might be regarded with suspicion.
3 The outdoor curriculum can be regarded with suspicion.
4 The outdoor curriculum should be regarded with suspicion.

a People sometimes express their doubts about the outdoor curriculum.
b It is possible that people will express their doubts about the outdoor curriculum.
c It is a good idea to doubt the value of the outdoor curriculum.
d People will certainly express their doubts about the outdoor curriculum.

5 Complete the following sentences using the correct passive form.

a People consider the five year old boy to be too young to have a mobile phone.
The five year old boy _____ to have a mobile phone.

b There have been rumours that the children's playground is going to become a car park.
It _____ to become a car park.

c The public think that the laws against underage drinking are too strict.
The laws _____ too strict.

d They suspect that a nine year old boy broke into his aunt's home and stole money.
A nine year old boy _____ his aunt's home and stealing money.

e The Government has estimated a 10% increase in the number of children under 14 who smoke.
The number of children under 14 who smoke _____ by 10%.

f People say that the missing boy was a loner and didn't have many friends.
It _____ many friends.

g Police believe she went missing somewhere between the bus stop and Walvern Road.
It _____ and Walvern Road.

➡ Grammar Reference 2.1, page 170

Passive form with *have* and *get*

6 Match the two sentences below with their grammatical use.

1 We had our house painted last month. _____
2 We had the roof of our house torn off in the storm. _____

a Replacement of a passive verb when talking about an accident or misfortune.
b Causative form, when someone else does something for the speaker.

7 Some verbs cannot be changed into the passive or they require other changes to be made. Make the following sentences passive. What needs to change or be added?

My Mum lets me have friends to stay at the weekend.

_____

My Mum made me do my homework before I could go out.

_____

Listening: sentence completion

EXAM SPOTLIGHT

PAPER 4, PART 2 Predicting information
In Paper 4, part 2 you will need to write down a word or short phrase that best completes a number of sentences. By studying the sentences before you listen, you can often identify important information that will help you complete the exercise.

1 Read the following sentence. How many words can you think of that could go in the gap?

By keeping his eye on the _____, Jack is able to choose the right equipment for the task.

Without hearing the tapescript, it will not normally be possible to guess the answer as several words may be possible, but you can limit the options by following the points below:
- Read the other sentences in this part of the paper to help you focus on the theme of the extract.
- Try to visualise the speaker and the situation and imagine what information they might be giving.
- Decide what part of speech (noun, verb, adjective, etc.) and quantity (singular, plural) is required in the gap. Is the word positive or negative in meaning?

2 Read the sentences below. How many words can you think of to go in each gap?

a   Some people think my methods are not _____, but I don't let that put me off.
b   Linda is staying with Simon _____, until her roof gets fixed.
c   Scientists have been analysing the effects of _____ on the local area.

Speaking: using visual prompts

1   Discuss. Look at the first set of photographs on page 193.
- Do you think the activities shown in the photographs are suitable for young children?
- At what age do you think they should be allowed to do them?

SPOTLIGHT ON SPEAKING

Expressing opinions
In the Speaking Paper, you'll be given the chance to express your opinions. You'll need to show that you can organise your thoughts and ideas coherently. There is no right or wrong answer to the questions you will be asked, so just concentrate on getting your views across. You will need to talk for about a minute.

2   ∩ 2.3 Work in pairs. Imagine you are a student taking the Speaking Paper. Listen to an interlocutor asking questions about these pictures.

Student 1: Answer the interlocutor's questions by expressing your own opinions for approximately one minute.

Student 2: Answer the interlocutor's question by expressing your own opinions for approximately 30 seconds.

3   ∩ 2.4 PAPER 5, PART 2
Work in pairs. Look at the second set of photographs on page 193, listen to the Interlocutor and answer the questions.

3   ∩ 2.2 PAPER 4, PART 2 You will hear an anthropologist talking about the way language developed in children. Listen and complete questions 1–8.

Most meat eating animals find that it is more effective to hunt in [_____ 1]

The first languages may not have had much [_____ 2] because they lacked refinement.

Deaf children may have problems learning to speak if they have never been [_____ 3] language.

Children under [_____ 4] don't need to make much effort to learn a language.

Most young mammals can [_____ 5] their basic needs to their mother.

Children in different [_____ 6] are likely to produce different kinds of babble.

The child's [_____ 7] voluntary syllable may be a result of imitating the sounds around him.

The [_____ 8] between mother and child may have contributed to the development of language.

Use of English: multiple choice cloze

PAPER 3, PART 1 Recognising option types

In Paper 3, part 1 you may be presented with any of the following multiple choice options.

1 **Words that appear similar in meaning, but may be used in quite different contexts.**

   a   What do the following words all mean?
       A unsuspecting B unaware C unconscious D unwitting

   b   Which of the words above cannot be used in the following sentence?
       He was totally _____ of the fact that I had lied to him.

   c   Which of the above options can be used in the following sentence?
       He was an _____ accomplice to the crime.

2 **Words that appear to be similar but whose meanings are quite different.**

   a   Which of the words below can be used in the following sentence?
       His _____ of the events that occurred that night are still a little hazy.
       A conception B perception C deception D reception

   b   What do the other words all mean? Write example sentences.

3 **Words that are all similar in meaning but are used in different contexts.**

   Match each of the words below to one of the sentences that follow:

A means	B tool	C method	D aid

   1   CD ROMS can be a useful _____ to language learning.

   2   John has his own _____ for making soup.

   3   Dancing can be an important _____ of emotional expression.

   4   A dog's tail is an important _____ for communication.

4 **Words that have similar meanings but may follow a different grammatical context.**

   Which three words would fit into the sentence below? Why could the other word not be used?

A findings	B reports	C studies	D research

   _____ have shown that populations tend to increase during long spells of mild weather.

5   **PAPER 3, PART 1** For questions 1–12, read the text below and decide which answer (A, B, C or D) best fits each gap.

Children and colour

Why is it that parents are so often egocentric when it comes to matters concerning their children? Although their (1) _____ are undoubtedly altruistic, they assume that the choices they make for their offspring are the right ones. Take the (2) _____ of colour, for example. Who decides what colour trousers to buy for young Jimmy? Who chooses the colours for his bedroom or bedclothes? (3) _____, parents condition their child's (4) _____ of colour from a very early age. Choosing a pair of pink trousers for their six-year-old son (5) _____ counter to most parents' idea of how to dress a boy, and they would be (6) _____ to decorate their daughter's bedroom in brown. In a similar way, a small child seen drawing a red tree may be quietly told that trees should be green. Yet the underlying criticism (7) _____ in that can be detrimental to the child's (8) _____ of the world around them.

Psychologists believe that allowing children to choose their own colours increases their self-confidence and their ability to express themselves. They use colour as a(n) (9) _____ of helping children to identify their feelings and discuss them. For instance, (10) _____ have shown that after listening to a sad story, children tend to draw in dark brown, black or grey, whereas one with a happy ending will (11) _____ a response in yellow or orange. So, a mother should be delighted to see her four year old drawing an orange tree or a yellow house, and perhaps be concerned if the child only uses grey. (12) _____ children free rein to choose colours for themselves may help parents to understand them better.

1 A desires	B intentions	C incentives	D concerns
2 A question	B type	C theme	D view
3 A Unerringly	B Unwillingly	C Unenthusiastically	D Unwittingly
4 A conception	B perception	C consideration	D observation
5 A plays	B runs	C goes	D comes
6 A likely	B incapable	C loath	D inept
7 A inferred	B implied	C inlaid	D imbued
8 A thought	B sense	C feeling	D instinct
9 A means	B tool	C method	D aid
10 A findings	B reports	C studies	D research
11 A lead	B evoke	C invoke	D envisage
12 A Giving	B Letting	C Entrusting	D Entitling

Writing: a review

1 Read the following examination question. Underline the two things you need to include in your answer.

PAPER 2, PART 2

> Your local newspaper has invited its readers to send in a review of one of the museums in your area. You decide to write about a museum you recently visited, describing what there is to see and do there and saying whether or not you recommend it to other people and why.

Write your review (220–260 words).

2 You are a teacher. One of your students submitted the following answer to the question.
Read it and report to the rest of the class, commenting on its organisation and use of language. Does it answer the question fully?

My family and I recently visited a toy museum. They have dedicated it to a local family who were among the earliest toy makers in my country, and they have built the museum on the site of the family's factory. They made toys mainly out of wood or metal, but the [museum shows the developments in toy making, from then until now.]

The Bryant Toy Museum is a new, interactive playground for children. When we arrived, they gave us a notebook called 'My Toy Scrapbook.' The cover shows a photograph of the original factory. As we [walked around] the museum, people encouraged us to fill it with pictures, stamps and notes, if we wanted. They designed each room to look like scenes from particular periods in history. For example, they have created one room to look like a scene from a Charles Dickens novel, another from around the time of the Second World War, and then suddenly, you're in a room filled with all kinds of electronic games. [My brother and I liked this.] In every room, they encourage children to play with some of the toys, and when they come to the final room in the museum, some people show the children how to [make] their own toys, if they want.

SPOTLIGHT ON WRITING

Sentence development

For Paper 2, your sentence structures should aim to be varied. Using the passive voice enables you to:
- make your style more formal
- emphasise an action rather than the agent
- talk about an action when you do not know or care who did it

3 Look at the museum review again, and replace the green structures with a suitable passive structure. You may need to make some other changes to the sentences.

4 The conclusion is an important part of any piece of writing. Choose the most suitable concluding paragraph for the student's museum review.

a The Bryant Toy Museum is believed to be informative and inspiring. It certainly was for me.

b At the end of the tour, we showed everyone the toys we had designed, and people commented on them. It was great!

c I came away from the museum inspired by the things I had seen and learned. The Bryant Toy Museum is well worth a visit, and I would recommend it to anyone who enjoys playing, irrespective of age.

In other words

5 Make the student's review on page 18 more descriptive, by varying the language presented in brackets [ ].

Use some of the words and phrases below to help you.

exhibits   innovative
revolutionary   let their imaginations run wild
design / create / build / construct
encourage / stimulate / inspire / fire someone's imagination
stroll around / through; make one's way around; wander
amusing / fascinating / delightful / imaginative
cleverly designed / attractive / well designed
inspiration / creativity

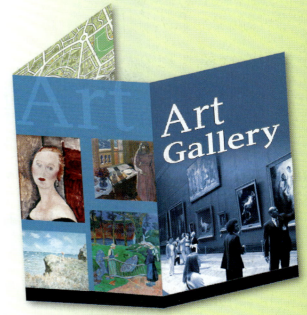

6 Imagine you are visiting one of the places shown on the right. Comment on what you see. Add to the list of words to describe your reaction to things.

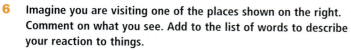

dull	mundane	_____
fascinating	nondescript	_____
imaginative	old fashioned	_____
innovative	poorly designed	_____
inspirational	well designed	_____

7 Answer the following examination question.

The local tourist board website has invited users to send in a review of a place that represents a day out for all the family in the area. You decide to write about a place that is special to you. Describe the place, say what there is to see and do there, and state why you would recommend it.

Write your review (220–260 words).

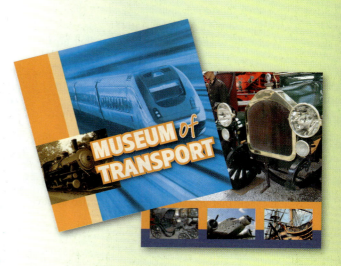

Vocabulary organiser 2

2.1 Getting started, page 11 Choose the correct word in italics.

1 The boys *waded / clambered* over the rocks on the shore.
2 The lively dog *tiptoed / bounded* up to Peter, wagging its tail in excitement.
3 'David and Paul are fighting over that toy again! They're on the floor *wrestling / heaving* with each other!'
4 Sally *paddled / waded* across the river to where her friends were waiting for her, on the other side.
5 Having stepped on a nail, Tim *hopped / skipped* round the room on one leg.
6 John sat on a plastic bag, and pushing himself along, began to *wander / slide* down the snow-covered slope.
7 The children *paddled / wrestled* at the water's edge, searching for pebbles and shells.
8 Karen *heaved / leaped* her bulging schoolbag on to her shoulder, and headed for the bus stop.

2.2 Reading, pages 12–13 Scan the reading texts for words which mean the following:

1 people who go to sea _____ (n pl)
2 wet and windy _____ (adj)
3 people who are the first to do something _____ (n pl)
4 a lack of enthusiasm to do something _____ (n)
5 unaware of the existence of something _____ (adj)
6 to grow and develop in a healthy way _____ (v)
7 a poisonous substance _____ (n)
8 without any movement or expenditure of energy _____ (adj)

2.3 Language development, page 14 Complete the sentences below with one of the body parts in the box.

foot	head	mouth	neck	shoulder

1 She really stuck her _____ out when she supported Tom, because lots of people criticised her for it.
2 I just can't say the right thing to Jake's mum. No matter what I do, I keep putting my _____ in it!
3 The government say they want to improve education, so they should put their money where their _____ is, and do something about it!
4 I can't remember the exact figure, but off the top of my _____ I'd say it was about £500.
5 Dave's got a real chip on his _____; he's always moaning about how unfair life is.

2.4 Choose which idioms can be used to mean …

a an annoying person _____
b very new and so inexperienced _____
c light-hearted and not serious _____
d in agreement with each other _____
e show that you are bothered or worried by something _____

2.5 Draw a body web in your notebook and add the idioms from exercise 2.4 to it, in addition to the idioms you learnt on page 14.

2.6 There are many other expressions with 'pick'. What do you think the following expressions mean? Use a dictionary and write example sentences of your own.

1 pick up the pieces
_____
2 pick somebody's brain
_____
3 take your pick
_____
4 pick holes in something
_____
5 pick your way
_____
6 pick-me-up
_____
7 pickpocket
_____
8 picky
_____
9 pick through
_____
10 pick over

BANK OF ENGLISH

Word partnerships

Use a dictionary. Find the difference in meaning between the words in the following groups:

1 *play* → reading text, *Pioneer nursery stays outdoors – in all weathers*, page 13
Use *play* with:
1 N UNCOUNT: fair play, foul play, horseplay, _____, _____, _____,
2 N COUNT: playboy, playmate, playwright, _____, _____, _____,
3 VERB: downplay, outplay, _____, _____, _____,
4 PHRASE: play on words, plug-and-play, _____, _____, _____,

Add the following words to the correct group above:

airplay	play act	playback
play off	play down	playtime

3

Are you game?

MAIN MENU

Topics:	endurance sports
Language development:	phrases with *up* & *down*; phrasal verbs with *take*; key word: *game*
Grammar:	modals for discussion

EXAM MENU

Reading:	attitude and tone
Listening:	recognising tone
Speaking:	suggesting solutions; justifying ideas
Use of English:	grammatical items
Writing:	appropriate register and language in letters

Getting started

1 **In pairs. These pictures all show different sports. Can you identify the type of sport in each?**

bodyboarding	cycling	hang gliding	ice skating	kite landboarding
mountaineering	paragliding	rowing	running	skiing
snorkelling	swimming	triathlon	white water rafting	yacht racing

2 🎧 **3.1 Listen to three people describing their feelings about doing some of the sports above. Circle any of the following words you hear.**

adrenalin rush	amazing	awesome	determined	exhausted	exhausting
exhilarating	fantastic	frightening	incredible	loneliness	petrified
terrifying	tiredness	reassuring	relaxed	relaxing	wild

3 Match what each speaker says with one of the activities in the photographs on this page.

4 Discuss. Tell your classmates about an experience you have had that was exhilarating, or frightening. Use some of the words mentioned in exercise 2.

5 ➡ Information File 3.1, page 202. **How game are you? Complete the questionnaire to find out how daring you are!**

Reading: multiple choice

1 Read the extract below and discuss what it would be like to be in these situations a) as the victim b) as the rescuer.

> The boy was barely hanging on, his feet dangling precariously over the rocks thirty feet below. For a moment I was unable to move, nauseated by the thought of that drop. I had to do something, but what if I wasn't up to it? What if my fear sent us both tumbling over the edge? Angrily pushing such thoughts aside, I struggled to focus on the boy. He couldn't hold on much longer. I lay down on my stomach, and edged forwards. I might be afraid, but I wasn't going to abandon another human being in need. I had no rope to help me, so I took off my belt, and threw the buckle end over to him. 'Get hold of the belt, and I might be able to pull you up!' I shouted. He turned two terrified eyes in my direction. Wrapping the other end of the belt round my wrist, and praying I could hold it, I yelled, 'Hurry, it's the only way!'
>
> He grabbed the buckle with one hand, and in the same moment, lost his grip on the branch he'd been holding on to with his other! The sudden weight of him nearly pulled me over the edge! Miraculously, a small bush broke my fall, and I managed to use it to lever myself up, and so pull the boy up to a point where my hand could grasp his. We both fell back on the grass with a thud. The wind was momentarily knocked out of me, and I just lay prostrate, devoid of all feeling but that of solid earth against my back ...

SPOTLIGHT ON READING

Understanding the writer's/narrator's attitude

Some questions require an understanding of the writer's (or their narrator's) attitude to the subject they're discussing. By this, we mean their attitude or feeling towards it.

2 **Look at the text above. How does the narrator seem to feel about the prospect of helping the boy? Underline which words and phrases helped you reach your conclusion.**

3 **Choose the best answer to the following question about the reading text above.**

The narrator hesitates before attempting to rescue the boy because he's
A worried his belt isn't strong enough to hold him.
B annoyed about being in this situation.
C overwhelmed by the thought of failing in his attempt.
D concerned the boy won't be able to hold on to the belt.

4 **Read the first paragraph of 'A Close Encounter' on page 23, and decide what *Aqua Quorum* is.**

5 **PAPER 1, PART 3 You are going to read an extract from an autobiographical account. For questions 1–7, choose the answer (A, B, C or D) which you think fits best according to the text on page 23.**

1 In what way did the writer misinterpret the distress call at first?
A He thought that it came from an Australian yacht.
B He believed the yacht in question was close by.
C He couldn't believe that anyone was in trouble.
D He didn't think it came from anyone he knew.

2 When he refers to 'one of us', we can infer that the writer is talking about
A a member of his team.
B another Australian.
C a fellow competitor.
D a fellow naval officer.

3 Why does the writer suggest he hesitated before sending his reply to Philippe?
A He couldn't decide whether to make a rescue attempt or not.
B He was afraid he would destroy his chances of winning the race.
C He needed to think about what might happen if he went.
D He needed a moment to consider the implications of his decision.

4 According to the writer, he decided to view the rescue mission as 'a fight',
A so as to dispel his fear and increase his determination to succeed.
B because he was angry about the situation in which he found himself.
C because he wanted to think of the wind and waves as enemies.
D in order to shake off his feelings of anger and fatigue.

5 As he turned the *Aqua Quorum* around, the writer was amazed by
A the boat's resistance.
B the force of the wind.
C the height of the waves.
D his feelings of anger.

6 Which of the following does the writer imply helped him face the task ahead?
A his faith in the boat
B his desire to win
C his previous military training
D his knowledge of the sea

7 Which word best describes the writer's attitude towards his rescue mission?
A horrified
B resolute
C resigned
D concerned

SPOTLIGHT ON VOCABULARY

Difficult words in a reading text

Sometimes when we read we encounter words which are technical or very specific to the topic. It doesn't matter if we don't understand every word as we can usually get a sense of meaning from the context. Sometimes it won't be necessary to understand all the words.

A Close Encounter

There was a tremendous crash and *Aqua Quorum* was knocked down again. I was thrown across the cabin as the boat groaned under the strain. Through the din I heard the satcom system bleeping away. I couldn't believe it was still able to work on what had practically become a yellow submarine. I struggled across to the chart table and called up the message. Mayday, mayday, mayday. It was a distress call being passed on by Marine Rescue and Control Centre (MRCC) Australia. The vessel in trouble was the yacht *Algimouss*. Poor sods. I wondered who they were and hoped I wouldn't be joining them. I assumed that she was somewhere near the Australian coast. I extricated a chart from the mess, plotted their position and did a double take. They were about 160 miles away. Who the hell would be daft enough to be down here? It never occurred to me that it might be one of us. The name *Algimouss* meant nothing to me as race communications had used the name of the skipper rather than the name of the boat.

The satcom bleeped again. This time the message was from Philippe Jeantot. The mayday was from one of us. *Algimouss* was Raphael Dinelli's boat and he was in trouble. Philippe asked if I could help. I took another look at the chart and realised that things were pretty bad: not only was Raphael 160 miles away from me but he was also to windward in atrocious conditions. But I had to go, I knew that. It was that simple; the decision had been made for me a long time ago by a tradition of the sea. When someone is in trouble you help.

However, I needed a minute to grasp the enormity of it. How could we make headway in this? Would *Aqua Quorum* hold together? The reality of what lay ahead grabbed at my guts. It was a cold and clammy grasp. Having made the decision I sat down to contemplate the consequences. It was only for thirty seconds, a minute – I'm not sure. I thought about what I was about to put on the line: my family, my boat, my life. In my own little world it was a profound moment that I shall never forget. To me, and I am sure it is different for everyone, if you keep chipping away at life you will eventually get to a clear and simple crossroads. I knew I had to stand by my morals and principles. Not turning back, whatever the stakes, would have been a disservice to myself, my family and the spirit of the sea. I fired off a quick fax to Philippe and expressed my doubts as to our ability to make our way back to Raphael – but I was going anyway.

I ventured on deck and the fight began. I had to think of it as a fight. I shouted at the wind and the waves, and the anger helped to strengthen my resolve. We had to gybe. Oddly it was easy and went like clockwork. I brought *Aqua Quorum* up to face the wind, feeling the full force of the hurricane, as the wind across the deck immediately increased by the twenty-five-knot speed that I had been travelling downwind. The gust put the guard-rail under and the lower spreaders touched the water. I couldn't believe the energy that was whistling past. I winched in the storm jib hard, put the helm down again and waited to see what would happen. *Aqua Quorum* was game, it was as if she knew what was at stake. The mast slowly came upright and she began to move to windward. I couldn't believe that she was making about eight knots – sometimes more – as she climbed steeply to the wild, topping crests at the apex of each huge wave, before accelerating down the fifty-foot slope on the other side and into the next trough. It wasn't quite the course I needed – eighty degrees to the wind was the best we could do – but it was a start and the wind would ease soon. It had to.

Meanwhile it screamed deafeningly through the rigging, sounding like a jet taking off, as *Aqua Quorum* gamely struggled away. It was impossible to breathe if I faced windward – the breath was sucked from my lungs – and I couldn't open my eyes.

Now that we were committed, I knew that we would do it somehow. The things I learned with the Royal Marines took over: be professional at all times, never give up and make intelligent use of everything to hand. I had asked a lot of my boats in the past, but never this much. I decided to take no prisoners. *Aqua Quorum* would do it or she would break up in the attempt; a man was out there and there could be no half measures. Night closed and we struggled on. The huge breaking seas and the waves were horrifying.

I fired off a fax to Tracey as I didn't want her to hear about all this from someone else. I made the mistake of telling her not to worry which was something I had never done before. She told me later that this was the only time during the race that she became really concerned.

Language development: phrases with *up* and *down*

1 **Discuss. The following phrase appeared in the first paragraph of the reading extract about a cliff top rescue on page 22: '... *what if I wasn't up to it ...*?' Explain what the writer means here.**

2 **In pairs. Discuss the meanings of the following sentences, and rephrase them without using *up* or *down*.**

a What *are* you *up to* nowadays? _____

b We must *get down to* some work. _____

c *It's up to you* what you do. _____

d The cancellation *is down to* Brian. _____

e *I'm down to* my last few pennies. _____

f The children *get up to* all sorts at their grandmother's house! _____

g *What's up?* _____

h *I'm feeling down* at the moment. _____

i Great! Finished that 'thank you' letter! *Five down, four to* go! _____

j That film *wasn't up to much*, was it? _____

Phrasal verbs with *take*

3 **In 'A Close Encounter' on page 23, you will find one phrasal verb with *take*: 'The things I had learned with the Royal Marines took over ...' (line 73). What does the writer mean here?**

4 **Complete the following phrasal verbs with a suitable preposition from the box below.**

after	apart	back	down	for	on	out	over	to	up

a You say you're working in the shop, and now at the restaurant as well? You've taken _____ too much.

b Have you heard? George Brown has taken _____ from Bill Coles as managing director!

c You're absolutely right. I shouldn't have said that. I take _____ everything I said against him.

d I've taken _____ a year's subscription of the National Geographic magazine.

e Sam took the DVD player _____ to see what was wrong with it, and found a piece of cheese stuck inside it!

f Your mum and mine seem to have taken _____ each other. They haven't stopped talking all afternoon!

g The lecture was really useful, and Helena took _____ a lot of notes.

h Oh! I'm terribly sorry, madam! I took you _____ a friend of mine!

i Nick really takes _____ his father. He's so like him!

j I've just taken _____ snowboarding. It's great fun!

Phrases with *take*

5 **Work in pairs. In the reading passage, the writer '*did a double take*' (line 13), and decided to '*take no prisoners*' (line 77). Choose the best explanation for these phrases below.**

a '*do a double take*' means

i look at something again in surprise

ii do something again because you doubt it

b '*take no prisoners*' means

i show no fear in the face of danger

ii fight to succeed, or die trying

Key word: *game*

6 **Match the phrases in A with their meanings in B.**

A

1 are you game?

2 fun and games

3 the name of the game

4 give the game away

5 beat somebody at their own game

6 play games with somebody

7 what's (your) game?

8 the game's up

9 game plan

10 big game

B

a someone's intended actions in order to achieve something

b used when asking somebody what their true intentions are

c used when asking somebody if they are willing to do something dangerous, new or difficult

d used to tell someone that their secret plan or activity has been discovered

e used to describe large wild animals that are hunted

f spoil a surprise or secret by letting someone know about it

g win against somebody by using the same methods as they do

h used sometimes to show disapproval of activities that are not serious

i behave in a dishonest or unfair way towards somebody to get what you want

j the most important thing in an activity or situation

7 **Use phrases from exercise 6 to complete the sentences below.**

a Right, team! Let's get to work, and remember, _____ is 'efficiency'!

b We were planning a surprise party for Mum, but Jonas _____ by asking her if his best friend could come!

c Sam, we're going to St. Moritz to do some extreme snowboarding. _____?

d OK, Kathy. _____. I know it's you making those noises, so you can stop now!

e Don't _____ me! I know you're not really my friend, so go away!

Grammar: modal auxiliaries in discussion

1 Work in pairs. What can you see in the picture above? Use the following structures to make suggestions:

It could be a …
It might be …
It must be …
It can't be …

→ Grammar Reference 3.1, page 171

2 Decide if the following statements show speculation (SP), suggestion (SU), assumption (A) or deduction (D).

a You could try phoning her to apologise. [...]
b You may find it works better if you turn up the volume. [...]
c I was wearing my glasses during the History lesson, so I must have left them in the classroom. [...]
d The phone's ringing, Mum! That will be Sarah. She said she'd call today. [...]
e He never thought she might leave him. [...]
f Mr Newton said he'd be wearing a black raincoat and hat, so that must be him over there! [...]
g It can't be Sally's husband! He's on a business trip in Spain. [...]

3 🎧 **3.2 Listen to a conversation between a man and his wife, and answer the questions below.**

a What does the man say is a possible reason for Jane's lateness?
b What assumptions does the woman make?
c What deduction does she make?

4 We use *may / might … but* when we want to refute someone else's argument or comment, or qualify someone's criticism of us. Complete the responses to the following comments. Then write whether the response refutes (R) or qualifies (Q) the comment.

a 'You don't know much about the Middle Ages!'
  'I might have studied History, but _____.' [...]
b 'You're a real chatterbox!'
  'I _____, but at least I've got something to say.' [...]

5 **PAPER 3, PART 5** For questions 1–8 below, complete the second sentence so that it has a similar meaning to the first sentence, using the word given. Do not change the word given. You must use between three and six words, including the word given.

1 I'm certain that's my umbrella, because it's got a brown mark on it.
  so
  That umbrella's got a brown mark on it, _____ mine.

2 James hasn't called. It's possible he's forgotten my birthday.
  have
  James _____, because he hasn't called.

3 I definitely didn't write that note, Lyn! That's not my handwriting!
  written
  I _____, Lyn, because that's not my handwriting!

4 Paul said he would call April to tell her he's not going to the party, and I'm sure he has.
  will
  Paul _____ her he's not going to the party, because he said he would.

5 I've definitely dropped my keys somewhere, because I remember putting them in my bag this morning.
  must
  I remember putting my keys in my bag this morning, so _____ somewhere.

6 'Has Anthea gone to Dubai yet?' 'I don't think so, because she hasn't called me to say goodbye.'
  would
  'Has Anthea gone to Dubai yet?' 'I don't think so. She _____ goodbye.'

7 It's true that I lost the match, but I played well.
  not
  I _____ the match, but I played well.

8 Although he's good with animals, he's not very comfortable with people.
  may
  He _____ animals, but he's unable to relax around people.

25

Listening: *multiple choice*

PAPER 4, PART 3 Understanding the speaker's attitude
In part 3 of the Listening Paper, it's often necessary to understand the speaker's attitude towards the subject they are talking about. This can be done by listening to the tone of their voices, and the language they use.

1 Work in pairs. Practise saying the following phrase using the various tones of voice below:
'How did you manage to do that?'

a amazed   b angry   c sarcastic   d excited

2 **3.3** Listen to four people. Choose the attitude A–E which best matches each speaker's feelings towards their subject. There is one extra option you do not need to use.

A critical
B dismissive
C frustrated
D noncommittal
E philosophical

Speaker 1: _____
Speaker 2: _____
Speaker 3: _____
Speaker 4: _____

3 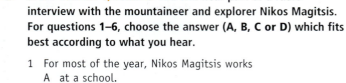 **3.4 PAPER 4, PART 3** You will hear part of a radio interview with the mountaineer and explorer Nikos Magitsis. For questions 1–6, choose the answer (A, B, C or D) which fits best according to what you hear.

1 For most of the year, Nikos Magitsis works
   A at a school.
   B for the local authority.
   C at a sports centre.
   D privately.

2 While kayaking, Nikos and his group were surprised by the sight of
   A an unusual animal.
   B a school of dolphins.
   C a sunken ship.
   D the local people.

3 According to Nikos, mountaineers
   A often misunderstand each other's intentions.
   B experience friction under extreme conditions.
   C form close bonds with the surrounding environment.
   D appreciate the importance of trust in the team.

4 Regarding the problem with frostbite on Everest, Nikos is
   A philosophical.
   B frustrated.
   C indifferent.
   D dismissive.

5 The team's first attempt to climb Carstensz Pyramid failed due to
   A mechanical problems with their helicopter.
   B disagreements with their sponsors.
   C disturbances caused by local dissidents.
   D a lack of sufficient time and funding.

6 Nikos's conquest of Carstensz Pyramid was special because it was
   A the first time a Greek had done this.
   B the second time he had climbed it.
   C a dream he had had since a child.
   D his second historic achievement for his country.

4 Discuss. Do you do any kinds of adventure sports? Why or why not?

Speaking: interactive

2 PAPER 5, PART 3 **In pairs, turn to page 194 and answer the questions.**

Use of English: open cloze

2 **Time reference words** Complete the following sentences with one suitable word. Explain your choice.

a _____ she left university, Marcia got a job in advertising.

b _____ going to university, Kevin had worked as a waiter in Rome for a year.

Secondary or relative clauses What is the missing word in the following sentences?

c Diana did not do well in the Maths test, _____ upset her.

d The party was a great success, with lots of people _____ to music from the eighties until three in the morning.

Text references Remember to think of the meaning of the whole text. One word may refer back to a previous sentence. What is the missing word in the following two examples?

e Annette is terrified of dogs. Her mother says _____ is probably because she was bitten by one at the age of five.

f Peter was terrified of heights. _____, he climbed the tree.

Prepositions and particles Complete the following sentences with a suitable preposition.

g Roberto has given up skiing to concentrate _____ his studies.

h Scientists have been conducting research _____ the potential health benefits of drinking tea.

3 PAPER 3, PART 2 **For questions 1–15, read the text below and think of the word which best fits each gap. Use only one word in each gap.**

Beyond the pain barrier

Alongside extreme sports, endurance sports are gaining in popularity.

(1) _____ its debut at the Sydney Olympic Games in 2000, the triathlon has become one of the world's fastest developing 'multi-sport' endurance challenges, with thousands of races (2) _____ held every year.

Usually, races consist (3) _____ a swimming section, followed by a cycling stretch, then culminating (4) _____ a run. The individual legs of each course may vary in distance, and events are held on different levels. For instance, the Olympic event (5) _____ a 1.5 km swim, a bike ride of 40km, with a 10km run to finish. This is (6) _____ as the 'standard course.' For those masochists who really want to push (7) _____ beyond the pain barrier, there are the Ironman long-distance triathlons, requiring competitors to swim 3.8km, cycle a gruelling 180km and then run 42 km. However, (8) _____ athletes have the stamina to endure such distances. Most (9) _____ the Olympic course more accessible.

In any typical triathlon event, competitors are separated into categories (10) _____ to age and gender. Some events (11) _____ include special categories called 'heavyweight' and 'lightweight' divisions, and shorter races are organised to allow children and teenagers to compete. The sport is popular (12) _____ all ages, but particularly 35–50 year-olds. Sociologists have suggested that (13) _____ is because of a need within this age group to break (14) _____ from the routine of their daily life, and a desire to push themselves (15) _____ the limit. Whatever the reasons, the triathlon now constitutes a major multi-sport event in many parts of the world.

Writing: a formal letter

1 **Discuss. Should schools be allowed to take students on activity holidays, or holidays abroad, or should they be restricted to day trips to museums and galleries? Explain your reasons.**

2 **Read the following question. It is the kind of question that appears in part 1 of the Writing Paper. Is it asking you to write a formal or informal letter?**

PAPER 2, PART 1

> You are a teacher. After a school skiing trip in which two teenagers were badly injured, an article appeared in your local newspaper criticising all school trips of this nature. You have decided to write a letter to the newspaper, expressing your views. Read the extract from the article below and the notes you have made on it. Then write a letter to the newspaper.

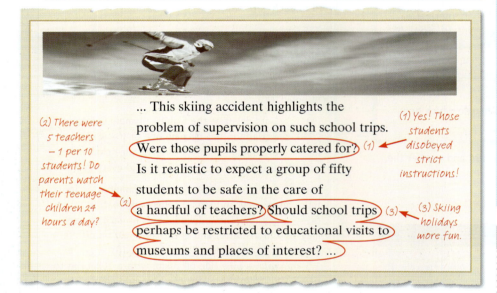

(2) There were 5 teachers – 1 per 10 students! Do parents watch their teenage children 24 hours a day?

... This skiing accident highlights the problem of supervision on such school trips. Were those pupils properly catered for? (1) Is it realistic to expect a group of fifty students to be safe in the care of (2) a handful of teachers? Should school trips (3) perhaps be restricted to educational visits to museums and places of interest? ...

(1) Yes! Those students disobeyed strict instructions!

(3) Skiing holidays more fun.

EXAM SPOTLIGHT

PAPER 2, PART 1 Writing a formal letter
In part 1 of the Writing Paper, you may be required to write a letter. It is important to read the instructions and the input material carefully and decide:

- who you are writing to
- why you are writing – to complain, request information, etc.
- what information you need to include
- what outcome you expect from your letter

3 **Work in pairs. Read the question in exercise 2 again, and make notes to cover the four points mentioned above.**

4 **Read the answer on page 29 to exercise 2. Has the writer considered the points made in the Spotlight carefully? Is the letter well organised? Is the language appropriate for the intended reader?**

5 **The writer fails to use the correct register consistently in their answer, and several phrases are rather informal. Decide which phrases are inappropriate, and use suitable phrases from the 'In other words' section on this page to improve the register of the letter. Not all of them are necessary.**

SPOTLIGHT ON WRITING

Using your own words
The writer of the letter on page 29 also 'lifts' many phrases directly from the question, and doesn't vary her language. She will lose marks for this.

6 **Using the lines provided, rewrite the following sentences in your own words.**

First, the students in question were properly catered for ...

_____

_____

There were five teachers in charge – one for every ten students ...

_____

_____

After all, do parents watch their teenage children 24 hours a day?

_____

_____

Skiing holidays give students and teachers the chance to relax together ...

_____

_____

In other words

Dear Sir/Madam,...

To whom it may concern, ...

I would like to present an account of the situation from my own point of view.

I would like to present my own account of the occurrence.

This event was unprecedented, and occurred as a result of ...

This occurrence was the first of its kind ...

Unfortunately, this kind of activity does not always interest students ...

Therefore, I feel it would be a mistake to suggest ...

I would be grateful if my letter could be published in the next issue ...

Dear Newspaper,

I read your article about the recent skiing accident, and I want to give my view of what happened.

First, the students in question were properly catered for, but disobeyed strict instructions to stay with the rest of the group. Something like this had never happened before! There were five teachers in charge – one for every ten students – so, I suppose there could have been more, but the teachers were with them the whole time. After all, do parents watch their teenage children 24 hours a day?

Your article suggests we restrict school outings to educational day trips to museums, but this is often boring. Not everyone is interested in history! Skiing holidays give students and teachers the chance to relax together, and improve relations between them.

So, I think you're wrong to suggest that such trips should be banned. Accidents like the one you mention don't happen every day. Please print my letter to show readers another view of the situation.

Yours,

7   **Discuss. The letter of response above is too short. What is missing?**

8   **PAPER 2, PART 1 Answer the following exam question.**

You **must** answer this question. Write your answer in 180–220 words in an appropriate style.

You are the physical education teacher. Recently, one of your students broke her leg during a lesson. Read the extract from a letter you received from the girl's parents below, and the notes you have made on it, and write a reply, expressing your views.

No! There was no problem with faulty equipment!

Sports training programme is carefully organised to suit students' age groups.

... We are very dissatisfied with the way the school's sports training programme is run. The equipment is not well maintained, and it is the teacher's responsibility to ensure that the safety mat is in place before each pupil attempts to use it, which did not happen on the day in question. We feel that there was insufficient supervision of the students during the Gymnastics session, resulting in our daughter being injured, ...

I had specifically told her not to get on the bar until it was!

Write your letter.

Vocabulary organiser 3

3.1 Getting started, page 21 Use the words in capitals at the end of each sentence to form a word that fits in the gap.

a The view from the top of Niagara Falls
is _____. **AWE**

b Flying in a helicopter was a _____ experience. Never again! **TERRIFY**

c His words were very _____, and I soon calmed down. **REASSURE**

d Standing at the summit after a long climb is _____. **EXHILARATED**

e I found the journey _____, and needed two days to recover from it! **EXHAUST**

3.2 Reading, page 22 Complete the sentences below with a word or phrase from the reading extract.

1 The gardener put his hand in the hole and _____ a large, fat worm.

2 'In this competition the _____ are high, as everyone is determined to win.'

3 Peter was not sure about his decision to enter the race, and the poor weather conditions did little to _____.

4 'You must be _____ to pay all that money just to see Madonna in concert!'

5 'Do you know what I had to _____ in order to marry you? My father nearly threw me out and disinherited me!'

6 'That was the worst restaurant I've ever been to! The service was _____, and the food was inedible.'

3.3 Reading, page 23 Find a word or phrase in the text which means the following:

1 noise [para 1] _____
2 message asking for help [para 1] _____
3 separated [para 1] _____
4 stupid [para 1] _____
5 terrible [para 2] _____
6 made me feel sick with fear [para 3] _____
7 place at risk [para 3] _____
8 the risks [para 3] _____
9 make me more determined [para 4] _____
10 willing to do something dangerous [para 4]
_____

3.4 Language development, page 24 Match the following definitions with one of the phrases with *up* and *down*.

1 be reduced to
2 misbehave
3 begin to concentrate on doing
4 experience slight depression
5 be not very good
6 be the fault of (someone)

3.5 List the definitions of the remaining phrases on page 24 in your notebook. Then find the definition for the phrase *'we've been having our ups and downs'* in your dictionary, and add it to your list.

3.6 Language development, page 24 Next to each of the following definitions, write the correct phrasal verb with *take*.

1 mistakenly think one person is another _____
2 regret having said something _____
3 resemble someone in your family _____
4 write something down on paper _____
5 accept responsibility _____
6 start a new activity _____
7 take control from someone else _____
8 obtain something by applying for it and paying the necessary fee _____
9 like immediately _____
10 separate something into pieces _____

Which of the definitions above can also mean:

11 return something _____
12 invite someone to go somewhere with you _____

Look in your dictionary to find more phrasal verbs with *take*.

BANK OF ENGLISH

Word partnerships: *take*

1 Which of the following phrases do not use *take*?
...it from me
...something lying down
...the bright side
...it out of you
...something as read
...a mountain out of a molehill
...the bull by the horns
...five
...your hat off to
...it or leave it
...or break it
...the wind out of somebody's sails
...no prisoners
...the hard line
...it with a pinch of salt
...kindly to

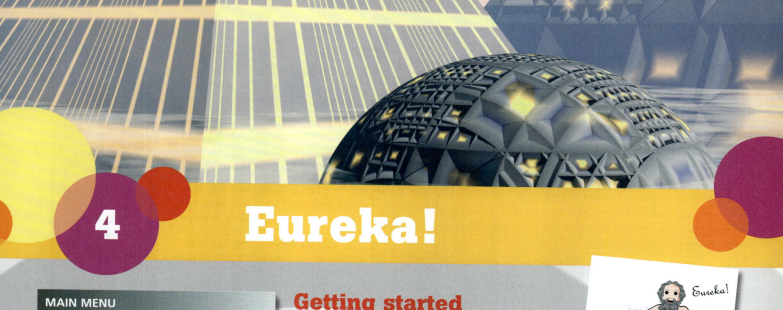

4　Eureka!

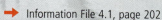

Getting started

1 Discuss. Do you know what 'Eureka' means? Where does the expression come from?

2 **GENERAL KNOWLEDGE** Work in pairs. Circle the correct answer.

1 The galaxy we live in is called the Milky Way. What is it shaped like?
  a a round ball
  b a doughnut
  c a flat spiral

2 Unlike most other fish, sharks have no
  a bones.
  b teeth.
  c gills.

3 The metal mercury is
  a the hardest known metal.
  b a liquid at room temperature.
  c highly radioactive.

4 If you were to take a lump of coal and squeeze for a long time at very high temperatures, would you end up with ...?
  a graphite
  b obsidian (a kind of volcanic glass)
  c a diamond

5 It is now believed that dinosaurs became extinct because of
  a viral diseases.
  b hunting by early humans.
  c a meteorite impact.

6 Charles Darwin began developing his theory of natural selection while voyaging on a ship named
  a *The Enterprise.*
  b *The Beagle.*
  c *The Santa Maria.*

7 An android is any robot that
  a has more than one basic function.
  b is built by other robots.
  c looks and acts like a human.

8 What is special about Sirius, the Dog Star?
  a It is the brightest star in the sky.
  b It always lies directly above the North Pole.
  c It emits staccato barking sounds which radio telescopes can detect.

→ Information File 4.1, page 202

3 Which of the photos on this page would you associate with the following categories? Some pictures may fall into more than one category.

archaeology	IT	astronomy
physics	genetics	geology
medicine	inventions	electronics
mathematics	chemistry	palaeontology
prehistory	forensic science	biology

Reading: multiple matching texts

1 **Discuss.** What functions or purposes do robots serve in today's society? What role do you think robots will perform in the future?

SPOTLIGHT ON READING

Scanning texts for information

Sometimes you have to read a number of texts to search for a particular piece of information. It's not necessary to fully understand everything you read, but it's important to be able to identify the main points.

2 Quickly scan Text A below to find ...

   a   the type of metal the robots were made of
   b   the name of the computer game designed by Steve Grand
   c   why Steve Grand was awarded an OBE

3 When scanning more than one text for a particular piece of information, it helps if you can identify the main theme of each text. Read the two book reviews, then summarise the main content of each in one sentence.

4 Read the following sentences. Decide which of the texts (**A** or **B**) each question refers to, or if it refers to both.

   a   This book seems to offer advice on building
       robots that can think.   A / B / BOTH

   b   This book seems to be about building robots
       that look like people.   A / B / BOTH

   c   This book was written by someone who has
       always been fascinated by robots.   A / B / BOTH

   d   This book is interested in understanding
       human intelligence.   A / B / BOTH

A

Growing Up With Lucy

by Steve Grand
Reviewed by Elizabeth Sourbut

Steve Grand learned about androids from comic books when he was a kid. They were built from shiny titanium and were much stronger and smarter than humans. He assumed that by the time he was an adult such machines would be commonplace. He grew up and became a programmer, designing the successful computer game *Creatures*. Years later, he was awarded an OBE for his work on artificial life. And still there were no androids – so he decided to build his own. Unfortunately, he quickly discovered that those sci-fi writers 'were glossing over a few of the snags'. Building a robot that can move around gracefully and think for itself is a lot harder than it seems.

This book seems to be about ...

_____

B

Understanding Intelligence

by Rolf Pfeifer and Christian Scheier
Reviewed by Inman Harvey

If you want to understand how a machine works, take it apart and put it back together. That's not, of course, an option for understanding the brain – you'd find yourself with nothing but a sticky mess. So why not do the next best thing: build your own simple creature, a robot, and see how that works. Surely with the power of today's computers we can put together something that has limited intelligence, and studying that might give us insight into the workings of a living brain. Unfortunately, when it comes to building mobile robots that can look after themselves, the classical artificial intelligence notion that 'brain equals computer' is a non-starter.

This book seems to be about ...

_____

5 **Discuss.** Do you know when dinosaurs disappeared from the earth? Do you know if any are still alive today? Scan the six book reviews on page 33 quickly to find the answers.

6 **PAPER 1, PART 4** You are going to read an article (on page 33) containing reviews of dinosaur books. For questions **1–15**, choose from the reviews (**A–F**). The reviews may be chosen more than once.

   In which review are the following mentioned?
   - a science that was once fashionable with the rich   1 _____
   - a book that illustrates evolutionary progress
     with artwork   2 _____
   - a book that is meant to be taken lightly   3 _____
   - the possible cause of the dinosaurs' extinction   4 _____
   - a book that is informative and visually appealing   5 _____
   - a book that conjures up a colourful portrayal
     of dinosaurs   6 _____
   - an explanation for the invention of a legendary
     creature   7 _____
   - related animals that exist in contrasting
     environments   8 _____
   - a writer who has the right credentials for the job   9 _____
   - information not strictly based on facts gleaned
     from fossils   10 _____
   - a book that details a period of time in Earth's
     history   11 _____
   - a description of dinosaurs that still exist today   12 _____
   - a place where the study of dinosaurs may
     have begun   13 _____
   - people who made an impact on a particular
     scientific field   14 _____
   - evidence that early humans shared an interest
     in fossils   15 _____

7 **In pairs.** A friend of yours is interested in dinosaurs. Which of the books on page 33 would you choose to give them as a birthday present? Explain why.

DINOSAUR BOOKS

Some recommendations of the latest books for dino fans.

 A

Dinosaurs of Italy by Cristiano Dal Sasso and **Mammals from the Age of Dinosaurs: Origins, evolution and structure** by Zofia Kielan-Jaworowska, Richard Cifelli and Zhe-Xi Luo

What is Italy famous for? Food, yes; flash cars, for some; footballers and fab fashions ... Italian dinosaurs? Italy was arguably the home of palaeontology more than 500 years ago, so it is surprising that its dinosaurs have not received too much publicity, and certainly high time the story of **Dinosaurs of Italy** is told. All is revealed in this nice little book by Cristiano Dal Sasso of the Museum of Natural History in Milan. As a legitimate member of the small international community of dinosaur experts, Dal Sasso is well placed and qualified to tell the story of the dinosaurs of Italy and their discovery for the general reader.

 B

The Cretaceous World edited by Peter Skelton
Reviewed by Douglas Palmer

If the Cretaceous conjures up anything at all, it is probably some vague association of chalk, school blackboards and big white cliffs on both sides of the English Channel. Bright sparks might also know that Cretaceous times were brought to an abrupt end by a bolt from the blue, a big bang and a sticky end for the dinosaurs. But do you know what chalk is actually made of? What was going globally between 142 and 65 million years ago? If you don't know, then you ought to, and **The Cretaceous World** is the book for you. OK, it is a textbook but it's how a textbook should be. To begin with it is actually a joy to look at. Now, if only the same team could address themselves to the remaining dozen or so periods of geological time ...

C

Dinosaurs of the Air by Gregory Paul
Review by Jeff Hecht

Dinosaurs no longer thunder across the land, but they do flutter among the trees and paddle around the pond. Evolutionarily speaking, modern birds from hawks to hummingbirds are avian dinosaurs, descended from swift two-legged predators like the velociraptors of Jurassic Park. Gregory Paul's title, **Dinosaurs of the Air** symbolises the compelling links that he documents. A sparrow perched on a twig is far from our usual view of the elephantine Apatosaurus (better known as Brontosaurus) or the terrifying Tyrannosaurus rex. Yet under the skin they share the same anatomical kinship as bats and whales, two mammals that evolved into profoundly different forms. The similarities among dinosaur and bird fossils are striking. Paul includes his own careful drawings that show how anatomical features shade gradually from dinosaur into bird.

 D

Chasing monsters by Michael Benton and **The Dinosaur Hunters** by Deborah Cadbury

People have always been fascinated by fossils, attracted by their curious shapes and rarity. A hand axe from the early Stone Age contains a fossil in its side. The ancient Greeks based their mythical giants on dinosaur skulls exposed in eroding cliffs. Fossil finds inspired dragons for the Chinese and suggested griffins to the Scythians.

These days, of course, we can unpick such myths and often identify some of the species that gave rise to them. Common fossils even acquired folk tales and names to match: thunderstones, or ammonites, were supposedly lightning-struck serpents, coiled in a spiral and bound in stone by the force of the shock. There's also a fossil mollusc whose shell resembles a large, ugly, claw-like nail. To early discoverers, these were obviously the devil's toenails.

E

The Dragon Seekers *how an extraordinary circle of fossilists discovered the dinosaurs and paved the way for Darwin* by Christopher McGowan
Reviewed by Simon Knell

Does every science have its heroic age? Geologists certainly think so: theirs spanned the first 50 years of the 19th century, when geology was born as a rigorous and essentially modern science. And historians agree. Of course, the science had really been gestating for more than a century, but extraordinary characters suddenly threw their energies into exploring the past. In the 1810s a coincidence of scientific and social circumstances turned this proto-science into a social phenomenon. Soon the most fashionable science in England, knowledge of geology was sought by the gentry, the scientific literati and provincial philosophers. Geology did not lose its appeal, even when it became preoccupied with the arcane details ...

 F

A Field Guide to Dinosaurs by Henry Gee and Luis V. Rey
Reviewed by Jeff Hecht

'This is a work of fiction,' says the introduction, but author Henry Gee and artist Luis Rey didn't make all of it up. They began with the facts known from dinosaur fossils, then extrapolated other details that aren't evident from the bones. In one sense, that's not a dramatic step beyond painting colour portraits of dinosaurs, since fossils preserve no clue of colour. Yet it is also a daring move because the casual reader won't know immediately what is based on solid science and what comes from the fertile imaginations of Gee and Rey. Your best bet is to relax and enjoy **A Field Guide to Dinosaurs** in the playful spirit the authors intended.

Language development:
colourful language

1 In one of the book reviews we learnt that *'Cretaceous times were brought to an abrupt end by <u>a bolt from the blue</u> ...'* What do you think the underlined expression means?

2 Choose the best option (A, B or C) to complete the sentences with the correct idiomatic expression.

1 You can complain about it until you go _____ – it won't make any difference at all.
   A blue moon   B blue in the face   C blue around the gills

2 If you don't pay your debts promptly, you could end up on someone's _____ and then you'll find it hard to get credit anywhere.
   A black mark   B black card   C black list

3 You'd better not spend any more money or you'll end up _____ again.
   A in the red   B seeing red   C in red tape

4 My grandmother used to have such _____ – her garden always looked so beautiful.
   A green fingers   B green hands   C green gloves

5 Stop complaining! You know the grass always looks _____ on the other side!
   A golder   B greener   C yellower

Key word: *tell*

3 In the reading texts, we learnt that 'Dal Sasso is ... qualified to *tell* the *story* of the dinosaurs of Italy ...' We can tell a *story*, we can tell a *lie*, we can tell a *joke*. How many other things can we tell?

4 Read the sentences and match each with the correct definition.

1 I told myself it would be all right in the end.
2 I could tell that she was lying.
3 Did she tell you the one about the turkey and the fox?
4 I can't tell the twins apart.
5 What this tells us is that she was here at 8 o'clock.
6 The pressure began to tell the night before the exam.
7 Michael was told off for talking in the lesson.

a to communicate a joke
b to put something into words in your own mind to give encourage or persuade yourself about something
c if facts or events tell you something, they reveal information in other ways (not speech)
d if an unpleasant experience begins to tell, it has a serious effect
e to reprimand or rebuke someone for something
f to judge a situation correctly based on evidence
g to differentiate between two or more things

5 🎧 4.1 Listen to a mini-dialogue between two friends and complete the gaps with an expression formed from *tell*.

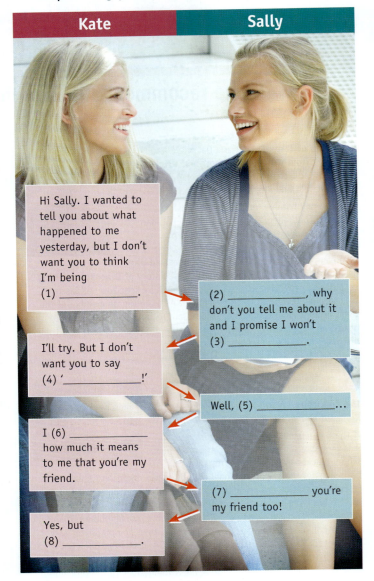

Kate   **Sally**

Hi Sally. I wanted to tell you about what happened to me yesterday, but I don't want you to think I'm being (1) _____.

(2) _____, why don't you tell me about it and I promise I won't (3) _____.

I'll try. But I don't want you to say (4) '_____!'

Well, (5) _____ ...

I (6) _____ how much it means to me that you're my friend.

(7) _____ you're my friend too!

Yes, but (8) _____.

Grammar: the future

1 Discuss. While there is no future tense as such, there are many ways to talk about the future in English. Underline the future forms in the sentences below.

1 The icebergs will melt within the next forty years.
2 By the end of this week I will have been working here for ten years.
3 This time next week we'll be flying to Mexico.
4 The match starts at two so you'd better hurry.
5 I'm going to visit Julie after I've picked up my dry cleaning.
6 James will be here for another hour.
7 I won't forget to write to you.
8 By the time you're ready everyone else will have left.
9 It looks like it's going to be one of those days!
10 I'm meeting Mark outside the cinema.

2 Now match the future forms on page 34 to these uses.

a programmed or scheduled events
b statements of fact
c predictions
d promises
e pre-arranged events
f intentions or plans
g statements based on present evidence
h actions in progress at a certain time in the future
i actions which will be finished by a given future time
j expresses the duration of an action or state at a given future time

➡ Grammar Reference 4.1, page 171

Other ways of expressing the future

3 Rewrite the sentences below in two different ways using the words provided.

a **I very nearly picked up the phone.**
I was just _____ up the phone. ABOUT
I was on _____ up the phone. POINT

b **John is sure to pass his exam.**
John is _____ his exam. BOUND
It is _____ his exam. CERTAIN

c **He is due for a promotion.**
He _____ promoted. SHOULD
It's _____ promoted. TIME

d **I think it's very likely that everyone will have a computer.**
In my opinion there's a good _____ have a computer. CHANCE
I very much _____ have a computer. DOUBT

GRAMMAR SPOTLIGHT

Future time in subordinate clauses
With certain time reference words, a different tense is sometimes used in the subordinate clause to the one used in the main clause.

4 Look at the following sentences (1–4) below and underline the time references. What tense is the verb in the main clause?

5 What tense is used in the subordinate clause? Match the sentences with the explanations (a–d) that follow.

1 I'll walk the dog while you cook dinner.
2 By the time Peter gets here, the show will have started.
3 As soon as they arrive, I'll take the cake out of the oven.
4 I won't do anything until I've heard from Dad.

a one action happening after another action has happened
b two actions happening simultaneously
c one action happening immediately after another
d one action that will be completed before another one happens

➡ Grammar Reference 4.2, page 172

6 Complete the sentences with the correct form of the verb in brackets.

a Once the roof _____ (be) fixed, I _____ (move) back to my house.

b I _____ (not / leave) until you _____ (tell) me where you put my keys.

c When you _____ (decide) to tell him the truth, he _____ (stop) bothering you.

d I _____ (phone) you as soon as the results _____ (arrive).

e By the time you _____ (get) this message, I _____ (leave) the country.

7 Read the text below and underline all the future forms. Correct the ones which are wrong.

Predictions for a new century

In December 1900 a magazine called *The Ladies Home Journal* contained an article which featured a variety of predictions about life in the 20th century. Here are a few of the predictions that were made.

1 There will have been almost 500 million people in America and countries in Central America and South America are wanting to join the American Union.

2 The letters C, X and Q will be disappearing from the English alphabet due to lack of use and spelling will have been phonetic. English will have become the most extensively spoken language in the world and Russian will have come second.

3 Automobiles are cheaper and more common than horses. Even ambulances, hearses, police patrols, hay wagons, ploughs and street sweepers are going to be becoming automobiles.

4 Giant guns will be able to shoot 25 miles or more and destroy whole cities. Aerial war ships and submarine boats are to be used in warfare.

5 Cameras will have been connected electronically with screens at the end of circuits thousands of miles away, enabling audiences in one part of the world to view something happening in another part of the world at the same time it happens. Giant telephones are going to provide the sound at the same time.

6 Strawberries will be being as large as apples and it won't not be necessary to eat more than one at each meal.

8 Discuss. Which of the above predictions have come true?

9 Write a list of predictions of your own describing how you believe things will have changed in 100 years from now.

Speaking: three-way task

1 Discuss. In the future do you think it will be essential to know how to use a computer to get a job in your country?

SPOTLIGHT ON SPEAKING

PAPER 5, PART 4 Developing topics for discussion

Paper 5, part 4 is an extension of part 3. The interlocutor will introduce some topics for further discussion, usually in some way connected to the themes already discussed in parts 2 or 3. This is a three-way activity, with both candidates expected to ask, answer and develop points of discussion.

2 🎧 **4.2** Listen to two students discussing the point in exercise 1 (above) in part 4 of the exam. What do you notice about their answers?

Sometimes you may think you don't have anything to say about a topic. The topic may not interest you or it may be something you have never thought about before, but the questions you will be asked are not meant to test your knowledge on the topic; they are just a prompt for you to demonstrate your speaking skills.

Sometimes you may find that your partner has covered the point you wanted to raise. What can you do in this case?

3 In pairs, discuss the following topic point:

How far do you agree that the computer is the greatest invention of modern times?

When you have finished making your point, prompt the second candidate, using expressions such as: *What do you think? Do you agree? How about you?*

4 **PAPER 5, PART 4** In pairs discuss the following point. Change roles so that Speaker 1 is now Speaker 2. Try to speak equally on the subject and prompt each other if necessary.

> Some people say that computers are helping to create a generation of people without social skills. What's your opinion?

Listening: getting the gist

1 Discuss. In your opinion, what is the most important item that has ever been invented? What would life be like today without it?

SPOTLIGHT ON LISTENING

PAPER 4, PART 4 Listening for gist

In Paper 4, part 4 you have to do two tasks simultaneously. Although you will hear each extract twice, you should aim to get the gist (the main idea) on the first listening so that you can catch the finer details the second time you listen.

2 🎧 **4.3** Listen to short extracts of five different people talking about inventions and jot down important key words to help you focus on the gist. The first has been done for you.

1 Speaker 1 *to get around, stress, pollution, driving, city*
2 Speaker 2 _____
3 Speaker 3 _____
4 Speaker 4 _____
5 Speaker 5 _____

3 🎧 **4.4** **PAPER 4, PART 4** Listen to the complete extracts. While you listen you must complete both tasks.

Task one
For questions **1–5**, choose from the list (A–H) the person who is speaking.

A a house-wife / -husband
B a school teacher
C a parent
D an artist
E a student
F a writer
G an architect
H a musician

Speaker 1 | 1 |
Speaker 2 | 2 |
Speaker 3 | 3 |
Speaker 4 | 4 |
Speaker 5 | 5 |

Task two
For questions **6–10**, choose from the list (A–H) what each speaker is describing.

A a centrally installed vacuum cleaning system
B the bicycle
C the wheel
D the radio
E the mobile telephone
F the internet
G computer software
H satellite TV

Speaker 1 | 6 |
Speaker 2 | 7 |
Speaker 3 | 8 |
Speaker 4 | 9 |
Speaker 5 | 10 |

Use of English:
prefixes

A prefix is a letter or group of letters which is added to the beginning of a word in order to form a different word. Here are some examples.

agree → **dis**agree	legible → **il**legible
develop → **re**develop	dress → **un**dress
regular → **ir**regular	possible → **im**possible
arrange → **pre**arrange	adequate → **in**adequate

1 Add a prefix to each of the word groups below:

a ___logical; ___literate; ___legal
b ___balanced; ___mutable; ___proper
c ___able; ___gender; ___list
d ___correct; ___decision; ___sane
e ___responsible; ___resolute; ___rational
f ___cultural; ___millionaire; ___lingual
g ___conscious; ___likely; ___necessary
h ___new; ___name; ___locate
i ___violet; ___marine; ___sound
j ___marine; ___conscious; ___directory
k ___meditated; ___historic; ___fixed
l ___associate; ___appear; ___arm

PAPER 3, PART 3 Forming words from stems

2 In a word formation task, you may have to make more than one change to a word. What other changes need to be made in the following sentences?

1 He was sentenced to eight years _____. PRISON
2 The road had to be _____ after the floods. SURFACE
3 I'm afraid to say they were _____ married for many years. HAPPY

3 **PAPER 3, PART 3** For questions 1–10, read the text below. Use the word given in capitals at the end of some of the lines to form a word that fits in the gap in the same line.

Mysteries of computer from 65BC are solved

A 2,000-year-old mechanical computer salvaged from a Roman (1) _____ in 1900 has astounded scientists who have finally unravelled the secrets of how the sophisticated device works. The machine was lost among cargo in 65BC when the ship carrying it sank off the coast of a Greek island. Since its discovery, scientists have been trying to (2) _____ the device, which is now known to be an (3) _____ calendar capable of tracking with remarkable (4) _____ the position of the sun, several heavenly bodies and the phases of the moon. Archaeologists working on the recovered objects noticed gear wheels, dials, clock-like hands and a wooden and bronze casing bearing ancient Greek (5) _____.
Thought to date back to 150–100 BC, the object had 37 gear wheels (6) _____ it to follow the movements of the moon and the sun through the zodiac, predict eclipses and even recreate the (7) _____ orbit of the moon.
(8) _____, scans showed the device uses a type of gear that was previously believed to have been invented in the 16th century. The level of miniaturisation and complexity of its parts is (9) _____ to that of 18th century clocks. Experts believe it to be the earliest-known device to use gear wheels and by far the most sophisticated object to be found from the ancient and medieval periods. No one knows why the Greek technology invented for the machine seemed to (10) _____. No other civilisation is believed to have created anything as complex for another 1,000 years.

1	SHIP
2	CONSTRUCT
3	ASTRONOMY
4	PRECISE
5	INSCRIBE
6	ENABLE
7	REGULAR
8	REMARKABLE
9	COMPARE
10	APPEAR

Writing: a newspaper or magazine article

1 **Discuss. Do you read articles in magazines or newspapers? What kind of style do they have? Are they formal and serious or informal and chatty? How do they catch your attention? What makes you want to read on?**

EXAM SPOTLIGHT

PAPER 2, PART 1 Analysing and organising input material
In the first part of the Writing Paper, it's essential that you make good use of the material you are given. Make sure you understand what the question is asking you, and then underline the key words that would help you to answer it.

2 **Look at the question below and the input material. Underline key words or phrases.**

A science magazine aimed at young people has invited readers to send in articles about how they envision the future. Read the readers' comments and write the article, referring to the points raised and describing your own vision of the future.

What does the future hold? It's a question we constantly ask ourselves and yet it's not easy to predict what may happen in different areas of our lives. Write to us and tell us how you think the future will unfold. The best articles will be published.

> Climate change is definitely going to affect the world.

> I'm not sure that every medical advance a good thing.

> I'm concerned about how an ageing population will affect society.

> Robots will be doing all the best jobs!

> What are we going to do about our transport problems?

3 **In pairs. Decide what information you would use and discuss how you would use it to answer the exam question above.**

4 **Discuss. The following two articles were sent in to the magazine. Which one do you think is more likely to be published? Why?**

Article 1:

Futurology – the survey

In a recent internet survey about the future, it was found that 78% of people believed climate change would make a significant difference during their lifetimes. Another 25% of coastal residents believed their homes would be underwater within the next 40 years, while 53% believed the earth is facing a global extinction crisis and that many species of animal will disappear forever.

When asked about medical interventions, 11% believed parents should have the right to genetically engineer their unborn children, while 65% said they supported research to wipe out genetic diseases in unborn children. Moreover, 52% believed living a longer life was a good thing, while 65% said they thought society would not be able to support an ageing population.

Asked about technological advances 40% said they thought robots would be doing all the best jobs. Concerning traffic problems, 88% said restrictions should be imposed for environmental reasons and 65% said they would use their cars less if they were charged by the kilometre. An astounding 78% said they would welcome a more efficient public transport system. It looks as if our traffic problems will soon disappear.

It looks as if everyone has a different idea about the future, but most people agree, it will certainly be different.

Article 2:

Unfolding the Future

Without a time machine, it's impossible to say for sure how things will turn out, but in my own – somewhat pessimistic – view of the future, I see a world where much of the earth's flora and fauna will have become extinct – a world with polluted skies and seas. Thanks to climate change icebergs will have melted and coastal waters will have risen. A soaring human population will live in overcrowded cities further inland. A select few, the super-rich, will have everything they need, while three quarters of the global population will face starvation.

And the population will continue to increase. In the western world, medical advances will have helped to eradicate most diseases and people will live much longer. However, societies will struggle to support this ageing population, many of whom will be forced to keep working until they are well into their nineties. Medical intervention will have made it possible for most infertile couples to have children, while the super-rich will be able to 'design' their babies, and select the qualities they would like them to have.

Technological advances will mean that many households will have a central computer and at least one robot to carry out menial duties. Most people will be walking or cycling to work as legislation will have made travelling by car very expensive, and only the very rich will be able to afford private transport.

That's the future I see if we don't change our ways. I think other futures are possible too, but we have to act fast if we want them to become reality.

5 Look back at both articles and circle all the key words you'd already underlined in the input material. Which article made better use of the topics that were given?

6 Underline the future tenses and future forms that the writers used in the articles above. What do you notice about them?

In other words

In the first article the writer used statistics and percentages. It's very tiring to read numbers in this way, so try to use a variety of phrases instead. For example, 99% of people could be written as 'almost everyone' or 'the vast majority of people'.

7 How else can we write the following numbers?

3% _____   51% _____
10% _____   100% _____

SPOTLIGHT ON WRITING

Editing your work
In part 1 of the Writing Paper, you have to write between 180 and 220 words (as opposed to up to 260 words in part 2). This means you are also being tested on your ability to write concisely.

8 Article 2 has 266 words and is therefore too long. Read it again and underline any superfluous sentences that could safely be removed to reduce the total length to 220 words or less without changing the meaning.

9 **PAPER 2, PART 1** Follow the steps in the Spotlight on page 38 to answer the question below.

> A family magazine has invited readers to send in articles about how they see the future of education. Read the extract and comments from parents below. Then write an article for the magazine, referring to the points raised and describing your own vision of the future of education.

In last month's edition of 'Modern Families', it was proposed that children can learn more from an hour on the web than they can from a whole month in the classroom. Send us your views in an article entitled 'The Future of Education'.

> Schools will just become a dumping ground for our kids!

> The traditional school teacher will become redundant as cyber teachers fill their roles.

> There'll be no need for a classroom at all, and children will just be sectioned off into computer cubicles to get on with it alone.

Write your answer in 180–220 words in an appropriate style.

Vocabulary organiser 4

4.1 Getting started, page 31 Which words mean ...

1 The study of fossils in order to learn about the history of life on earth _____
2 A robot that looks like a human _____
3 The study of space, planets and stars _____
4 The time in history before any information was written down _____

4.2 Reading, page 33 Scan the dinosaur book reviews (texts A–F) for words which mean the following:

1 genuine, lawful, recognised [adj; Text A]
2 obscure, not clear [adj; Text B]
3 connected with the air or flight [adj; Text C]
4 fast [adj; Text C]
5 animals that hunt other animals [n.pl; Text C]
6 disintegrating, dissolving [v.progressive; Text D]
7 snakes [n.pl; Text D]
8 developing, growing [v.progressive; Text E]
9 upper classes, aristocracy [n; Text E]
10 able to produce a lot of good ideas [adj; Text F]

4.3 Reading, page 33

1 *conjure up* – what's the meaning of this phrasal verb?
2 a *sticky end* – what does this refer to here?
3 *thunder* across the land – why is the word 'thunder' used here?
4 *flutter* among the trees – why is the word 'fly' not used here?
5 *paddle* around the pond – who or what would you normally expect to paddle around a pond?
6 *under the skin* – what does this expression mean?

4.4 Language development, page 34 Complete the sentences below with a suitable colour idiom.

1 After my first karate lesson, I was _____ all over. BLUE
2 After three years heavily in debt, the business is finally in _____ again. BLACK
3 The boys were caught _____ stealing Mrs Brown's apples. RED
4 Ernie was _____ when he saw the cake Molly got for her birthday. GREEN

4.5 Language development, page 34 Complete the sentences below with the correct particle and then match them to the definitions that follow.

apart	off	on

1 William was told _____ for speaking during the exam.
2 I find it increasingly difficult to tell the perfumes _____ – they all smell the same to me.
3 'If you don't give me back my pencil, I'm going to tell _____ you!'

a refer a person to someone in authority, for something they have done.
b reprimand, or speak to someone angrily about something they have done.
c recognise the difference between different things or people.

4.6 Use of English, page 37 Match a prefix to each of the words below ...

1 un –   a large
2 re –   b ability
3 super –   c religious
4 en –   d media
5 multi –   e decided
6 ir –   f consider
7 dis –   g functional
8 in –   h human

4.7 Writing, pages 38–39 The following words all appeared in the magazine articles. Replace the underlined words in the sentences with the most suitable alternative from the box. There is one extra word.

astounding	eradicate	flora and fauna
legislation	menial	pessimistic
residents	restrictions	soaring

1 I thought the things he said to Jane were absolutely <u>surprising</u>.
2 Unfortunately, settlers managed to <u>wipe out</u> the whole species.
3 There are a number of <u>limits</u> you have to be aware of at the college.
4 I was fascinated by the diversity of <u>wildlife</u> in the area.
5 He spent three years doing <u>tiring</u>, <u>unskilled</u> work in prison.
6 Stop being so <u>negative</u> all the time!
7 I looked up at the <u>elevated</u> peaks of the towers above.
8 Local <u>inhabitants</u> have complained about noise levels from the factory.

BANK OF ENGLISH

Word partnerships: tech-

Nouns: technology, technicality, Technicolor™, technique, techno, technocracy
Nouns (persons): technician, techie, technical support, technologist, technophobe, technophile, technocrat
Adjectives: technical, technocratic, technological
Adverbs: technically

Using the words above, find:

1 a person who hates technology _____
2 a special way of doing something _____
3 scientific knowledge used for practical purposes _____
4 a form of modern music with a heavy beat _____
5 a repair and advice service that some companies offer to their clients _____
6 a person whose job involves skilled practical work with scientific equipment _____
7 a system of colour photography used in making cinema films _____
8 a way of saying that something may be true according to fact, laws or rules, but may not be important or relevant in a particular situation _____

1 For questions 1–10, read the text below. Use the word given in capitals at the end of some of the lines to form a word that fits in the gap in the same line.

On the question of corporal punishment

We live in civilised times, or so we keep telling ourselves. Yet, the increasing level of
(1) _____ behaviour and violence in schools has led a number of teachers to start demanding the reinstatement of an archaic and, to most of us, (2) _____ law. They feel that the present laws regarding punishment in schools are (3) _____ to deal with adolescent students who are constantly (4) _____, leaving teachers feeling exposed and (5) _____. As a result, a group of teachers have petitioned the Government to (6) _____ the question of permitting corporal punishment in schools. Although this has caused some (7) _____ and debate among Government officials, the Minister for Education remains (8) _____ on the matter.
In a moving speech, he stated that a return to the age of beatings with the cane would be totally (9) _____, going against the UN convention on the rights of the child. The problems of (10) _____ behaviour should be dealt with in other ways, since it has been proved that treating violence with violence does not work.

1 DISCIPLINE

2 HUMANE

3 ADEQUATE

4 OBEY
5 PROTECT

6 CONSIDER

7 AGREE

8 FLEXIBLE

9 ACCEPT

10 ORDER

2 Choose the best option to complete the sentences.

1 I don't really see David any more, but once in a _____ he phones me and we talk of old times.
   A red sunset   C green field
   B blue moon   D purple heart

2 He was _____ to finish the race, despite being so tired.
   A exhausted   C relaxed
   B petrified   D determined

3 'Joe, you'd better lie down. You're _____ a temperature!'
   A making   C taking
   B running   D raising

4 I _____ when I saw how they'd destroyed my plants.
   A saw red   C was green
   B went red   D went yellow

5 'That was mean and unfair! I want you to take _____ everything you just said about me!'
   A out   C back
   B off   D down

6 That was fantastic! Your raft travels so fast, it's really _____!
   A exhausting   C reassuring
   B terrifying   D exhilarating

7 I made a real mess of my presentation! I was _____, kept dropping my notes, and knocked over the microphone twice!
   A wet behind the ears   C a pain in the neck
   B all fingers and thumbs   D down in the mouth

8 Until I find work as an actress, I'm working as a child minder to make _____.
   A it   C ends meet
   B my debut   D a name for myself

9 Nick really takes _____ his uncle. They even laugh in the same way!
   A after   C apart
   B for   D in

10 They thought of selling up and moving to Australia, but decided to stay and try to make _____ the business.
   A do with   C a go of
   B out   D up for

3 Circle the correct ending in italics to complete the phrases in each of the following sentences.

1 The children had a great morning, but as soon as their friends left, they got *up to / down to* work tidying up their room.

2 Kevin didn't bat *an eyelid / a finger* when Sara told him she was leaving, but just said, 'Oh, OK then.'

3 After the disastrous meeting, they agreed to wipe *a new leaf / the slate clean*, and start again with a different approach.

4 Give your child free *will / rein* to express herself, and you will help her build self-confidence.

5 I don't believe it! You've done some pretty stupid things in your time, but that really takes *the biscuit / the bull by the horns*!

6 'The change of plan is *up to / down to* Tom. If he'd come home earlier, we wouldn't have missed the train.'

7 Take paintbrush and some colours, and let your imagination run *wild / free*.

8 I didn't like the design, so I tore it up and started from *square one / scratch*.

4 Choose a suitable verb from the box below to complete the sentences. There are more choices than necessary.

activate	bound	bring about	clamber	embark on
generate	hop	initiate	instigate	launch into
leapmarch	paddle	prompt	provoke	skip
stride	stroll	trigger	wade	

1 The two little girls _____ happily off down the road to buy an ice cream.

2 The Mayor's speech _____ an angry reaction from the crowd.

3 A couple of Chelsea fans were accused of _____ the fight that had broken out after the match on Saturday.

4 Now we're retired, my wife and I often enjoy _____ along the sea front in the evenings.

5 Right! You stand on one leg and _____ towards the finish line, carrying an egg on a spoon!

6 His kind words _____ her to ask him if he was married.

7 My father doesn't walk along the street, he _____ as if he were still in the army!

8 Before _____ such a dangerous journey, it would be a good idea to pack a first aid kit.

9 When Andy goes salmon fishing, he _____ into the middle of the river before casting his rod.

10 The new headmistress has _____ discussions with the student council regarding the question of bullying in the school.

5 Complete the mini-dialogues below using the verbs in brackets in a suitable tense.

1 A: How are Ann and Tim, by the way? Do you hear from them?
  B: Oh, they _____ (move) to Spain! They _____ (go) last year, actually. Tim _____ (not be) happy at work for a long time, so they _____ (decide) to pack it all in and leave. Apparently, they _____ (open) a hotel in Alicante, and I believe it _____ (do) really well!

2 A: Right! I must dash! I _____ (go) to pop in and see my gran on the way home, but I don't want to miss 'Lost'.
  B: I thought you said Mike _____ (come) round for a meal tonight.
  A: Oh no, I _____ (forget)! I _____ (have to) go shopping! I've no idea what we _____ (eat)!
  B: How about making him a chilli? I _____ (really like) that one you _____ (make) for me last week.
  A: Good idea! Thanks! Bye ...

3 A So, how _____ (it happen)?
  B: Well, I _____ (ride) my bike along Price Street. It _____ (be) dark, but the moon _____ (shine), so I _____ (can) see fairly well. Then this car just _____ (come) from nowhere, and _____ (crash) into me!

6 PAPER 3, PART 5 For questions 1–8 below, complete the second sentence so that it has a similar meaning to the first sentence, using the word given. Do not change the word given. You must use between three and six words, including the word given.

1 People sometimes criticise Mr Smith's teaching methods.
  be
  Mr Smith _____ his teaching methods.

2 She learned how to dance the tango ten years ago.
  able
  She _____ the tango for ten years.

3 Although we've been friends for a long time, I don't always understand her.
  have
  We _____ a long time, but I don't always understand her.

4 There have been rumours that Peter and Jane are getting married.
  has
  It _____ Peter and Jane are getting married.

5 They finally got married last year, after living together for twelve years.
  been
  When they finally got married last year, _____ twelve years.

6 It is likely that local residents will be suspicious of the company's plans for development in the area.
  may
  The company's plans for development _____ with suspicion by local residents.

7 It definitely wasn't Paul you saw with that girl, because he's in Glasgow on business!
  seen
  You _____ that girl, because he's in Glasgow on business!

8 Jason intends to visit the ancient ruins of Machu Picchu when he goes to Peru next month.
  is
  When Jason goes to Peru next month, he _____ the ancient ruins of Machu Picchu.

7 PAPER 3, PART 2 For questions 1–15, read the text below and think of the word which bets fits each gap. Use only **one** word in each gap.

Sunshine and showers during dinosaur's heyday

Dinosaurs might have known an astonishing amount about what we think of as a quintessentially contemporary problem: global warming. Fossilised vegetation from 65 million years (1) _____ in the Cretaceous period, reveals that places like central Siberia were actually a lot like present-day Florida, (2) _____ lush ferns and lots of rain.
Academics from various universities in the UK examined fern leaves which had become fossils to estimate temperature at the time. (3) _____ of the 0 degrees centigrade that climate models (4) _____ led them to expect, the average temperature was far warmer. Based on this study, there are three (5) _____ reasons for the difference in results to their expectations.
Occurrences such as continental drift, differences (6) _____ atmospheric chemistry or the shape of the Earth's orbit round the sun (7) _____ have made the world so different then (8) _____ the models we use for today's atmosphere (9) _____ mimic it. However, some academics argue that (10) _____ explanations don't adequately explain the results. It (11) _____ well be that the fossil evidence (12) _____ been misunderstood.
(13) _____, there is a third explanation, for perhaps the internal physics of the models claiming to explain extreme warm climates is wrong. If so, that (14) _____ be very problematic for today's climate – for it hints that climate change models may be underestimating the magnitude of future temperature change, (15) _____ would turn out to be larger than currently predicted.

8 Complete the following sentences with a suitable future form of the word in brackets.

1 We're so late, that by the time we _____ (get) there, they _____ (finish) their meal!

2 In a few years, almost all university coursework _____ (conduct) online.

3 As soon as John _____ (finish) painting, I _____ (be able) to work on that project.

4 'So, what have you decided to do?' 'I _____ (tell) him the truth, and I hope he _____ (believe) me.'

5 'By this time next week, we _____ (trek) across the Gobi desert!

6 By 2020, people _____ (no longer use) landline phones.

7 I _____ (see) Anika later, and we _____ (think) of going to the cinema. Do you want to come?

8 'Fiona _____ (take) her driving test this afternoon.' 'She _____ (be bound to) fail, as she's hardly had any practice!'

5 Safe and sound?

MAIN MENU

Topics: Internet crime, DNA profiling, road and fire safety

Language development: verbs followed by prepositions; phrasal verbs with *turn*; key word: *law*

Grammar: verbs followed by infinitive or *-ing*

EXAM MENU

Reading: following a line of argument

Use of English: gapped sentences

Listening: distinguishing information

Speaking: giving personal information

Writing: a report

Getting started

1 Discuss. What do you think the connection is between these two photographs? What kind of crime is committed via the computer?

2 In pairs. Read items 1–5 in the 'Strange but true' box below. Number them in order of severity and decide how you think each one should be dealt with. Report your decisions to the rest of the class.

STRANGE BUT TRUE

Did you know …

1 A Chinese woman recently cut off her husband's right hand because of his addiction to the Internet. The man asked the court to forgive her because he said it was his fault for breaking his promise to stop.

2 Police in Florida, USA, are looking for a little girl, aged about seven, who tried to steal two boxes of Lego at knifepoint.

3 In Bulgaria, an escaped convict turned up at his old prison and asked to be let back in because he was missing his friends.

4 An Austrian toyshop owner who had gone bankrupt was arrested after he tried to rob a bank using a toy water pistol from his shop.

5 A Serbian man left a six foot snake inside his car because he couldn't afford an alarm. He was arrested after it escaped.

6 Police in Brighton, UK, are going to put on extra patrols on nights when there is a full moon, to combat an increase in violence.

3 Does the decision in point 6 above surprise you? Why or why not?

4 Discuss. Which of the following crimes do you think cause the greatest problem for law enforcement agencies? Give reasons for your choices.

| arson | computer hacking | drug trafficking | fraud | kidnapping | murder |

43

Reading: gapped texts

1 Read part of a headline from a newspaper article. What do you think the article is about?

Of Worms and Woodpeckers: the changing world of the virus-busters

2 Scan the first paragraph of the article to find out who the 'woodpeckers' are. Who or what do you think the word 'worm' might refer to?

3 Read the opening sentence of the article more carefully. Decide which two of the three paragraphs below could follow it.
   a   They have been working solidly for the last ten hours, developing some of the world's most sophisticated 'crimeware' to date.
   b   Inspired by such impressive surroundings, these young people are engrossed in their task, creating a new computer game for the American market.
   c   In a former life it was a nuclear research facility at the heart of the cold war. Now this dark skyscraper is home to a different kind of power struggle.

4 Read the second paragraph of the article again and decide which of the paragraphs in exercise 3 is correct. Explain your choice.

5 Read the following sentence. What kind of information would you expect to follow it?

'They examine and create antidotes to more than 200 pieces of code every day, but it is a task that is proving increasingly difficult.'

6 Look at the gaps between the paragraphs. Try to predict which of the support points in the Spotlight on Reading above (a, b, or c) you would expect to see in these paragraphs.

Of Worms and
the changing world of
fighting rise in

Inside a gloomy tower block on the north-western outskirts of Moscow a team of young computer programmers is deep in concentration.

0 [...]

Each day a dozen team members at the anti-virus firm Kaspersky Lab – mostly in their late teens or early 20s and nicknamed 'woodpeckers' – work in 12 hour shifts to crack, decode and eradicate some of the world's most malicious computer viruses, or 'crimeware'. They examine and create antidotes to more than 200 pieces of code every day, but it is a task that is proving increasingly difficult.

1 [...]

The danger of crimeware and hackers is being recognised by authorities and law enforcement around the globe. Last week Britain unveiled plans to stiffen its computer crime laws, doubling the maximum jail sentence for hacking to ten years and making it illegal to own 'hacking tools' such as password cracking software. And with good reason, say experts.

2 [...]

Eugene Kaspersky knows the mind of a cyber-criminal better than most. For 15 years he has worked on understanding viruses and their creators. His company is one of a host of anti-virus and internet security companies fighting to keep their customers secure. It is a battle that is getting bigger. According to figures released by the FBI last week, around 90% of people have experienced computer security problems recently. Research published last year suggested that the global cybercrime industry is now worth more than the international illegal drugs trade.

3 [...]

It is all a far cry from the earliest days of hacking, when viruses were created by bored teenagers. It is 20 years since the first widespread PC virus, *Brain*, which was created by brothers Amjad and Basit Farooq Alvi. *Brain* was a piece of trickery that began as a benign experiment but left corporate America shaking. Although there had been viruses before, business simply didn't understand the concept of security. As a result, *Brain* caused panic.

Woodpeckers:
the virus-busters internet crime

4 [...]

But the days of playing for fun are long gone. According to research, just 5% of malicious programmes are now written by bored teenagers. The rest are produced by ever increasing numbers of professional criminals and fraudsters. 'A lot of people are stuck in the 1990s, with their image of a virus writer as a kid eating pizza in their bedroom,' said Graham Cluley, an expert with Sophos. 'In fact, they are now much more serious, and much nastier.'

5 [...]

The hackers' change in attitude has also had other side effects. 'There are no global epidemics like there were in the past,' said Mr Kaspersky. 'Just local ones.'

Several years ago virus epidemics regularly hit the headlines. Now the smarter focus from criminals means they don't get as much coverage, despite being more successful. Some experts say this creates a sense of complacency.

6 [...]

Back in his Moscow laboratory, Mr Kaspersky directs his woodpeckers as they cope with a new influx of crimeware. Outside is winter, but inside the chill is warded off by the banks of screens. He knows that his job will never be over. 'Sometimes when you feel ill you can go to the chemist, and sometimes you need to go to hospital,' he shrugged. 'But people will never stop getting sick.'

SPOTLIGHT ON READING

Text organisation features

Comparison: When writers make a point, they often compare the present situation with the past. *'The modern computer is very different from Charles Babbage's invention. He envisaged a sophisticated mathematical tool, and could not have imagined how this would develop into today's tool.'*

7 Look back at the article and find a similar example of this kind of comparison.

Reference: Frequently in a formal text, more than one person may be mentioned. Each person will usually be introduced by their full name and title first. *'Eugene Kaspersky, the founder of Kaspersky Lab'*; then later referred to as *'Mr Kaspersky.'*

8 Read paragraphs A–G on the right and find references to another expert. Which one is likely to come first?

9 Read paragraphs A–G below and choose the one which fits each gap (1–6) in the article. There is one extra paragraph which you do not need to use.

A Mr Viveros agrees. 'Now that there's money involved, the threats have become a lot greater. The widespread adoption of broadband internet means that hackers have targets they can always access.'

B 'Hackers don't want to damage computers any more, they want to own them,' said Eugene Kaspersky, the founder of Kaspersky Lab. 'They've started to run direct attacks where just one business, or even just one computer, is infected.'

C 'If the guys on the News at Ten aren't talking about viruses, then the guy on the street doesn't think about it,' said Mr Cluley. 'But we're seeing fewer massive outbreaks, because actually clever criminals don't want access to 200,000 bank accounts at once, because they can't cope with that many. Instead they get access to 200, and just keep going back for more. The problems are less likely to get headlines,' he says, 'but that makes them more dangerous.'

D Over the weekend thousands of computers worldwide were crippled by the latest virus, *Kama Sutra*. The worm, which spread through emails and inside computer networks over the past month, was estimated to have caused tens of thousands of pounds of damage as it attempted to erase files on infected computers. Last week the Russian stock exchange, a short distance from Kaspersky Lab, shut down for an hour after a virus attack.

E A harmless but annoying virus which contained the names of its creators, *Brain* spread worldwide in just a few months, making it the first widespread PC virus. Then in 1992, the infamous *Michelangelo* came on the scene. One of the first viruses to get widespread media coverage, the reach of *Michelangelo* – at one point predicted to hit 5 million machines – turned out to be far smaller than anticipated.

F 'What we saw 20 years ago was really technical enthusiasts, and people creating proof of concept viruses,' said Sal Viveros, a security specialist with the anti-virus company McAfee. 'For the first seven or eight years that was really who made these things.'

G Through viruses and worms, hackers can control thousands of computers – turning them into 'zombies'. After that, they can steal people's identities, engage them in complex fraud or blackmail, send spam, attack websites, or run cyber-protection rackets. The internet security firm Sophos estimates that an unprotected computer connected to the internet has a 50% chance of being infected within 12 minutes.

Language development: verbs followed by particles

1 In pairs. In paragraph G of the Reading passage on page 45, we learn that *'hackers can ... engage [people] in complex fraud or blackmail ...'* How many verbs connected with crime and punishment can you think of? Make a list. What structures are they followed by (particles, infinitive, etc)?

2 Work in pairs. Complete the following newspaper report using suitable particles from the box below.

for	in	of	to	with

Jilted lover's plot for revenge

There may be an element of truth in the saying that 'hell hath no fury like a woman scorned', if the case heard recently at the Old Bailey* is anything to go by.

A top businesswoman was convicted (1) _____ inciting her new boyfriend to kill her former partner and his wife. Amy Hynde was furious when her lover of 22 years, Clive Layne, told her he'd found someone else. Unable to cope (2) _____ the rejection, Hynde resorted (3) _____ repeatedly sending Layne hate mail, accusing him (4) _____ abuse and unfair treatment. A year later, she began a relationship with another man, Adrian Lewis, and confided (5) _____ him about her feelings. When Layne changed his will, leaving everything to his new wife, Hynde and Lewis decided to act.

Lewis contacted an acquaintance in search of an assassin, but the police were informed (6) _____ his plans, and this led to an undercover officer being sent to pose as the 'hitman'. He met with Hynde, taped their conversation and subsequently arrested her. She was charged (7) _____ soliciting murder. At first, Hynde tried to blame her boyfriend (8) _____ forming the plan, but then admitted (9) _____ going along with the idea. Lewis confessed (10) _____ the crime, claiming he was 'blinded by love', and the jury found both guilty (11) _____ soliciting murder. They were sentenced (12) _____ 15 years' imprisonment.

*Note: The Old Bailey is the central criminal court in London.

Phrasal verbs with *turn*

3 In paragraphs E and G of the article on page 45, the phrasal verbs *'turned out to be'* and *'turned [them] into'* appeared. Match them to their definition below.

a was discovered to be _____
b made someone become _____

4 Choose one of the particles below to complete the phrasal verb in each of the following sentences:

down	in	to	out	over	on	in	off

1 'I'm exhausted from studying all day. I think I'll turn _____ and have an early night.'
2 When his business went bankrupt, Ken turned _____ his brother for help.
3 'This company's doing very well, and turned _____ a profit of $4 million last year.'
4 I know all about his illegal activities. I have decided to turn him _____ .
5 David asked Sarah to marry him, but she turned him _____ .
6 As Simon walked up the garden path, his neighbour's dog suddenly turned _____ him, and bit his arm.
7 They turned _____ the water supply for a while to repair the boiler.
8 Sam's landlord turned him _____ of his flat because he hadn't paid his rent for three months.

Key word: *law*

5 Use a dictionary to find out what the phrases in the box below mean.

be above the law	be against the law	break the law
by law	enforce the law	lay down the law	law-abiding
law and order	law enforcement	lawsuit	obey the law
take the law into your own hands	within the law

6 Complete the sentences below. Use phrases in a suitable form from the box above.

1 The problem of the Queen's missing dog has been keeping _____ agencies busy across the country.
2 'But officer, I wasn't _____. I was only driving at 40 miles an hour!'
3 Politicians sometimes make the mistake of thinking they _____, and can do what they want.
4 Kelly has decided to bring a _____ against her next door neighbours, regarding the noise they make.
5 All owners of a television are required _____ to have a TV licence.
6 Police have difficulty maintaining _____ in some inner-city areas.
7 It _____ to drive after you have been drinking alcohol in many countries.
8 'Joe's Dad was really angry, and we could hear him _____ through the closed door!'

Grammar: verbs followed by infinitive or *-ing*

1 **Place the following verbs into the correct category below.**

advise	agree	appreciate	arrange	ask	attempt	avoid	choose	contemplate
dare	decide	deny	encourage	enjoy	expect	face	fail	involve	let
make	order	persuade	practise	pretend	refuse	threaten	invite	remind

Followed by infinitive with *to*	Followed by infinitive without *to*	Followed by *-ing*
pretend to be	*make (someone) do*	*contemplate doing*

2 **Choose a suitable verb from exercise 1 to complete the following sentences. In some cases more than one answer may be possible.**

1 'You must _____ playing the piano for two hours a day.'
2 Tom _____ to break his brother's train set if he didn't shut up.
3 'I've _____ to have the kitchen painted next week.'
4 Ann _____ going to Switzerland for Christmas, but changed her mind at the last minute.
5 Claire _____ having an affair with her boss, but Kevin didn't believe her.

GRAMMAR SPOTLIGHT

3 **Some verbs can be followed by either *-ing* or infinitive with *to* (*like*, *remember*, etc). Look at the pairs of sentences below. How do the verb forms in italics change the meaning?**

1 I don't *like listening* to my teacher's stories.
   I don't *like to disturb* my teacher at home.
2 She *remembered seeing* Patrick at the beginning of the party, but not later on.
   She *remembered to see* John on his way home.
3 'Oliver *went on talking* for an hour, and some people fell asleep!'
   Trixie *went on to* thank the teacher for all his help.
4 'Sorry, I *meant to tell* you about the meeting!'
   'Sorry, but this *means having* a meeting at 7 o'clock in the morning!'
5 Helen stopped *to talk* to her neighbour.
   'Will you *stop talking* for five minutes!'

5 **PAPER 3, PART 5** **For questions 1–5, complete the second sentence so that it has a similar meaning to the first sentence, using the word given. Do not change the word given. You must use between three and six words, including the word given.**

1 'Give me your money or I'll shoot you!' said the thief to the old lady.
   threatened
   The thief _____ if she didn't give him her money.

2 'I didn't take the wallet from your bag, sir, honest!' cried Ronald.
   denied
   Ronald _____ from his teacher's bag.

3 'When you went into the room, Mrs. Smith, did you notice anything unusual?' asked the police officer.
   remembered
   The police officer asked if _____ when she went into the room.

4 'I can't phone her at this time of the night, it's too late!'
   like
   'I _____ so late.'

5 Diane told the police she hadn't intended to burn her ex-husband's house down.
   mean
   'I _____ fire to my ex-husband's house, officer. Really!'

➡ Grammar Reference 5.1, page 172

4 **Complete the cartoons below with one of the sentences from exercise 3.**

Listening: sentence completion

1 **Discuss. What do you know about forensic science and DNA analysis? Have you ever seen any TV series' or films about this?**

2 **In pairs. In science and technology, as well as in the area of government agencies, a lot of specialised terms are referred to by using initial letters. For example, the initials 'DNA' stand for *deoxyribonucleic acid*. Choose the correct full length phrase for the following well-known initials.**

    1 The initials 'CIA' stand for
       a Central Investigation of Advertising
       b Central Intelligence Agency

    2 The initials 'CSI', from the American television series about forensics, stand for
       a Criminal Science Institute
       b Crime Scene Investigation

3 ∩ 5.1 **Listen to someone talking about DNA analysis. The speaker mentions the following:**
    RFLP testing, STR testing and PCR testing.

    As you listen, match each abbreviated phrase with the correct description below:

    a Requires only a very small sample of DNA, which may be slightly degraded. However, this form of testing is highly susceptible to contamination. _____

    b Requires a small sample of DNA, but this must be recent, as degraded DNA is unsuitable for testing using this method. _____

    c Requires large amounts of DNA from recent samples. _____

4 **Listen to the extract again, and summarise the main point the speaker makes into one sentence. Is it necessary to understand all the terminology to answer the question?**

SPOTLIGHT ON LISTENING

Distinguishing key information
In part 2 of the Listening Paper, you have to complete eight sentences which summarise information you have heard. When you listen, you need to isolate the key word or phrase needed to complete each sentence.

5 **Read the following sentence. It is a completed sentence from a Paper 4, part 2 exercise.**

    According to the speaker, a national DNA database would act as a strong deterrent to potential criminals.

6 ∩ 5.2 **Now listen to the extract. Which word or phrase do you think has been filled in, to complete the sentence above?**

7 **PAPER 4, PART 2 Read the questions below but don't attempt to complete them until after you have listened. What *kind* of information is each one asking for?**

8 ∩ 5.3 **Listen to a criminologist giving a talk about DNA profiling. For questions 1–8 complete the sentences.**

    According to Daniel, before the advent of DNA testing (1) _____ was the main source of forensic evidence.

    Thanks to technological developments in DNA testing, one man was recently convicted of crimes he committed between (2) _____ and 1986.

    Daniel thinks the (3) _____ is responsible for creating an unrealistic image of DNA profiling.

    He regards the view that DNA testing alone can prove that a person is guilty as (4) _____.

    A number of scientists have expressed concern that forensic evidence presented in the case of Barry George was (5) _____.

    DNA analysis can now be carried out on a (6) _____ sample, which enables cases from years ago to be solved.

    Today, the odds of more than one match being found are approximately one in (7) _____.

    Daniel says that despite technological advances, DNA is not (8) _____, and mistakes are made.

9 **Work in groups. Read the following statement and brainstorm arguments in favour of a DNA database, and also arguments against it. Create a large table similar to the one below for your points.**

    A national DNA database containing DNA samples from every citizen is the best way to ensure our country becomes a safer place to live.

Points in favour of a DNA database	Points against a DNA database

10 **Class debate. Form two teams – one in favour of the statement, and one against forming a DNA database, and hold a debate.**

Use of English: gapped sentences

PAPER 3, PART 4 Finding the right word

In part 4 of the Use of English Paper you are given five sets of three gapped sentences, which have the same missing word. This word is in the same form and part of speech in each sentence. Sometimes a word may fit two of the sentences, but not the third. Make sure that the word you choose fits ALL the sentences.

1 **Find one word which fits the three sentences below.**

Graham's main _____ in life is to be happy.

'In order to achieve your _____, you'll have to work hard.'

Lizzie picked up the gun, took _____ and fired.

2 **Which other word could fit the first two sentences but not the third?** _____

3 **Circle the following phrases which cannot go with the word in bold. Use a dictionary to help you.**

a **show** (v) ... a leg, ... your face, ... somebody the door, ... off, ... your eye, ... your hand, ... the way

b **face** (n) put on a brave ..., ... factor, rock ..., a long ..., keep a straight ..., ... value, make a ...

c **press** (v) ... charges, ... home, ... on, ... out, ... for

d **light** (adj) ... relief, ... fingered, ... on your feet, ... mannered, ... sleeper, ... hearted, ... headed

e **keep** (v) goal ..., ... house, ... work, ... watch, ... going, ... a record, ... to yourself, ... in with

f **charges** (n) face, drop ..., lose ..., press ..., reverse ...

4 **PAPER 3, PART 4 For questions 1–5, think of one word only which can be used appropriately in all three sentences.**

1 'When you sit the examination, you'll need to have your passport with you as _____ of identity.'

Detective Sergeant Davies was convinced his suspect had committed the crime, but needed to find _____ of her guilt.

'Jane, did you check the _____ before it was printed?'

2 Although her neighbour had threatened her with a knife, Ali decided not to press _____ against him.

'Hello, operator, I'd like to make a call and reverse the _____, to ... Toronto, Canada.'

Our nanny is very fond of her young _____, Danny and Carrie.

3 The police decided to _____ the house over in search of the missing weapon.

The teacher thought that Steve had stolen his wallet, and made him _____ out his pockets.

'Don't worry. Tessa's always late, so she may _____ up yet.'

4 'I'm a very _____ sleeper, so the sound of breaking glass woke me.'

The teacher told a few jokes for some _____ relief from all the work the students had been doing.

It was still _____ when we arrived at the camping spot.

5 'Don't _____ wolf too often, or people won't ever take you seriously.'

The postman was too terrified of the dog to _____ out for help, and simply ran away.

'James keeps visiting Jen, but I think he just needs a shoulder to _____ on after his divorce.'

Speaking: giving personal information

1 🎧 **5.4 Listen to the first part of a CAE examination interview, where the examiner asks two candidates about themselves. Then compare the answers given by the two candidates.**

PAPER 5, PART 1 Talking about yourself

In this part of the Speaking Paper, candidates have to talk about themselves. Listen to the questions carefully, and try to give as many details about yourself and why you like or dislike something. Do not answer with one word or a short phrase.

2 **Work in pairs. Ask and answer the following question.**

What do you think is the most difficult thing about learning English?

3 **Listen again, and make notes on how Beret expands her answers to include more detail.**

4 **Look at some of Juan's answers below. Try to expand them, in a similar way to Beret.**

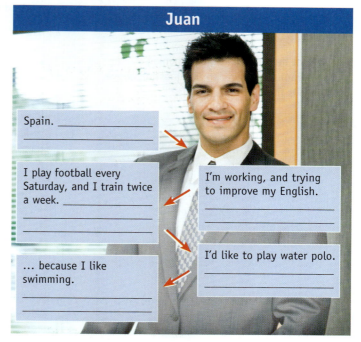

Juan

Spain. _____
_____

I play football every Saturday, and I train twice a week. _____
_____
_____

I'm working, and trying to improve my English.
_____
_____

... because I like swimming.
_____
_____

I'd like to play water polo.

Writing: a report

1 Discuss the following:

a Is there a lot of traffic in your area?
b Is your area safe for pedestrians?
c What about cyclists?

SPOTLIGHT ON WRITING

Accuracy and organisation
Writing a report needs careful organisation because each paragraph requires a heading. The question usually helps you with this by asking for specific points.

EXAM SPOTLIGHT

PAPER 2, PART 2 Look at the following question.

> A research group from your local council has asked you to write a report on road safety in your area. You should consider the amount of traffic, the presence and location of traffic signals and pedestrian crossings and cycle lanes. Make recommendations for improvements.

2 Plan an answer to this question by creating four paragraph headings.

1 _____
2 _____
3 _____
4 _____

3 Look at the following three opening paragraphs in answer to the question above. Which is the most appropriate?

> a The question of road safety in our area is a controversial issue, due to the fact that the level of traffic has increased drastically in the last few years, whereas the need for corresponding safety measures has largely been ignored.

> b In this report, I'm going to examine the amount of traffic in the area, and look at how effective traffic signals, pedestrian crossings, etc., are. I will also suggest some ways of improving the present situation.

> c The aim of this report is to evaluate road safety in this area, by examining the level of traffic, and the provision of traffic signals, pedestrian crossings and cycle lanes. It will consider their effectiveness, and make recommendations for improvements.

4 Discuss. What is wrong with the other two options?

In other words

5 Reports require formal language. Their purpose is usually to assess a current situation, and make recommendations for improvement. The opening paragraph outlines the aim of the report and the points it will address, and so its style is fairly standard. Make sure you build up a bank of useful words and expressions for your introductory paragraph.

a Use a dictionary, and add formal equivalents to the words below.
  * look at – examine, …
  * consider – assess, ….
  * suggest – ….

b Notice the use of nouns rather than verbs in formal language. Write the noun forms of the following words:
  * evaluate → _____
  * provide → _____
  * consider → _____
  * effective → _____
  * scarce → _____
  * recommend → _____
  * improve → _____

c Look at paragraph b in exercise 3. Rewrite it using some of the formal language you have found.

6 Now read the rest of the report. Does it answer the question? If not, make recommendations for improvements.

Heading: _____

The level of traffic in the area has increased dramatically during the last three years, as a result of the construction of a new industrial park on the edge of the town. Not only are there more cars on the roads, but also an increased number of heavy goods vehicles travelling through the town centre. A lack of parking facilities means that cars park on the roadside in the centre, often blocking the road for large vehicles. This causes congestion and delays, and has given rise to complaints from local shop owners and business people.

Heading: _____

Despite the rise in traffic, little has been done to improve road safety. The town centre itself is fairly well catered for, with a sufficient number of traffic lights and pedestrian crossings. The main problem lies in the residential areas of the town, particularly those in the direction of the industrial park, such as Rookwood, where there are several schools, yet traffic signals and pedestrian crossings are scarce. Several accidents involving schoolchildren have been reported on Hampton Road in the last few months, and local residents are extremely concerned about the fact that there are no cycle paths near the schools.

Heading: _____

There are several ways in which the situation could be improved. One would be to construct a by-pass for heavy goods vehicles to travel to the industrial park without having to pass through the town. Also, the construction of a multi-storey car park in the town centre would help reduce congestion in the streets, while the creation of more pedestrian crossings with warning signals near the schools in Rookwood would reduce the risk of accidents occurring.

7 Give each paragraph a suitable heading.

8 In pairs. Read the following exam question, then brainstorm ideas for your response. Plan your paragraph headings on the lines below.

> You work as a teacher, and the principal has asked you to write a report on the standards of safety in your school. You should consider the presence of fire escapes, fire doors and fire fighting equipment, in relation to the fact that class sizes have increased, and make recommendations for improvement.

1 _____
2 _____
3 _____
4 _____

9 ♫ 5.5 Listen to a schools safety inspector giving a talk on fire prevention, and write down any points and vocabulary which are useful for writing an answer to the question above.

10 PAPER 2, PART 2 Write your report. Use between 220 and 260 words.

Vocabulary organiser 5

5.1 Reading, page 44–45 Write definitions for the following words and phrases in connection with computers.

a programmer _____

b virus _____

c antidote _____

d crimeware _____

e cyber-crime _____

f cyber-criminal _____

g hacking _____

5.2 Language development, page 46 Replace the underlined words in the sentences below with a suitable verb structure.

1 Police <u>thought that Larry Jones committed</u> the crime.

_____

2 Sally <u>told Wayne she thought he had stolen</u> her money.

_____

3 Sergeant Vyne <u>caught Jones</u> and took him to the police station.

_____

4 After questioning, Larry <u>said that he had robbed</u> the bank, with help from his girlfriend. _____

5 Larry's girlfriend <u>said she hadn't helped</u> him. _____

6 The police <u>officially said that the couple had committed</u> the crime and prepared to take them to court. _____

7 The court <u>found Larry guilty of</u> robbing the bank. _____

_____

8 The judge <u>decided he should go to prison for three years.</u>

_____

5.3 Language development, page 46 Circle the correct preposition to complete the sentences below.

1 Mandy didn't know what to do, so she turned *in / to* her father for help.

2 Last night, Charlie was tired and turned *in / out* early.

3 The officer asked Maria to turn *out / off* her engine while he wrote the ticket.

4 The business turned *over / down* a profit of $30 million last year.

5 Mum said the eggs will need to be turned *to / over* in two minutes!

5.4 Language development (key word), page 46 Choose the best phrase to complete the sentences below.

1 The police met with opposition from local youths when they tried to _____.
A lay down the new law   B enforce the new law
C break the new law   D take the new law into their own hands

2 James thinks he is _____ and can do what he wants because his father is a friend of Prince Charles.
A a law unto himself   B within the law
C above the law   D law-abiding

3 At school, no one questions the headmaster; his word _____.
A is law   B is by law
C is within the law   D obeys the law

4 _____ agencies around the world are trying to stop drug trafficking.
A Law enforcement   B Law and order

5 You are required _____ to show proof of identity when entering this territory.
A within the law   B by law

5.5 Use of English, page 49 Decide if the definitions for the following phrases are true or false.

1 To 'press charges' means to make someone else pay for your phone call.   T / F

2 To 'put on a brave face' means to not show how upset or frightened you are.   T / F

3 To 'show your hand' means to make your real intentions clear.   T / F

4 To 'be light on your feet' means you have a tendency to run away from responsibility.   T / F

5 To 'keep in with someone' means to be friends with someone in order to gain something from them.   T / F

BANK OF ENGLISH

Word partnerships: *cry*

In the Reading article, we learn that computer hacking today is 'a far cry from the earliest days of hacking'.

Match the phrases with 'cry' in A with their definitions in B.

A

VERB:	cry foul, cry wolf, cry off, cry out for, a shoulder to cry on
NOUN:	a far cry from, battle cry
GERUND:	it's no use crying over spilt milk, for crying out loud
ADJECTIVE:	a crying shame

B
- *phrase used to encourage support for a protest or campaign*
- *need something desperately*
- *something very different from something else*
- *spoken phrase showing annoyance or impatience*
- *someone to listen sympathetically to your problems*
- *say you cannot do something you have agreed to do*
- *ask for help when you don't need it*
- *protest that something is wrong or unfair*
- *say that something is very sad or upsetting*
- *don't waste time feeling sorry about a mistake that cannot be changed*

6 Hale and hearty

Getting started

1 Discuss. Which of the following factors are the most important for a healthy life? Number them in order of priority, giving your reasons. Then match the pictures on this page to the points below.

a Consuming plenty of fresh fruit and vegetables ☐

b Avoiding stress and tiredness ☐

c Eating organically grown food ☐

d Not watching too much TV ☐

e Developing a strong immune system and exercising regularly ☐

f Not using chemicals in the home ☐

g Doing yoga and meditation ☐

h Going to the doctor and taking medication ☐

2 ∩ **6.1 Listen to three people discussing some of the above topics. Which topic (a–h) is each speaker talking about?**

Speaker one _____
Speaker two _____
Speaker three _____

3 In the Listening task above you heard the speakers use the following phrases:

1 'to treat the symptoms rather than the root cause'

2 'to boost the immune system'

Which was the speaker associating with …

a alternative health techniques?

b conventional western medicine?

4 In pairs. Discuss the advantages and disadvantages of alternative and conventional medicine.

Reading: text analysis

1 Discuss. How important is diet to a person's physical health?

2 Number the methods listed below in order of usefulness to you.

a Work out the meaning of new vocabulary from the context. ☐

b Read parts of the text several times if necessary in order to understand it. ☐

c Underline key words or phrases that seem to answer the question. ☐

d Eliminate wrong answers from multiple choice questions by identifying false or misleading information in the text. ☐

3 Read the text below. As you do so, try to utilise techniques a and b from exercise 2 above. Which ones helped you most?

Question:
Is it true chocolate is good for your heart health? Tell me more!
Answer:
Recent evidence suggests that chocolate – especially dark chocolate – is rich in substances that may actually help fend off heart disease. These substances are known as flavonoids and are not limited to chocolate; flavonoids are also present in onions, grapes, red wine and tea, among other plant-derived foods. It appears that flavonoids have powerful antioxidant effects. Additional preliminary research on chocolate shows it can also favourably affect blood clotting and the relaxation of blood vessels.

Will any chocolate do? Unfortunately no. Many chocolate products, such as cocoa powder and chocolate syrup, are typically processed with alkali, removing most of these beneficial flavonoids in the process. And milk chocolate has fewer of these beneficial chemicals than dark chocolate.

So what are you to do? Until further research is conducted, focus on foods proven to help enhance heart health and prevent disease – fruits, vegetables and whole grains for example. But, allow yourself to enjoy a small piece of dark chocolate or chocolate product once in a while. Remember, most chocolate products (candy bars, confections, cocoa powder, chocolate syrups) are traditionally high in calories and total fat, so incorporate these foods into your diet with discretion.

One day we may find we can 'have our cake and eat it too'. Until then, moderation is still key.

4 Look at the questions below. The correct answer is given in bold. Highlight the parts of the text where the answer can be found.

1 What do we learn about flavonoids?
   A They prevent heart attacks.
   B They appear in large quantities in milk chocolate.
   C They can easily be found in various plant-based foods.
   D They can slow down blood loss.

2 The writer advises readers concerned about their hearts to
   A eat chocolate whenever they have a sudden urge.
   B eat a larger quantity of healthy plant foods.
   C wait until we know more about the subject.
   D eat plenty of low fat chocolate foods.

5 Three of the options (the distractors) are wrong and may be deliberately misleading. In pairs, discuss why they are incorrect.

6 Answer the questions below about the devices used in the text about chocolate.

a Find and underline two rhetorical questions the writer asks. Discuss what effect do they have.

b Find and underline two sentences that begin with conjunctions. This is normally unacceptable in a formal piece of writing. Discuss the effect of it here.

c Find and underline a sentence that begins with an imperative. Discuss why the writer does this.

d Find and underline an idiomatic expression the writer uses. Discuss what you think it means, and why the writer chooses to use it here.

7   Read the text below and underline any unknown words.

A   What are phytochemicals?

Phytochemicals are non-nutritive plant chemicals that contain protective, disease-preventing compounds. More than 900 different phytochemicals have been identified as *components* of food, and many more phytochemicals continue to be discovered today. It is estimated that there may be more than 100 different phytochemicals in just one serving of vegetables. As early as 1980, scientists began evaluating phytochemicals for safety, *efficacy*, and applicability for preventing and treating diseases. Researchers have long known that there are phytochemicals present for protection in plants, but it has only been recently that they are being recommended for protection against human disease.

B   How are they beneficial?

Although phytochemicals are not yet classified as nutrients, they have been identified as containing properties for aiding in disease prevention. Phytochemicals are associated with the prevention and/or treatment of at least four of the leading causes of death in the West – cancer, diabetes, cardiovascular disease, and hypertension. They are involved in many processes including ones that help prevent cell damage, prevent cancer cell replication, and decrease cholesterol levels.

With health-care costs being a major issue today, it would be cost effective to continue the research needed to help promote the awareness and *consumption* of phytochemicals as a prevention strategy for the public.

SPOTLIGHT ON READING

Analysing unknown words

It is usually possible to work out the meaning of unknown words by trying the following techniques:
- Look closely at the words in context
- Identify the part of speech
- Look at the positive or negative meaning of the sentence
- Use other lexical clues around the word.

8   Look at the text above again. Match the italicised words in the text with the definitions below.

a   The parts that something is made of or that make it up.
b   The act of eating or drinking something.
c   Power or capacity to produce a desired effect or result.

9   You should now have a much better understanding of the text. From memory, decide if the following statements are true or false.

a   Phytochemicals are abundant in food.   T / F
b   Researchers have used phytochemicals to ward off diseases since 1980.   T / F
c   Phytochemicals can help to repair damaged cells.   T / F
d   Phytochemicals are thought to be able to stop the spread of cancer.   T / F
e   It would be more economically viable to teach people to eat plant foods than to spend money on health-care. T / F

10   PAPER 1, PART 1 **For questions 1–2 below choose the answer (A, B, C or D) which you think fits best according to the text.**

1   According to the text, phytochemicals
    A   evolved to protect plants.
    B   contain important nutrients.
    C   are too numerous to count.
    D   are difficult to digest.

2   According to the text, research into phytochemicals
    A   has been going on for nearly 25 years.
    B   will encourage healthier lifestyles.
    C   is expensive and cost-prohibitive.
    D   can help discover a cure for cancer.

11   **For questions 3–4 below choose the answer (A, B, C or D) which you think fits best according to the text below.**

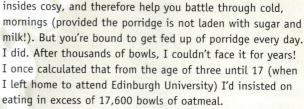

Growing up in Scotland, I know there's not a mother 'worth her salt' who will send her 'wee bairn'[1] to school in the winter without a hot bowl of oat porridge[2]. 'It'll stick tae yer[3] ribs,' my Mum used to say. That sounded pretty scary, but Mum actually had a good point. Biochemically speaking, warm oatmeal will keep your insides cosy, and therefore help you battle through cold mornings (provided the porridge is not laden with sugar and milk!). But you're bound to get fed up of porridge every day. I did. After thousands of bowls, I couldn't face it for years! I once calculated that from the age of three until 17 (when I left home to attend Edinburgh University) I'd insisted on eating in excess of 17,600 bowls of oatmeal.

So, what's an alternative? Enter quinoa. Make your loved ones a quinoa porridge instead. It'll be a welcome change for porridge oat addicts. Seriously though, quinoa will do for your kidneys what Scottish porridge is supposed to do for your ribs! It will warm them up, and give you a feeling of satisfaction. I'm not suggesting that you eat 17,600 bowls of quinoa during a major period of your life, but feel free to use it as a viable alternative some of the time.

1 young child (Scottish)
2 a thick sticky food made from oats cooked in water or milk and eaten hot, especially for breakfast
3 to your (spoken with a Scottish accent)

3   How did the writer's mother feel about porridge?
    A   She thought it was potentially dangerous.
    B   She felt it should be served with sugar and milk.
    C   She worried her daughter was eating too much of it.
    D   She knew it would keep her child warm all morning.

4   How is quinoa similar to porridge?
    A   It will stick to your kidneys.
    B   It's warming and nourishing.
    C   It tastes exactly the same.
    D   It's not as addictive.

Language development:
expressions with food

SPOTLIGHT ON VOCABULARY

Using idioms in speech

Native speakers tend to use idiomatic expressions a lot in speech but only in very informal situations and not very often in written form. An idiom used appropriately and wisely can add emphasis or description to what you say, but be careful! Do not overuse idioms – especially if you're not sure of the correct meaning or the appropriate situation, as it would sound rather odd.

However, you may very well come across idiomatic expressions in the Reading, Listening and Use of English Papers in the exam, and it's therefore important to build up your passive knowledge of English idioms.

1 ⌂ **6.2 Listen to four short dialogues and note down any food idioms that you hear.**
- Turn to the tapescript on page 210 and underline them.
- In pairs. Explain what each idiom means and in what context it could be used.

2 **Choose the best option to complete the sentences below.**

1 'Have you two been plotting something again? Something certainly smells _____ around here!'
   A greasy   C stale
   B meaty   D fishy

2 Gregory threatened to spill the _____ if we didn't tell him where the car keys were kept.
   A biscuits   C milk
   B eggs   D beans

3 I know I said it was a good idea to take on some extra work but now I think you've bitten off more than you can _____.
   A chew   C digest
   B swallow   D gnaw

3 **Discuss. In what situations do you think you might you use the following expression:**

'You can't make an omelette without breaking eggs.'

4 **Use a dictionary to find further expressions with the following words. Then write example sentences or mini-dialogues of your own.**

| bacon | bread | butter | cake | dough | egg | salt |

bread and but|ter also **bread-and-butter** **1** N-UNCOUNT [usu with poss] Something that is the **bread and butter** of a person or organisation is the activity or work that provides the main part of their income. ❏ *The mobile phone business was actually his bread and butter.* **2** ADJ [ADJ n] **Bread and butter** issues or matters are ones which are important to most people, because they affect them personally. ❏ *The opposition gained support by concentrating on bread-and-butter matters.*

Key word: *life*

5 **1** **Which of the following expressions may be used to talk about a car's engine suddenly starting?**

   a bring to life
   b spring to life
   c come to life
   d roar into life

2 **It could be said that growing old is …**

   a a fact of life.
   b true to life.

3 **If we say that someone was the '*life and soul of the party*', we mean he or she was …**

   a a lot of fun.
   b very healthy.

4 **If something gives you '*a new lease of life*', it …**

   a cures you from a serious illness.
   b fills you full of optimism or energy to start again.

5 **Which of the following expressions is the odd one out?**

   a a matter of life and death
   b to risk life and limb
   c to lay down one's life
   d to have the time of your life

6 **Arnold and Graham are _____ friends.**

   a lifetime   c lifelike
   b lifestyle   d lifelong

7 **She had a small, _____ model made of her cat, Hugo, after he died.**

   a lifesize   c lifelike
   b lifeless   d lifetime

6 **Which of the following words cannot follow the word *life*?**

achievement	belt	blood	boat
cycle	dream	expectancy	force
form	guard	history	imprisonment
insurance	jacket	killer	line
raft	sentence	support	vision

Grammar: conditionals

1 Look at the tapescript 6.1 on page 210. Underline one conditional sentence that each speaker uses. Which one is ...?

  a likely situation in the present with a possible solution

  b hypothetical situation in the present with a definite consequence

  c usual or habitual situation in the past

2 Read the sentences below and match them with the rules (a–f) that follow.

  1 If it rained we took the bus, but if the sun came out we always walked.

  2 If I didn't love chicken so much, I would become a vegetarian.

  3 If you look after your immune system, it will look after you.

  4 If the core body temperature drops by a few degrees, the immune system shuts down.

  5 If I hadn't been to that yoga class, I would never have learnt what it could do for me.

  6 If I hadn't smoked when I was younger, I'd be far healthier now.

  a what is *always* true – present facts [present + present]

  b real situations in the present and future [present + future]

  c hypothetical present situations [past + *would*]

  d what *used to* always be true – past facts [past + past]

  e past events with results in the present [past perfect + *would*]

  f hypothetical past situations and regrets [past perfect + *would have* + past participle]

3 Which of the sentences (a–c) in exercise 1 above is an example of the:

  a zero conditional   _____   d third conditional   _____

  b first conditional   _____   e mixed conditional   _____

  c second conditional _____   f false conditional   _____

➡ Grammar Reference 6.1, page 173

4 In addition to *'if'*, there are many different forms of conditional sentences.

  a Underline the conditional phrases in the clauses in A below.

  b Match the conditional clause in column A, with the best ending in column B.

A

  1 Unless I go on a diet,

  2 If I should give up eating hamburgers,

  3 Provided you exercise regularly,

  4 As long as you eat all your vegetables,

  5 Even if it rains,

  6 If you were to cut out the junk food,

  7 Had it not been for Judy,

  8 Supposing you gave up coffee,

  9 But for Helen's advice,

B

  a I would never have tried Chinese food.

  b I'll have to start eating vegetables.

  c I'll have to buy some new clothes.

  d you'll be fit enough to take part in the games.

  e what would you drink instead?

  f I'm still going to go for a walk.

  g I'll let you have some ice-cream.

  h I would still be taking antibiotics.

  i you'd feel so much better.

5 **PAPER 3, PART 5** For questions 1–8, complete the second sentence so that it has a similar meaning to the first sentence, using the word given. **Do not change the word given.** You must use between **three** and **six** words, including the word given.

  1 If his temperature increases, I'm going to call the doctor.
    intend
    Unless his temperature _____
    the doctor.

  2 I didn't have time today so I didn't have any lunch.
    had
    If I _____ had lunch today.

  3 If William hadn't advised me to continue, I would have given up.
    keep
    But _____ I would have given up.

  4 Drop in and see us if you ever come to Manchester.
    happen
    Should you _____ Manchester, drop in and see us.

  5 I was so short that I couldn't reach the top shelf.
    would
    If I _____ been able to reach the top shelf.

  6 You wouldn't visit the dentist so often, if you ate fewer sweets.
    cut
    Were _____ sweets, you wouldn't visit the dentist so often.

  7 I don't care if the doctor prescribes antibiotics – I'm not going to take them.
    even
    I object _____ the doctor prescribes them.

  8 You only beat me in that race because I am too old.
    would
    If I were _____ you in that race.

Listening: multiple choice questions

1 Underline the key words in the following question:
According to the speaker, why are enzymes essential in our diet?

2 ∩ **6.3 Listen to a woman answering the question: she explains what enzymes are. What is the main point she makes?**

3 ∩ 6.4 **PAPER 4, PART 3** You will hear an interview with a food writer about the benefits of eating raw food. For questions 1–6 choose the answer (A, B, C or D) which fits best according to what you hear.

1 Maureen says that one of the reasons why enzymes are essential in our diet is because they
   A stop us consuming poisonous substances.
   B are the main cause of chemical changes.
   C increase our resistance to disease.
   D prevent us contracting harmful diseases.

2 Maureen recommends reducing our intake of cooked food because
   A it cannot supply us with all the nutrients we need.
   B too much cooked food makes us feel heavy.
   C cooked food can cause health problems.
   D raw food tastes so much better.

3 The experiment with the cats showed that
   A each generation of cats responded differently to the foods offered.
   B there was a mixed reaction in the first group of cats.
   C the majority of cats developed health problems after starting the diets.
   D the fourth generation of cats eating cooked food had the most problems.

4 If we don't consume enough enzymes in our food
   A we force our bodies to use their own store of enzymes.
   B we will not be able to process any of the vitamins it contains.
   C our bodies will be forced to manufacture inferior enzymes.
   D we are likely to suffer from digestive problems.

5 Cooking food may cause some proteins to
   A break up into amino acids.
   B fail to function efficiently.
   C attack our bodies by mistake.
   D become damaged and dangerous.

6 The presence of too much cooked food in our bodies may
   A change the colour of our blood.
   B attract invasive organisms.
   C put our immune system on a state of alert.
   D set off an unusual chemical reaction.

Speaking: comparing pictures

1 Turn to page 195 and look at the pictures. Find two things that each set of three pictures has in common. Describe the different ways in which they deal with those themes.

2 **PAPER 5, PART 2** In groups of three, practise the speaking exercises that follow. One person should be the interlocutor and read the questions to the other students, who take turns to answer.

Interlocutor: [Student 1], here are your pictures. They show people eating different types of food. Compare two of the pictures and say what messages they are trying to give about food and diet.

Student 1: _____

Interlocutor: [Student 2], which type of food do you prefer to eat?

Student 2: _____

Interlocutor: [Student 2], here are your pictures. They show people engaged in different types of physical activity. Compare two of the pictures and say how the activities the people are doing may be beneficial to their health, and how these people may be feeling.

Student 2: _____

Interlocutor: [Student 1], which activity would you prefer to do?

Student 1: _____

Use of English: identifying collocations

1 Use a dictionary. How many collocations can you find for the word 'stand'?

2 Which of the following noun phrases cannot be used with the verb in bold? Circle your choice.

a	**take**	offence / the initiative / fault / into account
b	**do**	harm / luck / good / wonders for
c	**run**	a process / a risk / its course / for government
d	**make**	fun of / a mistake / an effort / justice
e	**give**	rise to / credit / fortune / notice
f	**fall**	to pieces / into disrepair / from grace / off power

3 PAPER 3, PART 1 For questions **1–12**, read the text below and decide which answer (**A, B, C or D**) best fits each gap.

NATUROPATHIC MEDICINE PHILOSOPHY

Illness is the body's way of letting us know that something is wrong, and according to believers in Naturopathic Medicine we should listen to the messages. This form of medicine (1) _____ the treatment of disease by stimulating, enhancing and supporting a person's own healing (2) _____.

One of the main underlying (3) _____ of naturopathic healing is to trust in the healing power of nature. The body has the (4) _____ ability to establish, maintain, and (5) _____ health by itself. It is also important to remember that no illness (6) _____ without a reason, and thus it is essential to identify and treat the cause of that illness. If the underlying causes of the disease are not removed or treated, a person cannot recover completely. A further directive that naturopathic doctors must consider is to do no (7) _____ to the body. Symptoms are actually an expression of the healing process and therapeutic actions should allow them to (8) _____ their course. Obstructing a symptom, or (9) _____ it, will only force it to reappear later, perhaps in a more damaging form. (10) _____ forms of treatment, which allow the body to heal itself, are encouraged.

It is also a key consideration in naturopathic healing to treat the whole person. Health and disease are conditions of the whole organism, and the complex interaction of physical, spiritual, mental, emotional, genetic, environmental, social, and other factors, all of which should be taken into (11) _____. Finally, let's not forget the old adage that 'Prevention is better than cure'. The (12) _____ goal of any health-care system should be prevention, which can be accomplished through education and the promotion of healthier habits. The emphasis is therefore on building health rather than fighting disease. This is not so profitable for the pharmaceutical companies, but that's another story.

	A	B	C	D
1	A approves	B endorses	C backs	D sanctions
2	A facility	B gift	C aptitude	D capacity
3	A codes	B principles	C moralities	D ethics
4	A inherent	B incoherent	C incompetent	D inconvenient
5	A restore	B remake	C reinstate	D renovate
6	A transpires	B establishes	C instigates	D occurs
7	A hurt	B harm	C impairment	D destruction
8	A go	B do	C run	D make
9	A aggressing	B oppressing	C suppressing	D depressing
10	A Balancing	B Corresponding	C Harmonious	D Complementary
11	A account	B thought	C report	D decision
12	A final	B consequential	C subsequent	D ultimate

Writing: developing an argument in an essay

1 Discuss. 'You are what you eat.' How important do you think diet is to our health? Explain your reasons.

EXAM SPOTLIGHT

PAPER 2, PART 2 What is an essay?
In Paper 2, part 2, you may be asked to write an essay. Essays need to present an argument, and give reasons for this. Therefore, an essay needs to be well organised, with an introduction, clear development and an appropriate conclusion. The main purpose of an essay is to develop an argument and/or discuss the issues surrounding a certain topic. You should give reasons for your views.

2 Read the essay title below and the beginning of one student's attempt to answer it. Does it begin to meet any of these requirements?

'You are what you eat.' Write an essay explaining how important you think diet is to our health and outlining your reasons.

You are what you eat.
The importance of diet to our health.

You are what you eat because if you eat good food then you feel good but if you eat bad food then you feel awful. If you eat lots of junk food you will get fat and you won't be able to go out and exercise because you'll feel heavy and you'll be tired all the time so you'll just sit on the couch and watch even more TV and eat lots of pizzas and drink lots of fizzy drinks and get even fatter. But if you eat lots of healthy food like fruit and vegetables and beans and rice then you will have lots of energy and it won't all turn into fat so you'll have more energy to do the things you want to do and then you'll feel really great.

SPOTLIGHT ON WRITING

Doing an essay plan
Follow these steps when writing an essay:
1 **Brainstorming:** write down your ideas or a list of points that would answer the question.
2 **Plan the paragraphs:** Remember there should be a clear development between your ideas, so keep your paragraph organisation simple.
3 **Write an introduction:** introduce the topic of the essay to the reader. Often the easiest way to write an introduction is to rephrase the question using your own words.
4 **Write the main body paragraphs:** Clearly state your main points. Use examples if necessary. Explain your reasons. Link your paragraphs appropriately.
5 **Write a conclusion:** A conclusion sums up your main message in the essay.

3 In which paragraphs would you write the following points (a–d)? Match them to the list (1–4) that follows.

a Why we need to eat healthy food
b Why we should avoid junk food
c Summary of main points (importance of paying attention to our diet in order to be healthy)
d Analysis of main statement (the fact that diet affects our physical health and makes us who we are)

1 Opening paragraph – introduction: ___d___
2 Main paragraph 1: ___a___
3 Main paragraph 2: ___b___
4 Closing paragraph – conclusion: ___c___

4 Look at the following introductory paragraphs. Which one would you choose for the essay title, 'You are what you eat'? Why wouldn't you choose the others?

a We are what we eat and therefore diet is very important to our health. This is for a number of reasons.

b It goes without saying that good health is dependent on the food we eat as well as a number of other factors. Our diet not only contributes to our physical health but also to the way we feel – our overall sense of wellbeing. This essentially means that we are what we eat.

c If people eat well they will be healthy and happy. If people eat badly, they will be unhealthy and therefore unhappy. For this reason it is clear that what we eat makes us who we are.

5 Using the points in the list below, write sentences to complete the main body paragraph plans (a and b in exercise 3 above).

nutrients (vitamins, minerals, protein, carbohydrates, fats, enzymes) repair tissues and cells, maintain healthy organs, provide energy, strong immune system, fight off illness, feel great …

nutrient deficiency
too much fat / salt / sugar, overweight or obese, bad health, lack of energy so limited physical exercise, weak immune system, illness and disease, feel bad psychologically …

6 You can show the development between your arguments by using examples. Look at the statements in the box below and notice how the examples used point towards a clear conclusion.

Statement	Example	Conclusion
1 Vitamins / minerals = healthy organs / repair tissues / cells	Vitamin C = healthy skin / immune system	Protects against illness / makes us look better
2 Too much junk food = feeling bad about yourself	Too much junk food = overweight = lack of exercise	Exercise releases endorphins = a sense of well-being and happiness

The first statement could be written like this:

We need vitamins and minerals to maintain healthy organs and repair tissues and cells. For instance, vitamin C is essential for healthy skin and boosts our immune system, as a result protecting us from illness and making us look better at the same time.

Rewrite the second statement in the same way:

Eating Too much junk food can make you feel bad because of the overweight and the lack of exercises

In other words

7 Look back at the student's attempt to write an essay in exercise 2. How many times have the words *and, but, because* and *so* been used? Replace as many as you can with a suitable word or phrase from the list below. Make other changes if it helps.

also   Another point is that   As a result of this/which   ... but on the other hand
Consequently   Despite the fact that   Finally   For which reason   Furthermore
However   In that   In view of this   Moreover   Nevertheless   On the one hand ...
Secondly   Subsequently   Therefore   Whereas   While   Which is why
→ in order to

8 Look at the following conclusion. It says the right things but it is all just one long sentence. This makes it sound clumsy. Can you rewrite it as two shorter sentences?

And so therefore, if we want to live long healthy lives we should follow a number of general guidelines, like for example not smoking and exercising more, but also we must be aware of the food we eat and we should aim to eat more of the right foods and less of the wrong ones because good health is fundamental to our sense of wellbeing and feelings of happiness and as good food equals good health, we should make every effort to eat well- because we are what we eat.

9 PAPER 2, PART 2 Read the essay question below.

Choose one of the statements and write an essay of between 220–260 words, explaining how much you think this statement is true and outlining your reasons.

'Everything in moderation. Too much of anything is bad for our health.'

'A healthy body means a healthy mind. You can't have one without the other.'

'Good health comes from within. External treatments alone are not enough.'

Vocabulary organiser 6

6.1 Getting started, page 53 Complete the sentences in your own words.

1 On a daily basis I try to consume _____ .
2 Generally it's best to avoid _____ .
3 One way of boosting _____ .
4 Organically grown vegetables are _____ .
5 Your immune system works by _____ .
6 Medication may be prescribed _____ .
7 Yoga is a form of _____ .
8 You should establish the root _____ .

6.2 Reading, page 54–55 Decide if the following statements are true or false. Correct the sentences that are false.

1 If you fend off something bad, like an illness, or an attacker, you fight back in order to keep it at bay. T / F (text 1)
2 If your blood clots, it becomes thinner. T / F (text 1)
3 Processed food has been through various procedures that destroy nutrients. T / F (text 1)
4 If you enhance a quality, you make it weaker and less powerful. T / F (text 1)
5 If you do something in moderation, you are doing it too much. T / F (text 1)
6 The efficacy of a drug or medicine is how well it achieves its purpose. T / F (text 2)
7 If you get fed up of something, it means you've been forced to eat too much of it. T / F (text 3)
8 If an idea or suggestion is viable, it means it can work successfully. T / F (text 3)

6.3 Language development, page 56

1 Match the following terms with their definition:
   a a bad egg
   b a nest egg
   c an egghead

   i   not a good person
   ii   money you save for a future purpose
   iii an intellectual person (often out of touch with social trends)

2 Which of the following words cannot be used to mean 'money'?
   a bread
   b dough
   c bacon
   d butter

3 If you were in a life threatening situation, you would probably do everything possible to save your _____ .
   a bacon
   b meat
   c burgers
   d chops

4 A friend of yours picks up a plate and accidentally drops it. What would you call her?
   a Jelly hands!   b Butter fingers!   c Oily palms!

5 What is the missing word in the following sentences?
   a My great aunt Mildred is the _____ of the earth – she'll do anything for someone in need.
   b I think Malcolm can be very interesting to talk to, but you should take whatever he says with a large pinch of _____ .

6 Complete the sentences that follow with one suitable word.
   a Unfortunately it's a _____ of life that we all must die one day.
   b I need some chocolate! It's a _____ of life and death!
   c Would you really _____ down your life just to help another person?

6.4 Use of English, page 59 Complete the collocations in the sentences below with the correct verb.

1 There are several factors you need to _____ into account if you are considering their offer.
2 Garlic is reputed to _____ wonders for one's health.
3 If you smoke, you _____ a much greater risk of getting cancer.
4 You shouldn't _____ fun of Natalie just because she has to wear glasses.
5 Low levels of vitamin D can _____ rise to a number of problems.
6 After her grandfather died, the house began to _____ into disrepair.
7 They tried to tease Nicole, but she wouldn't _____ for it.
8 Please _____ us know if you decide to visit our town.

BANK OF ENGLISH

Stem word: _heal_

1 How many words can you derive from the stem word 'heal'?
2 Which of the following words cannot be preceded by 'health'?

bus	care	centre
club	farm	food
provider	school	visitor

3 Which of the following sentences are incorrect? Can you correct them?
   a I've got a sore throat – I'm hoping it will heal by tomorrow.
   b It's just a little cut – don't worry, it will heal on its own.
   c Anna says she can heal people just by touching them.
   d The doctor has given me some pills to heal me.

7 Wish you were there ...

The open road, a timeless passage,
Has stoutly borne both car and carriage.
Travellers of leisure, travellers in need
Have followed its path wherever it may lead,
That whisper of promise floating in the air
Beckoning them onwards, who knows where?

Getting started

1 What kind of travel is depicted in the photographs?

2 ∩ 7.1 Listen to a tour operator making predictions about the future of travel. Which type(s) of travel does he think will be accessible to the masses?

3 Which of them are appealing to you? Why?

4 Discuss the poem. What image of travel does it evoke? Can you relate it to any of the pictures on this page? In what way?

Reading: multiple matching texts

1 In pairs. Think of a city you have visited that you really like, or the one you live in. Tell your partner about it.

2 ∩ 7.2 Listen to two people, Fiona and Nick, talking about a city they visited recently. Answer the questions below. Use F for Fiona, N for Nick and B for both. Who …?

  a thinks the architecture was impressive   _____

  b talks about the city in terms of smell   _____

  c is enthusiastic about the local people   _____

3 Read texts A and B about two cities that are special to the writers, and find out one thing they like about their chosen city.

B

St. Petersburg

I love St. Petersburg more than anyone I know; if it is possible to love a city more than a person, then that's how strongly I love St. Petersburg.

I was brought up in England, half-Russian, half-English, and I didn't actually go to Russia until I was 19. I was aware of family history and family stories but they did not mean anything to me until I stepped on to Russian soil in 1985. I felt I'd come home. It was a beautiful spring day, northern sun and sparkling snow, lovely fresh air and that wonderful feeling you get when you can see your breath.

We had all heard about the disgusting food and the horrible hotels in the Soviet Union, so I was not sure I would like the place. But I remember standing in the snow, looking at a church with domes, and I had this rush of being at home.

I visited my grandmother's palace, where she was brought up. I had heard about it and how they had left it, but I had only seen it in a black-and-white photograph. I was absolutely breathless – it was so much bigger than it appeared in the photograph. It was crumbling and full of this eerie spirit of the past. It had become a naval headquarters, and it was years before I could get inside.

Very few people are disappointed by St. Petersburg. It is dusty, falling apart and in desperate need of funding, but there is always the chance for you to feel that you have personally discovered a bit of the city yourself.

For me, the essence of St. Petersburg is walking through Rossi's triumphal arch into Palace Square and being hit by the Alexander column and the Hermitage and, beyond, the huge wide expanse of the Neva.

A

I lost my heart in … Dublin

I was born and bred in Dublin but, for me, it still has it all as a city. The only place I can compare it to is Rio de Janeiro because it is by the mountains and the sea.

Only after my travelling have I realised what an amazing city it is – it's walkable and the Dart* can get you down the coast in 15 minutes or into the mountains in 20. Visitors should go to a pub called Johnnie Fox's, in Glencullen, where they have bacon on the open fire. It's quite touristy but Dubliners go there as well.

I'm starting to get very protective of Dublin. It really annoys me that we sell out an awful lot and that shops are being bought up by English chains. People come to Ireland because they want to see Irish things.

One of the things I really like about Dublin at the moment is that when you go into a bar or cafe, there is usually one English person working there. The Irish have been living and working in London for years, so it's great that English people have decided that they can live in Dublin. It's a real sign that things have changed in the last few years.

[*Note: the Dart (Dublin area rapid transit) is a railway line]

4 Read the two statements below. What is the difference in their meaning? Which one is true of the texts above?

  1 Both writers are connected by birth with the place they write about.

  2 Both writers were born in the place they write about.

5 Decide if the following statements are true or false.

  1 The writer was surprised by how much they liked St. Petersburg.   T / F

  2 The writer thinks tourists' view of food and accommodation in Russia is misguided.   T / F

  3 The writer mentions their favourite place in Dublin. T / F

  4 The writer expresses concern about future developments in Dublin.   T / F

  5 The first writer's appreciation of their city is romantic, while the second writer's view is more pragmatic.   T / F

Calcutta

I was first attracted to Calcutta by the crumbling grandeur. I expected the place to be difficult, with terrible bureaucracy and endless frustration, but we settled in quickly. We found somewhere to live within ten days, were accepted right away into the neighbourhood and stayed for five months.

Calcutta is a huge city, but not particularly threatening. Things that would cripple a place like New York are dealt with as part of daily life: everyone keeps going even when the city floods. People seem to be looking out for each other, which you don't get in western cities.

There are squares that remind me of Italian piazzas, fascinating temples and sweet shops like Viennese cafes where people meet and talk. The most British areas are the least appealing.

Some tourists are disappointed if they don't go to visit the slums, but it is easy to get a distorted picture. If you go to Calcutta with an open mind, it is a remarkable place not a disaster zone.

Barcelona

Barcelona under Franco was rather sad and grey, but even then I loved it because it is Mediterranean and Latin but also sober and industrious with a north-European seriousness. In contrast, I find Madrid almost too jolly.

After Franco's death in 1975, the Catalans were given back their autonomy, and Barcelona was cleaned up and became brighter. There was a real sense that Catalans were recovering their identity and you could feel that passion in the city. There was a sense of a long wait before Franco's death, and then everything changed very quickly; it was a very exciting time.

The Olympics transformed Barcelona, especially the harbour. Before then, you could not really enjoy the sea, but now there is a sandy beach five minutes away from the centre. The port area used to be rather shoddy and run down. Now it is beautiful and safe with people flying kites and enjoying the sea.

The old, gothic part has never changed. I love walking through the courtyards and the palaces and finding little book shops. Although it used to be very quiet and now attracts lots of tourists, a big city needs development and the visitors have been a good thing. Everything was there before; it just needed doing up. I don't feel the restoration and development has been destructive.

6 PAPER 1, PART 4 **Read the texts C and D above and answer questions 1–10 that follow, by referring to the four texts A–D.**

Which writer(s) ...?

1 mentions the warmth and resilience of the local people _____
2 show concern about the city retaining its identity _____
3 talks about contrasting aspects of the city _____
4 discovered their initial fears about the city proved groundless _____
5 mentions two events which had a great impact on the city _____
6 compare the city of their choice with another _____
7 is pleased by how the city has developed _____
8 mentions some misconceptions people have about the city _____
9 talks passionately about buildings in the city _____
10 talk about the special atmosphere of the city _____

7 **Find words or phrases in texts A–D which mean the following:**

a companies which own a number of shops in different towns (text A) _____
b sudden strong feeling (text B) _____
c falling apart (text B) _____
d strange and a little frightening (text B) _____
e financial support (text B) _____
f marking victory (text B) _____
g complicated official system with lots of rules, and processes (text C) _____
h stop something from working properly or efficiently (text C) _____
i attractive (text C) _____
j mistaken impression or idea about something (text C) _____
k hardworking, busy (text D) _____
l falsely happy (text D) _____
m independence (text D) _____

Language development:
describing places

1 Which of the words and phrases below from the reading passages on page 64–65 could you use to talk about the following in a town or city?

a buildings _____

b atmosphere _____

c personal reaction _____

amazing	appealing	breathless	crumbling
disgusting	dusty	eerie	gothic
grandeur	horrible	industrious	it has it all
like home	lovely fresh air	magical	old
open mind	passion	threatening	remarkable
run down	shoddy	slums	sober
sparkling snow	the essence of	touristy	unique

Phrasal verbs and phrases with *look*

2 Read this sentence from the text about Calcutta:

'People seem to be looking out for each other, which you don't get in western cities.'

What do you think 'looking out for' means here?

3 Now match the following phrasal verbs with their meanings.

c	1	look forward to	a visit someone when you go to their town
e	2	look ahead	b investigate, try to learn the truth
a	3	look someone up	c be excited and pleased about something
g	4	look up to someone	d try to ensure the other person is treated well
b	5	look into	e think about what might happen in the future
	6	look to someone	f think you are better than another person
f	7	look down on someone	g respect and admire someone
	8	look out for each other	h depend on someone to provide help or advice

4 Decide whether the following sentences are true or false.

1 To 'look something up' means to find out what a word or phrase means in the dictionary.   T / F

2 If you 'look through someone' you don't understand what they are really like.   T / F

3 If you 'look on someone with affection', you watch them tenderly.   T / F

4 If you say that someone is 'not much to look at', you don't find them attractive.   T / F

5 If you say you'll 'look in on someone', you promise to make them a short visit, while you are going somewhere else.   T / F

5 Match the sentence beginnings with their endings.

A

1 'Look me in the eye and

2 'If you see someone being attacked,

3 'I can't believe anyone could

4 'Mrs Brown looked Jenny

5 'By the looks of it,

6 'The situation's getting worse, and I

7 'She just stood there

B

a overlook such an important detail!'

b up and down coldly.'

c you won't be going on that trip tomorrow.'

d don't like the look of it.'

e with a strange look on her face.'

f tell me you didn't break that window!'

g don't just look the other way!'

Key word: *road*

6 Choose the best ending for each of the following sentences.

1 If you are 'on the road to recovery', you are ...
   a making new plans for the future
   b becoming well after an illness

2 If you are 'on the road' you ...
   a are travelling for a while
   b have no fixed home

3 Someone says 'we've come to the end of the road' when ...
   a they've exhausted all possible solutions, and don't know what to do next
   b they've finished a process

4 Someone tells you not to 'go down that road' when they ...
   a want to harm you
   b think a course of action is wrong

5 If you say 'one for the road' you ...
   a are leaving
   b are asking for one more alcoholic drink before you leave

7 Which of the following words can follow *road*?

back	block	blog	credible	hog
house	map	rage	side	sign
show	value	wise	works	worthy

8 PAPER 3, PART 3 Read Sally's email to her French penfriend, Jeanette, and for questions 1–8, fill the gaps with a word formed from the words at the end of some of the lines.

Hi Jeanette!

How are you? Just wanted to tell you my news. Our school went on an (1) _____ to Blackpool yesterday, and the students had a great time.

1 OUT

You haven't been to this area of England before, so I'll tell you a few things about the place. Blackpool is a (2) _____ town, and so it's really (3) _____. It used to be really popular years ago, and if you ignore the run down and boarded up places, many of the houses along the sea front have kept that air of (4) _____ from the days when the town was booming. It's making a comeback now, though, with the help of (5) _____ from some local businessmen, and more people are starting to visit again.

2 SEA

3 TOUR

4 GRAND

5 INVEST

I took my class to Pleasure Beach fairground, and they went on all the rides. Julie Kerr was sick after going on the roller coaster, but that didn't stop any of the others going! Then Pete Jones won a prize in an Elvis (6) _____ contest and everyone teased him.

6 LOOK

We had some (7) _____ problems on the way home, caused by roadworks on the motorway, but that didn't dampen the kids' spirits. They sang all the way. All in all it was one of the most (8) _____ school trips I've ever been on.

7 FORESEE

8 MEMORY

Take care, and let me know when you're coming.

Love, Sally

Use of English: open cloze

PAPER 3, PART 2 Contrast and negative ideas in the text

In this part of the Use of English Paper, you're sometimes presented with a gap that requires a negative word. This can usually only be understood by looking carefully at the context and tone of the passage.

E.g. 'We had a barbecue on Saturday, but (1) _nobody_ turned up, because it was raining.'

Similarly, you may be required to fill a gap with a linking word that shows an opposing idea (contrast).

E.g. 'The TV can be a wonderful source of information. (2) _Nevertheless_, we need to monitor the programmes children watch.'

1 Look carefully at the contexts below, and decide which word fits each gap.

1 Paul had (3) _____ been to India, so this trip to Calcutta would be a new experience for him.

2 Kelly worked very hard at school. (4) _____ this, she didn't pass all her exams.

2 Use the words below to complete the sentences that follow.

despite	few	however	hardly
often	many	with	without

a Although she likes watching films, she _____ ever goes to the cinema.

b There are _____ ways in which you can enjoy yourself in Blackpool, as there is so much to do and see.

c _____ his fear of heights, Adam went up the Eiffel Tower.

d Most people find it difficult to be _____ a mobile phone nowadays.

e It was a beautiful sunny day. _____, she decided to stay in and do her homework.

f The beach was crowded, _____ colourful umbrellas and sunbeds covering almost every inch of sand.

g David _____ visits his grandmother, even though she lives 50 miles away.

h _____ people I know have ever visited Alaska, because they prefer going somewhere hot.

3 PAPER 3, PART 2 Complete the sentences. Use only one word in each gap.

Second Life

Until now, the word 'travel' has always conjured up visions of packed bags, the open road, and generally the idea of escape. (1) _____, an exciting new concept is changing all that. Not (2) _____ may you now travel to another country, but to another 'world', (3) _____ even leaving home.

'Second Life' is an interactive simulated world on the Internet which offers visitors the ultimate form of escapism: the ability to reinvent (4) _____ and live their dream life. (5) _____ you create your persona, called *an avatar*, and give it a name. Then you (6) _____ exploring the virtual environment, and choose to interact, or not, (7) _____ the other avatars you meet. For many, the beauty of the avatars is (8) _____ they can fly. You (9) _____ travel great distances, gaining a bird's eye view of various 'environments', (10) _____ the effect is rather surreal. The world changes while you watch, as other more experienced 'gamers' buy and sell property, using for currency the Linden dollar, (11) _____ has an exchange rate against the US dollar. Never before (12) _____ a game offered players so many options! You can shop, work, travel and (13) _____ relationships, go to parties, or hold your own parties if you want (14) _____.

'Second Life' is expanding rapidly, as more and more people are (15) _____ attracted to it, so don't miss out! Simply allow your PC to transport you there and let your imagination do the rest!

Listening: multiple extracts

1 Discuss. Would you like to travel in space? Why or why not?

2 Read the comment below on space travel. Does the speaker approve or disapprove of it? Then answer exercises 3–5 in the Spotlight on the right.

> The best spaceship is the one we live on. It's fully equipped with food, water and the natural resources necessary to sustain human life. Anyone who studies outer space for a living as I do can tell you that we have yet to discover a planet that comes close. So why pay extortionate sums of money to leave it, when we'd be better off protecting it from destruction?

3 **Who is making the comment on the left?**
   a An astronomer
   b A political activist

4 **Which words or phrases helped you choose your answer?**

5 **What is the speaker expressing?**
   a Fears that space travel will destroy the Earth's environment.
   b Concern that human beings fail to appreciate what they've got.

6 🎧 7.3 You will hear five short extracts in which people talk about commercial space travel.

Task One
For questions **1–5**, choose from the list A–H the occupation of the person who is speaking.

A a future 'space tourist'
B a medical expert
C a spaceflight representative
D a journalist
E a professor of science
F an environmentalist
G a businessman
H a university student

Speaker 1 ☐ 1
Speaker 2 ☐ 2
Speaker 3 ☐ 3
Speaker 4 ☐ 4
Speaker 5 ☐ 5

Task Two
For questions **6–10**, choose from the list A–H what each speaker is expressing.

A dismissal of the idea of space travel
B ignorance of the ethical problems surrounding space travel
C a desire to fulfil a lifelong ambition
D medical advice on travelling in space
E pride in personal involvement in developments in space
F an explanation of spaceflight procedure
G fears about safety in spaceflights
H concern that important issues are being ignored

Speaker 1 ☐ 6
Speaker 2 ☐ 7
Speaker 3 ☐ 8
Speaker 4 ☐ 9
Speaker 5 ☐ 10

7 Discuss. Which of the views expressed regarding commercial space travel do you agree with? Support your ideas.

Grammar: inversion

1   Sentence a below appears in 'Second Life' on page 67. The sentence has been inverted. Compare it with sentence b. What effect does it have?

   a   Not only can you now travel to another country, but to another 'world', without even leaving home.

   b   You can now travel to another 'world', as well as another country, and not leave home.

GRAMMAR SPOTLIGHT

Using inversion
We tend to use inversion:
- in formal situations
- to emphasise a point, especially in official/political speeches
- to make a statement more convincing or interesting
- to make a recommendation more persuasive
- to make a narrative more dramatic.

2   **Invert the following sentences, beginning with the phrases given.**

   a   'This tough cleaning gel will clean your kitchen surfaces, and also make your pans shine!'
       'Not only _____.'

   b   As soon as she opened the door, flames swept into the room.
       No sooner _____.

   c   'This is the first time anything like this has happened in this town!' said the Mayor.
       'Never before _____,'
       said the Mayor.

   d   Visitors must not take photographs inside the museum under any circumstances.
       Under no circumstances _____.

   e   'This is the only opportunity you will have to buy our product at this price!'
       'Never again _____!'

3   **Discuss. For each of the contexts presented below, choose the sentence you would be most likely to hear.**

   1   Politician at a press conference:
       a   'Never before has the country been more in need of positive action!'
       b   'The country really needs some positive action to be taken!'

   2   Four-year-old child to mother:
       a   'Not once have you let me watch TV this week!'
       b   'You haven't let me watch TV even once this week!'

   3   Newsreader:
       a   'Rarely has a politician had such a dramatic effect on opinion polls.'
       b   'A politician doesn't often have such a dramatic effect on opinion polls.'

   4   Friend to friend:
       a   'On no account am I going to Paul's party!'
       b   'I'm not going to Paul's party, and that is final!'

4   **Turn to Tapescript 7.3 on page 212, and underline the inverted phrases. In which extract does the speaker not use inversion?**

5   **In pairs. Make the speech in tapescript 7.3 sound more persuasive, by inserting some inverted phrases where appropriate. Make any necessary changes to the sentence structure.**

6   **Complete the second sentence in the following pairs of sentences with one of the phrases from exercise 3.**

   a   This is the first time a game has offered players so many options.
       _____ a game offered players so many options.

   b   As soon as the President began his speech it started to rain.
       _____ the President begun his speech than it started to rain.

   c   'Students must not talk during the exam.'
       _____ students talk during the examination.

7   **Make the statement below more persuasive.**

'Commercial space travel is now available to the public, and you can book tickets for the first flight. This is an opportunity for anyone who is interested in space.'

➡ Grammar Reference 7.1, page 174

Speaking: discussing possible future developments

1   **Discuss. Read the following statements, and decide whether you agree with them or not. Give reasons for your opinions.**

> One day, people will be going on virtual holidays in the comfort of their own home. It could become the only kind of holiday they'll be able to afford!

> Future weekends away will include trips to space station hotels.

> We could soon be coming to earth 'on holiday'.

> We spend too much time rushing around, and speed in travel seems to be a constant issue. I think people will veer towards the 'go slow' idea of pony trekking, as a reaction to all this.

2   **PAPER 5, PART 4 Discuss. Use the phrases in the box below to express your views about the following question.**

What do you think the future holds for travel and tourism?

USEFUL LANGUAGE

We can't say for certain how things will be, but …
It's very likely that …
There's a strong possibility that …
Contrary to popular opinion, I think that …
I disagree with the belief that things will …
One day, you may see …
There will still be people who …

Writing: a proposal

1 **Read the following question.**

PAPER 2, PART 1 You **must** answer this question. Write your answer in **180–220** words in an appropriate style.

You work at an art gallery. The number of people visiting the gallery has fallen, and the director has sent you the following email, asking you to help.

Read the email below, on which you have made some notes. Then, using the information carefully, write a proposal, suggesting the best ways to attract more visitors to the gallery.

workshops, to attract schools: gallery Art Club? Painting competition for different age ranges?

more variety of exhibits on display: vary art medium – photography exhibition? Sculpture? Tiles / textile design?Graphic Design?

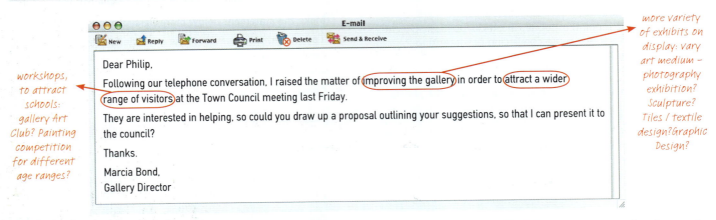

E-mail

New   Reply   Forward   Print   Delete   Send & Receive

Dear Philip,

Following our telephone conversation, I raised the matter of improving the gallery in order to attract a wider range of visitors at the Town Council meeting last Friday.

They are interested in helping, so could you draw up a proposal outlining your suggestions, so that I can present it to the council?

Thanks,

Marcia Bond,
Gallery Director

2 **Compare the two answers below. Look at whether the style and register are appropriate, and how effectively the student has used the input information from the question.**

A

Introduction
Here are some suggestions for ways to attract more visitors to the Gallery.

Exhibitions
One way is to exhibit a wider range of artistic work. We should include work from contemporary local artists, but also vary the art medium, by featuring photography, sculpture and tile or textile design. Graphic design could also be featured. To enhance the exhibits, we need to spend some money on improving the lighting in the Exhibition Halls.

Workshops for schools
To attract more visits from schools, we could hold painting workshops, with experts displaying their skills and techniques. This may be expensive, however, as extra staff would have to be employed. Also, we could encourage students to join our Art Club. A painting competition could be held for different age groups, and winners' work could be displayed in the gallery.

Conclusion
All in all, I feel that the suggestions mentioned above are practical, and would bring more visitors to the gallery.

B

Introduction
The aim of this proposal is to suggest practical ways to attract more visitors to the Terrigal Art Gallery.

Exhibitions
First, we need to vary the range of artistic work on display in the gallery. Until now, exhibitions have been restricted almost exclusively to paintings, and so attracted a relatively small group in the community. A good idea would be to offer stimulating alternative art forms. For example, we could hold a photographic exhibition, then one of sculpture, followed by fabric design or possibly graphic design. Not only would this cater for a broader range of contemporary specialist tastes, but the variety would also arouse the interest of the general public.

Workshops for schools
Another idea is to target schools and hold art workshops on a regular basis. The workshops should be related to a specific exhibition being held in the gallery, with artists demonstrating some of their techniques. Costs to the gallery could be kept to a minimum by charging participants a nominal fee. The workshop feature could be further developed by the creation of an Art Club for young people. Through this, painting and photography competitions could be held, with sponsorship from local businesses.

Conclusion
Only by developing a broader range of exhibits, more in line with contemporary interests, can we make the gallery successful once more.

Persuasive language

In part 2 of the Writing Paper, your answer will need to contain an element of persuasion. You may have to persuade your reader to follow a particular course of action, or, as is necessary when writing a proposal, you may need to convince them that your idea is a good one.

3 **Discuss.** Look back at answer B on page 70. How does the student make their ideas sound convincing?

4 Compare the following pairs of sentences. Which pair of sentences sound more persuasive and why?

1 a If we implemented these ideas, we would improve museum facilities.
  b This would attract more visitors, and also encourage businesses to invest in the area.

2 a The implementation of such ideas would dramatically improve museum facilities.
  b Not only would this attract more visitors, but it would also encourage businesses to invest in the area.

In other words

Use some of the words and structures below in appropriate ways to make answer A on page 70 more persuasive.

Displaying ... would arouse interest among ...
For example, modern innovations in ... could be exhibited.
Not only would this ... but also ...
This would certainly attract ...
Costs could be kept to a minimum by ...
Only if ...   attractive   inspirational
stimulating   innovative   effective

5 **PAPER 2, PART 1** You're a representative of the student union of your college. You have received the email below from the union president, regarding 'the end of year' college outing.

Read the email, and the notes you have written on it. Using the information given, write a proposal for making this year's outing a memorable one.

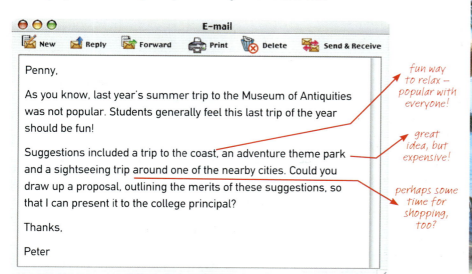

Penny,

As you know, last year's summer trip to the Museum of Antiquities was not popular. Students generally feel this last trip of the year should be fun!

Suggestions included a trip to the coast, an adventure theme park and a sightseeing trip around one of the nearby cities. Could you draw up a proposal, outlining the merits of these suggestions, so that I can present it to the college principal?

Thanks,

Peter

fun way to relax – popular with everyone!

great idea, but expensive!

perhaps some time for shopping, too?

6 Write your **proposal** in 180–220 words in an appropriate style.

Vocabulary organiser 7

7.1 Reading, page 65 **Complete the sentences below with a suitable word from exercise 7 on page 65.**

1   The National Art Gallery is in serious need of government _____ if it is to maintain the quality of its exhibitions.
2   In the village of Ashton Hayes, some _____ residents have launched a campaign to make the community carbon neutral.
3   The local power workers' strike has _____ business in the town, and entrepreneurs are calling for action to be taken.
4   Liverpool's _____ parade through the streets of their home town after beating Chelsea 3–2 yesterday stopped the traffic for over an hour.
5   After battling for many years, Scotland finally gained its _____, creating the Scottish Parliament in 1999.
6   The big supermarket _____ are threatening to wipe out all corner grocery stores.
7   As she stared at the doll's house she had played with as a child, Sally felt a sudden _____ of nostalgia for the blissful innocence of those days.
8   I worked at the town hall for a while, but I hated all the _____ involved in getting anything done in local government. There was so much paperwork!
9   From the outside, the cottage looked very _____, but when I walked through the door I could see it needed a lot of work doing on it to make it inhabitable!
10   There is a popular _____ that men aren't good at housework, but this is not true!

7.2 Language development, page 66

a   Place the descriptive words below into the correct column.

amazing	appealing	breathless	crumbling	cosy
disgusting	dusty	eerie	grand	horrible
industrious	magical	passionate	remarkable	run down
shoddy	sober	sparkling	threatening	unique

Positive description   Negative description

_____   _____
_____   _____
_____   _____
_____   _____
_____   _____
_____   _____
_____   _____
_____   _____
_____   _____

b   Discuss. Brainstorm other words to describe places and add them to the lists above.

7.3 Language development, page 66 **Write definitions for the following phrases with 'look'. Use a dictionary to help you.**

look ahead: _____
look down on somebody: _____
look forward to: _____
look in on somebody: _____
look into something: _____
look out for each other: _____
look through somebody: _____
look somebody up: _____
look up to somebody: _____
look somebody in the eye: _____

7.4 Language development (key word), page 66 **Decide whether the following statements are true or false.**

1   A 'road hog' is a farm animal that has got out into the road.   T / F
2   'Road rage' is angry behaviour by car drivers towards other drivers.   T / F
3   We say a person is 'roadworthy' when they are able to drive a car or motorbike.   T / F
4   'Road works' are repairs that are being done to a road.   T / F
5   A 'roadshow' is a type of carnival procession.   T / F
6   A 'road block' is an obstacle in the middle of the road that prevents cars from passing.   T / F
7   The 'roadside' is the edge of the road.   T / F

Write the phrases in your note book with their correct definition.

7.5 Grammar, page 69 **Complete the sentences below.**

1   Not only did she go to the party against my wishes …
2   Never before has anyone …
3   No sooner had I got home …
4   On no account must you write …
5   Not once did Winston …
6   Under no circumstances should you call …
7   Not until they arrived at the hotel …
8   Hardly had she walked into the classroom …

BANK OF ENGLISH

Word partnerships: *travel*

In the Listening section of this unit we talk about 'space travel'. There are various kinds of travel, and phrases associated with travel. Place the following phrases in the correct category below, according to how the word *travel* is used.

air travel	on their travels	rail travel
travel agent	travel by train, car, or plane	travel light
travel rug	travel sickness	travel widely
traveller's cheque	travelling expenses	travelling
musician	travelling salesman	travelogue

VERB: _____
NOUN: _____
ADJECTIVE: _____

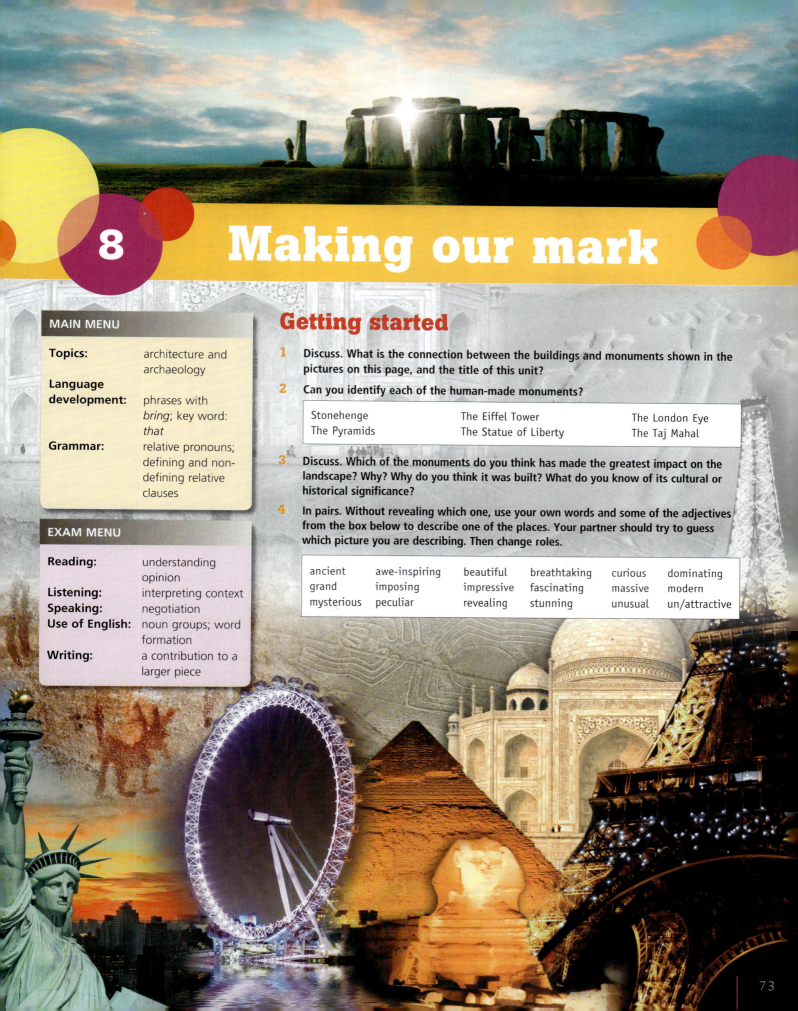

8 Making our mark

MAIN MENU

Topics: architecture and archaeology

Language development: phrases with *bring*; key word: *that*

Grammar: relative pronouns; defining and non-defining relative clauses

EXAM MENU

Reading: understanding opinion
Listening: interpreting context
Speaking: negotiation
Use of English: noun groups; word formation
Writing: a contribution to a larger piece

Getting started

1 Discuss. What is the connection between the buildings and monuments shown in the pictures on this page, and the title of this unit?

2 Can you identify each of the human-made monuments?

Stonehenge	The Eiffel Tower	The London Eye
The Pyramids	The Statue of Liberty	The Taj Mahal

3 Discuss. Which of the monuments do you think has made the greatest impact on the landscape? Why? Why do you think it was built? What do you know of its cultural or historical significance?

4 In pairs. Without revealing which one, use your own words and some of the adjectives from the box below to describe one of the places. Your partner should try to guess which picture you are describing. Then change roles.

ancient	awe-inspiring	beautiful	breathtaking	curious	dominating
grand	imposing	impressive	fascinating	massive	modern
mysterious	peculiar	revealing	stunning	unusual	un/attractive

73

Reading: understanding opinion

1 What do you know about green or sustainable architecture? Why do you think there is a growing interest in this kind of building in many countries today?

2 Which of the following criteria should be considered by architects planning to build an eco-house? Number in order of importance.

a Aesthetics (appearance) ☐

b Building materials (ecological impact, sustainability) ☐

c Cost (materials, labour) ☐

d Design features (modern or traditional) ☐

e Durability (lifespan of the building) ☐

f Efficiency (insulation, energy costs) ☐

g Environment (surroundings) ☐

h Energy (for construction, pollution) ☐

i Health (toxicity of materials) ☐

j Safety (fire risk, structural reliability) ☐

3 Look at the photo of a house made out of bales of straw below. What do you think would be the advantages and disadvantages of building a house like this?

4 Discuss. What would you normally associate a bale of straw with? Do you know a children's story that features three pigs and a house made of straw? Tell the story.

5 🎧 8.1 Listen to somebody listing the benefits of a straw bale house and see if you were right. Write down the seven main advantages that they mention.

SPOTLIGHT ON READING

Understanding opinion

In Paper 1, candidates are expected to show understanding of the writer's opinion, even if the writer's view contradicts other information. You should aim to read the text carefully in order to understand the main points the writer is making before you read the multiple choice questions.

6 Quickly read through the extract on page 75 from an information leaflet about straw bale buildings and answer the questions below according to the writer's view. Underline the part of the text which answers the questions.

[Para. 1] Why does the writer think that straw bale houses are at 'a pivotal point'?

[Para. 2] What's the atmosphere like on a straw bale house construction site?

[Para. 3] What does the writer think about working with straw as a building material?

[Para. 4] What does the writer think are the two main practical advantages of a straw bale house?

[Para. 5] According to the writer, what kinds of houses are ideally built out of straw?

[Para. 6] What kind of attitude does the writer think you should adopt when working with straw?

[Para. 7] Why does the writer think straw bale houses are better for our health?

7 PAPER 1, PART 3 For questions 1–7, choose the answer (A, B, C or D) which you think fits best according to the text on page 75.

1 According to the writer, straw bale building
   A is a novel variation of standard wall building techniques.
   B developed from experiments to build houses out of grass.
   C is favoured by people who have radically different views.
   D is about to be taken seriously by designers and builders.

2 The writer suggests that
   A building projects should be managed by authorised groups.
   B a straw bale houses can be erected quickly by people working together.
   C there are more women builders on a straw bale site than men.
   D it is only possible to build your own house if you join a co-operative.

3 The writer implies that
   A straw can be used in much the same way as traditional materials.
   B straw may cause some people to consolidate their ideas about construction.
   C straw houses may not be suitable for complex or insecure people.
   D straw houses are solid and safe despite misinformation to the contrary.

4 The writer points out that
   A straw bale buildings use far less energy to keep warm in winter.
   B the majority of brick houses do not have super insulated walls.
   C a conventional family house costs at least £10,000 to build.
   D a house owner can cut their heating bills by one quarter once they moves in.

5 In the writer's opinion, straw
   A can only be used to build houses that do not need a precise design.
   B is an ideal material for flexible and organic designs.
   C has to be used in a particular rounded style of house.
   D makes traditional stone or brick houses appear colder.

6 The writer insists that when building with straw,
   A it's easy to make mistakes if you don't know the material.
   B novice builders should seek expert advice about building techniques.
   C a good team effort and sense of logic is essential.
   D you are given the power to do anything you want.

7 In the writer's view
   A more people are becoming affected by the atmosphere inside their houses.
   B all modern building materials emit poisonous contaminants.
   C a straw bale house can remove the toxins in the air and walls.
   D people with breathing problems would be better off in a straw bale house.

Straw Bale Futures

Straw bale building is a smart way to build. It's more than just a wall building technique that has yet to come into its own. It's a radically different approach to the process of building itself. Like all innovative ideas, it has been pioneered by the passionate, and used experimentally by those with the vision to see its potential. Its background is grassroots self-build; it is firmly based in that sustainable, 'green building' culture that has brought to the construction industry many new and useful ideas about energy efficiency and responsibility towards the environment. It is now at a pivotal point in its development, ready to be taken on by construction firms who see its value in terms of cost-effectiveness, sustainability, ease of installation and energy efficiency. The building method itself is based on a block system, making the designs very easy to adapt from one project to another, and giving great flexibility in its use.

The accessible nature of straw means that people unfamiliar with the building process can now participate in it. This opens the door for interest groups to work together on joint projects. Local authorities and housing associations, for example, are ideal managers for self-build straw projects that won't take years to complete, and which will engender an excitement and motivation that gets the job done. The atmosphere on a straw bale building site is qualitatively different to that found on the vast majority of other sites. It is woman-friendly, joyful, optimistic and highly motivated. Knowledge and skills are freely shared, and co-operation and teamwork predominate, all of which has a positive effect on health and safety on site.

Working with straw is unlike working with any other material. It is simple, flexible, imprecise and organic. It will challenge your preconceptions about the nature of building and the correct way of doing things; not everyone will be able to meet this challenge. Its simplicity can be disarming, or alarming. If you need complexity for security, then this may not be for you. Don't be put off by nursery tales about the big bad wolf – we should be wise enough to realise that the wolf probably worked for the cement manufacturers! And don't pay too much attention to colloquial tales about 'hippie' houses – read on, and make your own mind up.

Straw as a building material excels in the areas of cost-effectiveness and energy efficiency. If used to replace the more traditional wall-building system of brick and block, it can present savings of around £10,000 on a normal three-bedroomed house. Of interest to the home owner is the huge reduction in heating costs once the house is occupied, due to the super insulation of the walls. Here the potential savings are up to 75% compared to a conventional modern house.

One of the biggest attributes of straw bale building is its capacity for creative fun, and its ability to allow you to design and build the sort of shape and space you'd really like. It lends itself very well to curved and circular shapes, and can provide deep window seats, alcoves and niches due to the thickness of the bales. It's also a very forgiving material, can be knocked back into shape fairly easily during wall-raising, doesn't require absolute precision, and can make rounded as well as angular corners. Partly due to its great insulation value and partly because of its organic nature, the inside of a straw bale house feels very different to a brick or stone one, having a cosy, warm quality to it and a pleasing look to the eye.

Straw is a flexible material and requires us to work with it somewhat differently than if it was rigid. Accurate measurement and precision is impossible and unnecessary with straw, but working without these aids can be worrying to the novice, and threatening if you're already used to 20th century building techniques. You have to develop a feel for the straw. You have to give it time, absorb its flexibility. More than any other material (except perhaps cob and clay) it is susceptible to your own spirit and that of the team. Straw bale building is not something to do alone. It requires co-operation, skill-sharing and common sense. Many of the inspirational and artistic features occur in this atmosphere. It is empowering, expanding the world of opportunities for you and making possible what you thought to be impossible!

The atmosphere and environment in which we live is becoming increasingly a matter of concern to homeowners and designers alike. There is a growing body of knowledge on the harmful effects of living long-term with modern materials that give off minute but significant amounts of toxins, the so-called 'sick-building syndrome'. Living in a straw house protects you from all that. It is a natural, breathable material that has no harmful effects. Hay fever sufferers are not affected by straw, as it does not contain pollens. Asthmatics too find a straw bale house a healthier environment to live in. Combined with a sensible choice of natural plasters and paints, it can positively enhance your quality of life.

Language development:

phrases with *bring*

1 Complete the sentences with the correct particle from the box below. There is one extra particle.

| ab~~o~~ut | back | ~~down~~ | forward | ~~out~~ | ~~o~~n | ~~up~~ |

a Brian always manages to bring ___out___ the best in his boys, doesn't he?
b All those industrial strikes in the 70s finally managed to bring ___down___ the government.
c It's funny you should bring that ___up___ – I was just thinking of mentioning it myself.
d Jackson managed to bring ___about___ a complete change in the way we worked.
e Mr Johnson has brought ___forward___ the meeting to this morning at 11 o'clock.
f They think his illness was brought ___on___ by all the stress and anxiety in his work.

2 Match the sentences below with the correct definition.

g 1 They were hoping for a good review; they hadn't expected to *bring the house down*.
d 2 Against all the odds, she managed to *bring* three healthy boys *into the world*.
f 3 He added a few jokes to the telling in order to *bring it alive*.
a 4 Her tone of voice *brought it home to me* that we were no longer friends.
b 5 Listening to that song again *brought it all back* to me.
c 6 The smaller children marched in front and Tim and George were told *to bring up the rear*.
h 7 Doing a university degree while raising four children nearly *brought her to her knees*, but she did it!
e 8 He couldn't *bring himself* to tell her the truth.

a to make somebody realise something
b to make somebody remember something
c to be the last person in a moving line
d to give birth to
e to make oneself do something difficult
f to make something more interesting
g to greatly impress an audience or critic
h to defeat someone

3 Read the text below and underline the two phrasal verbs that use *bring*. Explain what each phrase means.

Carbon footprint

The phenomena of global warming and climate change have <u>brought about</u> a much greater awareness of the consequences of human activities and lifestyles. The term 'carbon footprint' has come into existence in recent years as a way of describing the amount of carbon dioxide that is released into the earth's atmosphere by any one particular activity or thing. For instance a trans-Atlantic flight on a supersonic aeroplane will leave a much larger carbon footprint than travelling an equivalent distance by ship. Likewise the manufacture of plastic objects leaves a much larger carbon footprint than the use of many natural and sustainable materials. Some individuals and organisations are working hard to <u>bring down</u> their own carbon footprints to almost nothing. This is known as becoming 'carbon neutral'.

Key word: *that*

That can be used:

1 As a relative pronoun (instead of *who* or *which*)
2 To introduce reported speech
3 As a reference device (to refer back to something previously mentioned)
4 To refer to something the speaker is physically distant from or not involved in
5 After adjectives

4 Match the sentences below to the rules above.

4 a *That* smells delicious. What is it?
2 b They announced (that) they were going to resume excavations in the spring.
5 c It's obvious (that) they will never approve of his house plans.
1 d We've been invited to a house-warming party by the woman *that* moved in next door.
3 e For *that* reason, we decided it was time to move out.

5 ***That*** can often be omitted altogether. Put brackets around the instances of *that* that can be omitted in the above sentences.

6 Look back at 'Straw Bale Futures' on page 75. The word *that* has been used several times. Underline them and count how many times has it been used. 12

1 How many times can *that* be replaced by 'which'? ___6___
2 How many times can *that* be replaced by 'who/whom'? ___0___
3 How many times can *that* be omitted altogether? ___3___
4 How many times is *that* used as a reference device? ___3___
5 How many times is *that* used to introduce speech? ___2___

Speaking: reaching a decision through negotiation

Reaching a decision through negotiation

In Paper 5, part 3 you need to sustain an interaction with your partner and will probably be asked to decide something about the pictures you will be shown. You don't have to agree with each other but you need to try to persuade your partner to agree with you by giving your reasons for your choice or reasons why you don't agree with their choice. Be flexible and listen to your partner's ideas too.

1 Read the Student A statements below and choose the most suitable response as Student B. Give reasons for your choice.

1   Student A: I think the Parthenon in Athens is the most impressive monument.
   a   *I don't think it is the most impressive monument. I think the Colosseum is the most impressive monument.*
   b   *I can't disagree with you totally but personally I would prefer the Colosseum.*

2   Student A: I would like to visit the Pyramids in Egypt.
   a   *While I'm inclined to agree with you to a certain extent, I actually think that Macchu Piccu has much more to offer.*
   b   *No, I would like to visit Macchu Piccu because it has more to offer.*

3   Student A: I would probably choose the Great Wall of China – it has to be the biggest human-made object on earth. What about you?
   a   *No. Stonehenge. It's older.*
   b   *While you've got a point there, I would have to say that Stonehenge would probably be more mysterious and fascinating.*

2   PAPER 5, PART 3 In pairs. Look at the pictures on page 196. Practise the following speaking.

> Interlocutor: Now, I'd like you to talk about something together for about three minutes. Here are some pictures showing different human-made monuments. First, talk to each other about how the monuments in each picture may have been important to the people who built them. Then decide which monument would be most interesting to visit. You should try to talk together for about three minutes.

Listening: interpreting context

PAPER 4, PART 1 Interpreting context

In Paper 4, part 1, you may be required to interpret the context of the pieces you hear in order to answer the questions correctly. You may not actually hear the answer in the dialogue, but there will be other verbal clues to help you identify it.

1 **8.2 Listen to a man being interviewed about his work.**

The man is
A   an architect.
B   a fine artist.
C   a philosopher.

Write down three phrases or clues which give away his occupation.

2 You may also hear words or phrases that may lead you towards an incorrect answer.
Listen to the dialogue again and write down any words or phrases that the speaker uses which may lead you to think B and C may be correct. Explain why they are wrong.

3 Listen to the extract one more time and answer the question that follows. Make notes for each point A, B, and C that explain why each answer may be right or wrong.

He thinks it is important to
A   keep his clients satisfied.
B   make a mark on the landscape.
C   maintain harmony between his work and the landscape.

4 8.3 **PAPER 4, PART 1** You will hear two different extracts. For questions 1–4, choose the answer (A, B or C) which fits best according to what you hear. There are two questions for each extract.

Extract One: You hear two people discussing a significant moment in the woman's career.

1   The woman is most probably
   A   a student.
   B   an archaeologist.
   C   an explorer.

2   She is describing
   A   the moment she made a significant discovery.
   B   the main motivations behind the project.
   C   an Egyptian artefact excavated 10,000 years earlier.

Extract Two: You hear part of an interview with the rock star Angel Jacobs.

3   Angel is talking about
   A   her childhood.
   B   her education.
   C   her main reason for becoming a rock star.

4   What does Angel regret most about being famous?
   A   That she can't be left alone when she wants to be.
   B   That she can't totally disappear from the public eye.
   C   That reporters follow her wherever she goes.

Grammar: relative pronouns / defining and non-defining relative clauses

1 Complete the sentences below with *which, who, whose, when* or *where*.

a That's the man _whose_ dog keeps following me home.

b It was almost dark _when_ Samuel got here.

c Isn't that the expedition _which_ you wanted to go on?

d If I ever go back to the place _where_ I was born, I'll let you know.

e Is that the man _who_ bought your car?

2 In which of the above sentences can the pronoun be replaced by *that* or be omitted altogether?

3 Complete the sentences with one of the phrases below.

all of whom	as a result of which	at which point
both of whom	by which time	in which
neither of whom	some of which	the person whom

a We arrived at the station at ten past three _by which time_ the train had left.

b Julian is _the person whom_ I was telling you about.

c We missed the train _as a result of which_ we were both late to work.

d That's the church _in which_ my grandparents were married.

e Two hundred immigrants, _all of whom_ were looking for a better life, had fled their homes.

f Mike and Jill, _neither of whom_ had ever eaten asparagus before, thought it was delicious.

g The houses, _some of which_ were still unfinished, were put up for sale.

h Andy and Karen, _both of whom_ are unemployed, have offered to look after my house next summer.

i We spread out the rug and opened the picnic basket _at which point_ the rain came pouring down.

→ Grammar Reference 8.1, page 175

4 Look at the pairs of sentences below. Decide which sentence contains a defining relative clause (D) and which contains a non-defining relative clause (ND). What's the difference in meaning between each pair of sentences?

n.d. 1 a The Indians, who lived in these parts, respected the land.
d   b The Indians that lived in these parts respected the land.

n.d. 2 a Petra, the architect who built this house, studied in London.
d   b The architect that built this house studied in London.

d 3 a The trees that had been growing for over a century were cut down.
n.d.   b The trees, which had been growing for over a century, were cut down.

5 Why are commas used in some of the sentences in exercise 5? What other differences are there between the pairs of sentences?

6 Rewrite each of the following sentences twice, so that the information in brackets is clear in the meaning.

1 The exhibits were in the Egypt section. They were very old. *(All of them / Some of them)*

2 The students got part-time jobs. They wanted some extra money. *(Some of them / All of them)*

3 The girls were waiting for the bus. They were wearing a school uniform. *(Only one girl / All the girls)*

4 The house is going to be knocked down. It has a beautiful garden. *(There are many houses / Only one house)*

GRAMMAR SPOTLIGHT

Reduced relative clauses

7 It is quite usual to alter or reduce sentences which contain a relative clause. Look at the following sentences. What changes have been made?

1 Many species which are growing in the rainforest have not yet been discovered.
Many species growing in the rainforest have not yet been discovered.

2 The box, which was broken in the accident, was a family heirloom.
The box, broken in the accident, was a family heirloom.

3 Neil Armstrong was the first man who walked on the moon.
Neil Armstrong was the first man to walk on the moon.

→ Grammar Reference 8.2, page 175

8 Read the following sentences and underline the relative clauses. Then rewrite each one as a reduced relative clause.

a The tunnel which was weakened by years of neglect, was no longer considered safe.

b Children who are attending that school have all their lessons in French.

c Gillian was the only person who volunteered to help organise the event.

d Rebecca, who was embarrassed by what she had done, decided not to tell anyone.

e Adrian, who was expecting to be paid that week, offered to buy drinks for everyone.

Monday July 21 1969

1969: Man makes his first sp

On the moon after perfect touchdown

Use of English: word building (noun groups)

1 Transform the following words into nouns and put them under the relevant heading below.

combine	cosmic	deliver	dependent	develop	encourage	inhabit	naughty
persuade	obsessed	racist	redundant	sensitive	stupid	tense	tired

-ism	racism	-ology	cosmology
-ity	sensitivity / stupidity	-ment	development / encouragement
-ation	combination	-cy	redundancy / dependency
-ness	tiredness / naughtiness	-ant	dependant / inhabitant
-sion	obsession / tension persuasion	-ry	delivery

SPOTLIGHT ON VOCABULARY

Compiling noun groups

Be careful! Some nouns have more than one form.

2 How many noun forms does the word *inhabit* have?

3 Discuss. What do you know about the statues in the picture below? Have you seen them before? Who do you think made them and why?

4 PAPER 3, PART 3 For questions 1–10, read the text below. Use the word given in capitals at the end of some of the lines to form a word that fits in the gap in the same line.

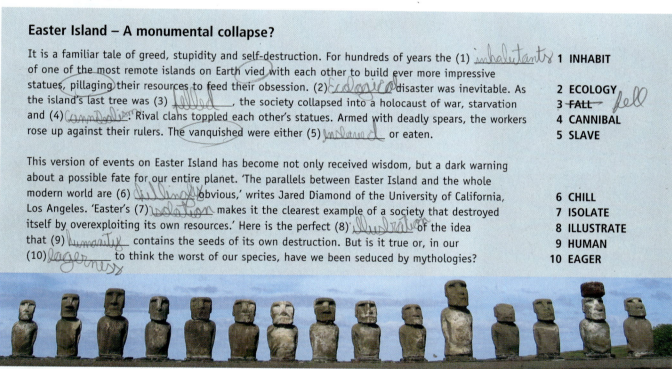

Easter Island – A monumental collapse?

It is a familiar tale of greed, stupidity and self-destruction. For hundreds of years the (1) inhabitants **1 INHABIT**
of one of the most remote islands on Earth vied with each other to build ever more impressive
statues, pillaging their resources to feed their obsession. (2) Ecological disaster was inevitable. As **2 ECOLOGY**
the island's last tree was (3) felled , the society collapsed into a holocaust of war, starvation **3 FALL** *fell*
and (4) cannibalism. Rival clans toppled each other's statues. Armed with deadly spears, the workers **4 CANNIBAL**
rose up against their rulers. The vanquished were either (5) enslaved or eaten. **5 SLAVE**

This version of events on Easter Island has become not only received wisdom, but a dark warning
about a possible fate for our entire planet. 'The parallels between Easter Island and the whole
modern world are (6) chillingly obvious,' writes Jared Diamond of the University of California, **6 CHILL**
Los Angeles. 'Easter's (7) isolation makes it the clearest example of a society that destroyed **7 ISOLATE**
itself by overexploiting its own resources.' Here is the perfect (8) illustration of the idea **8 ILLUSTRATE**
that (9) humanity contains the seeds of its own destruction. But is it true or, in our **9 HUMAN**
(10) eagerness to think the worst of our species, have we been seduced by mythologies? **10 EAGER**

5 Discuss. Do you think the people of Easter Island really brought about their own destruction? What else could have happened that led to their disappearance?

6 ∩ 8.4 Listen to the extract and answer the questions below. Turn to the tapescript on page 213 and underline the key words that helped you find the answers.

1 The islanders may have _____ with each other by trying to build the biggest statues.
2 There is a lack of _____ to prove that the people of Easter Island brought about their own destruction.
3 The island was "discovered" on _____ by a Dutch explorer called Jacob Roggeveen.
4 The island had once been home to around _____ palm trees.
5 Due to _____ the trees were all gone by the year 1500.
6 It is thought that _____, introduced by colonisers, may have eaten the palm nuts.
7 Many of the oral stories contain contradictory information and are therefore considered to be _____.
8 Missionaries may have _____ the idea that the islanders were cannibals.
9 What some people consider to be spearheads may in fact have been made for _____ purposes.

Writing: contributing to a larger piece

1 Discuss. Describe the kind of house or building you live in. Is it typical of the main architectural styles in your country? In what ways?

Writing a contribution to a longer piece

In Paper 2, part 2 you may be asked to write a contribution to a longer piece of writing. This type of piece is written for someone who is in the process of collecting information to use in a longer document (e.g. a book, a guidebook or a piece of research). The main purpose is to supply information and opinion. The choice of register is likely to be influenced by the purpose of the longer document, as indicated in the task instructions. A contribution should be clearly organised and may include headings.

2 Look at the question example below and answer these questions.

   a   What register would you use to answer this question? Formal, neutral or informal?

   b   What information are you being asked for?

   c   How would you organise your paragraphs? What headings would you use?

PAPER 2, PART 2

> A friend of yours is writing a book on architecture in your country and has asked you to collect some information for her. She would like you to write a general description of the buildings in your town/city/country, especially houses, churches, or other public buildings.

3 Read the contribution that was written by someone from Greece, describing the architecture there. Have they dealt with the task in the same way that you planned in exercise 2?

Subject: Architecture in Greece – Public and private buildings

Personal residences: flats

In towns and cities most people tend to live in blocks of flats, usually between five and six stories high. The older buildings, built during the 1960s-1980s, are rather dull, rectangular blocks of grey cement, with protruding balconies on most sides. There is very little garden space and they have usually been built very closely together. However, since the 90s architects have made an effort to incorporate more visually appealing styles and modern apartment buildings tend to have rounded balconies, circular columns, and more attractive colours.

Personal residences: houses

In the country or where space is less of an issue, people tend to live in one or two storey dwellings. In Greece this varies from location to location, depending on the geographical features of the place. For instance, the Cyclades islands are famous for their small, white-washed cubic houses built into the island rock. In other areas, houses or villas are usually built to blend as much as possible into the natural landscape although there is no great diversity of style.

Public buildings: churches

Churches abound all over Greece and vary from small village shrines large enough to barely hold a priest and a handful of worshippers, to enormous cathedrals in the centre of the city. Most churches reflect the Byzantine style of round domes and huge vaulted ceilings. Spires and minarets are not common. On the outside churches are usually painted white, but not invariably, while inside every single centimetre of wall and ceiling space is painstakingly painted with scenes from the Bible, in particular those commemorating the saint after whom the Church has been dedicated.

4   In what ways is the piece of writing on page 80 similar to a report? How is it different?

In what ways is the piece of writing on page 80 similar to a report?

SPOTLIGHT ON VOCABULARY

Brainstorming vocabulary

Examiners will be looking for good use of descriptive language, so think carefully about the words you use. Before you start writing it's a good idea to brainstorm descriptive adjectives and phrases that you could use.

5   Read the paragraphs again and underline all the descriptive adjectives and phrases.

6   Brainstorm. Write down three to four adjectives or phrases to describe the following in your country, town or city.

a	town/city residences	
b	public buildings	
c	places of worship	
d	country residences	

In other words

It's a good idea to substitute synonyms for a particular word that you may be using repeatedly in order to not sound repetitive. The following words can all mean 'the place/area or building where someone or something lives'.

7   Use a dictionary to compare differences in meaning and complete the sentences that follow using one of the words below.

abode	dwellings	habitat	housing	place	residence

a   The _housing_ provided by the council was in very poor condition.
b   The natives live in straw hut _dwelling_ made from natural materials.
c   In its natural _habitat_ the elephant lives for over 70 years.
d   Buckingham Palace is the Queen's formal place of _residence_ in London.
e   He claimed he had no telephone and no fixed _abode_
f   He invited me back to his _place_ but told me to be quiet so as not to disturb his landlady.

8   Read the following task and write your contribution. Spend time planning the paragraph layout and headings and brainstorm vocabulary before you begin.

PAPER 2, PART 2

One of your professors is writing a book on the architecture of educational establishments around the world and has asked you to collect some information for him. He would like you to write a general description of the schools, colleges or universities in your town/city, to describe the buildings themselves, and to explain why they are architecturally interesting.

Write your contribution. (220–260 words).

Vocabulary organiser 8

8.1 Getting started, page 73 Choose the most appropriate adjective to complete the sentences below

awe-inspiring imposing massive peculiar unattractive

a The Sphinx was absolutely _____ – much larger than it looks in pictures.

b The Great Pyramid of Giza is totally _____ – it just fills you with wonder.

c Those Easter Island statues are quite _____ really. It's odd that nobody really knows why they made them.

d Stonehenge is beautiful but rather _____ – it makes you feel ever so small.

e I think the Great Wall is fairly _____ actually. What's so elegant about miles and miles of solid stone cutting through the landscape?

8.2 Reading, page 75 Look at the reading text and find a suitable adjective to fill each gap.

a Something that is _____ is new and original. [para 1]

b Something that is _____ (such as a natural resource) is kept at a steady level and is not likely to be wiped out by overuse. [para 1]

c If something is _____ to people, they can easily use it or obtain it. [para 2]

d Something that is _____ is not clear, or accurate. [para 3]

e _____ substances are of the sort produced by or found in living things. [para 3]

f A _____ substance or object is stiff and does not bend, stretch, or twist easily. [para 6]

g Something that is _____ provides you with a feeling of enthusiasm and gives you new and creative ideas. [para 6]

h Something that is _____ gives you the feeling that you can achieve something, for example by becoming stronger or more successful. [para 6]

8.3 Language development, page 76 Match the phrasal verbs in the box below with their definitions.

bring about	bring along	bring back
bring down	bring forward	bring in
bring off	bring out	bring up

a manage to do something successfully

b cause a government, an aeroplane, or a person to fall

c take someone or something with you when you go somewhere

d introduce a new product; cause a particular behaviour in someone

e arrange for a meeting or event to happen earlier than previously arranged

f recall a memory, reintroduce a rule or law

g cause something to happen

h to mention a subject or to raise children

i invite someone to do a job

8.4 Language development, page 76 Complete the sentences below with one suitable word.

a Fred is thinking of bringing a/an _____ against the newspaper.

b Seeing the farm again brought it _____ to me how happy I had been there.

c Angela could not bring _____ to sell the old house.

d He had a difficult illness that almost brought him to his _____, but he's fine again now.

e The doctors brought all their skills to _____ on the patient, but were unable to save him.

f Why don't you use a few good adjectives to bring your description _____?

8.5 Use of English, page 79 Derivatives of the following words all appeared in the text. Write the nouns and explain what they mean.

a destroy _____

b obsess _____

c remote _____

d inevitable _____

e rival _____

f vanquish _____

8.6 Writing, page 81 Complete the definitions.

a _____ – the buildings provided for people to live in [general]

b _____ – the place where someone lives [formal]

c _____ – the place where someone lives [formal address]

d _____ – the place where someone lives [usually indicates simplicity]

e _____ – the place where you live, usually rented

f _____ – the natural environment in which an animal lives or a plant grows

---

BANK OF ENGLISH

Word partnerships: *house*

Verb forms: to house someone or something
Type of house: boarding house, clearing house, council house, doll's house, full house, open house, opera house, outhouse, public house, Wendy house, White House,
Idiomatic phrases: get on like a house on fire, eat someone out of house and home, safe as houses
Fixed phrases: on the house, get or put one's house in order
Adjective phrase: house to house
House: arrest, boat, bound, boy, breaker, coat, guest, hold, husband, keeper, lights, maid, master, mate, owner, party, plant, proud, room, warming, wife, work
House of: Commons, God, Lords, Representatives, Houses of Parliament
Housing: association, benefit, development, estate, project

Which of the above is ...?

a an outside toilet or storage room _____

b a phrase which means 'to have a good relationship' _____

c a person who is in charge of the day to day running / management of a house _____

d the main government building in London _____

e money some people receive from the state to help them pay their rent _____

Review 2 Units 5–8

1 Complete the sentences below with a suitable verb from the box below. There are two extra words you do not need to use.

beckon	confess	confide	consume	convict	digest
enhance	erect	incite	overlook	run	sustain

1 The man they were holding in custody eventually _____ to the crime.
2 If you eat fruit after a meal it will be harder for the stomach to _____ it.
3 The temple was probably _____ in honour of a goddess.
4 A number of essential nutrients are needed to _____ life.
5 I'm sorry I must have _____ that small detail in my rush to finish.
6 A strange man _____ us to follow him but we were suspicious.
7 In the west we _____ far too much junk food.
8 Lillian promised to _____ her secret to me if I told her mine.
9 The police don't yet have enough evidence to _____ him.
10 A few people tried to _____ the crowd to start shouting.

2 Complete the sentences below with a verb from the box below in its correct form, and one or more particles to form a phrasal verb that means the same as the word in brackets.

bring x 2	look x 2	turn x 3	ward x 1

1 Harold has proposed to Madge six times but she keeps _____ him _____. (refuse)
2 You need to eat plenty of oranges to _____ _____ a cold. (deter)
3 I have always really _____ _____ Grant. (admire)
4 It would be great if they _____ _____ sixties fashions! (revived)
5 This has _____ _____ to be one of the happiest days of my life! (become)
6 I promised Michael I would _____ _____ the mystery of what's been eating his lettuces! (investigate)
7 I'm absolutely exhausted. I think I'll _____ _____. (go to bed)
8 It was tactless of Augusta to _____ _____ the subject of her wedding. (mention)

3 Replace the underlined part of the sentences that follow with an expression which uses the word in capitals.

1 If you don't tell me what you did with the money I'm going to <u>tell someone your secret</u>. BEANS
2 Even though we are all aware of the suffering that exists in the world, most of us choose to <u>ignore it</u>. LOOK
3 I wouldn't <u>do something that might lead to trouble</u> if I were you. ROAD

4 Martha would <u>do absolutely anything at all</u> for Robbie. LIFE
5 Seeing that photo of the children <u>made me realise</u> how quickly they grow up! BROUGHT
6 Sam is <u>getting better</u> after his operation. ROAD
7 Slow down! I think you've <u>taken on a larger burden than you can cope with!</u> CHEW
8 Just because his father owns the company, it doesn't mean that Julian <u>can do whatever he likes!</u> ABOVE

4 Write down the verb that collocates with each word or phrase in the sentences below.

1 _____ offence / the initiative / into account
2 _____ harm / good / wonders for
3 _____ a risk / its course / for government
4 _____ fun of / a mistake / an effort
5 _____ rise to / credit / notice
6 _____ to pieces / into disrepair / from grace

5 Choose the **best** word from the options A, B, C or D to complete each of the sentences below.

1 The most _____ moment of my life was when I stood on the top of Everest!
   A appealing   C unusual
   B awe-inspiring   D stunning

2 The view from the top of the Empire State Building is _____!
   A breathtaking   C revealing
   B sparkling   D threatening

3 Despite its history, Cairo is a fascinating, _____ modern city.
   A antiquated   C crumbling
   B shoddy   D industrious

4 There was a/an _____ air of mystery surrounding the Inca temple.
   A mysterious   C unique
   B eerie   D remarkable

5 I felt so small and insignificant, standing under the _____ structure of the Eiffel Tower.
   A peculiar   C imposing
   B curious   D impressive

6 Complete the gaps in the sentences with a suitable verb from the box below and one suitable particle.

accuse	charge	deter	implicate	refrain	work

1 Miriam tried to _____ Rupert _____ going to the police.
2 Arnold _____ Ethel _____ eating the last cookie.
3 A witness tried to _____ Miles _____ the robbery because they said they saw him inside the building.
4 Police have not _____ Liam _____ burglary, but they are holding him for further questioning.
5 I tried to _____ _____ opening my big mouth and saying something I might regret.
6 Andrea _____ _____ advertising on the fourth floor.

7 PAPER 3, PART 3 For questions 1–10, read the text below. Use the word given in capitals at the end of some of the lines to form a word that fits in the gap in the same line.

What should we eat?

The more we read about our health, the more we learn about how important diet is. It seems we have a number of (1) _____ about what's good for us and what isn't. Most people assume that the (2) _____ of great quantities of fish and meat will provide us with plenty of protein. The truth is that cooking meat and fish all the way through results in the (3) _____ of up to 95% of its protein content, yet we are not able to eat raw meat. In fact most plant foods can provide us with all the protein we need. We also believe that our (4) _____ systems were designed for large heavy meals high in animal protein. Actually our very long intestine is ideal for breaking down plant foods – animal proteins are difficult for us to digest and create acids in the stomach. One good (5) _____ for eating more raw fruit and vegetables is that it allows for the (6) _____ of a strong immune system, especially if it has been weakened by illness, (7) _____ or stress. A strong immune system in turn ensures the body receives proper (8) _____, protects us from disease and other (9) _____, and reduces the number of times we have to rely on (10) _____ drugs.

1 PRECONCEIVE
2 CONSUME

3 DESTROY

4 DIGEST

5 MOTIVATE
6 RESTORE
7 TIRED
8 MAINTAIN
9 CONTAMINATE
10 PRESCRIBE

8 PAPER 3, PART 4 For questions 1–5, think of one word only which can be used appropriately in all three sentences.

1 It irritates me that Martha thinks she can lay down the _____ every time she comes here.
The new government has promised to increase spending on _____ enforcement.
Someone who takes the _____ into their own hands is known as a vigilante.

2 Due to failing _____, Mr Rogers has decided to cancel his business trip.
The chemicals present a _____ hazard to workers and so should be banned.
Although she's physically very well, it's her mental _____ I'm worried about.

3 Building that house in the country has given Claudia a new lease of _____.
Gerald risked _____ and limb to get Angela to the church on time!
Of course I'm going to invite Bruce! He's the _____ and soul of the party.

4 You need to _____ into account the money we spent on advertising.
I hope Marjory won't _____ offence if I make a few suggestions about her work.
Susan decided to _____ the initiative and she switched on the machine without waiting for me.

5 She's determined to _____ for president when she grows up!
They warned him that it was economically unviable but he still decided to _____ the risk.
You have to let the rumour _____ its course, but people will soon forget about it.

9 PAPER 3, PART 5 For questions 1–8, complete the second sentence so that it has a similar meaning to the first sentence, using the word given. **Do not change the word given.** You must use between **three** and **six** words, including the word given.

1 'I didn't burn the house down!' said June.
on
June _____ fire.

2 Alison continued to talk for hours about her children.
went
Alison _____ her children for hours.

3 I got the job because I arrived just in time.
would
_____ got the job.

4 If Jasper hadn't warned me about the dog, I would have stroked it.
warning
But _____ touch the dog, I would have stroked it.

5 No matter what happens you mustn't open this door.
account
On _____ open this door.

6 This is the best opera I have ever seen.
have
Never _____ a good opera.

7 I got the sack because I was late for work.
result
I was late for work, _____ I was given the sack.

8 Timmy and Paul have started a business even though they don't have any experience.
whom
Timmy and Paul, _____ any experience, have started a business.

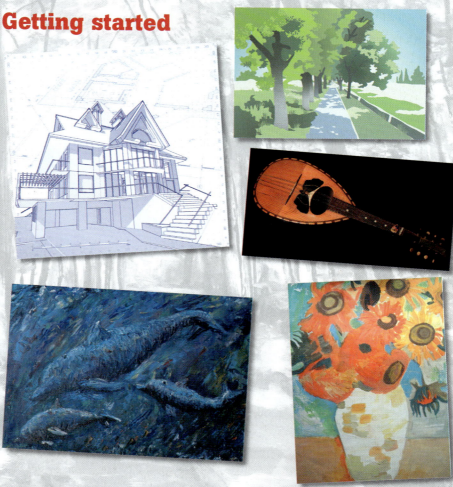

9 Brushstrokes and blueprints

MAIN MENU

Topics:	forms of art and craft
Language development:	compound nouns, phrases with *pay*
Grammar:	changing structures: a change in emphasis or meaning?

EXAM MENU

Reading:	understanding implication
Listening:	understanding stated opinion
Speaking:	suggesting solutions, justifying ideas
Use of English:	key word transformations
Writing:	competition entry

Getting started

1 **Discuss.** Look at the different styles of art and design. Which, if any, do you like, and why?

2 **Match the written extracts below with one of the pieces in the photographs, and explain where you might expect to find them.**

a 'People claim the sea may be cold, but the sea contains the wildest, hottest and most desperate blood of all!'

b The classic perspective illustration: observe that vertical lines remain vertical; horizontal edges converge at a vanishing point (or points) on the horizon line (which is always at the artist's eye level). In a nutshell, that's one point perspective.

c Form the neck completely, including the preparation of the head for the tuning gear, but do not fit the latter yet.

3 **Which of the pictures above would you choose to hang in (a) a living room (b) an office and (c) a school? Give reasons for your choice(s).**

Reading: understanding tone and implication in a text

1   Discuss. Which of the everyday objects shown in the photographs on the right do you think are cleverly designed? Explain why you think they are clever.

SPOTLIGHT ON READING

Understanding tone and implication
At first glance, a writer's attitude towards what they are writing about is not always clear. Below are three of the main ways in which a writer may express their views indirectly.

1   Use of positive or negative vocabulary to describe something
2   Presenting an opposing point or opinion in order to refute it
3   Leaving something unexpressed when describing feelings in a narrative

2   **Match the following extracts (A–C) to one of the techniques (1–3) above.**

A   *'Wellington boots, and the people who wear them, are the subject of many a comedian's funny stories. After all, they're not very stylish, and certainly don't show off the shape of your legs. Yet put yourself in the middle of a muddy field on a wet Sunday afternoon, and you'll soon feel differently about them.'*

B   *'I'm leaving you, Petunia,' he said. Words momentarily failed her, but she quickly recovered her composure. 'If that's what you want, Geoffrey,' she replied simply.*

C   *'This eyesore of a building, a blot in an otherwise attractive urban landscape, is said to be at the cutting edge of architectural design.'*

3   **Now answer the questions that follow:**

1   In Extract A, does the writer think that wellington boots …
    a   are funny?
    b   are useful?

2   In Extract B, how does Petunia react?
    a   She is indifferent to the man's revelation.
    b   She tries to conceal her feelings.

3   In Extract C, the writer
    a   likes the building?
    b   dislikes the building?

4   **Quickly read Text 1 below, and decide whether the following statements are true or false.**

According to the writer …

a the paperclip is old-fashioned.	T / F
b the paperclip is uninteresting.	T / F
c the paperclip is unappreciated.	T / F
d the paperclip is admired for its versatility.	T / F
e people waste time with the paperclip.	T / F

5   **PAPER 1, PART 1 Read Text 1 and answer the questions below.**

1   The writer attributes the ingenuity of the paperclip's design to
    A   its indispensability.
    B   the fact that it is springy.
    C   its ubiquity.
    D   the fact that it is simple.

2   The writer also suggests that the paperclip
    A   is not particularly useful.
    B   has an amusing name.
    C   is extremely versatile.
    D   may replace the toothpick.

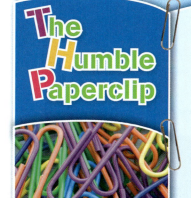

TEXT 1

The Humble Paperclip

When I asked for your favourite everyday designs a fortnight ago, someone nominated the paperclip. First patented in Germany by Johan Vaaler (1866–1910), a Norwegian inventor, in 1899, the paperclip remains indispensable. It has yet to be superseded by some modish, bleeping computer-controlled digital device demanding a PhD (or four-year-old computer whizz) to operate it, while gobbling up equally fashionable 'sustainable' green energy generated by rooftop windmills to keep it going …

In its utter simplicity lies the genius of the paperclip. Ubiquitous, it's so banal that the very word paperclip is somehow funny. Yet this little bit of minimalist springy folded metal does its job well enough and, besides, can be used as an all-purpose miniature tool, for shaping desk-top animals, cleaning fingernails, making miniature buildings, or simply as something to fiddle with in times of bureaucratic stress. According to an enjoyably time-wasting survey conducted by Lloyds Bank some while ago, of every 100,000 paperclips made in the United States, 19,143 were used as poker chips, 17,200 held clothing together, 15,556 were dropped and lost, 14,163 were absent-mindedly destroyed during telephone calls, 8,504 cleaned tobacco pipes and finger nails, while 5,434 served as stand-in toothpicks.

The Photographer's Apprentice

TEXT 2

The late spring days of 1941 are cold and largely dull. Not great weather for a photographer, but Helmut is keen to improve his skills. He saves what he can from his wages, managing enough for a roll of film each week. Gladigau allows him long lunch breaks, and even occasional half days out, if his duties are done. On Sundays, with Gladigau in the darkroom to guide him, Helmut spends hours printing up his precious rolls. Rows and rows of tiny experiments on Gladigau's leftover paper: all strips and scraps.

Almost all of the prints have people on them, usually considerable numbers of people, too. Helmut gravitates towards crowds, busy streets, enjoys capturing the milling, moving mass. Gladigau admires Helmut's photos, squinting and nodding at the prints pegged up on the lines across the darkroom to dry. 'That's Berlin', he says. 'All that life.' He points out the sense of movement in the pictures, clears his throat and tells Helmut he has a true photographer's eye.

The compliment is heartfelt, jealous and not easily voiced. Gladigau's chest feels tight in the chemical dark. His apprentice, however, shows little sign of hearing the praise: standing silently next to him, running his pale, critical eyes across the prints with a frown.

Art and poetic metaphor

TEXT 3

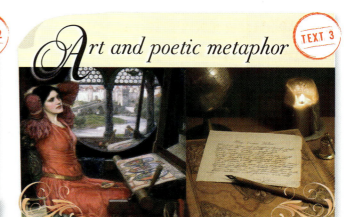

How true Horace's words were when he wrote, 'As is painting so is poetry'! For the poet creates wondrous images with the stroke of his pen, much as the painter does with the stroke of his brush. Both weave intricate patterns: the poet through his use of rhythm and metaphor, the artist through his use of colour and form. Both present a clarity and sharpness of thought and vision that often become obscured in the wordiness of prose. A poem of quality conveys a profound message in a few poignant lines. Similarly, a masterful painting can capture a whole story in one scene. Perhaps for this reason they are both often overwhelmed with feelings of mutual admiration, as can be seen in the reams of poems that pay homage to works of art, and paintings that claim inspiration from poetry.

With this in mind, I have taken the liberty of compiling this anthology, in an attempt to bring together poet and artist for the benefit of visitors to this gallery, that they might enrich their own appreciation of some of the works they view, by looking at them through a poet's eyes, and drawing their own parallels between poem and painting. I have endeavoured to present pairs whose connections serve only to stimulate the imagination and facilitate appreciation of both.

Poem and painting are presented adjacent to one another, without the adornment of an introduction or explanation, and this is intentional. I do not presume to restrict the reader's enjoyment by inserting comments. Nor do I presume to lead the viewer's imagination in a certain direction. The matching of poem and painting is designed to make its own statement to the individual, in the hope that they will create a harmonious synergy, enabling the one to enhance appreciation of the other.

Now read texts 2 and 3 and answer the questions that follow.

3 In the first paragraph of Text 2, the writer *implies* that Gladigau
   A gives Helmut a lot of work to do.
   B encourages his apprentice to learn.
   C is over indulgent towards Helmut.
   D does not pay Helmut very well.

4 In Text 2, what can we *infer* from the passage about Gladigau's feelings towards Helmut's work?
   A He is irritated by Helmut's lack of enthusiasm for his work.
   B He is amazed by Helmut's choice of photographic theme.
   C He is jealous of Helmut's photographic printing skills.
   D He realises that Helmut's talent exceeds his own.

5 In Text 3, what is the writer's view of art and poetry?
   A He believes they are essentially the same art form.
   B He thinks that they share visions that are often obscure.
   C He feels they share a number of admirable qualities.
   D He claims they are both easy to understand.

6 In Text 3, the writer's intention in not commenting on his choices in the anthology is to
   A direct the reader's interpretation of the connection between poem and painting.
   B prevent any misunderstandings from arising between himself and the artists.
   C highlight the special relationship between each painting and poem in the book.
   D allow observers and readers the freedom to draw their own conclusions about them.

Language development:
compound words

1 Join words from group A with words from group B to make compound nouns. In some cases, more than one combination may be possible.

A
paper
roof
wind
desk
finger
foot

B
print
top
nail
top
mill
clip

SPOTLIGHT ON VOCABULARY

Compound words

When we join two nouns together to form a compound noun, no hyphen (-) is usually required. e.g. *paperclip*. You may see a hyphen used for some activities, such as bird-watching, or train-spotting.

When we form a compound adjective, we often need to insert a hyphen between the words we are joining, especially when the two words are different types (noun + verb). e.g. *radio-controlled*.

However, there is no clear rule about this.

---

2 We often create compound adjectives in order to say what we want more briefly.

Look at Text 1 on page 86, and find compound adjectives and adverbs for the following definitions.

a that is used regularly in our daily lives _____

b that is operated through a computer _____

c that can be used in many ways _____

d that takes up time unnecessarily _____

e without thinking clearly _____

f used as a replacement for something _____

3 Complete the sentences below with compound words from exercises 1 and 2 above.

a After leaving the building, the thief left muddy _____ on the driveway, which helped the police to find him.

b 'Julia Roberts is ill, so we'll have to use a _____ actress for today's rehearsal.'

c The Swiss Army knife is a useful, _____ tool, which is indispensable on camping trips.

d 'Attach these papers together with a _____.'

e Martin is rather _____, and often loses his keys.

f The cat climbed to the top of the building, and agilely leapt across the _____, to escape from the dog.

Key word: *pay*

4 In the Text 3 on page 87, we came across the phrase '*pay homage to*'.

'Perhaps for this reason they are both often overwhelmed with feelings of mutual admiration, as can be seen in the reams of poems that pay homage to works of art, and paintings that claim inspiration from poetry.'

What do you think this means? What else could one 'pay homage to'?

5 Choose the most suitable word(s) to complete the following sentences:

1 In his speech, the headmaster paid _____ to the hard work of the students who had participated in the school play.
   a homage   b attention   c tribute

2 'All I did was pay _____ about how attractive you look today, and you slap my face!'
   a you respect   b you a compliment   c my respects to you

3 'Look, if you can just take me with you to Paris, I promise I'll pay _____ the trip.'
   a the penalty for   b my way on   c through the nose for

6 Explain the meaning of the phrases in italics in the following sentences:

'Hi, Tanya! I thought I'd *pay you a visit* on my way back from Moscow. Will you be home?'

'Solar heating is quite expensive to install, but after the first three years, it starts to *pay for itself*.'

7 PAPER 3, PART 4 For questions 1–4, think of **one** word only which can be used appropriately in all three sentences.

1 'I saw some fabulous _designs_ at the London Fashion Show.'
   'Carl has _designs (plans)_ on that cottage on the corner, and thinks he can turn it into a pub!'
   'Jane has grand _designs_ for her singing career, but I'm not sure she has enough talent.'

2 I am interested in graphic _art_.
   'Kevin has been practising making paella, and he's now got it down to a fine _art_.'
   'Let me teach you the _art_ of public relations!'

3 After Mr. Jones' funeral, I went to the house to _pay_ my respects to his family.
   They travelled all the way to Lourdes to _pay_ homage to the shrine there.
   'After having to _pay_ through the nose for the tickets, we could still hardly see the stage!'

4 Tom's doctor believed it was the new drug that _arrested_ the disease.
   An antique chair in the shop window _arrested_ his attention.
   Police _arrested_ three men yesterday in connection with last Saturday's robbery.

Listening: interview with an artist

1 Discuss. How do you feel about the kind of art shown in the photographs? What do you like or dislike about it?

2 What difficulties do you think the artist might have had in creating these pieces?

3 🎧 9.1 Listen to two people discussing one of the pieces shown in the photographs above. Which photograph are they talking about?

4 From what the speakers say, we can understand that ...

- A they both like the powerful use of materials in the piece.
- B Joe doesn't think the colours in the piece are garish.
- C Clare thinks the piece is bulky.
- D Joe is impressed by the symbolism in the piece.

SPOTLIGHT ON LISTENING

Understanding stated opinion

In **PAPER 4, PART 3** some questions may require an understanding of the speaker's opinion of the subject they are is talking about. You need to listen carefully and decide whether the speaker is criticising something or praising it.

5 Discuss. What opinion did the two speakers express about the paintings above?

Joe: _He was impressed about it, he found it really meaningful_

Clare: _She didn't like it, cause she found it garish_

6 🎧 9.2 **PAPER 4, PART 3** Listen to an interview with the artist whose work is shown in the photographs, and answer the questions below.

1 According to Vasilis, his art
- A is an exploration in colour.
- B has influenced another artist.
- C appeals to his sense of touch.
- D is a reflection of his mood.

2 When did he become interested in three-dimensional art?
- A After he became tired of painting landscapes.
- B As a boy, while watching his father painting.
- C While he was studying photography at university.
- D After experimenting with painting techniques.

3 Vasilis attributes his present choice of materials to ...
- A the fact that they are strong and will last.
- B a desire to use only natural materials.
- C his use of them in his work as a dentist.
- D a sense of responsibility towards the environment.

4 What aspect of his artwork does Vasilis particularly enjoy?
- A Its versatility.
- B Its escapism.
- C Its symbolism.
- D Its unpredictability.

5 What reason does Vasilis give for not holding an exhibition of his work?
- A It is too personal to him.
- B He sees his art as a means of escape.
- C He thinks it's wrong to make money out of it.
- D A combination of A and B.

6 Anyone who wants to buy one of Vasilis' pieces
- A must make a dental appointment first.
- B cannot do so at present.
- C will have to wait for months.
- D can ask him for a price list.

Grammar: changing sentence structure: a change in emphasis, or a different meaning?

1 Compare the sentence below from Text 1 on page 86 with the two sentences that follow it. Which one has a different meaning?

'[The paperclip] has yet to be <u>superseded</u> by some modish, bleeping computer-controlled device.' (Text 1)

a Yet another modish, bleeping, computer-controlled device has superseded the paperclip.

b A modish, bleeping, computer-controlled device has not superseded the paperclip yet.

2 Work in pairs. Sentence (a) is from Text 3 on page 87. Compare its meaning with that of sentence (b) below. How do they differ?

completed

a *'Poem and painting are presented <u>adjacent</u> to one another, without the adornment of an introduction or explanation, and this is intentional.'* (Text 3)

future

b *'I intend to present poem and painting adjacent to one another, without the adornment of an introduction or explanation.'*

3 Compare the following pairs of sentences. How do slight changes in their structure or punctuation affect the meaning?

1 a As I thought, this poem wasn't written by W.H. Auden.
  b This poem wasn't written by W.H. Auden as I'd thought.

2 a Karl started learning to drive two years ago.
  b Karl has been driving for two years.

3 a It was <u>Sally</u> that borrowed my Shakira CD.
  b It was <u>my Shakira CD</u> that Sally borrowed.

4 a Paul bought the painting which had belonged to an Italian nobleman.
  b Paul bought the painting, which had belonged to an Italian nobleman.

5 a She'd paint flowers and trees unlike the others in her class.
  b She'd painted flowers and trees, unlike the others in her class.

4 🎧 9.3 By inverting the normal word order in a sentence we can create emphasis. Listen to two people saying the pairs of sentences 1–5 below. In each case, what is the effect of changing the word order?

1 *'I don't know where she finds the time to do all those activities.'*
✱ *'Where she finds the time to do all those activities, I don't know.'*

2 *'Although this exercise may seem boring, it is useful.'*
✱ *'Boring though this exercise may seem, it is useful.'*

3 *'You need a complete break from the office.'*
✱ *'What you need is a complete break from the office.'*

4 *'They are creating unnecessary waste.'*
✱ *'What they are doing is creating unnecessary waste.'*

5 *'Don't get upset. You just need to go and talk to your teacher about the problem.'*
✱ *'Don't get upset. All you need to do is talk to your teacher about the problem.'*

5a 🎧 9.4 Listen to the following sentence with varying intonation. How does the meaning of each sentence differ?

'Vincent Van Gogh cut off his ear after a quarrel with his good friend Gauguin.'

b Write the question that might have been asked to obtain each sentence as an answer.

➔ Grammar Reference 9.1, page 176

Use of English: key word transformations

Key word transformations

PAPER 3, PART 5 In this part of the Use of English Paper, you are sometimes asked to transform a sentence in a way which makes it more emphatic. It is important to make sure that the changes you make do not alter the meaning of the sentence.

1 Transform the following sentences. Make sure that your second sentence has the same meaning as the first one:

a Mary said Pete crashed her car last night.
who
According to _____ crashed her car last night.

b 'Although it's cold, we're still going rowing.'
may
'Cold _____ still going rowing.'

2 **PAPER 3, PART 5** For questions 1–7, complete the second sentence so that it has a similar meaning to the first sentence, using the word given. **Do not change the word given.** You must use between three and six words, including the word given.

1 'I like going on holiday, but not the journey.'
what
'I like going on holiday, <u>what I don't like</u> is the journey.'

2 'Paul didn't break the window, John did,' said Claire.
it
According to <u>Claire it was John</u> who broke the window.

3 'She has so many commitments that I can't understand how she manages to stay calm.'
how
'With all her commitments, <u>how she manages to stay calm</u> is a mystery to me.'

4 Susan's music is bothering the neighbours; not me.
but
'It's <u>not me but the neighbours that</u> Susan is bothering with her music.'

5 'Even if it rains, we won't cancel the match.'
may
'Rain <u>though it may, the match</u> won't be cancelled.'

6 Some children in Class 3 painted pictures of the sea and won an award.
whose
The children in Class 3 <u>whose pictures were of the sea</u> won an award.

7 We'd thought Helen would be angry, and she was.
as
Helen <u>was angry as</u> we'd expected.

Speaking: suggesting solutions, justifying ideas

1 Colours symbolise different things in different cultures. What do you associate black and white with in your culture?

2 In western cultures, colours are sometimes associated with certain emotional responses. Match the colours, 1–10 below, with the emotional associations, a–j , that are suitable for you. Compare your answers with the rest of your class.

Colour matching test

1	Red *b*	a is cool and calm, and is associated with making time pass more quickly
2	Blue *a*	b is known for raising blood pressure, and is associated with excitement and danger
3	Yellow *d*	c is associated with sophistication and rebelliousness
4	Green *h*	d is associated with happiness, but also cowardice and deceit
5	Purple *g*	e is warm and encouraging, and is often associated with transition
6	Grey *i*	f is calm and gentle, and is associated with women and nostalgia
7	Navy Blue *j*	g is a balance between cool and warm colours, and is associated with being unique and mysterious
8	Lavender *f*	h is cool and calm, and is associated with balance, harmony and stability
9	Black *c*	i is a neutral colour, and seldom evokes strong emotion
10	Orange *e*	j is a strong, dominant colour, associated with importance and confidence

3 In pairs. Which of the colours listed above would you choose to decorate ...?

(a) a bedroom   (b) a living room?   (c) a kitchen   (d) a classroom

Report back to the class, giving reasons for your choices.

4 PAPER 5, PART 3 Work in pairs. Below are some pictures showing proposals for the front cover of a book on contemporary design. First, talk to each other about the merits of each option. Then decide which one you think is the most suitable as a front cover. Use the 'In other words' box on the right to try and persuade your partner to agree with you.

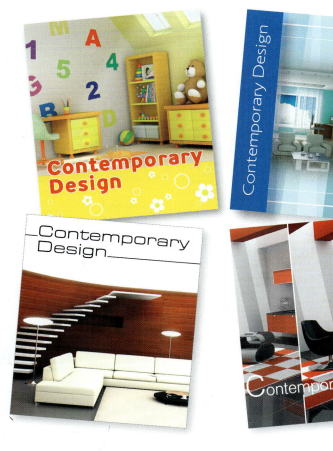

In other words

Emphatic phrases can be persuasive. Compare the following pair of sentences:
'We need an effective advertising slogan to make people remember our product.'
'What we need is an effective advertising slogan to make people remember our product.'

Use the following phrases to make the sentences below more emphatic:
What we need here is ...
It is this that will attract ...
All we have to do is ...

1 A bold logo is something that will attract people's attention.

2 Bright colours create an impression of dynamic creativity.

3 A catchy title is what attracts readers' attention.

4 We need lots of photos of different kinds of design.

5 I think we should keep it simple.

6 One bold design on a neutral background will make people curious.

7 Colours which reflect sophistication and originality.

8 Warm, inviting colours that stimulate interest.

Marc Chagall

Wassily Kandinsky

Paul Klee

Gustav Klimt

Takashi Murakami

Writing: competition entry

1   Look at the paintings on the left. They are by famous artists. Which, if any, would you like to hang on the wall in your room? Explain why.

2   **PAPER 2, PART 2** You have read the following announcement in a newspaper.

Favourite Artist Competition

The Arts Council is compiling a book on the most popular artists of the twentieth century. We would like to hear the views of all you art lovers before making our choices. Nominate your favourite artist, and say why you think your choice deserves to be included. All those whose nominee is chosen will have their names entered in a raffle, and the winner will receive a week's free tuition at an art school in Tuscany, Italy.

Write your **competition entry**.

SPOTLIGHT ON WRITING

Justifying choices
This kind of question in Paper 2 requires you to justify your choice for nomination. You must give reasons for your choice which will convince the organisers of the competition that your nomination should be accepted.

3   ∩ 9.5 Listen to five students brainstorming ideas about which artists to nominate for the competition above. Fill in the table below, with the name of each student, their choice of artist, and the reasons they give for their choice.

Student	Artist of choice	Justification
Maria	Marc Chagall	his pictures represent his subconscious dream qualities
Caitlin	Gustav Klimt	speaks more directly / passion
Alice	Takashi Murakami	works reflects reality in Japan / his women
Michele	Wassily Kandinsky	sense of music in painting
Tony	Joan Miro	love colours on his pictures

4   Discuss. Would you nominate one of the above artists for the book, or someone else? Justify your choice.

5 Read the following competition entry from one of the students, and underline the parts where she justifies her choice.

Jasmine

For the Arts Council's book on the most popular artists of the twentieth century, I would like to nominate the Japanese artist, Takashi Murakami. To my mind, any book on twentieth century artists cannot fail to include mention of this remarkable painter.

His work reflects trends in modern popular culture, and the influence of mass-produced entertainment on both Eastern and Western cultures more than any other contemporary artist. Murakami is influenced by animated images from comics and cartoons, and much of his artwork shows this. Many people like his work for its 'happy' colours. In particular, his smiley flowers are cheerful, and remind me of a child's bedroom. However, some of his well-known Mr DOB paintings seem threatening, and, to my mind, express the emptiness of popular culture today. His cartoon-like sculptures are bold in style, too, and not popular with everyone, but they are very impressive, also.

Another point worth noting is that Murakami is commercially successful. He is very versatile, and understands the importance of marketing if you want to survive as an artist. His organisation, Kaikai Kiki, is an art production company which manages and promotes artists, organises art festivals, and is generally involved in marketing art-related products. So, he is very much a twentieth century artist.

For these reasons, I strongly recommend that Takashi Murakami be included in the book.

Miltos

6 Do you find the competition entry above convincing? Why or why not?

> **Useful language for justifying choices and recommendations**
>
> *To my mind, this person/writer/singer etc. displays a wonderful talent for ...*
> *She uses a remarkable number of ...*
> *His work has been inspirational to many people ...*
> *She has a unique style ...*
> *Their music defined the style of music in the 80s ...*
> *Her painting has been inspirational ...*
> *He is versatile in his choice of theme ...*
> *To my mind, she employs an impressive range of materials ...*
> *For these reasons, among others, I strongly recommend ...*
>
> Add more useful words and phrases from the model competition entry above, and from Tapescript 9.5, on page 215.

Nikolaos

Nikos

7 Look at the following question.

PAPER 2, PART 2

> 'Your school is participating in a national arts competition, and your teacher has asked your class to nominate a picture to enter the artwork category, giving reasons for your choice. The student whose nomination is chosen will win a prize. You have decided to nominate one of the artworks on the right.'

8 Choose one of the artworks, and note down reasons for your choice. Then write your **competition entry** for exercise 7. Use the 'Useful Language' box to help you justify your choice.

Spiros

Vocabulary organiser 9

9.1 Reading, page 86 Find the words in Text 1 and its corresponding questions which mean the following.

Verbs

1 _____ recommend for an award or special attention
2 _____ gain the right to be the only maker or seller of a particular product
3 _____ replace an older model
4 _____ use up or eat very quickly
5 _____ produce energy or power
6 _____ move something around with your fingers, often when you are worried

Nouns

7 _____ very great ability or skill
8 _____ small, plastic counters used in gambling to represent money
9 _____ lasting strength
10 _____ ability to be used in different ways
11 _____ ability to bend and stretch without breaking
12 _____ ability to be trusted to do a job

Adjectives

13 _____ essential, necessary
14 _____ fashionable
15 _____ that can be used at a steady level
16 _____ common, appearing everywhere
17 _____ ordinary and boring
18 _____ simple
19 _____ which returns quickly to its original shape after you press it
20 _____ very small
21 _____ involving complicated rules and procedures (usually in an office)
22 _____ forgetful, not able to concentrate well

9.2 Reading, page 86–87 Choose the best word or phrase from Text 1 or 3 to complete the sentences below.

1 Sally _____ her hair when she's anxious, twisting it round her fingers.
   a) gobbles up   b) dwells on
   c) fiddles with   d) pays homage to

2 'I find your lessons boring!' Paul told his teacher _____.
   a) absent-mindedly   b) impertinently
   c) ubiquitously   d) modishly

3 The _____ of this multi-purpose food mixer makes it ideal for the creative chef.
   a) versatility   b) synergy
   c) durability   d) adjacency

4 The bold colours of the design _____ Jane's attention.
   a) generated   b) confined
   c) compiled   d) arrested

5 The professor gave a(n) _____ lecture on black holes, and I came away with a clearer picture of what they are.
   a) indispensable   b) illuminating
   c) sheer   d) banal

9.3 Language development (phrases with *pay*) page 88 Choose the correct phrase in italics to complete the sentences.

1 'Please pay *attention / tribute* to what I am about to say!'
2 Sam surprised his mother by paying her *respect / a compliment* about her hair.
3 The underfloor heating system only began paying *its way / for itself* after the first three years.
4 I was forced to pay *the penalty for / through the nose* for not studying by failing all my exams.
5 'I've come to pay you *my respects / a visit*; I'm so sorry for your loss.'

9.4 Speaking, page 91 Complete the sentences below with one of the words in the box.

balance	nostalgia	harmony	deceit	joy
rebellious	sophisticated	stability	transition	unique

1 The smell of jasmine arouses feelings of _____ in me, reminding me of times spent at my grandmother's house.
2 Teenagers are sometimes _____, and refuse to follow rules.
3 I was particularly hurt by her _____, because I'd thought I could trust her.
4 The teenage years represent a period of _____ from childhood to adulthood.
5 Everything in the room seems to be in _____, creating a pleasant, relaxed atmosphere.
6 Tom has changed jobs and moved town a lot in recent years, but now he's looking for some _____ in his life.
7 The new baby brought _____ to the family.
8 My father is a _____ man; there's no one like him!
9 Parents nowadays struggle to find a _____ between work and family.
10 Laura is a charming, _____ woman, who is able to mix well in any social event.

BANK OF ENGLISH

Word partnerships: *design*

1 **Describe a design feature of your mobile phone, or the chair you are sitting on.**
2 **Why is a design fault something undesirable? Give an example.**
3 **Read sentences a–e below, and explain the use of the phrases in italics.**
a It is unknown whether the house was set on fire by accident or *by design*.
b 'Maria has *grand designs* for her hat-making business.'
c 'Jason *has designs on* that restaurant in the town centre.'
d 'Beth is taking a course in *Graphic Design*.'
e Developments in genetic engineering have given rise to the idea of *designer babies*.

10 The good life

Getting started

The term 'ethical living' is used to describe a way of life that aims to do no harm to other people, animals or the world in which we live.

1 **Discuss.** Look at the statement above. Do you live 'ethically'? What factors do you think contribute to an ethical lifestyle?

2 What ethical or unethical choices do the photographs on this page suggest we may have to make in our lives?

3 Rank the following criteria in order of importance according to your own view of what would constitute a 'good life' for you. Tell your partner about the choices you made.

a good health ☐
b happy family ☐
c material wealth ☐
d personal success ☐
e social standing ☐
f successful career ☐

Reading: gapped texts

1 Discuss. 'Quality of life' versus 'quality time'. How much should spouses or parents be willing to sacrifice in order to provide a comfortable and secure lifestyle for their families?

EXAM SPOTLIGHT

PAPER 1, PART 2 Text structure, paragraph cohesion and coherence

Part 2 of the Reading Paper is designed specifically to test a student's understanding of the way a text is structured. It's therefore important to be aware of the way that paragraphs are joined together (cohesion) in such a way that they make sense (coherence).

2 The article that follows can be divided into three clear sections, each section talking about a different family. Skim read the text below and the missing paragraphs on page 97 to complete the table below.

Surname of family	Names of the couple	Information about the children
1 The Chitnis family		
2		Four children (names not given)
3	Laurie and Jim	

3 Which paragraph does not belong to any of these sections?

4 In order to understand the way the text is organised, it's also important to understand the gist of the article. Read the text and paragraphs again more carefully. What effect has long distance separation had on each family?

Nice week at the office, darling?

You want the kids to grow up in the country, living in a nice house, going to a good school. There's only one problem: you could never afford it without your metropolitan salary. Joanna Moorhead meets the long-distance families.

Anthony Chitnis doesn't need to consult his diary to tell me that this week, like every week, Tuesday will be his most difficult day. Or that – whatever deals he does or doesn't manage to pull off in his City office – Thursday will give him his easiest ride and his happiest moments. Why is he so sure? Because Anthony is one of a growing tribe of long-distance dads in the UK: fathers (and it almost always is fathers) who live apart from their family for all or part of the week because their job is based hundreds, sometimes even thousands, of miles away. So for Anthony, Tuesday is the day when he kisses his wife, Jane, and children, Asmita, Daisy and Arthur, goodbye for three days: and he doesn't like what that means for any of them.

1 [...]

Leaving Jane and the children behind for half of every week hasn't, Anthony admits, got any easier. 'The truth is that I just miss them all an awful lot. I'm lucky in that I've got a small flat in London. Hotels are soulless for business travellers; I don't think I could do this at all if I had to live in a hotel. But the thing is that you're on your own, it's not home. You phone a lot, and you try to know everything that's going on, but it's hard. And it's hard telling the children why you're doing it as well. Arthur said to me the other day, "Why do you have to work in London, Daddy? I like it so much better when you're here with us." It's a tough one to explain.'

2 [...]

The Chitnises have been friends of mine for the past decade; they're one of the closest and most family-oriented couples I've ever known. They're both completely committed to why they're doing what they're doing, and they're both extremely supportive of the other's point of view: what's more, Jane's parents live next door, so she has plenty of practical back-up when Anthony is away. But even they are finding long-distance family life tough going, and they're certainly not alone.

3 [...]

These considerations were very much to the fore ten years ago for the Yardley family when Jonathan, a marketing director, arrived back at the family home in Kingston upon Thames to tell his wife Jean that he'd been offered an exciting new job ... in Germany. 'It was a good career move for him,' says Jean, now 54. 'But we knew uprooting our four children would be impossible – our older kids were doing their GCSE courses, and their lives were here. We thought it would work: he'd be home every weekend; Germany is only a two hour flight away.' And at first, says Jean, it was fine. 'We really trusted one another, which was important. And though the children missed him, we worked hard to make the weekends special.'

4 [...]

Two years ago, Jonathan took a new job in Tokyo, returning only every other month or so. Jean knew it was the beginning of the end, and the couple divorced earlier this year. When she looks back, says Jean, she can see that what undermined their marriage was the loss of opportunities to share the nitty-gritty of life. 'You think it's the big set-pieces, the romantic dinners, that keep you together, but

actually it isn't. It's the small stuff: the impromptu giggles, the little nagging worries, the everyday sharing: that's what binds a marriage together, and no amount of emails and phone calls can make up for it. I honestly think if Jonathan had stayed here, though we might have had some tough times, we'd have rocked on together somehow.'

5 [...]

'We exchange lots of emails and we talk on the phone several times a day: he'll usually phone at lunchtime and then again in the evening, and he tries to speak to the girls every day. On the upside we've been together a long time and we're very comfortable about guessing what the other one would say or do in a particular situation, which helps a lot. But the downside is that you don't enjoy one another the way you used to: when he's home there often seems to be just the niggles and the nagging stuff. There's a danger of the little frustrations taking over and not having time to appreciate the good things about one another.'

6 [...]

The bottom line is that family life is all about being together: take one key player out of the equation, and you inevitably rock the boat and add to the stresses and strains that every family inevitably experiences anyway. And even though some families can handle it – maybe for part of the week like the Chitnises, maybe for a few years like the Veningers – the truth is that, for others like the Yardleys, it can add up to an intolerable strain that ends up with the family splitting permanently. Which is ironic, given that – for most families that take this path – the prime motivating factor in the first place was their children's quality of life.

5 In pairs. Answer the following questions in your own words to see how much you have understood of the text.

  a Which days of the week is Anthony away from home?
  b Where does Anthony stay when he is in London and why?
  c Which factors help Jane to get through the week when her husband is away?
  d Why did Jean and the children not go to Germany with Jonathan?
  e Which factors does Jean feel contributed to the eventual break-up of her marriage?
  f What is it sometimes difficult to appreciate and why?
  g Why, according to the writer, is it 'ironic' that some families decide to spend part of their lives apart?

6 Read paragraph A below. Underline any key words that may help reveal where in the original text it belongs. Who does 'he' refer to? Does this help you find where the paragraph belongs?

7 Look back at the main article and underline any key words or reference devices at the beginning and end of paragraphs.

8 Read paragraph B. Underline any key words or phrases. Which of the three families is it referring to? Does it refer to anything mentioned in the main text?

9 Read paragraph C. Who is mentioned here? Is this person mentioned anywhere in the main text or in any other paragraph? What kind of information is given here?

10 Which paragraph seems less relevant to the main body of text?

11 PAPER 1, PART 2 Choose from paragraphs (A–G) the one which best fits each gap in the text (1–6). There is one extra paragraph which you do not need to use.

A 'But the years went by, and somehow it all went wrong. He started going back to Germany earlier and earlier on a Sunday, and he found it hard to switch from his weekday bachelor existence into this frenetic, four-kids household at weekends. And I started to feel I couldn't share stuff with him because I didn't want to upset him and risk a disastrous couple of days when that was all the time we had.'

B No one is collating the figures on how many families live apart for some or all of the week, but there are plenty of reasons why it's a reasonable guess that the figure is on the up. Job insecurity, a new kind of employment fluidity, technological change, cheap flights: all this adds up to a world in which it is no longer unthinkable for a thirty- or forty-something parent to say yes to a job that's many miles from home.

C Anne Green, a researcher at the Warwick Institute for Employment Research who has studied long-distance commuting and its effect on family life, says that while 20 years ago it would have been unthinkable for a wife and children not to up sticks if a husband got a new job, these days things can be very different. 'Women's employment has changed things: more and more families are dual-career, so one partner getting a new job in another part of the country doesn't necessarily mean the other one's career can automatically be grafted there too,' she says.

D 'We've been living this life for the last four and a half years – we left London for Lancashire because we wanted the children to go to school here, and Jane's family were here,' he says. 'And it's all worked out extremely well – we're very happy here. But I knew from the beginning that, to make the money I need to support them, I needed a metropolitan income: I can work in my company's Leeds office on Mondays and Fridays, but from Tuesday to Thursday I'm in London.'

E One of the biggest dangers, says Laurie, is that it's easy to get tough and hardened. 'You haven't got the support for the little things, and you do need that,' she says. 'I think we've survived it and we'll be OK, but it takes its toll: I'm glad I can see an end to this way of life for us now, and I think things will be a lot easier in the future when we're back together.'

F For Jane, the days when Anthony is away are always unsettling. 'I think I'm always subconsciously waiting for him to come home – I just can't quite get used to it. I tend to stay up too late doing the ironing and putting things away. It's in the back of my mind that things aren't quite right, that we're not all together.'

G For Laurie Veninger, 44, the alarm bells have already started to sound: her husband, Jim, also 44, currently works in Holland from Monday to Friday, but is giving up his job in the next few months and returning to the UK to a new job in Cambridge. The couple's daughters, 14-year-old Madeleine and 13-year-old Emma, are happy in their school near the family home in Lancashire, but Laurie and Jim have made the difficult decision to uproot them so the four of them can be together again in Cambridge by the end of next year. 'I think Jim taking a job abroad was right at the time, but it's been much harder than we realised it would be to live this way,' says Laurie. 'It's been three years, and the girls have never got entirely used to it. And the person it's been hardest on, far and away, is Jim himself. The stress on him of all this commuting and of being away from us is visible. I worry about him out there all on his own, and I worry about all the travelling he has to do.'

Language development:
fixed phrases

1 The following fixed phrases were all used in 'Nice week at the office, darling?' on pages 96–97. Match the expressions with the definitions that follow:

a	alarm bells started to sound	e	take [its] toll on
b	nitty gritty	f	the bottom line
c	rock the boat	g	tough going
d	stresses and strains	h	up sticks

1 The most important or interesting facts of a situation or activity. ☐
2 The most basic or most important factor that you have to consider about a situation. ☐
3 To upset a calm or stable situation by causing trouble. ☐
4 To have a bad effect or cause a lot of suffering. ☐
5 Something that makes people feel worried or concerned about something. ☐
6 To get up and leave a place to go somewhere else. ☐
7 A situation that is difficult or problematic may be described as this. ☐
8 The various problems and pressures that are a part of a situation. ☐

Key word: *pull*

2 The following phrasal verb appeared in the reading text:

…whatever deals he does or doesn't manage to <u>pull off</u> *in his City office.*

What do you think it means?

3 Complete sentences 1–8 below with a suitable phrasal verb formed from *pull* using one of the particles provided.

back	down	off	out of
over	through	together	up

1 Armed forces were _____ from the front, but kept in position in case there was an escalation of the conflict.
2 It's about time they _____ that old building – it was about to fall down anyway.
3 'Oh come on, Amanda – _____ yourself _____ and stop crying about this boy.'
4 Everyone clapped when the trapeze artist managed to _____ a triple backwards somersault in mid air.
5 A leg injury forced the athlete to _____ the next race.
6 The police car flashed its sirens in order to tell the driver to _____ to the side of the road.
7 He was so ill we weren't sure if he was going to _____ or not.
8 'James, why don't you _____ a chair and come and join us?'

4 Complete the sentences with one of the phrases below in its correct form.

pull a face	pull out the stops
pull a fast one on someone	pull someone's leg
pull a muscle	pull strings
pull yourself together	pull your weight

1 He didn't warm up properly before the race, so it's not surprising he _____.
2 If you want to win this match, you're going to have to _____.
3 The little girl _____ as soon as her teacher's back was turned.
4 Kelvin told me he'd won the lottery, but I think he must have been _____ again.
5 If you don't _____ Annie, I'm going to have to slap you!
6 She only got the part in the play because her uncle was able to _____ with the theatre manager.
7 If you don't start _____ around here, you'll have to find somewhere else to live!
8 Jimmy is a bit of a prankster. He tried to _____ _____ the new teacher by changing the signs on the staff toilet doors!

5 How many phrases with *pull* are depicted in the cartoons below?

Listening (1): identifying speakers

1 Discuss. What do you think the term 'sustainable living' means? What aspects of your life would you have to change if you wanted to be totally self-sustaining?

2 Read the list of options (A–H) in tasks one and two below, and underline the key words. Then brainstorm a list of words that could be associated with those keywords.

3 PAPER 4, PART 4 You are going to listen to five people talking about how their parents would reuse and recycle natural resources when they were growing up. You will hear each extract twice. While you are listening, attempt tasks one and two.

🎧 10.1 **Task One:** For questions 1–5 below, choose from the list (A–H) the main message each speaker is giving.

A recycling old clothing
B reusing everyday objects
C growing organic vegetables
D creating homemade produce
E economising on electricity use
F conserving water
G recycling kitchen waste
H cutting down on chemical use

Speaker 1	1
Speaker 2	2
Speaker 3	3
Speaker 4	4
Speaker 5	5

Task Two: For questions 6–10, choose from the list (A–H) a childhood memory that each speaker expresses.

A excitement caused by a parent's innovations.
B a parent recycling organic material in the garden.
C discomfort caused by a parent's economising.
D a parent doing a chore on a particular day of the week.
E getting into trouble for forgetting to do something.
F a parent's suggestion for home-made cosmetics.
G a parent imposing a penalty for not doing something.
H a parent reusing a natural resource in a different way.

Speaker 1	6
Speaker 2	7
Speaker 3	8
Speaker 4	9
Speaker 5	10

4 Discuss. Which of the tips above do you find useful? Have you adopted them? Would you like to adopt any of them?

Grammar: direct and reported speech

1 In order to make their articles more engaging and lively, journalists use direct speech frequently in articles and interviews. Look back at the article on pages 96–97 again and underline every time direct speech is used. What effect does this have?

GRAMMAR SPOTLIGHT

Direct speech to reported speech
In the Reading text, we saw the following sentence:
… Arthur said to me the other day, 'Why do you have to work in London, Daddy? I like it so much better when you're here with us.'

In a more formal or literary text, this could have been rewritten as:
The other day, Arthur asked me why I had to work in London. He said he liked it so much better when I was there with them.

2 Underline the changes that have been made to the sentence. What rules can you identify?

➡ Grammar Reference 10.1, page 177

3 Rewrite the following direct speech sentences from the article on pages 96–97 using reported speech.

a Anthony: 'I miss them all an awful lot but I'm lucky I've got a small flat in London.'

_____

_____

b Jean: 'It was a good career move for my husband, but we knew uprooting our four children would be impossible.'

_____

_____

c Laurie: 'It's been three years since Jim started working in Holland and the girls have never got entirely used to it. Today my younger daughter said she was missing her daddy.'

_____

_____

GRAMMAR SPOTLIGHT

Reported speech to direct speech
As we saw, using direct speech in a piece of writing can make an article, informal letter or narrative or descriptive account more lively and interesting. The following sentence also appeared in the article:
Jonathan, a marketing director, arrived back at the family home in Kingston upon Thames to tell his wife Jean that he'd been offered an exciting new job … in Germany.

This could also be rewritten as:
Jonathan, a marketing director, arrived back at the family home and said: 'Jean, I've been offered an exciting new job … in Germany!'

4 What changes have been made?

5 Rewrite the following reported statements as direct speech.

a Paul told me that he'd really had a good time in Spain and couldn't wait to go back the following summer.
'_____

_____!' said Paul.

b Liam said he had been to the concert the night before and was feeling rather tired.
'_____

_____,' Liam told me.

c Amelia refused to come with us because she said she hated the theatre.
'_____

_____.' Amelia said.

6 When reporting direct speech, avoid using 'said' and 'told' too often. To enrich your sentences use a variety of reporting verbs. Choose the best option in italics in each of the sentences that follows.

1 She *admitted /complained / doubted* that she had not been listening to a word I said.
2 I *deny / report / propose* that we all listen to what Georgina has to say.
3 He *believed / demanded / repeated* that he be released from custody.
4 She *announced / considered / swore* to leave if he ever did it again.
5 He *begged / mentioned / insisted* her not to break off their relationship.
6 She *decided / objected / suggested* going for a walk.

➡ Grammar Reference 10.2, page 177

7 For questions **1–6**, complete the second sentence so that it has a similar meaning to the first sentence, using the word given. **Do not change the word given.** You must use between three and six words, including the word given.

1 'I had nothing to do with the robbery!' said Adrian.
   denied
   Adrian _____ the robbery.

2 'You are coming home for some lunch and I won't take no for an answer!' Tom said to me.
   insisted
   Tom _____ home for lunch.

3 'It's going to snow this week – I can tell,' William announced.
   predicted
   William _____that week.

4 'I'm sorry for what I said yesterday,' said Andrew.
   for
   Andrew _____ the day before.

5 'I really don't want you to get a tattoo!' Mum said.
   objected
   Mum _____ tattoo.

6 'You really should try our local Thai restaurant – it has fantastic food,' said Lewis.
   recommended
   Lewis _____ our local Thai restaurant because it has fantastic food.

Speaking: organising a larger unit of discourse

EXAM SPOTLIGHT

PAPER 5, PART 2 Organising a larger unit of discourse
This part of the Speaking Paper consists of an individual 'long turn' for each candidate. You will be given three pictures and expected to talk about two of them for one minute. It's not enough at this level simply to describe what the pictures show. The focus is on organising a larger unit of discourse – by comparing, describing, expressing opinions, and speculating.

1 Look at the pictures on page 197 and decide which two pictures are the most interesting, or which you think have the most things you can talk about. If they are very different there will be more things to contrast. In order to organise your one minute discourse, think about:

a What the pictures show (*describing*) or might be showing (*speculating*);

b How the pictures are similar or what common themes they share (*comparing*);

c How they differ or can show different points (*contrasting*);

d How you can best answer the question you have been asked based on the pictures (*expressing your opinion*).

2 **PAPER 5, PART 2 In pairs. Answer the questions below as Student 1 and Student 2.**

(A)

Student 1:	Look at the three pictures on page 197. They show three different forms of food production. Compare two of the pictures and say how you think the methods used might be better or worse for consumers' health and the environment.
Student 2:	Which picture shows the least ethical method of food production in your view?

(B)

Student 2:	Look at the three pictures on page 197. They show different forms of energy production. Compare two of the pictures and say how you think the methods used might be better or worse for the environment.
Student 1:	Which picture shows the cleanest method of energy production in your view?

Use of English: gapped sentences

1 **Discuss. Look at the following set of three sentences. What does the underlined word mean in each context?**

a If you don't put that back where you found it, you'll be in trouble!

b Gillian had to put up with incompetent staff when she worked in the restaurant.

c If you don't put your back into it, you won't get any results!

SPOTLIGHT ON VOCABULARY

Lexical contexts
The fourth part of the Use of English Paper is designed to test your knowledge of a lexical item in different contexts. You'll be given three different sentences with a gap. The word that fits the gap in each sentence is the same word and the same part of speech, but it usually has a different meaning in each case. There will often be one more familiar use of the word and one or two slightly less familiar or less common uses of the word. A good idea is to find the easiest ones first and focus on those.

2 **Which meaning of shut in the following sentences is more frequently used and which is less familiar, or used idiomatically?**

a She tried to shut her eyes to the suffering around her.

b Peter couldn't shut out the memories of being bullied at school.

c The shops shut in an hour, so you'd better get a move on.

3 **Sometimes the word you are expected to find may have an idiomatic or metaphorical meaning. Which of the sentences below are idiomatic or metaphorical? Which sentence has the most common or easily recognised meaning?**

a Bob won't be adversely affected by his negative experiences due to his thick skin.

b He made himself a huge sandwich with two very thick slices of bread.

c Ulrich speaks English with a thick German accent.

4 **PAPER 3, PART 4 For questions 1–5, think of one word only which can be used appropriately in all three sentences.**

1 He was the first person in his family to get a _____ from a university.
Martin infuriated me to such a _____ that I threw a plate at him.
We decided to go for a walk – even though it was barely one _____ above freezing outside!

2 Arnold and Lillian have been _____ friends since they were children.
It's no _____ saying you don't like mushrooms now – I've cooked the meal.
I know you don't like taking your medicine, but it's for your own _____.

3 Did you know that tomatoes belong to the same _____ as potatoes?
They decided to start a _____ almost as soon as they were married.
Cornelius has traced his _____ tree right back to Roman times.

4 Lizzie put a _____ in the newspaper about the cat she found.
Samuel threatened to hand in his _____ if they didn't reduce his overtime.
Emmanuel only gave me a week's _____ to find another driver before he left for Spain.

5 £50 was a small _____ when I was your age!
I had the good _____ to work with one of the best writers of the time.
Jennifer didn't believe in it, but she decided to let Madame Rosa read her _____.

Listening (2): note-taking

1 **Discuss.** Have you heard of 'freecycling'? If not – what do you think the term means?

2 🎧 **10.2** Listen to three people (Dave, Julia and Anna) talking about what 'freecycling' means to them. In each case write down the things that each person has acquired and given away and what other items freecycle members might offer.

Dave	Acquired	*bathroom cabinet*
	Given away	
	Other items	
Julia	Acquired	
	Given away	
	Other items	
Anna	Acquired	
	Given away	
	Other items	

3 **Discuss.** What are the main advantages of freecycling according to what you heard?

Writing: an information sheet

1 **Read the exam question below and write down five possible headings for paragraphs.**

PART 2

Some friends of yours have just set up a 'Freecycling' centre in your town and they have asked you to write an information sheet to distribute. They have asked you to write about 'Freecycle', outlining its aims, describing how it started, how it works, its rules and guidelines and giving information about who can participate and how.

2 **Read the leaflet on freecycling on page 103 and decide if it has answered the question well. Complete the gaps with appropriate headings.**

3 **Look back at the exam question. In your answer, you'll be expected to demonstrate appropriate use of two or more functions. Tick the functions below that the writer is being asked to fulfil in this task.**

comparing	complaining	describing
evaluating	explaining	expressing opinion
giving advice	hypothesising	justifying or judging priorities
narrating	outlining	persuading
recommending		

4 **Look again at the above leaflet. What register is used? Is it formal, informal or neutral? Think about the purpose of the leaflet. Who is the intended audience? Underline the sentences that make this clear.**

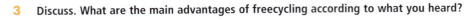

Freecycling For Everyone

1 _____
The Freecycle Network™ is made up of many individual groups across the globe. It's a grassroots and entirely non-profit movement of people who are giving and getting stuff for free in their own towns. Membership is free.

2 _____
The Freecycle Network was started in May 2003 to promote waste reduction and help save the landscape from being taken over by landfill sites. The Network provides individuals and non-profit bodies an electronic forum to 'recycle' unwanted items. One person's junk can truly be another's treasure!

3 _____
When you want to find a new home for something – whether it's a chair, a fax machine, piano, or an old door – you simply send an email offering it to members of your local Freecycle group. Or, maybe you're looking to get something yourself. Simply answer a member's offer, and you just might get it. After that, it's up to the giver to decide who receives the gift and to set up a pick-up time for passing on the treasure.

4 _____
Everything posted on the website must be free, legal, and appropriate for all ages. Non-profit organisations also benefit from The Freecycle Network. Post the item or items you want to give away and specify that you wish the gift to go to a non-profit cause. It's entirely your choice! It's a free cycle of giving.

5 _____
The Freecycle Network is open to all communities and to all individuals who want to participate. Freecycle groups are moderated by local volunteers from across the globe, who facilitate each local group. Think globally, recycle locally.

---

5 **Decide which of the following sentences is formal (f), informal (i) or neutral (n).**

1 a So get yourselves down town and join the team! [...]
  b You are invited to attend the organisation's first community event in the town hall. [...]
  c We would be happy to see you at our first meeting on Friday. [...]

2 a The purpose of this information leaflet is to offer a definitive account of our aims. [...]
  b By writing this leaflet we hope to offer you an insight into what we hope to do. [...]
  c Read our leaflet to find out about what we are planning to do – with or without you! [...]

3 a The charitable organisation was established with a view to dispensing aid and assistance to those without a permanent residence. [...]
  b We set up the group to help folks with nowhere to live. [...]
  c The charity was founded in order to offer direct aid to the homeless. [...]

6 **In pairs. Discuss the sentences above. Which sentences tend to be longer? Which sentences tend to use the passive more often? Which sentences tend to use slang or colloquial language more often?**

7 **Rewrite the first three paragraphs of the Freecycle leaflet in a more formal tone. Use language from the 'In Other Words' box below.**

In other words

acquire	beneficial	communicate by
consists of	comprises	dominating
exchanging	handover	recyclable waste
reduce the number of	re-housing	respond to
worldwide		

8 **PAPER 2, PART 2 Read the question below. Follow the steps that follow to prepare your information sheet for it.**

> An ancient woodland in your area is going to be cut down to make way for a road. Together with some friends you have decided to form a protest group to try to prompt the town planners to reverse their decision. The aim is to persuade people to join your group to make your protest stronger. You have decided to write an information sheet describing the group's aims, background and policies and giving information about how people can join and when meetings will be held.

1 Write down or underline possible headings for each paragraph.
2 For each paragraph heading brainstorm ideas about what information that paragraph might include. You can make up the details.
3 Think about who your intended audience is and decide what register is required: formal, neutral or informal.
4 Look at your plan and check that you have covered at least two of the functions you selected in exercise 3 on page 102. Remember you need to decide how much of your answer to devote to each function required so that your response is appropriately balanced.

9 **Write your information sheet.**

Vocabulary organiser 10

10.1 Getting Started, page 95 Use a dictionary to bank these words:

1 sustainable (adj) → _____ (definition)
   _____ (antonym)
   _____ (v)
   _____ (n)

2 ethical (adj) → _____ (definition)
   _____ (antonym)
   _____ (n pl)
   _____ (adv)

10.2 Reading, pages 96–97 Look back at the text and find a word that means:

a to look in a book, map or diary for information (v)

b to travel long distances every day between home and work (v)

c to gather together different pieces of information, statistics, numbers (v)

d to leave, or be forced to leave, a place that has been your home for a long time (v)

e to make something less likely to succeed, especially deliberately (v)

f an unmarried man (n)

g something that causes you to worry slightly over a long period of time (n)

h something that is not planned or organised in advance (adj)

i fast, energetic but uncontrolled (adj)

j so bad or so extreme that nobody can bear it (adj)

10.3 Language development, page 98 Complete the sentences below with one suitable phrase. Make any changes that are necessary.

1 Martha started to tell me about what had happened, but her brother walked into the room, just as we were getting down to the _____.

2 We said we would let Martin come along, as long as he promised not to _____ by mentioning Robert's name to Mary.

3 Fossil fuels and greenhouse gases are beginning to _____ the environment.

4 Elizabeth thought it would be easy to change course in the middle of the year, but she now admits it's been _____ all the way.

5 All the _____ of working in a fast-paced career caused his hair to turn white when he was still only in his thirties.

6 Archie had never really looked after his health, so when he got this nasty cough last winter _____.

7 It was too cold for us in Manchester, so we decided to _____ and move to Florida.

8 _____ is this: if you don't get your act together by the end of the week, you'll be out of a job, my friend.

10.4 Language development, page 98 Replace the underlined parts of the following sentences with a phrasal verb or an expression formed from *pull*.

1 I think Chris was <u>teasing you</u> when he said you'd won the lottery. _____

2 Mum was always moaning at Dad for not <u>doing his fair share of the work</u>. _____

3 He managed to <u>succeed at</u> three bank robberies in one week. _____

4 The factory is going to be <u>demolished</u> to make way for a shopping centre. _____

5 How long has Lionel been <u>deceiving us</u>? _____

6 Miriam had been diagnosed with a terminal illness, but she managed to <u>recover</u>. _____

7 I bet he only got promoted because his father <u>used his influence</u>. _____

8 '<u>Drive to the side of the road and stop</u>. I want to look at the map.' _____

10.5 Use of English, page 101 In your notebooks, write three example sentences for each word, so that it has a different meaning in each case.

1 shut   4 family
2 puts   5 lodge
3 degree   6 recall

BANK OF ENGLISH

Words with similar meanings

conscience	dilemma	ethics	morals	scruples

Choose the correct word for each definition below.

1 _____: the awareness of a moral or ethical aspect to one's conduct, together with the urge to prefer right over wrong. *'One of the things that make us different from animals is that we have a _____.'*

2 _____: a situation that requires a choice between options that are or seem equally (un)favourable or mutually exclusive. *'I found myself in a _____ – what was I going to do?'*

3 _____: a set of principles of right conduct; a theory or a system of moral values. *'According to our society's code of _____, treating people in this way is wrong.'*

4 _____: rules or habits of conduct, especially of sexual conduct, with reference to standards of right and wrong. *'Historically she was portrayed as a woman of loose _____, though there is no evidence that this was so.'*

5 _____: motivation deriving logically from ethical or moral principles that govern a person's thoughts and actions. *'Mike didn't have any _____ about pushing his way on to the bus first.'*

11 Making ends meet

MAIN MENU

Topics: making a living, earning and borrowing money

Language development: phrases with *out* and *money*; key word: *money*

Grammar: modal auxiliaries

EXAM MENU

Reading: interpreting literature; literary devices

Use of English: words of similar meaning, different uses

Listening: listening for dates / statistics

Speaking: responding to other people

Writing: a report

Getting started

1 **Which of the following views do you agree with? Why?**

> There is joy in work. There is no happiness except in the realisation that we have accomplished something.
> **Henry Ford**

> Working gets in the way of living.
> **Omar Sharif**

> The reward for work well done is the opportunity to do more.
> **Jonas Salk**

> All I ever wanted was an honest week's pay for an honest day's work.
> **Steve Martin**

2 **Discuss the following statement:**

'There are those who work to live and those who live to work.'
Which phrase applies to you?

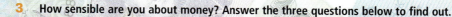

3 **How sensible are you about money? Answer the three questions below to find out.**

MONEY MANAGEMENT QUIZ

1 You've been given some money for your birthday, and need to decide what to do with it. Do you …
   A add it all to your savings?
   B add some of it to your savings?
   C spend it all and save none?

2 A friend of yours keeps borrowing money from you and not paying it back. He has just asked to borrow some more. Do you …
   A refuse to lend him any more money until he pays you some back?
   B agree to lend him some, but say this is the last time?
   C agree to lend him some more, and not worry if he pays it back or not?

3 You have borrowed some money from a friend and realise that you won't be able to pay her back when you said you would. Do you …
   A talk to her about it and agree to pay it back in small amounts over a set period?
   B tell her you can't pay it back now but will do so soon?
   C not say anything, since you're sure she won't mind waiting?

➡ Information File 11.1, page 203

105

Reading: interpreting literature

1 Discuss. What do you think the difficulties would be in finding work and living in another country?

2 Read through the extract on the opposite page. Decide whether the following statements about Chanu and his family are true or false. Underline the parts of the text which give you the answers.

1 The family seems wealthy.   T / F
2 Nazneen is self-opinionated.   T / F
3 Chanu has been unable to find work.   T / F
4 Shahana is satisfied with the family circumstances.   T / F
5 Chanu associates work with self-respect.   T / F
6 The family are immigrants.   T / F

3 PAPER 1, PART 3 Read the extract again. For questions 1–7, choose the answer (A, B, C or D) which you think fits best according to the text.

1 In the first paragraph, Chanu insists on 'calling the girls' because he wants
   A to tell them why he married their mother.
   B them to learn how to use the sewing machine.
   C to show them how hard their mother has been working.
   D to mark the significance of their mother starting work.

2 From the way she reacts, how does Shahana appear to feel about this?
   A unimpressed
   B angry
   C delighted
   D concerned

3 What do we learn about Chanu from the way he goes about helping Nazneen?
   A He is an astute businessman.
   B He needs to feel a sense of purpose.
   C He doesn't trust Nazneen to work on her own.
   D He is an official in a clothing factory.

4 Why does Nazneen pick up one of Chanu's books?
   A She would like him to read to her.
   B She wishes he would start reading again.
   C She feels he's working too hard.
   D She hopes he'll do some tidying up.

5 Why is Nazneen happy when Chanu goes out all day?
   A She's relieved he's stopped working for a while.
   B It means he trusts her to work on her own.
   C He seems happier when he returns.
   D She likes to see him wearing a suit.

6 Why does Chanu show the family his driving licence?
   A He's fiercely proud of having it.
   B He's just passed his driving test.
   C Its frame has broken.
   D It is proof of his qualifications.

7 From the passage, what impression do we gain of Chanu's character?
   A He wants to be respected.
   B He is arrogant.
   C He is mean with money.
   D He is pessimistic.

4 Discuss. Speculate what is going to happen next in the story.

5 VOCABULARY Find a word or phrase in 'The Middleman' which means the following:

a face cream (para 2) _____
b smiled broadly (para 3) _____
c express something uncertainly (para 3) _____
d briefly (para 3) _____
e a type of large bag (para 4) _____
f simple, basic (para 4) _____
g an item of clothing (para 4) _____
h performed a ritual to get rid of (para 7) _____
i make something easier (para 8) _____
j to make something vanish (para 10) _____

SPOTLIGHT ON READING

Literary devices
Literature differs from factual writing in style. Novelists employ various literary devices to create emphasis and dramatic effect.

6 Which of the following sentences from the text (a–c) are examples of the literary devices below (1–3)?

a *But he had to take what was going and the calculations themselves were a low-margin endeavour.*
b *It was a good sign.*
c *Every couple of days he went for new loads.*

1 Short, 'chopped' sentences, representing a character's thought patterns.
2 Sentences beginning with adverbs of time.
3 Sentences beginning with a conjunction.

7 Find at least one more example of each type of literary device in the text.

The Middleman

Nazneen wanted to begin at once but Chanu insisted on calling the girls. 'When I married her, I said she is a good worker. Girl from the village. Unspoilt. All the clever-clever girls – ' He broke off and looked at Shahana. 'All the clever-clever girls are not worth one hair on her head.'

Bibi opened and closed her mouth. Her white lacy socks had fallen around her ankles and her shins looked dry and dusty. Shahana had begun to use moisturiser. Yesterday she had refused to wash her hair with Fairy Liquid. She wanted shampoo now.

Nazneen held on to the casing of the sewing machine. Chanu waggled his head and beamed at her. She fixed the thread and began. One trouser leg, then the other. When she had finished, they clapped and Bibi became sufficiently carried away to venture a small cheer, and Chanu's applause was emphatic, and Shahana smiled fleetingly and marched back to the bedroom.

Chanu brought home holdalls of buttonless shirts, carrier bags of unlined dresses, a washing-up tub full of catchless bras. He counted them out and he counted them back in. Every couple of days he went for new loads. He performed a kind of rudimentary quality control, tugging at zips and twiddling collars while probing his cheeks with his tongue. Chanu totted up the earnings and collected them. He was the middle-man, a role which he viewed as Official and in which he exerted himself. For a couple of weeks he puzzled feverishly over calculations, trying to work out the most profitable type of garment assignment, the highest-margin operation. But he had to take what was going and the calculations themselves were a low-margin endeavour. Then he had time to supervise in earnest and he made himself available at her elbow, handing thread, passing scissors, dispensing advice, making tea, folding garments.

'All you have to do,' he said, 'is sit there.'

She got up to stretch her legs. She picked up one of his books and blew off some lint, hoping something in him would respond to the call of neglected type.

'We're making good money this week.' He pulled at his lower lip, working it out. 'Don't worry. I'll take care of everything.'

For two whole months she did not even know how much she had earned. It was a relief when, for the first time since the piecework began, Chanu retired to the bedroom one evening and called for a page-turner. The next day, a Saturday, he made a kind of fortress of books around him on the sitting-room floor and delivered a pungent oration on the ancient history of Bengal. On Sunday he shaved with extra care and limbered up in front of the mirror in a suit, but did not go out. The next day he went out all day and came back singing fragments of Tagore.

It was a good sign.

Tuesday and Wednesday passed in the same pattern and Nazneen completed the linings of thirty-seven mini-skirts. She had no more sewing to do.

Chanu gathered his family together and exorcised some troublesome blockages in his throat. 'As you are all aware.' He noticed Shahana's dress. She had hitched up her uniform at school so that it bloused over the belt and rode up towards her thigh. Without changing her expression she began to inch it slowly downwards.

'As you are all aware, we have decided – as a family – to return home. Your mother is doing everything possible to facilitate our dream through the old and honourable craft of tailoring. And don't forget it was we who invented all these weaves of cloths – muslin and damask and every damn thing.' He seemed uncertain. He looked at his daughters as if he had forgotten who they were. Only when his darting gaze fixed on Nazneen did he remember himself.

'Ahem. So. We are going home. I have today become an employee at Kempton Kars, driver number one-six-one-nine, and the Home Fund will prosper. That is all I have to say.'

Nazneen and Bibi clapped their hands. It came as a surprise that Chanu could drive a car.

As if to dispel their silent doubts he took a tattered piece of paper from his pocket. 'Driving licence,' he said in English. He inspected the document. 'Nineteen seventy-six. Never had it framed.'

So Chanu became a taxi man and ceased to be a middleman. And on the first hot day of the year, when the windows were closed against the ripening of waste bins and the flat hummed to the tune of its pipes, and Nazneen had mopped up the overflow from the blocked toilet and washed her hands and sighed into the mirror, a new middleman appeared. Karim, with a bale of jeans over his broad shoulder.

This was how he came into her life.

Language development: idiomatic phrases with *out* and *money*

1 Look at the sentences below from the text on page 107. Explain what the underlined phrasal verbs mean.

a 'For a couple of weeks he puzzled feverishly over calculations, trying to <u>work out</u> the most profitable type of garment assignment...'

b 'Chanu <u>totted up</u> the earnings and collected them.'

2 Complete the sentences below with one of the phrases in the box.

out of	out of it
out of luck	out of order
out of the blue	out of the question
out of this world	out of your mind

1 'You can't go to the cinema on a school night, when you've got school tomorrow,' said Jane's Mum, 'It's _____!'

2 'I hadn't seen her for months, and she just turned up _____ _____!'

3 'You must be _____ _____ to spend 150 euro on a ticket for the U2 concert! It's far too expensive!'

4 'You should go to the farewell dinner _____ respect for your boss. He's been good to you over the years.'

5 'The view from the top of the London Eye is _____ _____! On a clear day, you can see for miles.'

6 'I didn't enjoy the party yesterday. All my younger brother's friends were there, so I felt a bit _____ _____.'

7 'You can't use this machine; it's _____, I'm afraid.'

8 'Have you got change for a twenty-pound note?'
'Sorry, but you're _____ _____. I've only got a fifty.

➡ Grammar Reference 11.1, page 178

Key word: *money*

3 What can you do with money?

borrow	charge	clean	drive	earn	hire	heighten
inherit	launder	lend	lose	lower	make	owe
pay	raise	refund	save	spend	trade	waste

4 Choose the correct meaning of the following phrases in italics:

1 'Why don't you offer him a fiver to take her a message? Everybody knows *money talks*!'
   a you get things if you pay for them   b you can communicate with money

2 Dallas knew he couldn't beat Karen at chess, but he was determined to *give her a good run for her money*.
   a not let her win easily   b to cheat

3 'You can't hope to win Molly's love by *throwing money at her*!'
   a repeatedly telling her how rich you are   b spending lots of money on her

5 Match the money phrases below with their definitions.

A
1 pump money into something
2 not be made of money
3 have money to burn
4 get your money's worth
5 put your money on something
6 put your money where your mouth is

B
a bet money on the result of a race or competition
b get something that is worth the money you paid for it
c show by your actions that you really believe what you say
d give money to a company or business to help it become successful
e not be able to afford everything
f have enough money to be able to buy a lot of unnecessary things

6 PAPER 3, PART 3 For questions 1–10, read the text below. Use the word given in capitals at the end of some of the lines to form a word that fits in the gap in the same line.

Just for the fun of it!	
A (1) _____ law student found a novel way to free himself	1 PENNY
from (2) _____ difficulty. Using his computer, he embarked	2 FINANCE
on a number of (3) _____ activities which involved	3 FRAUD
obtaining credit card and bank details from (4) _____	4 SECURE
websites. He then used them in (5) _____ to buy cars,	5 TRANSACT
clothes and cash to the grand sum of £250,000. 'It felt like a	
bit of fun,' he said, when questioned, 'and a pastime which developed	
into an easy way of making money.' He even sent one of his victims a	
bouquet of flowers, paid for by their stolen bank details! He admits he	
became too confident. 'I thought it would be impossible to get caught,	
and just got carried away!' His (6) _____ ways soon aroused	6 CARE
the (7) _____ of the fraud prevention service, eventually	7 SUSPECT
leading to his arrest. He was charged with (8) _____ to	8 CONSPIRE
defraud, and served a three and a half year prison sentence.	
The general view among (9) _____ who specialise in	9 CRIMINAL
studying the motivation of such fraudsters is that the apparent ease of	
fraud conducted via the internet is encouraging people to commit	
crime, since they believe the risk of getting caught is negligible.	
However, one of them did get caught, and, needless to say, any	
(10) _____ law firm is hardly likely to employ a graduate	10 RESPECT
from the wrong side of the prison bars!	

Listening: sentence completion

1 Discuss. Which of the following views on the use of credit cards do you agree with? Explain why.

> It's so much easier than carrying a load of cash around, ready for someone to steal!

> The problem with cards is, you don't know how much money you're spending!

> It's easy to run up a lot of debts!

> Credit cards aren't very secure any more. It's easy for someone to steal your number, without you realising it.

> I'm less likely to buy silly little things if I don't carry cash. I feel more in control of my spending with a card.

EXAM SPOTLIGHT

PAPER 4, PART 2 Listening for dates, statistics or figures
In Paper 4, part 2, you may be asked to listen for a date, or piece of statistical information. So, when you read through a sentence completion listening task, try to predict where a gap may require a number or date.

2 **Look at the following sentences, and decide what kind of information you should listen for in each case.**

a In 1980, British families spent an average of _____ a week on household goods.

b They spent approximately £62 a week on motoring between 2002 and 2003, which had almost doubled since _____.

c Surprisingly, fuel and power expenditure was approximately £12 in 2003, which was _____ than it had been in 1980.

3 ∩ **11.1 Listen to an analyst comparing weekly family spending between the years 1980 and 2003, and complete the sentences in exercise 2. Were your predictions correct?**

4 Read the questions for the sentence completion task below, and try to predict the kind of words you need to fill the gaps. Make a note where you need a date or statistics.

5 ∩ **11.2 PAPER 4, PART 2 Listen to an interview with someone who works for a credit card fraud agency. For questions 1–8, complete the sentences.**

1 Recently, credit card fraud has been responsible for a loss of approximately _____ US dollars worldwide.

2 Fraud to the value of £411.6 million was committed on UK-issued credit cards in _____, a rise of over £5 million in two years.

3 Rodney claims that consumers are _____ with regard to credit card security.

4 Consumers are at risk when paying by card, because unscrupulous _____ may copy their card details, and then use them fraudulently.

5 Some criminals will even go so far as to search through household _____ to obtain credit card details.

6 As long as you inform the card issuer of any suspicions you have that your card has been copied, the most you are likely to have to pay is _____.

7 Rodney advises people to be more _____ when making payments by credit card.

8 Rodney suggests that British people are not as _____ as Americans about revealing their personal card details.

Grammar: modal auxiliaries (2)

1 **Match the following sentences with their uses.**

1 'What were you doing? You might have had an accident!'
2 'It would be easy. She'd tell her teacher she'd had her schoolbag stolen on the bus.'
3 'As it's raining, we might as well go home.'
4 'Oh no! There *would* be a traffic jam when I've got an important meeting!'
5 'It's eleven o'clock, so the headmaster will be in his office now.'

a *Modal for criticism*
b *Modal for prediction*
c *Modal for resignatio*n
d *Modal for a plan*
e *Modal for annoyance*

2 **Which of the uses above are the following sentences from this unit examples of?**

a 'I thought it would be impossible to get caught, and just got carried away!' ('Just for the fun of it', Language Development, page 108) _____

b 'But some [shop assistants] are not, and will try to steal their details.' (Listening, tapescript 11.2, page 217) _____

c 'The most you will have to pay is £50 ...' (Listening, tapescript 11.2, page 217) _____

GRAMMAR SPOTLIGHT

Making plans
For making decisions about future plans, **'will'** and **'would'** can be used:
'I think I *will go* to see Maria this afternoon.'
That was it! She *would give* her Mum a surprise birthday party.

Making predictions
'Will' and **'would'** can also be used to make predictions:
'It *won't be* easy to park in town today, because of the carnival.'
He sighed and thought it *would be* difficult to avoid going to the party.

Criticism
To express criticism or annoyance, **'might'** and **'could'** can be used:
'Drive more carefully! You *might have killed* that little boy!'
'You *could at least apologise* to her!'

Annoyance
'Will' and **'would'** can also be used to express annoyance:
'She *will keep* practising on the violin while I'm trying to study!'
'There *would be* a power cut now, just when I want to watch a film!'

Resignation
To express acceptance of a situation when there is no better alternative, **'may as well'** and **'might as well'** can be used:
'You're never going to be good at gymnastics, so you *may as well* stop.'
'I don't think Penny's coming, so we *might as well* leave.'

3 **Complete the sentences in the following mini-dialogues with a suitable modal structure.**

1 A: I think I _____ go shopping this afternoon.
  B: Remember there's a demonstration going on against the building of a new shopping centre. Some of the roads _____ closed.
  A: Oh, yes! I'd forgotten! I _____ stay home and do some homework, then!

2 C: I wish you _____ stop making so much noise! I'm trying to work!
  D: Well, you _____ give up and go out for a walk, because I'm putting these shelves up, and I _____ have time later.
  C: You _____ told me about this earlier!

3 E: Peter's called to say he _____ be coming to the concert tomorrow.
  F: Typical! He _____ cancel at the last minute! Now what am I going to do with the extra ticket?
  E: We _____ try and sell it outside the hall. Someone _____ want it!

4 **PAPER 3, PART 5** For questions 1–5 below, complete the second sentence so that it has a similar meaning to the first sentence, using the word given. Do not change the word given. You must use between three and six words, including the word given.

1 'I don't know why you bother going to that German class, since you never do your homework!'
  well
  'You never do your homework for German, so _____ _____ give it up!'

2 Sally decided then and there to go to France as a nanny for a year.
  become
  'I know! I _____ go to France for a year!' said Sally.

3 'Why didn't you offer to pay for the damage to that woman's car, seeing as the accident was your fault?'
  offered
  'You _____ for the damage to that woman's car, since the accident was your fault!'

4 'Kathy doesn't like David very much, so she's not going to be easily persuaded to go to his party,' said John to himself.
  persuade
  John realised that _____ Kathy to go to David's party, as she didn't really like him.

5 'Those kids next door keep playing basketball against my living room wall!'
  stop
  'I wish those kids _____ against my living room wall!'

Use of English: multiple-choice cloze

Words of similar meaning, different uses

In the Use of English Paper, it may be necessary to look at more than the target sentence in order to see the development of an argument and then decide which word or phrase is correct.

1 Choose the correct phrase to complete the following sentences:

1 Simon hated crowds. So, he _____ go to a football stadium.
   a would often   b might not   c would never   d would prefer to

2 'I've been studying in my room all week! Can we do something _____ staying indoors today?'
   a as well as   b but for   c except for   d other than

2 Make your own sentences using the other options in each sentence in exercise 1.

3 **Paper 3, part 1** For questions 1–12, read the text below and decide which answer (A, B, C or D) best fits each gap.

The Philosophy behind the Monopoly game: lessons for life?

I recently asked my multilingual English class which board games they most enjoyed playing. Monopoly won hands down.

Published in 43 countries, Monopoly is available in 26 languages (1) _____. So, what is it about this game that makes it (2) _____ popular? Searching on the Internet later that day, I was astounded by the number of websites offering information, instructions and (3) _____ advice on understanding the rules, how to improve your (4) _____ of winning the game, and also inviting you to play online. Besides this, there are several sites (5) _____ the use of Monopoly in the classroom, to teach accounting, the laws of economics and even sociology!

And therein (6) _____ the secret of the game's success. Or at least that's what some teaching experts will tell you. There are important lessons in life to be learned from playing a game of Monopoly. (7) _____ the game has evolved over the years, and there are now several versions, its guiding (8) _____ remains the same – to become the richest player through buying, selling and renting property. It is all about money, but doesn't adhere to the 'get rich quick' philosophy; (9) _____ it. The most important lesson we can learn from the game, say the experts, is not only how to get rich, but how to stay rich, by investing (10) _____. And that idea appeals to people the world over, (11) _____ of nationality, age or gender. Monopoly makes players think not only about how to make money, but also how to make money work for them.

So, if you're wondering how to teach your 12 year old child about finance, you could do a lot (12) _____ than introduce him or her to this game.

1	A worldly	B worldwide	C throughout	D together
2	A universally	B generally	C overall	D ultimately
3	A valued	B invaluable	C worthy	D fruitful
4	A possibilities	B chances	C probabilities	D opportunities
5	A advising	B sponsoring	C counselling	D advocating
6	A falls	B hides	C lies	D runs
7	A Despite	B However	C Although	D Notwithstanding
8	A idea	B thought	C concept	D principle
9	A in spite of	B far from	C instead of	D nothing of
10	A prudently	B rarely	C openhandedly	D wastefully
11	A disrespectful	B regardless	C disregarding	D thoughtless
12	A better	B more	C worse	D less

4 Discuss. Do you think the way you play a game like Monopoly can tell you something about what kind of career you will follow in the future?

Speaking:
disagreeing with someone else's opinion

1 🎧 **11.3** Listen to two candidates, Fernando and Katrina, answering the following question: *'Some people say that having any job is better than no job at all. What do you think?'*

Tick any of the useful phrases below that they use to respond to each other's comments.

> USEFUL PHRASES ... for disagreeing with each other
>
> I think it depends on ... ☐
> Perhaps, but don't you think ... ☐
> Yes, but if you've no other choice, what then? ☐
> I'm afraid I can't agree! ☐
> For me, doing such a thing would be ... ☐
> That might become a problem if ... ☐
> I cannot say the same for me ... ☐

2 In pairs. Answer the following question in a similar way. Use some of the phrases in the box, where appropriate.

> Some people believe that money is the most important thing in life. Do you agree?

Writing: A report – being concise

1 **Discuss.** Which of the two places depicted in the photographs on the left would you prefer to shop in? Give reasons for your choice.

2 **Look at the following writing task. What is it asking you to do?**

PAPER 2, PART 1

'You are the marketing manager of a large department store chain. The managing director has asked you to investigate the recent fall in sales. You asked the shop's customers their views on the various departments in the store. Read some customers' comments below, and write a report, briefly outlining the situation, and making recommendations for improvements.'

'There's hardly anything for boys in Children's Clothing, and what is available is too pricey!'

'The stationery department is well laid out, making it easy to find what you need.'

'Well, I don't think much of the furniture in the store. Choice is limited, and rather old-fashioned in style. Not worth travelling all the way to the fifth floor for!'

'My husband and I buy all our clothes here. There's plenty of choice, and the changing rooms are spacious, too!'

3 **Read the following report. What's wrong with it?**

Reason for writing

The aim of this report is to examine the reasons behind the recent fall in sales in the store. The report aims to provide an overall view of the current situation, and is based on points raised by the store's customers with regard to the various departments in the store. We asked customers to tell us which departments they visited most frequently, and which departments they hardly ever visited, and why.

Departments visited most frequently

Many customers told us they were more than satisfied with both the ladies' and the men's clothing departments. Some people even went so far as to say that they bought all their clothes there. They expressed the view that there was plenty of choice, and also said that the changing rooms were spacious. Another very popular department was the stationery department. Here, customers commented particularly on the successful layout, which helps the customer find what he or she needs very quickly and easily.

Departments that customers are dissatisfied with

By far the least popular department in the store is the furniture department, with many customers complaining that there is little choice, and what is available is rather old-fashioned in style. Some said it just wasn't worth travelling all the way to the fifth floor to visit this department. Besides this department, complaints were also made about the children's clothing department. Several customers complained about the lack of items in stock for boys, and also suggested that prices were too high.

Conclusion

It is clear from the comments customers made that improvements should be centred around the furniture and children's clothing departments. The Buyers for these departments need to alter their approach, and search for more varied and modern products. Considerable investment should perhaps be made in expanding the furniture department, while the buyer for children's clothing should search for new brands, and concentrate more on striking a balance between girls' and boys' clothing. If all this can be achieved, then sales will almost certainly improve in these departments, and the store in general will surely benefit.

PAPER 1, PART 1 Being concise

In part one of the Writing Paper, you are expected to write **180–220 words**. It is necessary to be concise when expressing your points, and to avoid repetition.

One way you can make sure you keep within the required word limit, is to keep your opening and concluding paragraphs as brief as possible.

4 In pairs. Reduce the opening paragraph of the model answer on page 112 to one sentence.

5 Discuss. What's good about the page 112 model answer? Note down the most important points you need to keep when reducing its length.

6 Make the rest of the model answer more concise, using the box below to help you.

In other words

Join points together in one sentence by using a variety of language.

- **Improve the opening paragraph above, by using some of the following phrases.**

  This report aims to provide an overall view of the current situation ..., based on ..., and to make suggestions for ...

- **Do the same for the main paragraphs.**

  There has been a dramatic / significant / considerable decrease / drop / fall in the number of ...
  As opposed to this, the Ladies' and Men's Clothing departments are experiencing ...
  This can be attributed to ...
  A possible reason for this is ...

- **Reduce the length of the concluding paragraph to one or two sentences.**

  Investment is needed in renovating / renewing / redesigning ...
  We need to expand / develop / modernise ...
  This will certainly encourage more people ...

7 Choose the best heading for each paragraph from the options below:

→ Paragraph 1	→ Paragraph 2	→ Paragraph 3	→ Paragraph 4
a Introduction	a The Good Points	a Problem areas	a The Future
b Aims	b Successful departments	b The Bad Points	b Recommendations

8 Look at the picture of the rollercoaster (above right). Have you ever been on a ride like this? Have you ever visited a theme park such as Disneyland or Legoland? Would you like to? Why (not)? Are there any parks like this in your country?

9 Answer the following question:

PAPER 2, PART 1

> 'You are the assistant manager of a large theme park. The manager has asked you to investigate the recent decrease in the number of visitors to the park. You asked visitors to fill in a questionnaire about the rides.
> Read some of the comments customers made about particular rides below. Then write a report, summarising the findings and making recommendations for improvements.'

'*Captain Hook's Ship is brilliant!*'

'While my ten year-old son can go on everything, there's nothing for my three year-old daughter, so she gets fed up quickly.'

'*You can't buy much to eat, apart from cakes and biscuits.*'

'*Boone's Park down the road has got more rides to choose from, and you pay one entrance fee, instead of paying for individual rides.*'

Write your report (180–220 words).

Vocabulary organiser 11

11.1 Reading, page 106 Circle the correct word or phrase in italics to complete the following sentences.

1 Nancy *ventured / endeavoured* a nervous smile in response to her teacher's words of praise.

2 At the end of the night, the bartender *worked out / totted up* the money in the till.

3 'I have some *troublesome / rudimentary* neighbours in the flat upstairs,' sighed Mandy, as a loud crash made the ceiling shudder.

4 Harry quickly showed them his passport in order to *dispel / exorcise* any suspicions they might have regarding his identity.

5 His excitement mounting, Ian *fleetingly / feverishly* worked out how much a trip to Peru would cost.

11.2 Language development, page 108 Decide if the following statements are true or false.

1 If you feel 'out of it', you feel you don't belong in a group or place.   T / F

2 If something is 'out of the question', it is irrelevant to the discussion in progress.   T / F

3 When something is 'out of order', it is not in the correct position.   T / F

4 We say something is 'out of this world' when it is amazing.   T / F

5 When something occurs 'out of the blue', it happens in the sky.   T / F

6 When you are 'out of your mind' you are happy.   T / F

11.3 Language development, page 108 Complete the following sentences with one of the phrases from the box below, making any changes to the tense etc, as necessary:

give him a good run for his money	money is no object
pump money into	put my money on it
put your money where your mouth is	

1 'I'll buy you whatever you want for your birthday. Honestly, _____!'

2 'Well, I may not have beaten James in that match, but I ___ _____.'

3 'You keep saying you could do the job better than me, so why not _____?'

4 'I may be wrong, but I'd _____ a woman becoming the next President.'

5 'Tom wants to develop the company, so he _____ _____ product development.

11.4 Use of English, page 111 Use a dictionary to find derivatives of the following words and complete the chart.

Noun	Personal noun	Verb	Adjective	Antonymous adjective
value				valueless
worth				
counsel	counsellor		sponsored	
sponsor			world-famous	
world				world-weary

11.5 All the unit Add more words and their derivatives from other sections in this unit.

BANK OF ENGLISH

Word Partnerships: *work*

Work can be used in many ways, and it can form many phrases.
PHRASES: *work in, work out, work off, work through, work up, have your work cut out, work your fingers to the bone, make light or heavy work of something, work ethic, work in progress … etc*

1 Using a dictionary to help you, make a list of example sentences using the phrases above.

2 Match the following compound nouns with their meanings:

A		B	
1	workaholic	a	person or machine that does a lot of hard, heavy work
2	workbench	b	total number of people in a country or region who are available for work
3	workbook	c	a heavy wooden table on which people use tools to make or repair things
4	workflow	d	person who works most of the time and finds it difficult to stop
5	workforce	e	the way a project is organised by a company, including who is going to do which part
6	workhorse	f	period of physical exercise, particularly in a gym
7	workmanship	g	book of practice exercises
8	workout	h	skill in making things well
9	worksheet	i	room or building where people use tools to make things
10	workshop	j	piece of paper with questions and exercises for students

12 Behind the silver screen

MAIN MENU

Topics:	film, scripts, Hollywood
Language development:	modifiers and intensifiers; key word: *quite*
Grammar:	present and past participle clauses

EXAM MENU

Reading:	humour, irony and sarcasm
Listening:	purpose and function
Speaking:	exchanging ideas
Use of English:	recognising parts of speech
Writing:	a film review

JACKIE CHAN

Getting started

1 How much do you know about cinema?

1 What do we call a film which has suspense and mystery?
2 What do we call a film or TV programme that tells us something about real life?
3 What is the group name for all the people who act in a film or on stage?
4 What's another word for the music in a film?
5 What kind of film tells a story with music and songs?
6 What kind of special effects are used in many modern films?

2 Which of the following do you consider the most important elements in a film? Rank in order. The ...

acting	☐	music / score	☐
cast	☐	cinematography	☐
setting	☐	script / screenplay	☐
costumes	☐	special effects	☐
direction	☐	story / plot	☐

3 Discuss. Which of the following factors influence your decision to go and see a film?

• Film trailers on TV or at the cinema
• Recommendation from someone you know
• Film reviews in newspapers, magazines or on TV
• The type of film it is (thriller, romance, comedy etc)
• Who stars in it, directed it etc
• The number of awards it has won

Reading: understanding humour, irony and sarcasm

1 Do you know any jokes from your country that can be translated into English? With a partner tell each other a joke you know. Does it work? Is it funny?

2 Read the definitions below for 'irony' and 'sarcasm'. Would either of these be considered as a form of humour in your own language?

> **irony** (n) /irony/ a subtle form of humour which involves saying things that you do not mean or the opposite of what is true. e.g.: *'What could be more enjoyable than going for a picnic in the pouring rain!'*
> DER ironic (adj), ironically (adv)

> **sarcasm** (n) /sarcasm/ speech or writing which actually means the opposite of what it seems to say, and is sometimes intended as a joke or to mock or insult someone. e.g.: *'You look absolutely gorgeous in those orange wellington boots and red plastic trousers!'*
> DER sarcastic (adj), sarcastically (adv)

SPOTLIGHT ON READING

Understanding humour, irony and sarcasm

In any part of the Reading Paper, you may be presented with a text that contains elements of humour, including irony or sarcasm. Every culture and nation has its own type of humour that may not always be shared with other cultures. One of the hardest things to 'understand' in a foreign language is humour. While you will not be expected to 'appreciate' humour in the CAE exam, it is important to recognise when the writer is being sarcastic, or using irony, to get their message across.

3 Read the film review that follows and decide ...

a Is the writer using any sarcasm or irony?
b Which humorous elements can you spot?

Happy Feet (Cert U)

This animated family picture offers a sucrose-enriched upgrade to the documentary *March of the Penguins*. It's as if executives watched that film and thought: 'Mmm, not bad, sick-makingly anthropomorphic, sure, but only a fraction as anthropomorphic as we'd really like: the penguins still aren't actually singing and dancing and doing Elvis Presley impressions.' It is a deficiency that is remedied in this schmaltzy comedy with an environmentalist message. Our little penguin hero is captured and displayed in an aquarium, where he finds he can entrance the crowd with tap-dancing skills; the humans respond, not by raising ticket prices to $10,000 per head, but by instantly restoring him to his habitat so they can learn more about how to protect him and his kind. Thank God those penguins can dance just like humans, eh? It means they deserve to live!

4 Based on the writer's review of the film 'Happy Feet', decide if the following statements are true or false.

a The reviewer believes 'Happy Feet' is more realistic than another film with similar subject matter. **T / F**

b The reviewer thinks the penguins resemble people too much. **T / F**

c The reviewer thinks the film contains a realistic portrayal of a famous person. **T / F**

d The reviewer thinks only species which possess special abilities deserve to be saved. **T / F**

5 You are going to read six different film reviews by Peter Bradshaw. Skim the texts and decide:

a which reviews are meant to be humorous.
b which reviews use irony or sarcasm.
c which films the reviewer liked.
d which films the reviewer disliked.
e which films you would most like to see.

6 **PAPER 1, PART 4** For questions 1–15, choose from the reviews (A–E). The reviews may be chosen more than once.

- a well-written script that is smart as well as funny **1** _____
- a character who reveals a contrasting side of his nature **2** _____
- an actor who is the perfect choice for the role he plays **3** _____
- a film that's so bad it should get a prize **4** _____
- a film set during a period of historic conflict **5** _____
- a storyline scenario that the reviewer finds hard to believe **6** _____
- a character who channels negative energies into positive action **7** _____
- the portrayal of a character by an actor that set a high standard to live up to **8** _____
- a film with a theme that the reviewer thinks has been overdone **9** _____
- a film that should have a shorter and slicker storyline **10** _____
- a character that makes a fool of himself **11** _____
- a well-known film that has recently been released to cinemas again **12** _____
- a film that is better for having fewer jokes than before **13** _____
- a character we are beginning to tire of **14** _____
- a film that could have been longer **15** _____

7 In Review B, the writer describes the 'romcom' (romantic comedy) as 'deathly' and 'wooden'. What do you think he means?

8 Look back at the reviews and find the adjectives the writer uses to describe each of the following aspects in the films. Explain what you think he means in each case.

1 _____ dialogue (text A)
2 _____ film-making (text A)
3 _____ leading man (text A)
4 _____ moment (text A)
5 _____ storyline (text C)
6 _____ music (text D)
7 _____ gags (text E)
8 _____ casting (text F)
9 _____ role (text F)

A Casablanca
(Cert U)

Michael Curtiz's rereleased 1942 classic is irresistible, big-hearted film-making – a unique kind of romantic noir – with cracking dialogue and a thrilling leading man in Humphrey Bogart as bar owner Rick: a stateless, cynical American in second world war Casablanca, where desperate refugees plead for transit papers. Rick is coolly at the centre, apparently needing nothing and wanting nothing, but nursing a broken heart after an affair with Ingrid Bergman, who is married to legendary Resistance fighter Paul Henreid. Rick comes to transform his emotional pain into a gallant and passionate support for his love rival's battle against the Nazis. There are too many spine-tingling moments to list.

B The Truth About Love
(Cert 15)

The Worst Film of 2007 awards race has now been called off. It has been rendered redundant by this wooden and deathly romcom* that was made three years ago, and is now being dragged out of the freezer. Jennifer Love Hewitt is a doctor living in Bristol. Jimi Mistry plays her love-rat husband. Most worryingly of all, poor Dougray Scott has to play the decent guy who is tragically, secretly enamoured of Hewitt. You can tell how adorably macho yet sensitive he is by the way he is seen caulking his boat in the harbour. Maybe the worst moment comes at the beginning when Scott, allegedly moonstruck with love for Hewitt and walking home alone, has to go into a goofy and horrifically embarrassing sort of hopscotch. Not one for the showreel.
* romantic comedy

C Spider-Man 3
(Cert 12A)

Tobey Maguire is back for the third and probably not last time in the role that he almost deserted mid-series. All superheroes have to be 'dark' now of course, to demonstrate their seriousness, and Spider-Man is no exception. This, evidently, is the film in which he goes over to the dark side, with a new dark costume, kept in a separate trunk under the bed and worn – sans mask – under his shirt, when he wants to feel super-bad. SM3 has its moments, but it's over-long and messy with a number of disjointed storylines. There's no clear villain to boot and, by the end, no clear hero to cheer. Instead of one obvious, compelling enemy, there are two. Or three if you count another who pops up right at the end. Where once a single baddie would do, now you need two or three. As he scampers around the bathtub of popular culture, Spidey is beginning to exhaust everyone's patience. The time has come for someone to produce a rolled-up newspaper the size of a subway train and bring it down with an almighty crash.

D Rocky Balboa
(Cert 12A)

Euphorically running up those Philadelphia steps to the pounding music must take a little longer for Rocky these days, you'd think, but he's back for one last wildly implausible shot at heavyweight boxing glory – in a movie called *Rocky Balboa*. Just that. Not *Rocky 10* or *Rocky 18*, but *Rocky Balboa*, which is evidently supposed to have a dignified, end-stopped ring to it: simply his full name, a man movingly rendering up a final account of himself. Incidentally, Sylvester Stallone is 60. It could be that Rocky the Italian Stallion, the legendary boxer he first created in 1976, is supposed to be younger than that, but no one in this film ever has the bad taste to mention his precise age. At any rate, Rocky is now a melancholy widower running an Italian restaurant. Then he gets a chance to prove himself in the ring. Again.

E The Simpsons Movie

The Simpsons are finally, triumphantly, here, after much whingeing and whispering that we've all got Simpsons fatigue and that the movie was only going to be a feature-length version of the TV show. To which I can only say 'only'? It's only going to be superbly funny and well-written all the way through? With a creative IQ that easily outpaces 99% of everything else Hollywood churns out? And as for Simpsons fatigue, I was too busy laughing to notice any. The gags are razor-sharp and lightning-swift; they keep coming, and the writing just puts everything else to shame, in the cinema just as on television. So many movies promise what they could never deliver in a million years. *The Simpsons Movie* gives you everything you could possibly want, and maybe it's a victim of its own gargantuan accomplishment. Eighty-five minutes is not long enough to do justice to 17 years of comedy genius. It's still great stuff.

F Casino Royale
(Cert 12A)

Daniel Craig has taken on the mantle of 007, and the result is a death-defying, sportscar-driving, cocktail-recipe-specifying triumph. Daniel Craig is a fantastic Bond, and all those whingers out there who think otherwise should hang their heads in shame. Craig was inspired casting. He has effortless presence and lethal danger; he brings a serious actor's ability to a fundamentally unserious part; he brings out the playfulness and the absurdity, yet never sends it up. He's easily the best Bond since Sean Connery, and perhaps, even … well, let's not get carried away.
It is all ridiculously enjoyable, because the smirking and the quips and the gadgets have been cut back. Mr Craig brings off cinema's most preposterous role with insouciant grit: I hope he doesn't quit too soon. For the first time in ages, I am actually looking forward to the next James Bond movie.

Language development:
modifying and intensifying adjectives

1 In the film reviews, the writer used certain adverbs to intensify or modify the meaning of the descriptive adjectives. Look back at the text on page 117 and underline the phrases below. What are these phrases describing?

a horrifically embarrassing (B) _____

b wildly implausible (D) _____

c superbly funny (E) _____

d ridiculously enjoyable (F) _____

SPOTLIGHT ON VOCABULARY

Emphasising adjectives

In addition to the standard quantifying adverbs (such as *extremely, very, incredibly, terribly, really* etc), you can often emphasise what you want to say by forming an adverb from an adjective with a similar meaning to the adjective you want to use. For example: hilarious + funny = hilariously funny.

2 Form adverbs from the words below to complete the sentences that follow. In some cases more than one answer may be possible.

back-aching	delightful	genuine
ridiculous	strange	tedious

1 I didn't like the music but the children's dance was _____ entertaining.
2 That was one of the most _____ boring films I've ever had to endure.
3 The plot was _____ silly, but I watched it anyway.
4 Although it was a bit weird, the programme was still _____ fascinating.
5 The documentary was _____ interesting despite being far too long.
6 I enjoyed the opera, despite having to sit in _____ uncomfortable seats.

---

3 What's wrong with the following sentences?

a Angelina Jolie is very brilliant. She's my favourite star.
b It was an absolutely good film. You really should go and see it.

4 Which of the following adjectives are gradable and can therefore be preceded by *very* and other intensifying adverbs?

annoying	delightful	disastrous	dull
exciting	fascinating	funny	good
hilarious	interesting	original	perfect
ridiculous	scary	unbelievable	

5 Which of the following intensifying adverbs can be used with non-gradable adjectives, such as *brilliant*? Can any also be used with both gradable and non-gradable adjectives?

absolutely	awfully	completely	extremely
fairly	incredibly	pretty	quite
rather	really	totally	very

6 Some adverbs and adjectives form collocations. Choose the option below that would not normally follow the word in bold?

1 **highly** (a) unlikely (b) amused (c) angered (d) qualified
2 **bitterly** (a) embarrassed (b) cold (c) disappointed (d) resentful
3 **deeply** (a) hurt (b) ill (c) offended (d) moved
4 **greatly** (a) confused (b) mistaken (c) changed (d) different
5 **seriously** (a) injured (b) ill (c) wounded (d) kidnapped
6 **fully** (a) aware (b) insured (c) amused (d) conscious
7 **perfectly** (a) simple (b) cold (c) fair (d) reasonable
8 **most** (a) kind (b) generous (c) helpful (d) nice

7 In pairs. Discuss the following questions. Use adjectives and intensifying adverbs from the boxes above. What do you think of ...?

1 Musicals
2 Old classic black and white films
3 Hollywood films with happy endings
4 Chinese martial arts films
5 Romantic films
6 Horror films

Key word: *quite*

Quite can be used:

1 to indicate that something is true to a fairly great extent, but is less emphatic than *very* or *extremely*.
2 with non-gradable adjectives to mean *absolutely*.
3 to emphasise what you are saying.
4 after a negative to make what you are saying less definite or weaker.
5 in front of a noun group to emphasise that a person or thing is very impressive or unusual.
6 to express your agreement with someone.

8 🎧 12.1 Listen to the sentences below. Which of the points above (1–6) do they demonstrate?

a 'I think it's time Roger retired.' 'Yes, well, quite!'
b Gillian is quite a little trouble maker, isn't she!
c I think it's quite a good idea to take her advice.
d It's quite clear to me that you were not listening.
e After the accident, he was never quite the same.
f I thought the script was quite ridiculous.

Listening: understanding purpose and function

1 Work in pairs. Discuss the following points:

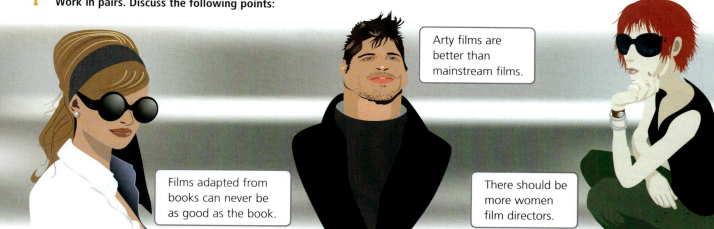

Films adapted from books can never be as good as the book.

Arty films are better than mainstream films.

There should be more women film directors.

SPOTLIGHT ON LISTENING

Understanding purpose and function
Understanding the purpose and function of what you're listening to can help you answer questions correctly. By reading the questions carefully before listening, you may be able to work out the purpose or function of each extract.

2 Read questions 1–6 in the listening task below. Decide what the purpose of each extract is. Which extract attempts to …?

a   establish a socio-political message
b   inform us of how someone got started on their career
c   highlight the differences of opinion between two speakers

3 🎧 12.2 **PAPER 4, PART 1** You'll hear three different extracts. For questions 1–6, choose the answer (A, B, or C) which fits best according to what you hear. There are two questions for each extract.

Extract one
You hear part of an interview with a filmmaker called Richard Morrison. Now look at questions 1 and 2.

1   Richard's main influences in filmmaking were
A   directing and cinematography.
B   his father's eight millimetre camera.
C   films that diverged from mainstream cinema.

2   Why does Richard claim he is not interested in making 'arty' films?
A   He doesn't think they are ever good.
B   He wanted to express his message in a different way.
C   He thinks they follow a predictable pattern.

Extract two
You hear two people talking about adaptations of children's books into films. Now look at questions 3 and 4.

3   The woman says that adaptations of children's books into films
A   cannot correspond with her childhood memories of them.
B   can renew an interest or give a deeper understanding of the original.
C   can put her off ever reading the books again.

4   What does the man think about adaptations of children's books into films?
A   He never sees films which are adaptations of children's books.
B   They are offensive to people who read the books.
C   He is unwilling to give up his own personal interpretation of the books.

Extract three
You hear a programme in which two women are discussing female film directors. Now look at questions 5 and 6.

5   The first woman's main point is that
A   there should be more female directors.
B   women should make more commercially successful films.
C   there is too much ambivalence in the film industry.

6   According to the second woman, the main reason why it is difficult for women to become film directors is
A   because there are too many men in the film industry already.
B   because women lack the skills and confidence to do a man's job.
C   because woman are not so adept at raising the money to make the film.

4 Discuss. Besides Hollywood movies, what other kinds of films are there? Talk about the films that your country produces, arty films, or films that are not in the mainstream of popular culture.

Grammar: participle clauses

1 **Read the sentences below and match each one to one of the options that follow.**

1 Climbing out of the pool, he reached for his towel.
2 Carrying a heavily-laden tray, she walked into the restaurant.
3 Emptying the bag, he dropped all the coins on the floor.

a two actions occurring simultaneously
b the second action is caused by, or is a result of the first action
c one action is immediately followed by another

GRAMMAR SPOTLIGHT

Participle clauses

Participle clauses are often used to join separate sentences or clauses together and they can make a sentence more descriptive or interesting. They tend to be used more often in formal or written English than spoken English. They are formed with the present or past participle form of the verb and often replace a noun, pronoun, relative pronoun or conjunction.

2 **Look at the sentences below and note the changes that have been made.**

a Present participle clauses

Joe walked into the room. He was humming a tune.
→ *Joe walked into the room **humming** a tune.*
It was a sunny day so we decided to go for a walk.
→ *The day **being** sunny, we decided to go for a walk.*
He didn't know if his parents would agree, so he decided to ask them.
→ ***Not knowing** if his parents would agree, he decided to ask them.*

b Past participle clauses

She opened the door and looked down the street.
→ ***Having opened** the door, she looked down the street.*
As / Since / Because she had passed with top marks, she got into Cambridge.
→ ***Having passed** with top marks, she got into Cambridge.*
As / Since / Because the house was designed by a top architect, it should be impressive.
→ ***(Having been) Designed** by a top architect, the house should be impressive.*

➡ Grammar Reference 12.1, page 178

3 **Replace the underlined words in the sentences below using a participle clause. Make any other changes that are necessary.**

1 <u>Because</u> I didn't know what else to do, I called Mum.
   _____
2 The sea <u>was</u> so warm that they decided to go for a swim.
   _____
3 <u>Since</u> we had been told off, we stopped talking. _____
4 <u>As</u> I had told Annette my secret, I wasn't surprised that everyone knew about it. _____
5 Jackson was looking for a film to watch. <u>He</u> switched on the TV. _____
6 <u>Seeing as</u> she had fallen in love with him, she decided to write him a poem. _____
7 <u>As</u> the manager had retired, Victoria was hoping for a promotion. _____

4 **Replace the underlined parts of the film review below with a participle or participle clause. Put brackets around words that could be left out.**

In the second Tomb Raider film, *The Cradle of Life* Academy Award Winner Angelina Jolie once again brings glamour and strength to her role as <u>Lara Croft, who is one of the world's most celebrated action heroines</u> ever to hit the big screen. <u>As she faces</u> her greatest challenges yet, the intrepid tomb raider must travel the world on a spectacular adventure. <u>She demonstrates her physical prowess and reveals her courage as never before, and Lara proves</u> that nothing can prevent her from searching to find the mysterious whereabouts of a hidden site known as 'The Cradle of Life'. <u>She knows that Pandora's box is concealed there, and that she must protect the secret</u> of its location in order to save the world from <u>the most unspeakable evil that anyone has ever known</u>.

SPOTLIGHT ON VOCABULARY

Participles as adjectives

Participles can be used as adjectives before nouns when the meaning is to describe a general quality, not a current event.

5 **In which of the following sentences is the present participle used as an adjective?**

a *Gillian was an **annoying** child.*
b *Gillian was **annoying** the grown ups.*

6 **Sometimes the past participle adjective has to be used after the noun, not before it. Which of the following sentences is correct?**

a *any **discussed** questions at the meeting …*
b *any questions **discussed** at the meeting …*

When a participle has an object the whole expression can sometimes be used as an adjective before a noun.
For example, '*a triumph that defies death, drives a sports car and specifies cocktail recipes*' could be written as '*… a death-defying, sportscar-driving, cocktail-recipe-specifying triumph.*'

7 **Rewrite the following sentence:**

The vegetables were grown organically.
They _____ .

8 **Rewrite the following sentences using a participle phrase.**

a We felt tired after the journey. → It was a _____ .
b The people this concerns should come to the meeting. → The people _____ .
c They are Swiss but they speak French. → They _____ .
d The colours on the curtains had faded. → The curtains had _____ .
e The dogs that were barking were getting on my nerves. → The _____ .
f The teacher had retired. → He was a _____ .
g The only seats that were left were in the balcony. → Only _____ .
h Her children have grown up. → She has _____ .

Speaking: exchanging ideas (parts 3 & 4)

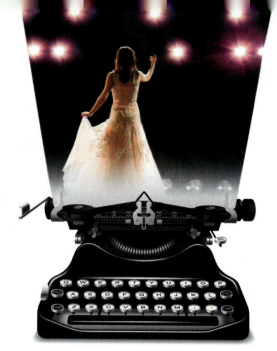

SPOTLIGHT ON SPEAKING

Exchanging ideas

In Paper 5, part 3, you and your partner will be asked to talk together for about three minutes. Sometimes you may be in groups of three, but then you will need to talk for about five minutes in total. The interlocutor and invigilator will be assessing each of you separately, but you'll be awarded points for your ability to interact with your partner/s and exchange ideas.

1 **In pairs or groups of three. Turn to page 198 and look at the pictures. They show different aspects of the film industry. Talk together for about three minutes.**

- First, talk to each other about how these pictures show different aspects of film.
- Then decide which picture best reflects the film industry.

2 **PAPER 5, PART 4 In pairs. Discuss the following points.**

- In what ways can film and television influence our lives? Is this a good or bad thing in your opinion?
- Sometimes millions of dollars are spent on a film. With so much poverty in the world, what is your view on this?
- Do you think films should be used as a vehicle for expressing political or religious beliefs?
- Do you think violence on television and in film has contributed to the violence in the world today?

Use of English: open cloze

EXAM SPOTLIGHT

PAPER 3, PART 2 Identifying parts of speech

As we have seen, in Paper 3, part 2, it's advisable to read the whole text carefully in order to understand the gist and to look out for negative meaning, inverted structures, conjunctions and so on. Make sure you know what part of speech should go in each gap as this will make it easier to guess the missing word if you do not know it.

1 **Read the sentences below and decide what part of speech the underlined word is.**

adjective	adverb	article	auxiliary
conjunction	modal	noun	particle
preposition	pronoun	quantifier	relative
pronoun	verb		

1 It was, <u>without</u> doubt, one of the best evenings I've ever had.
2 You have to be <u>absolutely</u> certain that you want to go into the business.
3 If you don't hurry <u>up</u>, you're going to miss the show.
4 Why don't you <u>make</u> an effort with Steve?
5 You really <u>should / must</u> try harder!
6 Amy, <u>who</u> knew nothing about the film industry, enjoyed herself enormously.
7 Very <u>little</u> is known about his childhood.
8 She ordered the pizza <u>although</u> she knew she wouldn't eat it.
9 <u>Anyone</u> who has been to Greece will know that the light is different there.
10 Given <u>the</u> lack of knowledge we have, it's amazing that we don't do more research.

2 **PAPER 3, PART 2 For questions 1–15, read the text below and think of the word which best fits each gap. Use only one word in each gap.**

Writing a Great Screenplay

When talking about a film we may comment on the acting, the directing and the plot, but only very rarely (1) _____ we think about the scriptwriting. Scriptwriters in general are denied most of the glory, and (2) _____ from two Academy Awards given out for writing each year (Best Original Screenplay or Best Adapted Screenplay), even the (3) _____ talented screenwriters tend to remain to all effects anonymous. And this (4) _____ the fact that the script is the fundamental tool of the film. (5) _____ it, there would be no film to speak of. The screenwriter must think (6) _____ an original story, develop the characters, and (7) _____ life to a piece of blank paper that will eventually, hopefully, yield a film. The journey will be long and arduous, but (8) _____ if the script is one of the few to be taken (9) _____ by a director, the writing process doesn't end there. Everyone on the set may (10) _____ a go at embellishing it, tweaking it, and building up its layers.

A writer can only get better with infinite amounts of practice. It was (11) _____ stated that a writer won't sell a script (12) _____ he's written a million words. Obviously, it's not going to be easy to achieve fame and fortune as a screenwriter and you will need a great (13) _____ of patience, perseverance and self-belief. Difficult though it is to reach the top, there is a demand for good scripts. Even in Hollywood, (14) _____ thousands of scripts are read weekly, there is a desperate shortage (15)_____ material that is fresh in voice and vision.

Writing: a film review

1 ∩ **12.3** Listen to some people describing their favourite films. Can you guess which films they are describing? Have you seen these films?

2 **PAPER 2, PART 2** Read the exam question below and underline the key words.

> Your college magazine has invited its readers to send in a review of a film they've recently seen, briefly outlining the plot, and giving their opinions on the acting, directing and any other elements of the film that stood out. You recently saw a film at the local cinema and have decided to write a review.

SPOTLIGHT ON WRITING

Planning your review

3 Before you start writing your film review, think carefully about how you are going to plan it. In your notebooks, answer the questions that follow.

- Choose a film: write down the names of three films you know you could write about (one you loved, one you hated and one that failed to move you either way).

- Write a brief summary of one of the films you chose above, using no more than 100 words. Be succinct. Don't waffle.

- Do you know the names of any of the cast, the director, the writer, etc? If not it doesn't matter, just use the character names when you talk about the story. If you can, fill in the names of the people involved in the film you summarised above.

- Talk about the elements of the film that really impressed you or failed to achieve a positive effect. Write a word or short phrase about the following elements in the film that you chose above: acting, setting, costumes, plot, script, directing etc.

TIP:
your favourite film is not necessarily the best one to describe. The best one might be a film you hated, or were indifferent to. Try to think of a film that is clear in your mind and you know a few things about (i.e. who was in it, or who directed it).

TIP:
Try to keep your words down here. You don't need to tell the whole story in detail – only the main idea. Don't give away the ending or destroy any moments of suspense for your reader. Sometimes you only need to describe the scenario at the film's opening.

TIP:
If you do know the names of the main characters, then either put them in brackets after the character's name or say: '[Actor's name] who plays [character's name]...' If you don't know the character names, use generic terms like: the hero, the heroine, the protagonist, the villain, etc.

TIP:
If possible avoid saying: 'I loved ...' or 'I hated ...' too often. Use the passive or describe the effects or results of the film on the audience.

4 Rewrite the sentences below so that they do not use the first person. For example, *I really loved the music because it was so powerful and it added emotion to the film.*

The powerful music added emotion to the film.

- a I didn't like the script because it was dull and failed to bring life to the story.
- b I wasn't impressed by the wooden actors and their performances didn't convince me.
- c I thought the story was quite interesting but I think it could have been developed further.

In other words

Think about the words you can use to describe elements of the film. Try to use descriptive adjectives with modifying or intensifying adverbs – and try to avoid saying 'very', 'really', or 'good' or 'bad' too often. Some noun and adjective groups often form collocations. For example: 'wooden acting', 'two-dimensional characters', 'a moving story', 'a complicated plot'. Read film reviews as often as you can, and make a note of any you come across.

5 Rewrite the underlined words in the sentences below with other words of your own choice.

- a The scenery was <u>very nice</u>.
- b The actor who played the main role was <u>really good</u>.
- c The script was <u>very boring</u>.
- d The directing was <u>not very good</u>.

6 Read the review below and tick the elements in the box that have been mentioned.

acting	directing	cinematography (filming)	costumes
editing	genre	music	plot
script	sets	special effects	the reviewer's opinion

7 Rewrite the parts of the text in italics using a participle clause and deleting any unnecessary words.

The Illusionist

(2006, USA, Thriller/Period/Romance, cert PG, 109 mins)

Set in Vienna at the turn of the century, the film centres around an enigmatic showman, Edward Abramovitz, *who is charismatically played* by Edward Norton. *He discovers that he has a talent for magic, and he* soon charms a beautiful young duchess called Sophie with his tricks. Unfortunately, *because he is* the son of a low-born cabinet-maker, he knows they are not destined to be together. She begs him to use his magic so she can disappear with him but the pair are soon tragically parted and forced to go their separate ways.

Years go by and Abramovitz is now appearing on stage in the capital, staggering the audience with his tricks. *He has changed his name, and he is known* as Eisenheim the Illusionist: clearly a brilliant magician and a phenomenal success.

In need of an assistant one night, fate brings him face to face with the beautiful fiancée of the Crown Prince Leopold, *who is played* very convincingly by Rufus Sewell. The supercilious prince allows his intended bride, (Jessica Biel), to descend from the royal box and assist Eisenheim with a trick. *As he looks* into her eyes, in front of hundreds, the young magician recognises her as his beloved Sophie and fate begins to take its course once again.

Adapted from a 1997 short story *which was written* by Pulitzer prize-winner Steven Millhauser, director Neil Burger has created a slick and subtle piece of work. The film skilfully sketches in the background historical detail, *and makes* it the setting for an elegant 19th century tale.

EXAM SPOTLIGHT

PAPER 2, PART 1 + 2 **Writing reviews**

In Paper 2 you may be asked to write a review. This could either be a review of a film, a book, a musical concert, a theatrical performance, an art exhibition, a set text or something similar. You may be asked to write a review in part 1, in which case you would be given additional information, or in part 2, where you have to use your own imagination or experiences to write a review of your own.

8 Try to think of a subject for each of the different review types mentioned below so that you will be prepared if you are asked to write about any of them in the exam.

A book: _____

A musical concert: _____

A theatrical performance: _____

An art exhibition: _____

9 Write one of the following.

Write a review of one of the films you've outlined in exercise 3 on page 122.

or

A bookshop website has invited its readers to send in a review of a film they've seen that's been adapted from a book. You have just seen the film version of a book that you've also read and you decide to write a review, commenting on how successful you think the adaptation to screen has been. Say whether you would recommend it to other readers and why.

Write your review.

Vocabulary organiser 12

12.1 Getting Started, page 115 Choose the best option (a, b or c) in each case.

1 When I go to the cinema, I often watch the _____ to decide what I want to see next.
   a credits   b trailers   c advertisements
2 I don't like horror films which just try to scare you, but I don't mind a good _____ with lots of suspense and adventure every now and then.
   a thriller   b documentary   c film noir
3 The composer's job is to write a good _____ for the film.
   a music   b lyric   c score
4 No matter how good the script is, if you don't have a good _____ it's not going to be worth watching.
   a crew   b cast   c actors
5 The _____ consisted of two or three different storylines which all converge in the final scene, and that's when you finally understand what's been going on!
   a plot   b direction   c production

12.2 Reading, pages 116–117

cynical	disjointed	enamoured	euphoric
gallant	gargantuan	preposterous	implausible
melancholy	redundant		

Find each of the words above in the film reviews and use each one to complete the definitions below.

1 A _____ person believes the worst of other people. [Text A]
2 If you describe someone as _____, you mean that they possess or display great dignity or nobility. [Text A]
3 Something that is _____ is no longer needed because its job is being done by something else, or is no longer useful or necessary. [Text B]
4 If you are _____ of something, you like it or admire it a lot. [Text B]
5 If something seems _____ it lacks order and cohesion. [Text C]
6 If you do something in a _____ manner, you feel very happy or elated. [Text D]
7 If someone is _____ they look and feel sad. [Text D]
8 If you describe something as _____, you think it is unlikely to be true. [Text D]
9 If you describe something as _____, you mean it is huge, enormous, bigger than could be expected. [Text E]
10 If you describe something as _____, you think it is extremely foolish. [Text F]

12.3 Reading (vocabulary), page 117 Complete the sentences that follow with a suitable phrasal verb.

1 Ms Roberts has had to _____ her engagements this evening due to a cold.
2 She plans to _____ a foundation for young actors with physical disabilities.
3 With a little make-up she can be _____ a plausible princess.
4 Mark has already agreed to do three films this year; I don't think he can _____ any more.
5 I think the film would be better if they _____ on the clichéd dialogue.

12.4 Language development, page 118 Choose one word from A and one word from B to form a collocation to complete the sentences below.

A	most highly seriously perfectly deeply bitterly
B	offended kind simple disappointed injured amusing

1 I thought it was very funny. In fact I found it _____ _____.
2 I thought the play was a complete waste of money. I felt _____ _____.
3 Thank you very much for your hospitality. You've been _____ _____.
4 You shouldn't have said such a terrible thing. He was _____ _____.
5 He was in an accident. Fortunately he wasn't _____ _____.
6 It's not complicated at all. In fact it's _____ _____.

12.5 Grammar, page 120 Rewrite the following phrases as participle or compound adjectives.

1 The clothes were made by hand. They were ….
2 The book amused me. It was an …
3 The fruit had been modified genetically. It was …
4 The watch was resistant to water. It was a …
5 The river had debris floating on it. There was …

12.6 Use of English, page 121 Use a dictionary. Find the words below in the text about screenwriters and write an example sentence of your own. Make a note of any derivatives.

a anonymous (adj)   d embellish (v)
b yield (v)   e tweak (v)
c arduous (adj)   f perseverance (n)

12.7 Writing, pages 122–123 What can the adjectives below be used to describe when talking about a film?

1 wooden _____
2 two-dimensional _____
3 moving _____
4 complicated _____
5 inspired _____
6 imaginative _____

BANK OF ENGLISH

Humour is a form of entertainment or communication, intended to make people laugh and feel happy. The origins of the word come from ancient Greek, the word meaning 'fluid'.

1 How many derivatives of the word 'humour' can you find? Write an example sentence with each of them.
2 Which one of the following words does not have anything to do with humour?

amusing	comedy	comical	deadpan
dehydrated	dry	farce	funny
giggle	hilarious	humorist	hysterical
irony	jesting	joke	laughable
mirthful	prankster	uproarious	sarcasm
satire	side-splitting	slapstick	wit

Review 3 Units 9–12

1

Match the following adjectives with their intensifiers or modifiers to complete the sentences below.

> bitterly
> deeply   deliciously
> fully   greatly   most
> perfectly   ridiculously
> tediously   thoroughly

> annoying
> aware   disappointed
> dull   kind   mistaken
> mouthwatering   offended
> reasonable   small

1 The film was _____, and we left half way through it.
2 Her handwriting is so _____ that you can hardly read it!
3 I was _____ by your unkind words, and expect an apology!
4 It's _____ of you to give me flowers, Mr. Jones! Thank you!
5 Sally was _____ not to be chosen for the part of Alice in the school play, and cried all the way home.
6 I am _____ of all the hard work you've put in, Mary, but I'm afraid your essay is irrelevant.
7 Ron has a(n) _____ habit of repeating the end of your sentence when you're talking to him.
8 You are _____ if you think I'm going to the party with you dressed like that! Go and get changed!
9 The food in that restaurant was good, but the _____ desserts were the best part of the evening!
10 Your reaction to the news is _____, and I do understand how you feel, so don't apologise.

2

PAPER 3, PART 3 For questions 1–5, think of one word only which can be used appropriately in all three sentences.

1 Penny waved to Mike, but he took no _____ of her.
I promise I'll give you plenty of _____ if the plans change.
Have you seen the _____ outside the headmistress's office about bringing mobile phones into the school?

2 No! I'm not buying you a PSP! I'm not made of _____, you know!
The school is holding a sponsored walk to raise _____ for charity.
She blindly pumped _____ into her boyfriend's new business, and then he ran off with his secretary.

3 Be careful with those matches! These chemicals are _____ inflammable!
It's _____ unlikely that James will come, as he hates parties.
A PhD in Applied Science makes you too _____ qualified to be a lab technician.

4 When dedicating the book, the author _____ tribute to the inspirational work of his father.
On her way home, Sarah _____ a visit to the hospital to see how her grandmother was.
David _____ the penalty for oversleeping by missing the school trip.

5 Lynne made short _____ of finishing her essay, and was soon ready to go to the party.
Tom's a good horse trainer, but with that stallion, he's got his _____ cut out!
We have a strong _____ ethic in this family; you don't get anything without putting in some effort!

3

Choose a suitable phrase from the box below to complete the sentences. Make any necessary changes.

> bottom line   nitty gritty   out of luck
> out of order   out of the blue   out of the question
> out of your mind   rock the boat   take its toll
> tough going

1 That last part of the race was _____, as it was mainly uphill and our legs were tired.
2 Sorry, but you're _____! We sold the last one this morning.
3 The long wait for news of her whereabouts had _____ on Jane's parents, and they looked tired and drawn.
4 Right, team! Let's get down to the _____! Who's going to be responsible for feeding the pigs?
5 Don't use the toilet on the third floor! It's _____.
6 It's _____ for a seven-year-old to go skydiving, Milton! You're too young!
7 I know things have been going well between you and Fred lately, and I don't want to _____, but I'm afraid I have something to tell you.
8 I know packaging is important, but the _____ is this: will the product sell?
9 You must be _____ to want to take four six-year-olds camping!
10 I hadn't heard from Claire for years, and then, _____ she phones me!

4

PAPER 3, PART 4 For questions 1–10, read the text below. Use the word given in capitals at the end of some of the lines to form a word that fits in the gap in the same line.

Swap Shop Revisited!

The last few years have seen a revival of interest in recycling old clothes and textiles. There is a growing (1) _____ of the negative impact the clothing industry has on the environment, and anti-consumerism (2) _____ are vociferous in their criticism of the (3) _____ nature of the fashion industry. As a result, buying brand new clothes from a retail store is now seen by many as (4) _____. A growing number of websites market clothes which have been manufactured using (5) _____ practices, and several offer tips on how to revamp your wardrobe at very little cost. No longer is it (6) _____ to buy your clothes from second-hand outlets or charity shops, and (7) _____ university students are now being joined by professional women in doing so!

A new craze has taken things a step further. Clothes (8) _____, once restricted to friends and family, has taken hold on a grander scale, (9) _____ by networking schemes on the Internet. In addition to private swap parties, public 'Swap Shop' events are now held, to which you take your (10) _____ clothes along, and are awarded points according to the estimated value of each garment. Then, using these points, you 'buy' other items on offer. And clothes aren't the only things available. Handbags, shoes, and even jewellery made from reclaimed materials can also be obtained.

1 AWARE
2 ACTIVE
3 MATERIAL
4 ETHIC
5 SUSTAIN
6 FASHION
7 PENNY
8 SWAP
9 FACILITATE
10 WANT

5 Make the following sentences more emphatic.

1 You should go out and meet people more.
What _____.

2 Because I didn't want to disturb them, I left without saying goodbye.
Not _____.

3 I don't understand how he managed to work it out that way.
How _____.

4 Calm down! You just need a break from working on the computer.
All _____.

5 The weather was so cold that they decided to light a fire.
So cold _____.

6 Since she had dreamed of going to Alaska all her life, Grace was extremely excited.
Having _____.

7 I don't know where he gets his bad temper from!
Where _____.

8 Because she hoped to become an Olympic swimmer, Hannah trained very hard.
Hoping _____.

9 As I hadn't seen Mike and Helen for several years, we had a lot to talk about.
Not _____.

10 Although this car is old, it is reliable.
Old _____.

6 Complete the following dialogue with a suitable modal auxiliary phrase.

Andy: Neville's late. It's not like him.
Sharon: I suppose he (1) _____ (get) lost.
Andy: He (2) _____ (not get) lost! My instructions were pretty clear! Anyway, he (3) _____ (phone) if he was stuck.
Sharon: Knowing Neville, he (4) _____ (not have) a mobile phone. He hates them! It's annoying, though. He (5) _____ (be) late when we want to go to the cinema!
Andy: Well, seeing as he hasn't come, we (6) _____ (go).
Sharon: What if he turns up and we're not here?
Andy: That (7) _____ (be) his fault for being ...
Neville: Hi, guys! Sorry, I'm late. I missed the bus!
Sharon: Well, you (8) _____ (call) us!
Neville: I (9) _____ (do), but my mobile wasn't working.
Andy: Anyway, we're too late for the cinema now, so what shall do? We (10) _____ (order) a pizza and watch a DVD.
Sharon and Neville: Yeah, why not!

7 Replace the underlined words in the sentences below with a suitable reporting verb. Make any other necessary changes.

1 He said he was sorry he had missed her party.
2 Tommy said he hadn't put worms in the teacher's bag.
3 She said she would kill herself if he left her.
4 He said she had lied to him.
5 We told him that the Indian restaurant on the corner was good.
6 Clare said she had taken the money.
7 Julie said she thought it would be a beautiful wedding.
8 They told us it was dangerous to go near the railway tracks.

8 **PAPER 3, PART 5** For questions 1–8, complete the second sentence so that it has a similar meaning to the first sentence, using the word given. **Do not change the word given. You must use between three and six words, including the word given**

1 I think it's terrible that you didn't apologise to her for breaking that vase!
might
You _____ breaking that vase!

2 'I demand to see the Manager at once!' said the angry customer.
insisted
The angry customer _____ immediately.

3 We went for a coffee because the train was delayed.
been
The train _____, we went for a coffee.

4 The Managing Director of the company was an old schoolmate of her father's, so she got the job.
strings
Maria got the job after her father _____ Managing Director of the company, with whom he'd been at school.

5 We'd thought Dale would cancel dinner, but he didn't.
as
Dale _____ we'd expected.

6 Although she had no idea where she was going, she packed her bags and left.
knowing
She packed her bags and left, _____ she was going.

7 Although I don't particularly like my work, I do enjoy going on business trips.
what
My job is nothing special, _____ going on business trips.

8 My poor head! Someone please tell Nick to stop practising on his drums!
would
I wish _____ stop practising on his drums! I've got a headache!

13 Getting the message across

MAIN MENU

Topics: sending messages, talking to aliens, communicating ideas

Language development: nouns followed by prepositions; key word: *set*

Grammar: text references; introductory pronouns

EXAM MENU

Reading: predicting information
Use of English: educated guesses
Listening: doing multiple tasks
Speaking: sustaining interaction
Writing: contribution to a longer piece

Getting started

1   Discuss. How are the pictures on this page connected with the idea of 'getting the message across'? What other ways of communicating can you think of?

2   In pairs. Place the following 'communication' verbs into the suitable columns below. Many of them fit into more than one column. Explain the reasons for your choices. For example, you can *'instil ideas in someone'*, but not *'information'*.

broadcast	clarify	convey	exchange	explain
impart	instil	publicise	publish	reveal
send	share	transmit		

Ideas	Information	Messages	Knowledge
convey	broadcast	transmit	
	send	send	
		convey	

3   Complete the following sentences with one of the verbs from exercise 2. Please note that more than one answer may be possible.

a   'I'm not sure I understood you there, Dan. Could you give me an example to _____ your idea?'

b   The soldier struggled to get the radio to work so that he could _____ a message to headquarters and warn them that the enemy was advancing.

c   The artist uses powerful images to _____ his ideas about life and death.

d   As a teacher, Jack endeavoured to _____ not only knowledge but also wisdom to his students.

e   The sales manager tried to _____ determination into his sales team.

Aa Bb Cc Dd Ee Ff Gg

Hh Ii Ji Kk Ll Mm

Reading: predicting information

1 Discuss. Have you ever watched any science fiction films involving humans making contact with aliens? Do you believe this could really happen? Why or why not?

3 Read the title of the extract page 129, and look at the pictures. What do you think the article is going to be about?

4 **PAPER 1, PART 2** Read the extract from an article on the next page. Six paragraphs have been removed from the extract. Choose from the paragraphs (A–G) the one which fits each gap (1–6). There is one extra paragraph which you do not need to use.

5 **VOCABULARY** Find words or phrases in the text on page 129 which mean the following definitions.

a being that is not from earth (para 1)
b important official (para 2)
c unsuitable, because outdated (para 3)
d work out what something means (para 4)
e an unpleasant thick, slippery substance (para 7)
f unable to be heard due to so many others speaking (para 8)
g think carefully (para A)
h long narrow hole dug in the ground (para C)
i bring together a number of people for a purpose (para D)
j deliberately, for a reason (para E)

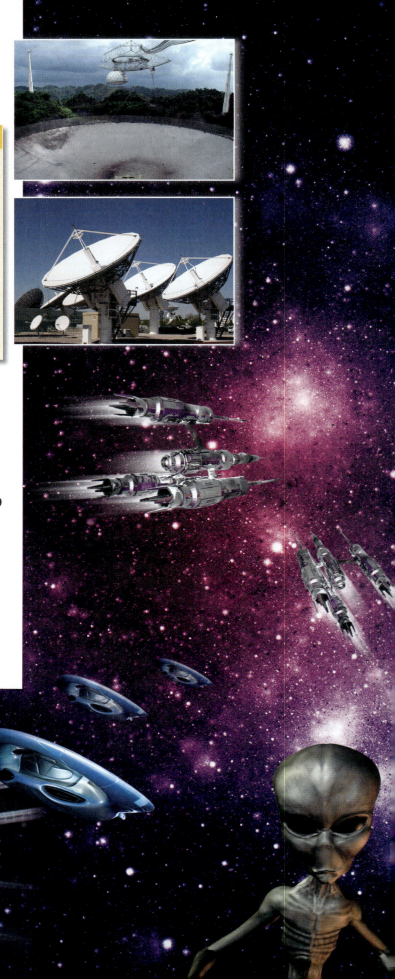

How to Talk to Aliens

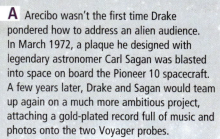

On November 16, 1974, astronomer Frank Drake dedicated a new observatory in Arecibo, Puerto Rico, by sending humankind's first deliberate communication to extraterrestrials.

The message, made up of 1,679 seemingly random zeros and ones, was shorter than the first four paragraphs of this article, but it still took three minutes to send. While the message began its voyage to the cosmos – a 24,000 year trip to M-13, a cluster of stars in the constellation Hercules, to be exact – visiting dignitaries listened over a loudspeaker while each bit played as a short, high-pitched tone. Some participants later said it brought tears to their eyes.

1 [...]

To a large extent, modern technologies have made these suggestions irrelevant. Since the 1920s, human radio and TV broadcasts have spammed the galaxy and anyone listening has already gotten an earful. 'In some sense, this is all
10 academic, because we have been broadcasting to aliens for decades,' says Seth Shostak, senior astronomer at the SETI Institute, a non-profit organisation dedicated to the search for extraterrestrial intelligence. 'They're already watching re-runs of our TV shows!'

2 [...]

The Arecibo broadcast represented one approach. Those 1,679 zeros and ones carried hidden meaning for any intelligent species who noticed that 1,679 is the product of two prime numbers, 73 and 23. Arrange the message in 73 rows of 23 numbers, and you get a picture painted in bits. It was a novel approach, but the message was hidden, and it depended on aliens making leaps of logic in order to decipher it.

3 [...]

20 These efforts are notable because so few other attempts have been made to craft a message to alien civilisations. But as actual attempts at communication, the spacecrafts fall flat. They're too small to notice and move too slowly. Far better to use a broadcast signal, which we can target at a specific star, and which moves at the speed of light.

4 [...]

And we could do it with style. 'One nice thing about light is that creatures develop eyes, and it would be possible to make optical radiation bright enough to see,' says Paul Horowitz, a professor of physics at Harvard University. 'That's an unmistakable signature. You look up, and there's a star, blinking in code, and the colour's changing, too.'

5 [...]

30 Other researchers say that the best way to get an alien's attention is to send it a significant numeric pattern, perhaps prime numbers or the value of Pi. 'Maybe the most fundamental way to initiate a message would be with mathematics,' says Horowitz. 'A lot of stuff will surely be understood by anybody, no matter what slime they're made out of, because it's so basic.'

6 [...]

The discussion might seem academic. But many astronomers are confident they'll detect an extraterrestrial intelligence in the next few decades, and when that happens, we'd better have an official reply ready, or risk being drowned out by the public.

* Search for Extra Intelligence

A Arecibo wasn't the first time Drake pondered how to address an alien audience. In March 1972, a plaque he designed with legendary astronomer Carl Sagan was blasted into space on board the Pioneer 10 spacecraft. A few years later, Drake and Sagan would team up again on a much more ambitious project, attaching a gold-plated record full of music and photos onto the two Voyager probes.

B If you're sending a message to extraterrestrials, what you want to send is what's special about us and our planet – what's unusual. Now that's not basic chemistry or mineralogy, it's pretty much the cultural stuff and the consequences of evolution.

C Humans have debated the best ways to contact our interstellar neighbours for centuries. In 1820, German mathematician Karl Friedrich Gauss proposed cutting an enormous right-angled triangle into the Siberian pine forest, creating a monument to the Pythagorean theorem big enough to see from outer space. Twenty years later, Austrian astronomer Joseph von Littrow expanded on that idea, suggesting the excavation of huge trenches in the Sahara desert, which would be filled with kerosene and set ablaze. Flaming triangles, circles and squares would be a beacon to our solar neighbours, at least until the fire went out.

D Next comes the question of what the message should say. Drake says if he could do it again, he might convene an international committee of scientists, artists, politicians and religious figures to produce a holographic movie about life on Earth.

E But what if we decided we wanted to send a message with intent, something that will say more about us than simply popular culture? What's the best way to send a message that will be received, understood and useful?

F The mathematical approach has its critics. 'You're not going to send the value of Pi,' says Shostak. 'If aliens sent us the value of Pi, wouldn't you be disappointed? You learned that in seventh grade.' Instead, why not transmit everything we've got? 'I would just send the entire contents of Google's servers,' says Shostak. 'To begin with, you don't have to worry about the fact that they don't speak English, because there's a lot of redundancy, so they'll learn it. And every subject is in there ...'

G We could use the same radio frequencies as the Arecibo message, but why not do something a little more dramatic? The universe is pretty transparent to optical light; that's how we can see far away galaxies. If we used a bank of high-powered lasers, we could beam a high-bandwidth message across the cosmos.

Language development:
nouns followed by particles

1 Complete the following sentences taken from the text on page 129 with the correct particle.

a The SETI Institute [is] dedicated to the search _____ extraterrestrial intelligence.

b But as actual attempts _____ communication, the spacecrafts fall flat.

c Karl Friedrich Gauss proposed ... creating a monument _____ the Pythagorean theorem big enough to see from outer space.

d Next comes the question _____ what the message should say.

2 Choose the correct particle to complete the sentences below.

1 The Moon alphabet was developed as an alternative _____ Braille.
   a for   b to   c of   d over

2 Scientists are in dispute _____ what kind of message should be sent into space.
   a for   b with   c on   d over

3 Kathleen is an authority _____ communication in dolphins.
   a on   b over   c for   d about

4 For years, the SETI Institute has been trying to set up a channel _____ communication between humans and extraterrestrial intelligence.
   a in   b of   c over   d with

5 Few people have been privileged enough to have had contact _____ dolphins or whales in the wild.
   a over   b to   c with   d between

6 I've been in communication _____ an expert in New York, and he is going to send me some information.
   a to   b on   c for   d with

7 The Internet allows us access _____ more information than ever before.
   a on   b in   c to   d for

8 There has been a breakdown in communication _____ the workers and the management.
   a from   b with   c between   d for

Key word: *set*

In the Reading text on page 129, one of the suggestions for contacting aliens was to dig long trenches in the ground and 'set them ablaze'. To *'set something ablaze'*, *'set something alight'* and *'set fire to something'* all mean to *'start a fire'*. Many other phrases with *set* mean 'start' something, or 'establish' it.

3 Which of the words below can follow set?

... an example	... a trend	... a desire
... a precedent	... in motion	... to work
... a goal	... the alarm	... money
... a pattern	... a point	... a standard

4 Match the following actions in column B with the person who does them in column A.

A		B	
1	a surgeon	a	set sail
2	a happy couple	b	set a record
3	a teacher	c	set a date
4	an athlete	d	set up a business
5	a hunter	e	(try to) set the world to rights
6	a waiter	f	set a test
7	a writer	g	set the table
8	an idealist	h	set a bone
9	an explorer	i	set pen to paper
10	an entrepreneur	j	set a trap

5 **PAPER 3, PART 5** For questions **1–8** below, complete the second sentence so that it has a similar meaning to the first sentence, using the word given. **Do not change the word given.** You must use between **three** and **six** words, including the word given.

1 There is a lot of disagreement among politicians about government spending on space travel.
   dispute
   Politicians are _____ government spending on space travel.

2 A teacher is responsible for providing her students with knowledge and ideas.
   impart
   It is the job of a teacher to _____ her students.

3 An impression of what life was like thousands of years ago can be gained from the cave paintings.
   convey
   The cave paintings _____ what life was like thousands of years ago.

4 'Don't bother trying to stop Steven – he's determined to go.'
   set
   'Steven _____, so don't bother trying to stop him.'

5 Scientific information is available to the general public via the university website.
   access
   The university website allows _____ scientific information.

6 'Last night I saw a terrible car accident as I was walking home from work.'
   witness
   'As I was walking home from work last night, _____ car accident.'

7 Darren used examples of local businesses to illustrate his idea.
   clarified
   Darren _____ putting forward examples from local businesses.

8 'Just as we were leaving to go on holiday, my boss called me to say there was an emergency meeting!'
   set
   'We _____ holiday, when my boss called me to an emergency meeting!'

Grammar (1): text references (*this, that, it, such, these, those*)

GRAMMAR SPOTLIGHT

Reference words

Every written text contains several features which enable the reader to understand how it is organised. Reference words are used to refer to something that has already been mentioned, or they may point forward to an example, or the next point. '*This*', '*that*', '*it*', '*these*', '*those*' and '*they*' are reference words.

1 The following sentences all appear in 'How to Talk to Aliens' on page 129. What does each of the underlined words refer to?

a 'In some sense, <u>this</u> is all academic ...' (line 9)

b '<u>Those</u> 1,679 zeros and ones carried hidden meaning for any intelligent species who noticed that 1,679 is the product of two prime numbers, 73 and 23.' (line 14)

c '<u>These</u> efforts are notable because so few other attempts have been made to craft a message to alien civilisations.' (line 20)

d 'And we could do <u>it</u> with style.' (line 25)

e '<u>That's</u> an unmistakable signature.' (line 27)

2 *Such* is also a reference word. What does it refer to in the text below?

Many scientists believe that studying communication in animals like dolphins and chimpanzees can help us to come closer to understanding the reasons for our own ability to speak. <u>Such</u> ideas have given rise to a number of research projects around the world.

3 Complete the following text with suitable reference words.

Dolphin chatter

Dolphins are social creatures. Like humans, they form attachments to each other and live in 'families'. Following a 'safety in numbers' policy rather like our own, dolphins hunt for food in numbers and defend themselves more effectively in numbers. A mother needing to look for food will leave her offspring in the care of another adult female in the group. They also play together. (1) _____ behaviour would not be possible without good communication.

They achieve (2) _____ by producing whistles and other sounds. Since it is difficult to see underwater, dolphins send out high-pitched signals to find food, or detect danger. (3) _____ signals bounce back from whatever they hit and the dolphins are able to interpret what (4) _____ are. (5) _____ process is known as 'echolocation'. The human ear is unable to hear the dolphins' signals, but we have managed to develop machinery which can pick 6) _____ up. After years of careful study, scientists have ascertained that they use (7) _____ system to call each other when they find food, and to ask for help or warn each other of danger. Dolphins also appear to 'chat' rather like we do, and while scientists are still far from being able to decipher exactly what they say, they are able to recognise certain sounds, along with the dolphins' use of body language. For instance, when they rub fins after being apart for a while it signifies a form of greeting. They clap their jaws together when there is a fight, and (8) _____ seems to mean 'back off'.

Another area of study which scientists are particularly interested in is (9) _____ of communication between mother dolphins and their offspring. In one experiment, a mother and her calf were placed in separate tanks which were connected by an audio link. They proceeded to chatter by squawking and chirping to each other, and appeared to know who they were talking to.

The question is, will we ever be able to communicate with dolphins? Now (10) _____ would really be something worth talking about!

➡ Grammar Reference 13.1, page 179

4 Discuss. Why might it be useful to be able to communicate with animals such as dolphins and chimpanzees? What, if anything, could we learn from them?

Use of English: gapped sentences

EXAM SPOTLIGHT

PAPER 3, PART 4 Making educated guesses
In Paper 3, part 4, it may not be obvious what the missing word is. When this happens, don't get anxious, experiment! Use what you know to help you make a reasonable guess.

1 Look at the sentences below. All three options are idiomatic, and so you may not know them. First, what part of speech are you looking for – a verb, a noun or an adjective?

1 *'Wendy may be able to help you! I'll have a _____ with her.'*
2 *'_____ has got round that Jane is going out with Gary. Is it true?'*
3 *'Joe likes to have the last _____ in any argument, and hates being wrong.'*

2 Use the context of each sentence to try and think of a word which fits into that sentence. For example, 'talk' and 'chat' could fit into sentence 1, but do they fit into sentences 2 and 3? Sentence 2 needs something which means 'gossip', but this option doesn't fit into the other sentences.

3 Look at the options you've eliminated – *talk, chat, gossip.* What do they have in common? Brainstorm possible alternatives. What have you found?

4 **PAPER 3, PART 4** For questions 1–5, think of one word only which can be used appropriately in all three sentences.

1 'Dr Drake is going to give a _____ on how we send non-verbal messages using body language.'
'Jake says he's going to leave his job and travel the world, but he's all _____!'
'I've heard there's _____ of a new shopping centre being built on the site of the old school.'

2 'Sandra lives in a small, white cottage _____ back from the road.'
'OK, runners! On your marks, get _____, ... go!'
'She is so _____ against going to the party, I don't know whether I'll be able to persuade her.'

3 'Officer Brown? Yes, I've got some information in _____ with that robbery last night.'
'The vacuum cleaner's not working. There must be a loose _____.'
'The train from London was delayed, so I missed my _____ for Plymouth.'

4 'My brother lives in Zurich, so we _____ mostly by email.'
'Parents sometimes unintentionally _____ a lot of their anxieties to their children.'
'Teachers need to be able to _____ ideas to their students.'

5 The politician worked hard to improve her public _____.
'Sarah's the _____ of her mother – even the way she moves is like her!'
I have a clear _____ in my mind of how my ideal home would be.

Speaking: sustaining interaction (Paper 5, part 3)

1 🎧 **13.1** Listen to two candidates discussing the photographs on page 199. How successful are they at interacting?

SPOTLIGHT ON SPEAKING

Sustaining interaction

Sometimes your Speaking Paper partner may not have much to say, perhaps because they're nervous. However, in Paper 5, part 3, it's necessary to keep the conversation flowing between you. Make sure you give your partner time to express a view, perhaps by asking them a direct question about a picture, before you comment on it yourself. Remember, this will gain *you* marks, for attempting to *interact*, while at the same time giving your partner the chance to speak!

2 Look at the tapescript on page 219, and suggest ways Carlos might encourage his partner Magda to respond in a more convincing way.

3 Work in pairs. Talk together about how successful you think the advertisements above and on page 199 are. Then decide which advertisement is the most effective in getting its message across. Remember to give each other the chance to speak, in a natural manner.

Listening: multiple matching

1 Discuss. The pictures on the right involve people using different means to get a message across to others. Think of other situations in which we need to communicate ideas.

2 ∩ **13.2** Listen to a short extract once, and complete the tasks below.

1 The person speaking is a
   a zoologist
   b young mother

2 The speaker's tone is one of
   a enthusiasm
   b disbelief

3 The speaker is expressing
   a wonder at the birth of the gorilla in captivity
   b fascination at the gorilla's attempt to communicate

3 ∩ **13.2** Now listen again. Do you need to change any of your answers?

4 What words tell you which options are correct? Why are the other options incorrect?

5 ∩ **13.3** You will hear five short extracts in which different people are talking about communicating. While you listen, complete tasks one and two below.

Task One
For questions **1–5**, choose from the list A–H the person who is speaking.

A a neighbour
B a sociologist   Speaker 1 [1]
C a sales representative Speaker 2 [2]
D a charity official   Speaker 3 [3]
E a hospital official
F a teacher   Speaker 4 [4]
G a marketing consultant Speaker 5 [5]
H a prison officer

Task Two
For questions **6–10**, choose from the list A–H what each speaker is expressing.

A pride in their communicative skills
B frustration over an inability to communicate with their neighbour   Speaker 1 [6]
C advice on how to avoid conflict   Speaker 2 [7]
D fascination in the complexities of language
E a commitment to addressing a social   Speaker 3 [8]
   problem effectively
F fears that a service is operating   Speaker 4 [9]
   inefficiently
G concern that children are receiving the   Speaker 5 [10]
   wrong messages from the media
H advice on expressing an idea successfully

6 A number of communication issues were raised in the listening extracts. Work in groups. Discuss one of the following:

• Children often receive the wrong messages from the media.
• In a multicultural society, the problem of communication within public services needs to be addressed.
• Communication skills should be taught in schools.

Grammar (2): *'it / there'* as introductory pronouns

1 Work in pairs. What is the difference between the following pairs of sentences?

1   a *'It's very windy.'*
     b *'There's a lot of wind.'*

2   a *'It's a long way to Glasgow.'*
     b *'There's a long way still to go before we reach Glasgow.'*

3   a *'It's time to do your homework.'*
     b *'There's time to do your homework and go to the cinema, if you start now.'*

GRAMMAR SPOTLIGHT

Introductory *'it'*
We usually **introduce** the sentence with *it* when …
1 … an infinitive is the subject of a sentence.
2 … we're beginning a sentence with a comment.

We also use *it* **before** …
3 … impersonal verbs followed by *that*.
4 … some verbs which require it before them.

Introductory *'there'*
We use *there + be* when …
5 … the subject of a sentence is an indefinite noun.
6 … asking a general question
7 … introducing a noun followed by a relative clause.
8 … *there* can be followed by another auxiliary + *be*.

2 Which point in the Spotlight above are the following sentences an example of?

a It appears that he isn't coming after all.
b It's odd you don't like this painting.
c There's something I have to do in town.
d It struck me how like her father she was.
e There may be something stuck behind the door.
f It's better to check what you write.
g There's a man on the phone for you.
h Is there anything I can do?

3 Complete the following sentences with *it* or *there*.

1 'How far is _____ to Brighton?' '150 kilometres.'

2 _____ is no time to go home and get changed. We have to leave now.

3 _____'s a book on the table. Whose is _____?

4 Mum, _____'s nothing to do here. _____'s boring!

5 _____'s too cold to go out today. Is _____ anything on TV?

6 _____ may be some sense in going that way, but _____ is advisable to check the traffic news first.

Writing: contribution to a longer piece

WWF   unicef   GREENPEACE

1 These are the names of different international charity organisations. Do you know any of them? Are you a member of any such organisation? Have you ever raised money for, or donated money to one?

2 Discuss. Should your answer to the writing task below be formal or informal?

PAPER 2, PART 2

> A friend of yours is a member of an international charity organisation, and is compiling an information book for new volunteers and campaigners. She has asked you to contribute a section advising campaigners on how to give presentations to companies in order to raise money and support for the charity.

3 Which of the following points should you include in an answer to this question?

- Learn something about the target company before you visit them.
- Keep your tone and the level of your language formal at all times.
- Emphasise the positive marketing effects support of the charity will have on the company.
- Make sure you know a great deal about the charity, so that you will be able to answer any questions that may be asked.
- Use an informal language and a relaxed tone, so that your audience can feel totally at ease.
- Make your audience feel guilty that they haven't supported the charity until now.
- Try to assess the level of your audience when talking to them, in order to achieve the right tone.

4 Read the answer to the writing task on page 135. Check how many of the points mentioned in exercise 3 it includes.

5 Does the model answer strike the right tone? After looking at the second paragraph on page 135 again, read the alternative paragraph below. Which one is more appropriate for the task in exercise 2? Give reasons for your choice.

> First, it's important to recognise the level of your audience. Aim to achieve the right balance in tone. Avoid sounding too formal, or you may distance your audience. On the other hand, a tone that is too informal may imply a lack of respect. So, the best approach is to be friendly, yet polite.

Giving Presentations

Fundraising is a fundamental part of charity work. In order to do this successfully, volunteers will need to approach companies who might be potential supporters. It may be necessary to give a presentation, and so good communication skills are essential.

An important aspect of giving a presentation is recognising the level of your audience. *Without doubt, it is very important to achieve* the right balance in tone. *One shouldn't be too formal, for instance,* because this can distance the audience, while a tone that is too informal may imply a lack of respect. *A friendly, semi-formal approach is invariably the most desirable.*

The value of research before preparing one's presentation cannot be ignored. It is important to know as much as possible about the charity's work and its achievements, as well as its needs, and also to know a fair amount about the target company. Knowledge of the concerns of an organisation and interest shown in these will appeal to any business executive.

Another point to consider is appealing to the audience ethically, without making them feel guilty. Present them with a good reason for supporting the charity – such as free advertising – while explaining the ethical advantage in doing so. *Emphasis of the fact that* the charity receives regular attention from the media also has a positive effect on members of the marketing team.

There are a number of websites available which give online advice about giving presentations to companies, as well as helping charities prepare press releases. Take advantage of these when preparing your first presentation.

skill

media

fundraising

helping

charity

support

care

6 Some of the language in the model answer is too formal. Use some of the phrases in the 'In other words' box below to replace the phrases in italics, and make the piece more direct.

In other words

Try to achieve the right balance ...
You shouldn't be too formal, ...
Do some research into ...
Make sure that you know something about ...
Appeal to their sense of justice ...
Avoid making your audience feel guilty ...

A useful trick is to ...
You may find it useful to ...
It may be wise to ...
There may be some sense in ...
but be careful not to ...
It is advisable to ...

7 Read the writing task below. How does it differ from the model task above? Brainstorm ideas about:

- the intended audience
- the style of your contribution
- whether you need headings
- the kind of language you should use in your answer

PAPER 2, PART 2

> The local council where you work is writing a new guidebook for visitors to the area. You have been asked to contribute a section, giving advice on the best places to eat in the area, giving a brief description of the type of food on offer, and an indication of the restaurants' reputation and price range.

8 Write your contribution (220–260 words).

Vocabulary organiser 13

13.1 Getting started, page 127 Complete the sentences below with a suitable 'communicating' verb. In some cases, more than one verb may be possible.

1 The producer decided to _____ this week's chat show live.
2 The newspaper reporter refused to _____ the source of his information.
3 The research findings are being _____ in this month's 'New Scientist'.
4 The town council is running an advert in the local newspaper to _____ the new recycling campaign.
5 The American physicist has agreed to _____ information with a Japanese scientist based in Tokyo.
6 The coach spoke to the team before the match in order to _____ confidence in them.
7 The staff training officer said to the group of new trainees, 'It is my job to _____ knowledge to you about how to sell our products.'
8 The chef _____ the plans for the party to his staff.

13.2 Reading, pages 128–129 Complete the sentences with a suitable word or phrase from the Vocabulary task on page 128.

1 She _____ how to tell him the news without upsetting him.
2 'I find it impossible to _____ my doctor's writing, and can never read my prescriptions!'
3 The chairman decided to _____ a meeting of the board of directors to discuss the sale of the company.
4 The Royal Gala night in honour of the Queen was attended by several _____, including the Mayor of London.
5 'Your findings are interesting, professor, but quite _____ to what we are trying to do here, which is something entirely different.'

13.3 Language development, page 130 Complete the table below with the words in the box.

access	admiration	alternative	approach
argument	authority	communication	connection
contact	dispute	effect	matter
product	question	respect	result
search	solution	threat	witness

Nouns followed by	
of	
for	
to	
on	
over	
with	

13.4 Language development, page 130 Explain the meaning of the following phrases and phrasal verbs with *set*.

1 set a date: _____
2 set a precedent: _____
3 set a task: _____
4 set your heart on: _____
5 set your eyes on: _____
6 be set against: _____
7 set about (doing): _____
8 a set menu: _____
9 set the stage for: _____
10 set the scene: _____

Make sure you add any new ones to your list!

13.5 Writing, page 135 Match the words and phrases from the model answer in A with their contextual meaning in B.

A		B	
1	fundamental	a	information sheet given to newspapers
2	potential	b	reason to do something
3	benefactor	c	basic, essential
4	asset	d	interest
5	concern	e	possible
6	incentive	f	advantage
7	press coverage	g	person who provides financial support
8	press release	h	news reports on a particular organisation's work

BANK OF ENGLISH

Word partnerships

The prefix **co-** is placed at the beginning of verbs or nouns that refer to people doing things together or sharing things.

Verbs	Nouns
cooperate	colleague
collaborate	co-worker
coexist	co-writer
communicate	co-director
connect	
contact	
converse	

Complete the sentences below with one of the verbs in the box in its correct form.

1 Renee and I _____ on writing a book about marine life a few years ago.
2 'Have you ever _____ with a parrot? It often has a lot to say!'
3 'Prisoner 225, if you don't _____ and tell us who sent you, you'll be shot!'
4 'I just can't _____ with my little brother! He doesn't understand me at all!'
5 'Have you _____ the doctor yet? Her temperature's gone up to 40 degrees!'

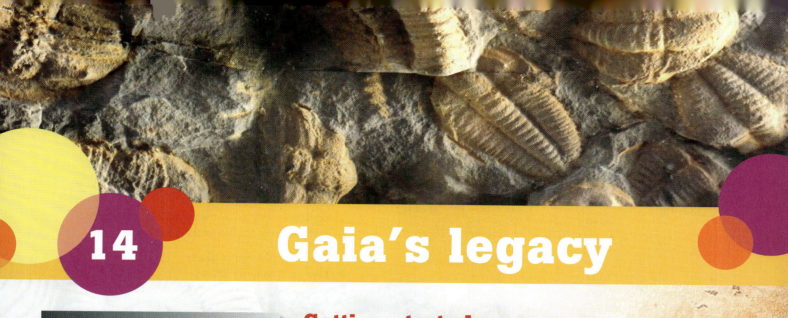

14 Gaia's legacy

Getting started

1 Discuss. What do you know about the history of the Earth? Do you know how old it is or how long human beings have lived here?

2 Look at the timeline below left. It represents the age of the Earth. See if you can guess when the following events happened. Mark the corresponding letter on the time line.

a Life begins on Earth
b Homo Sapiens (modern humans) appear

3 ∩ **14.1** Listen to a palaeontologist talking about the appearance of life on Earth and fill in the table below.

Event	Time (millions of years ago)
a The first multi-celled animals (sponges) appear	*700*
b Animals without back bones (invertebrates) appear (jelly fish)	
c The first animals with backbones (vertebrates) appear (fish)	
d Plants appear on land	
e Insects appear on land	
f Fish develop lungs and leave the sea (amphibians)	
g Reptiles (snakes, lizards) appear	
h Dinosaurs appear	
i Mammals appear	
j Birds appear	
k Primates (monkeys, apes) appear	
l Apes that use their hands to make tools appear	
m Apes that walk on two legs appear	
n Modern humans appear	

BILLIONS OF YEARS

4.7 — Earth is formed
4
3
2
1
0 — Present time

Reading: multiple choice questions

1   Discuss. Have you heard of 'Gaia' before? Who or what is it?

2   Skim read the text on page 139 and write down the answer to exercise 1 in your own words.

SPOTLIGHT ON READING

Matching gist to detail

Very often multiple choice questions will ask you to match detailed information in the text to more generalised question stems. Read the paragraph below.

> It is almost impossible to know how many species there used to be or calculate how fast they disappeared, but in studying the vertebrates and molluscs in the fossil records over the past 65 million years, one notices that the average life of a species is approximately two to three million years, and one species per every million seems to have become extinct per annum during that time.

3   Look at the statement below. Underline the words in the paragraph above which have been used in the statement and circle or highlight the words that have been changed but have the same meaning.

> According to the fossil record, one species out of every million would disappear every year on average.

4   Assume that option A below is the correct answer and write a sentence of your own that could be used as a false option but still contains information taken from the paragraph above.

According to the fossil record …
A   one species out of every million would disappear every year on average. ✔
B   _____ ✗

5   Read the following paragraph and decide which of the options that follows (A, B, C or D) is the most accurate summary.

> In other words, he knew that when looking at the Earth in this way, what he was seeing was not so much a planet that just happened to be suitable for sustaining life, but a self-evolving and self-regulating living system, that could adjust itself to support life. This seemed to qualify the Earth as a living entity in her own right.

He realised that he was looking at a system

A   that had multiple life-support systems.
B   that was suitable for sustaining evolved life.
C   that qualified as a living being in order to sustain life.
D   that had the means to adapt conditions for life to exist.

6   Underline the parts of the paragraph that provide the answer. Do not try to answer multiple choice questions from memory or after one reading because false options will deliberately try to confuse you and may be very similar to the correct answer.

7   **PAPER 1, PART 3** Read 'Planet Earth – the Gaia hypothesis' again. For questions 1–7, choose the answer (A, B, C or D) which you think fits best according to the text. Underline the answers in the text.

1   The first astronauts in space were
   A   conscious of the lack of physical boundaries between nations.
   B   forced to adjust their perspective of their place in the cosmos.
   C   profoundly affected by the symbolism of the Earth.
   D   made aware of the life-forces operating on Earth.

2   Dr James Lovelock had originally
   A   been an inventor in Britain.
   B   been employed to compare Mars with Earth.
   C   been looking for Martian life.
   D   proved Mars was a dead planet.

3   Lovelock surmised that
   A   Earth's inconstant atmosphere was a bi-product of life on the planet.
   B   the chemical condition of the Earth had come about by accident.
   C   the imbalance of gases on Earth had created life.
   D   life had evolved to survive in Earth's planetary conditions.

4   Research has shown that
   A   the various planetary systems are regulated by different mechanisms.
   B   clouds are formed by metabolic chemical changes in the sky.
   C   the saltiness of the seas is due to the presence of oceanic algae.
   D   Gaia can ultimately control her own survival.

5   According to Gaia theory
   A   the planet has physical biological organs similar to a person's.
   B   the oceans control the temperature of the Earth's atmosphere.
   C   the rainforests can remove all the pollution from the Earth.
   D   each species on Earth has a part to play in the planet's survival.

6   According to Lovelock,
   A   higher forces were at work behind the Earth's existence and survival.
   B   the Earth had developed senses and was conscious of its purpose.
   C   the complex life-forces on earth are equal to the sum of a living being.
   D   bacteria and plants are alive but can only produce simple processes.

7   The Gaia hypothesis may ultimately ensure the immediate survival of
   A   the planet Earth.
   B   the human species.
   C   the ecosystem.
   D   all life on Earth.

Planet Earth – the Gaia hypothesis

According to accounts, when the first astronauts in space looked down and saw the Earth floating in the vast black void, they had what can only be described as a profound spiritual experience; in an instant they had attained a 'global consciousness' in which all national and international boundaries disappeared, and they were left with the awesome realisation that they were mere 'planetary citizens'. To the astronauts, the planet looked as if it were some huge single living system. The photographs they brought back touched us all in some way, and the blue sphere in space came to symbolise the oneness of all humanity and life on Earth. The idea that the planet might be alive, strange though it sounds, was soon to gain credence, even among the scientific community.

Not long afterwards in the 1970s, the hypothesis that the Earth's biosphere actually functions as a single living system was put forward by Dr James Lovelock, a British scientist and inventor who had been commissioned by NASA to help determine whether or not there was life on Mars. By comparing the atmospheres of both planets, he soon realised that, while Mars had a stable, unchanging, 'dead' atmosphere, Earth had no such equilibrium, and that there were some complex processes going on. It was this imbalance that made the planet suitable for sustaining life. He postulated that: *'the physical and chemical condition of the surface of the Earth, of the atmosphere and of the oceans has been, and is, actively made fit and comfortable by the presence of life itself … in contrast to the conventional wisdom which held that life adapted to the planetary conditions as it, and they, evolved their separate ways.'*

Suffice it to say, Lovelock knew that when looking at the Earth in this way, what he was seeing was not so much a planet that just happened to be suitable for sustaining life, but a self-evolving and self-regulating system that adjusted itself to support life. This seemed to qualify the Earth as a living entity in her own right, so he named her 'Gaia' – after the Greek goddess who was said to have drawn the living world forth from Chaos – and the 'Gaia hypothesis' was born.

Lovelock first published his idea in 1979 in his book, *Gaia, a New Look at Life on Earth*, although the science behind the hypothesis was still imprecise. The ideas in the book provoked a storm of criticism, but also generated a lot of research, which has since led to profound new insights about life on Earth. For instance, Lovelock knew that the heat of the sun had increased by 25% since life began on Earth, yet he did not understand by which process the temperature on the surface had been kept at the optimum conditions suitable for sustaining life.

Since that time, many of the mechanisms by which Gaia regulates her systems have been identified. For example, it has been shown that cloud formation over the open ocean is almost entirely a function of the metabolism of oceanic algae. Previously, it was thought that this cloud formation was a purely chemical phenomenon. Further research suggested that Gaia has automatically been controlling global temperature, atmospheric content, ocean salinity, and other factors in order to *'maintain the conditions suitable for its own survival'*, in much the same way that any individual organism regulates its body temperature, blood salinity etc.

Similarly, all the life forms on the planet are a part of Gaia, in a way analogous to the different organs in a body, each with its own function. The oceans and atmosphere act as the planet's circulatory and temperature control systems, while the tropical rainforests could be compared to the liver, cleansing the body of toxins. In their diversity, the myriad life forms of earth co-evolve and contribute interactively to produce and sustain the system as a whole.

Some of Lovelock's critics took his hypothesis to imply that the Earth was behaving with a sense of purpose, that it was a teleological* being, actively controlling the climate and so on. However, Lovelock had never stated that planetary self-regulation was purposeful, only that it was a living, highly complex system. No one doubts that plants or bacteria are alive, yet they do not produce processes nearly as complicated as the Earth's.

The Gaia Theory has already had a huge impact on science and has inspired many leading figures of the past 20 years, who have written and spoken eloquently about how we can model human activities that are beneficial to the living systems of our planet. By making us more aware of the damage we are doing to the eco-system, Gaia theory may also help us to survive. We are just one part of a larger system, and are reliant on that system for our continued existence. As Lovelock said: *'if we see the world as a superorganism of which we are a part – not the owner, nor the tenant, not even a passenger – we could have a long time ahead of us and our species might survive for its 'allotted span'. It all depends on you and me.'*

* A being with an ultimate purpose/design towards an end.

Language development:
idioms from nature

1 In the Reading text on page 139 the expression *'a storm of criticism'* was used to show that the criticism was sudden and violent. Many words from nature are used in idiomatic expressions. Choose the best option in each of the following sentences.

1 If we say that someone has *come up in the world* we mean
   a they have reappeared after a very long absence.
   b they have more money and/or a better social position that they had before.

2 If we say that two people or situations are *worlds apart* we mean
   a they are very different.
   b they are far away from each other.

3 If you are in *deep water* you are
   a potentially in a lot of trouble.
   b stranded far from home.

4 If you get *bogged down* in something you are
   a stuck in an uncomfortable situation.
   b prevented from making progress or getting a job done.

5 The *tip of the iceberg* refers to
   a a very small part of a much larger problem.
   b a very cold and uncomfortable place.

6 You may say that you're *not yet out of the woods* if you are
   a still having difficulties or problems.
   b lost.

7 If you *get wind of something* you
   a are suspicious of someone's activities.
   b hear of something that you weren't supposed to hear about.

8 If you decide to *clear the air* you probably need to
   a resolve a problem or disagreement with someone.
   b tell someone you lied to them.

2 The following adjectives appeared in the Reading text on page 139. Which particles follow them?
   a analogous _____   b reliant _____

3 Complete the sentences with the correct particle.

about	at	by	for	from
in	of	on	to	with

1 Miranda was ashamed _____ her past and refused to talk about it.
2 If you are serious _____ becoming a quantum physicist, you'd better start doing your homework.
3 Julian was becoming obsessed _____ his butterfly collection.
4 Unfortunately, I was never much good _____ maths, but I've always loved biology.
5 I had measles when I was younger, so I'm immune _____ the disease now.
6 The group was very distressed _____ the news that the river dolphin is now presumed to be extinct.
7 The species is now endangered and eligible _____ government legislation to protect it.
8 People who don't eat enough fresh fruit or vegetables may become deficient _____ essential enzymes.
9 The word 'geology' is derived _____ the Greek words for 'earth' and 'study'.
10 Lizzie has never really been keen _____ insects, so I'm surprised she has joined an entomology study group.

Key word: *earth*

4 Match the words in column A with the definitions in B.

A		B	
1	Earth / the Earth	a	very surprising or shocking
2	earth	b	face reality again after a period of great excitement
3	come back down to Earth		
4	where / what / who on Earth ..?	c	something that is unable to fly or is on the ground, not in the air
5	down-to-earth person	d	the planet in space, where we live
6	cost the Earth or paid the Earth	e	used for emphasis
		f	someone who is practical minded
7	hell on Earth	g	ground, soil, sand, mud
8	earthbound	h	when something is very expensive
9	earthly	i	a very bad or unpleasant experience
10	earth-shattering	j	of the material, physical plane (not the spiritual or metaphysical plane)

Grammar: unreal past

1 In the Reading text we saw the following sentence: *'To the astronauts, the planet looked as if it were some huge single living system.'*

Which of the following statements was true at the time the astronauts looked at the Earth?

a The planet appeared to have been a 'single living system'.
b The planet appeared to be a 'single living system'.

GRAMMAR SPOTLIGHT

Unreal past
We sometimes use past tenses to describe things in the present or future that are imagined or unreal.

2 Underline the verbs in the sentences below. What time are we talking about in each case?

1 If only I were rich enough to save the world's forests!
2 Suppose you had the chance to do one selfless act. What would it be?
3 I'd rather you didn't smoke in here.
4 You wouldn't have been fined if you hadn't dropped that litter.
5 It looked as if it was going to be a beautiful day.
6 Were I able to go back in time, I would probably visit the Jurassic era.
7 It's time we did something about global warming.
8 If only I hadn't had that extra burger!

➡ Grammar Reference, 14.1, page 179

3 Match the sentences in the Grammar Spotlight with one of the functions below.

a comparison or prediction
b hypothetical past situation
c wishes
d regrets
e advice or suggestions
f preferences
g imagining
h hypothetical or impossible present situation

4 Complete the sentences below with the correct form of the verb in brackets.

1 I wish I _____ (be) able to travel all over the world.
2 It looked as if it _____ (be) about to start raining.
3 If only we _____ (not / make) such a mess of our planet.
4 It's about time we _____ (take) some responsibility for our actions.
5 I'd rather you _____ (take) the bus every day instead of driving.
6 _____ (be) I rich enough, I would buy a ticket into space.
7 Lilla wishes Richard _____ (not / buy) that expensive motorbike.
8 I'd sooner he _____ (not / tell) me about his stomach problem – I feel sick now.
9 If the house _____ (be) demolished, I wouldn't want to know about it.
10 Russ looked as if he _____ (see) a ghost.

5 PAPER 3, PART 2 For questions 1–12, read the text below and think of the word which best fits each gap. Use only one word in each gap.

From time to time I find myself wishing that things could be different. If (1) _____ we lived in a world where everyone (2) _____ at one with their environment, and respected the Earth and all the creatures that dwell on her. We mostly act (3) _____ if we were the most superior beings on the planet. Imagine if we (4) _____ in fact merely the guardians instead! If we (5) _____ not believed the Earth belonged to us in the first place, we would never (6) _____ hurt her in the way we have. I would much (7) _____ contribute something to the Earth (8) _____ be constantly taking from her. I (9) _____ we all could stop thinking about what we want for ourselves and think about what the planet needs instead. Isn't it about (10) _____ we ended the destruction? I'd sooner we (11) _____ in a world full of natural wonders than a world we had trashed for our pleasure! It's almost as (12) _____ we had no imagination!

6 PAPER 3, PART 5 For questions 1–8, complete the second sentence so that it has a similar meaning to the first sentence, using the word given. Do not change the word given. You must use between three and six words, including the word given.

1 Why don't you turn off the television and get some fresh air!
high
It's _____ the television and got some fresh air!

2 Instead of colonising another planet I think we should try to save this one.
rather
I _____ this planet than colonise another.

3 It's a pity I was so careless and ignorant in my youth.
wish
I _____ so careless and ignorant in my youth.

4 It will be amazing if you see a blue whale!
if
Imagine _____ a blue whale!

5 The Yangtze River Dolphin became extinct because the river was so polluted.
been
If the river _____, the Yangtze River Dolphin would not have become extinct.

6 It would be better if we could go to an organic health food shop than a supermarket.
sooner
I'd _____ an organic health food shop than a supermarket.

7 I'd like to join an environmental group but I'm not going to change career.
would
If _____ an environmental group.

8 Miriam doesn't know everything but sometimes she behaves like she does.
if
Sometimes Miriam behaves _____ she doesn't.

Listening: sentence completion

1 **Discuss. Despite overwhelming odds, life exists on Earth. What are some of the things that make life on Earth possible, yet we tend to take for granted on a daily basis?**

2 **Answer the following questions.**

   a   Which words or phrases in the sentence above appeared in the listening tapescript?

   b   Which words or phrases in the sentence are a paraphrase of those used in the tapescript?

   c   Are there any words from the tapescript that may appear to fit in the sentence above, but which would be wrong in meaning?

3 **Study the sentences below and underline any keywords to listen out for.**

There have been animals living on land for approximately (1) _____ years.

Today's atmosphere consists of approximately (2) _____ per cent oxygen in relation to other gases.

With an abundance of oxygen many animals were free to leave the water and (3) _____ the land.

When oxygen levels were greater many animals underwent a much faster stage of (4) _____.

Around 400 million years ago, many species of animal became (5) _____ when oxygen levels fell sharply.

Around 300 million years ago higher oxygen levels enabled (6) _____ to flourish.

Many animals (7) _____ and died because they could not adapt quickly enough to periods of low oxygen levels.

Birds can fly at high (8) _____ due to the air sacs near their lungs which they inherited from dinosaurs.

4 **Discuss. Which words would you expect to hear in each of the gaps? What part of speech and what possible meaning could they have?**

5 🎧 **14.2 PAPER 4, PART 2 You will hear a palaeontologist called Jeremy Sargon talking about atmospheric conditions in Earth's past. Complete questions 1–8 above.**

Speaking: evaluating

1 **Discuss. Do you have a favourite or a least favourite wild animal? Can you explain why you like or dislike it?**

2 🎧 **14.3 Listen to two students who have been asked to evaluate some information and make a decision. Note down the issues they mention below. Do they change their minds while they are speaking?**

Elisabeth mentions: _____

Giovanni mentions: _____

3 **PAPER 5, PART 3 Work in pairs. Turn to page 200, where you will see some pictures showing different critically endangered animal species in the world today. First, talk to each other about how these pictures reflect what is happening to the world's animal species today. Then decide which species you would prefer to protect and explain your reasons. Talk for three minutes (five minutes for groups of three).**

Use of English: word formation

Suffixes

A suffix is a letter or group of letters that is added to the end of a word in order to form a different word. There are many different kinds of suffix in the English language, which form adjectives, nouns or verbs.

1 Look at the words below and underline the suffix in each case.
E.g. <u>globe</u> → global, globalise, globalisation, globally

Which suffix do they all use? Which extension to the suffix is used for ...?

a a noun   b a verb   c an adverb

2 Add the correct suffix to the following stems.

a   affection (n) → _____ (adj)   e   diverse (adj) → _____ (n)
b   evolve (v)   → _____ (n)   f   develop (v)   → _____ (n)
c   active (adj)   → _____ (v)   g   modern (adj)   → _____ (v)
d   history (n)   → _____ (adj)   h   child (n)   → _____ (adj)

3   **PAPER 3, PART 3** For questions 1–12, read the text below. Use the word given in capitals at the end of some of the lines to form a word that fits in the gap in the same line.

Biodiversity and humanity's place in it

It is estimated that approximately 1.4 million species of organisms have been discovered, yet the total number alive on Earth is unknown. Some experts estimate that there are somewhere between 10 and 100 million species, although no one can say with (1) _____ which of   **confident**
these figures is closer. Fewer than one in ten of all the species that have been given (2) _____ names have been closely studied.   **science**

We have to (3) _____ our goals in studying species because,   **broad**
unlike the rest of science, the study of biodiversity has a time limit. Species are disappearing at an accelerating rate as a consequence of human activities, primarily the (4) _____ of natural habitats   **destroy**
but also ever-increasing pollution and contamination of pristine environments by introduced species. Twenty per cent or more of the species of plants and animals could vanish or be doomed to early (5) _____ by the year 2020 unless we do something drastic   **extinct**
to save them. The loss of many species will mean that new sources of scientific information and incalculable potential (6) _____   **biology**
wealth will be destroyed. We should also be aware of the dangers of overlooking the services that ecosystems provide humanity. Human beings coevolved with the rest of life on Earth. It would be (7) _____ to suppose that we can continue to diminish   **mad**
biodiversity (8) _____ without threatening our own existence.   **define**

One of the reasons why humans have failed (9) _____ to save   **intellect**
life on Earth is because we prefer to be ignorant of our common origins with the rest of life. We therefore have a misplaced sense of (10) _____ over the other species on Earth. But human beings   **superior**
are a part of nature, a species that evolved among other species. The more closely we (11) _____ ourselves with the rest of life,   **identity**
the more quickly we will be able to acquire the (12) _____ on   **know**
which to build a new direction for the Earth as a whole.

Writing: an essay (discussing issues that surround a topic)

1   Look at the writing question below.

> Your class has been discussing global issues and your teacher has asked you to write an essay with the title: **The most serious issue facing the world today.**

Discuss. What do you think is the most serious issue facing the world today?

2   One way to sort out your ideas is to put them into categories. Look at the spidergram below and add the ideas on the right to the most appropriate category.

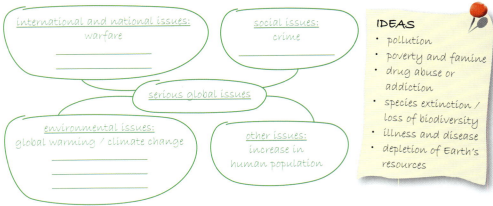

international and national issues:
    warfare
_____
_____

social issues:
    crime
_____

serious global issues

environmental issues:
global warming / climate change
_____
_____
_____

other issues:
    increase in
human population

IDEAS
- pollution
- poverty and famine
- drug abuse or addiction
- species extinction / loss of biodiversity
- illness and disease
- depletion of Earth's resources

3   In order to answer the question, you need to identify one issue that stands out as being more serious than the others. Look at the essay below written by a student. Which issues does she think is the most serious issue facing the world today and what reasons does she give? Which of the reasons mentioned above may not be appropriate here and why wouldn't they be?

> **The most serious issue facing the world today**
>
> I think that the most important issue facing the world today is in fact the increase in human population on the Earth. That's because it is actually the main cause of all the other problems which the world is facing today and it makes them worse. Because the number of people on Earth is increasing very fast, the human population on Earth is responsible for using up the Earth's resources. Also, because there are so many people there is more and more pollution and this causes climate change which is causing species extinction and bringing about the loss of different species. In the end this affects us all because with all the animals and plants gone we would not be able to survive anyway.

4   Discuss. What do you think about the essay above? How can it be improved?

In other words

5   Use a dictionary to find out the meaning of the following words. Which words or phrases in the above essay could they be used to replace?

a   exacerbate (v) _____
b   exponentially (adv) _____
c   deplete (v) _____
d   biodiversity (n) _____

Discussing issues that surround a topic

As we learnt in Unit 6, an **essay** is usually written for a teacher and may be written as a follow-up to a class activity. Your essay should be organised clearly. It begins with an introduction, and then develops the argument, and concludes with an appropriate ending. The main purpose of an essay task is to develop an argument, or to discuss the issues surrounding a certain topic. You're usually expected to give a reason(s) for your opinion.

6 Look at the more detailed spidergram. The central issue is the human population. Read the issues that surround it and complete the gaps with one of the global problems listed in exercise 2.

Global issues caused by the human population

1 _____:
the Earth's human population has to be fed, clothed and accommodated. This means we have to use the Earth's resources which are fast running out.

2 _____:
Almost seven billion people on Earth using fossil fuels for energy releases carbon dioxide into the atmosphere, which heats the Earth, thereby affecting the global climate.

**Human Population
6.5 billion people and
counting …**
The total world human population, now at 6.5 billion, at the moment is climbing by almost 90 million a year but this amount is about to rise exponentially to nine billion in less than a century.

3 _____
_____: the vast number of people on Earth means there is not enough space for other species to exist in harmony.

4 _____: nobody knows how many people the Earth can support but at the moment millions of people are living below the breadline.

5 _____:
there are so many human beings on the planet that if a particularly contagious viral outbreak were to occur, it would spread very quickly.

6 _____:
because we have conquered every last scrap of land and sea, wars based on the claim for territory are increasing as population increases.

7 Using the spidergram above, write your own paragraph plan to the topic. Decide which points you would keep, and which you would leave out. Write a suitable introduction and conclusion.

8 PAPER 2, PART 2 Choose **one** of the following essay topics to discuss. Brainstorm your ideas by drawing a spidergram as in exercise 2 on page 144, with your main idea at the centre and reasons for reaching your conclusion pointing to it.

> Your class has been discussing social issues and your teacher has asked you to write an essay with the title: **The most serious issue facing modern society today.**

> Your class has been discussing global issues and your teacher has asked you to write an essay with the title: **Human beings – our place in the world around us.**

9 Write your **essay** using the techniques outlined above (220–260 words).

Vocabulary organiser 14

14.1 Reading text, page 139 The following nouns all appeared in the Reading text. Match them to their definitions.

biosphere	diversity	entity
equilibrium	metabolism	myriad
phenomenon	salinity	void

a   the saltiness of a liquid or substance
b   the rate at which food is converted into energy
c   something that is observed to happen or exist
d   something that exists separately and has an identity of its own
e   part of a planet's surface and atmosphere that sustains life
f   the different elements to be found within something
g   a large and empty space
h   a very large number or great variety of something
i   balance, harmony

14.2 Reading, pages 139 Complete the sentences below with a verb or adjective taken from the text. The word(s) in brackets will help you.

a   He was a great philosopher, who came up with many _____ (deep, philosophical) insights into human nature. [para 1]
b   By meditating every day he was able to _____ (reach) a state of absolute tranquillity. [para 1]
c   Some scientists _____ (theorised) that life on Earth had in fact come from outer space. [para 2]
d   The accusations made against him were vague and _____ (not totally accurate). [para 4]
e   His comments about climate change _____ (generated) a negative response from environmentalists. [para 4]
f   Traditional farming methods in the area have created the _____ (most suitable) conditions for biological diversity. [para 4]
g   They learnt how to dry meat and fruit to _____ (support) them during the lean season. [para 4]
h   We were each given our _____ (selected) share of the land to grow our own vegetables. [para 7]

14.3 Language development, page 140 Decide which particle follows the adjective groups below.

a   aware, capable, conscious, fond, jealous _____
b   anxious, excited, pleased, sorry, upset _____
c   incompatible, bored, happy, pleased, connected _____
d   surprised, bad, annoyed, angry, excellent _____
e   addicted, attentive, grateful, indifferent, liable _____
f   baffled, detained, shocked, surprised, ridiculed _____
g   famous, responsible, liable, ready, sorry _____
h   experienced, interested, absorbed, fascinated, disinterested _____
i   absent, different, missing, safe, distant _____
j   dependent, reliant, keen, hooked, based _____

14.4 Use of English, page 143 Complete the sentences with the correct form of the word in brackets.

a   I couldn't believe the _____ of the situation. (ridicule)
b   Do you know how much the _____ is for Australia? (post)
c   He may be a very small dog, but he's ever so _____. (courage)
d   Ava is such an _____ little girl – she's always giving me hugs. (affection)
e   I don't use _____ on my vegetables – I prefer organic gardening methods. (insect)
f   Thousands of _____ were trying to get over the border and away from the war zone. (refuge)
g   After millions of years of _____, the variety of species in the forests are beginning to disappear. (diverse)
h   I've decided to switch to _____ light bulbs in an effort to save energy. (ecology)

14.5 Writing, page 144 Replace the underlined phrases in the sentences below with one word from the 'In other words' box in order to improve the vocabulary.

1   The human population is increasing <u>very fast.</u>
2   <u>Using up the majority</u> of all the Earth's resources means that the planet will not be able to support us.
3   Policies implemented in ignorance may only <u>make</u> the situation <u>worse.</u>

BANK OF ENGLISH

Word partnerships

Geo- is used at the beginning of words that refer to the whole of the world or to the Earth's surface.

geography, geographer, geographical geology, geologist, geological geometry, geometrics, geometrical geophysics, geophysicist, geophysical geopolitics, geopolitical

Bio- is used at the beginning of nouns and adjectives that refer to life or to the study of living things.

biochemistry, biodegradable, biodiversity, bioengineering, biographer, biology, biomedicine, biometric, biopsy, biotechnology, biosphere

1   Which of the terms in the boxes on the left is defined by the following?

a   the part of the Earth's surface where there is life
b   the study of the countries of the world, the land, seas, towns etc.
c   the science which is concerned with the study of living things
d   the study of the Earth's structure, surface and origins
e   a person who writes an account of someone else's life
f   the mathematical study of lines, angles, curves and shapes
g   the existence of a wide variety of plants and animals in their natural environments
h   something that breaks down or decays naturally in nature
i   a person who uses physics to determine the Earth's structure, climate and oceans
j   affected by a country's position or relationship with other countries

15 Our global village

Getting started

1 Discuss. Do you recognise any of the customs shown in the pictures? With which countries are they usually associated?

2 GENERAL KNOWLEDGE Look at the quiz below and see if you can answer any of the questions. Turn to the Information file to check your answers.

1 A piñata is
   a a paper container filled with sweets
   b a type of cold drink
   c a long stick used in dances

2 A jack o'lantern is
   a a Chinese paper light
   b a man who carries a flaming torch
   c a pumpkin carved with a face

3 In Japan, Sado is
   a a special kind of dress
   b a tea ceremony
   c something worn in the hair

4 Lobola is an African
   a custom of paying for a bride
   b type of cow
   c game

5 Henna is
   a a type of Indian coffee
   b a bridal dress
   c a red dye used to paint hands and feet

6 Eggs are traditionally painted or dyed because
   a they symbolise new life
   b they're abundant in spring
   c they are a Christian tradition.

7 Chinese New Year is often celebrated in
   a December
   b February
   c July

3 Describe a special or unique custom, tradition or taboo from your country or culture.

➡ Information File 15.1, page 203

147

Reading: purpose and main idea

1 In pairs. Does your culture have any traditional dances? Do the dancers wear traditional costumes? Try to describe the dance to your partner.

2 Skim read the text below and decide

a what the source might be.
b what its purpose is.
c what the main idea is.

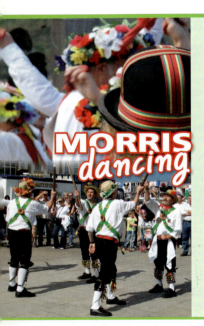

MORRIS dancing

Morris Dancing is a traditional English form of folkdancing, performed by groups of men or women. It has been danced for hundreds of years, and passed down through the generations in the villages of rural England. The dances are usually performed at festivals such as May Day, Whitsun and Christmas.

Origins

There are several thoughts to the origins of Morris Dancing. The name may refer to the possibility of the form of dancing coming to England from the Moors of North Africa; or it may have been called 'Moor-ish' simply because the dancers sometimes painted their faces black, and people compared this to the dark-skinned Moors. There are different forms of Morris Dancing:

Border Morris

Border Morris dances are usually performed with heavy wooden sticks which are clashed together, often accompanied by shouts from the dancers. Dancers generally black their faces – probably originating as a form of disguise. Border costumes consists of black trousers or skirt, black shoes and black tatter jackets. Each person wears their own individual style of black hat and shades.

Cotswold Morris

The dancers wear dozens of bells on each leg, wield handkerchiefs and/or sticks and dance to lively folk tunes.

Sword Dancing

Dancers are linked in a ring holding blunt swords. The dance form is distinctive for its fast, elegant weaving movements created by the dancers passing over and under the swords whilst remaining linked. The dance usually ends with the final woven "star" being held aloft by one of the dancers.

Music

The dances are performed to live music, traditionally played on instruments such as the accordion, penny whistle, fiddle and tabor. The songs are mainly traditional in origin, and each dance goes with a particular tune.

3 Answer the questions true or false according to the text. Underline the true answers in the text. Correct the false answers.

1 Morris Dancers often learn the dance from their parents. T / F

2 There is one standard Morris Dance. T / F

3 Morris dancers always have black painted faces. T / F

4 The dance may have been inspired by dancers from Africa. T / F

5 Border Morris dancers may shout out while they hit sticks together. T / F

6 Cotswold Morris wear black clothes and hold handkerchiefs. T / F

7 Sword Morris wear bells on their legs and carry swords. T / F

8 Morris dancers make up the dance to suit the music. T / F

SPOTLIGHT ON READING

Texts from different sources

Part 1 of the Reading Paper consists of three short texts from a variety of sources which share a broad common theme, such as extracts from books, magazines, newspapers, advertisements, publicity materials etc. Each text is followed by two four-option multiple choice questions which test comprehension. Some of the questions may require you to understand the overall *function* or *purpose* of texts or sections of texts.

4 Skim the three texts on page 149 very quickly to find information that may be from:

a the blurb on the back of a novel.
b information from an encyclopaedia.
c information extracted from an article.

5 **PAPER 1, PART 1** The following three extracts are all concerned in some way with different cultures and customs. For questions 1–6, choose the answer (A, B, C or D) which you think fits best according to the text.

A Customs are those activities that have been approved by a social group and have been handed down from generation to generation until they have become habitual. However, many customs vary from culture to culture, and those who visit other countries may suddenly discover that the simplest of customary actions in their own society may be misinterpreted as improper in another. For example, whether they are being introduced to someone for the first time or greeting an old friend, men and women in western nations are accustomed to shake hands. While the clasping of hands is intended as a gesture of friendship by Westerners, the people of many Asian countries may be alarmed by the boldness of a stranger who extends a hand, for they prefer to bow as a sign of goodwill.

Some travellers to foreign countries have also discovered much to their dismay that even the most innocent of hand gestures in their home culture may be considered offensive in another. It must soon become apparent to any fairly objective observer that the traditional values and customs of one culture may be considered very strange by another.

When an action or activity violates behaviour considered appropriate by a social group, it is labelled a 'taboo', a word that we have borrowed from the Polynesian people of the South Pacific. An act that is taboo is forbidden, prohibited, and those who transgress may be ostracised by others or, in extreme instances, killed.

1 The purpose of this text is to
A act as a guide for travellers in regard to foreign etiquette.
B introduce a narrative account of taboo behaviour.
C inform us of some cultural differences between nations.
D define the differences between eastern and western cultures.

2 The writer uses the word 'dismay' in line 16 to show that some travellers have
A felt upset that they had unintentionally caused offence.
B found their gestures were disregarded by local people.
C been frustrated by not being able to communicate.
D considered the values and customs abroad very peculiar.

B After nearly two decades in Britain, Bill Bryson took the decision to move back to the States for a while, to let his kids experience life in another country, to give his wife the chance to shop until 10 pm seven nights a week, and, most of all, because he had read that 3.7 million Americans believed they had been abducted by aliens at one time or another, and it was thus clear to him that his people needed him.

But before leaving his much-loved home in North Yorkshire, Bryson insisted on taking one last trip around Britain, a sort of valedictory tour of the green and kindly island that had so long been his home. His aim was to take stock of the nation's public face and private parts (as it were), and to analyse what precisely it was he loved so much about a country that had produced Marmite, a military hero whose dying wish was to be kissed by a fellow named Hardy, place names like Farleigh Wallop, Titsey and Shellow Bowells, people who said 'Mustn't grumble', and *Gardeners' Question Time*.

3 The purpose of the extract is to
A highlight the idiosyncrasies of British culture.
B explain why Bryson wanted to return to America.
C justify the author's reasons for writing the book.
D promote the book by affording an insight into it.

4 Why are specific objects and places mentioned in lines 14–17?
A Bryson intended to analyse their functions.
B Bryson considered them endearing British oddities.
C Bryson thought they sounded strange and amusing.
D Bryson has always felt disturbed by them.

C In many Western cultures, married people usually live together in the same home, often sharing the same bed, but in some other regions this is not the tradition. In south-western China, for example, 'walking marriages', in which the husband and wife do not live together, have been a traditional part of the Mosuo culture. In walking marriages, the women open their doors to their spouses every evening, and the men walk home to work in their mother's household every morning. A man is responsible for supporting his sisters' children, rather than his wife's.

The traditional Mosuo culture is strongly matrilineal – a system in which one belongs to one's mother's lineage in contrast to the more currently common pattern of patrilineal descent. But patrilineal descent systems have not always been so common and there is evidence of many ancient societies following the line of decent from mother to daughter. This may be because logically it is easier to identify who the mother of a child is than the father. And today it is scientifically easier to identify a matrilineal line of descent due to mitochondrial DNA, which is normally inherited exclusively from one's mother – both daughters and sons inherit it all the same.

Walking marriages have also been increasingly common in modern Beijing. A similar arrangement in Saudi Arabia, called *misyar* marriage, also involves the husband and wife living separately but meeting regularly.

5 In a 'walking marriage' the husband
A never spends the whole night with his wife.
B probably doesn't know who his own father is.
C lives with his wife, her mother and his sister.
D is not obliged to support his children financially.

6 Matrilineal systems
A were once more common than they are today.
B are more logical than modern day systems.
C make it easier to identify the child's mother.
D exist only between mother and daughter.

6 Discuss. Which of the above texts was most interesting to you? Why?

Language development:
phrasal verbs and phrases with *pass*

1 In the text about Morris Dancing we learned that it 'has been danced for hundreds of years, and **passed down** through the generations in the villages of rural England'.

   a What does the phrasal verb 'pass down' mean?

   b Look back at Text A on page 149 and find another phrasal verb that means the same thing.

2 Fill the gaps in the sentences with the correct particle to complete the phrasal verbs.

as	away	by	off	on	out	over	up

   1 Arnold's been passed _____ for promotion again – it's no wonder he's upset!

   2 Could you pass the message _____ to Roger when you see him?

   3 Do you really think I would pass _____ the chance of a free holiday to Florida?

   4 She tried to pass him _____ as her brother but I know she doesn't have a brother.

   5 Unfortunately, his father passed _____ last week after a long battle with cancer.

   6 His skin is so dark that he could easily pass _____ an Italian.

   7 Emily passed _____ at the sight of the cut on my finger.

   8 If you pass _____ the supermarket on your way home, could you get some milk?

3 Choose the best option for the sentences below.

   1 Julian passed his exam with flying _____.
     a clouds   b colours   c balloons

   2 What can I do to pass the _____ until the party starts?
     a hour   b day   c time

   3 Parliament recently passed a(n) _____ to abolish blood sports.
     a Act   b check   c tab

   4 You know whether you were right or wrong. It's not up to me to pass _____.
     a verdict   b sentence   c judgement

   5 Michelle was angry about the broken vase but she decided to _____ it pass.
     a let   b make   c give

   6 Never fear! Not a word of what I saw here tonight shall ever pass my _____.
     a mouth   b tongue   c lips

   7 And so, after many years spent locked in the tower, it _____ to pass that the princess escaped on the back of a dragon.
     a ran   b came   c flew

   8 It's time William took responsibility for his actions instead of always trying to pass the _____ to someone else.
     a buck   b dollar   c bill

Key word: *pass*

4 Which of the following sentences is incorrect? Why?

   a Julian passed me in the street.

   b Julian walked right passed me in the street.

5 In the text on Morris dancers, we also saw the following sentence.

> 'The dance form is distinctive for its fast, elegant weaving movements created by the dancers passing over and under the swords whilst remaining linked.'

Which of the following definitions goes with the meaning of *pass* above?

   a To go past someone or something without stopping.

   b To go in a particular direction.

   c If something such as a road passes along a particular route, it goes that way.

   d If you pass something through, round, over or under something, you move it or push it that way.

   e If you pass something to someone, you give it to them.

6 For which of the definitions above can the following example sentence be used?

'He passed a hand through his hair in exasperation as he realised they could not understand him.'

7 In pairs. Write example sentences for five of the definitions of *pass* below, then swap them with your partner to match them with the definitions a–i.

   a If something passes to someone, it means they inherit it.

   b If you pass information to someone, it means you give them information.

   c If you pass a ball to someone in a game or match, it means you throw or kick or hit it to them.

   d When a period of time passes, it has finished.

   e If you pass a period of time in a particular way, you spend it that way.

   f If you pass through a stage or phase, you experience it.

   g If something passes a level or amount, it goes above it.

   h If you pass a test, it means you have reached the required standard.

   i If a government passes a law, they formally agree to it.

Listening (1): multiple speakers

1 Discuss. What does a 'kiss' mean in your culture? Does it mean different things with different people? Are there different ways of kissing different people? Are there any times or occasions when it would be considered inappropriate, or taboo?

SPOTLIGHT ON LISTENING

Attitude and opinion

The speakers in part 3 of the Listening Paper may express conflicting attitudes or opinions about a topic, so it's important to pay attention to what each speaker says and to make notes about their opinions.

2 🎧 **15.1 You will hear part of a radio interview in which the function and origin of kissing is being discussed. As you listen, decide which speaker gives us the following information:**

A Professor Rosemary O'Bryan
B Dr Andrew Peters

1 A mother may kiss her child to cement the bond between them.
2 The biological function of kissing allows an individual to choose the right mate.
3 Chimpanzees kiss to make up after fights.
4 In ancient Rome husbands kissed their wives to see if they'd been drinking.
5 The first romantic kiss happened in France in the sixth century.
6 Before the Second World War romantic kissing was largely a western habit.
7 In Polynesia and Lapland they rub noses to show affection.
8 Bonobo monkeys will kiss for just about any reason.

3 **PAPER 4, PART 3 Now listen again. For questions 1–6, choose the answer (A, B, C or D) which fits best according to what you hear.**

1 According to Professor O'Bryan, kissing may have originally developed from a mother
   A using her mouth to clean and educate her child.
   B massaging or touching her child to increase affection.
   C chewing solid food for her child to eat more easily.
   D teaching her child to show respect to others.

2 According to Dr Peters, women kiss prospective mates in order to
   A decide who has the most attractive smell.
   B groom and bond with their partners.
   C choose the best providers for their children.
   D increase the survival chances of their offspring.

3 Kissing is also a means of
   A social bonding in chimpanzees.
   B chemical pairing in mammals.
   C avoiding fights by primates.
   D establishing social order in ape societies.

4 In ancient times a kiss was
   A not necessarily a sign of affection.
   B never given on the lips.
   C only bestowed by a husband.
   D used as a form of wine tasting.

5 Romantic kissing
   A became common during World War II.
   B spread to other cultures via cinematic films.
   C was invented in North America and Europe.
   D was not instinctive to Asian people.

6 Andrew and Rosemary disagree about whether
   A rubbing noses constitutes a form of kissing.
   B kissing denotes affection for a partner.
   C kissing is instinctive behaviour in all mammals.
   D kissing exists in all cultures.

Speaking: talking about your country, culture and background

1 With a partner take turns talking about your country, culture, customs, traditions and taboos. Ask each other questions and try to find out as much as possible.

2 **PAPER 5, PART 1 Answer the following questions.**

1 Are there any traditions, customs or taboos in your country which are unique to your culture or are particularly meaningful to you? Why?

2 Which international traditions, festivals or ceremonies are celebrated differently in your country? What are the differences?

3 Many of the world's more ethnic traditions are dying out. Are there any customs or traditions that you think will never disappear from your culture? Why?

> **USEFUL LANGUAGE**
>
> In [country] the people are …
> We have many unique cultural traditions, for example …
> In my country it is customary to …
> My favourite tradition is …
> I consider myself quite (un)traditional / (un)conventional …
> One of the strongest taboos is …

151

Grammar: adverbial clauses

1 Read the extract from Listening 15.1 below, and decide what the words in bold tell us.

'... correct, and **thus** we get more information about our biological compatibility. Women are more attracted to men who are more genetically compatible to them, and a woman picks this up **by** breathing in his pheromones. Any resulting offspring will have better resistance to a greater number of diseases, and will **consequently** have a better chance of survival. **That's why** we still like to kiss – **to** maximise our chances of sampling each other's aroma.'

GRAMMAR SPOTLIGHT

Clauses of time, purpose, reason, concession and result
Adverbial clauses give information about the circumstances of the event described by the verb in the main clause. They can tell us about when or where an event happened, the manner or place in which it happened, the reason why it happened, or the purpose for which it was intended. Or they can tell us about the result of an event, or indicate comparison or contrast (concession) with other events or circumstances. Adverbial clauses are usually preceded by a word or phrase which gives this information.

2 What does the adverbial clause in the following sentence tell us?

'I won't be able to meet you **until** I've finished my homework.'

3 Add the sentences below to the table.

- It got **so** hot **that** I couldn't concentrate.
- It was as bad **as** I'd feared.
- I walked fast **because** it was late.
- She wanted to know **where** I'd been.
- He asked me **how** I had done it.
- She smiled **so that** I'd feel welcome.
- **If** I'd known you'd be late, I'd have started without you.

Time	I'll meet you **when** I've finished.
Place	
Manner	
Comparison	
Cause / reason	
Purpose	
Result	
Condition	
Concession	She won the game **although** she'd never played before.

➡ Grammar Reference 15.1, page 180

4 Choose the best option in italics in the sentences below.

1 *As a result / Due to / Consequently* the fire, many birds lost their nests.
2 I wrote the book *so that / in order that / in order to* highlight the social problems.
3 I want you to call me *the minute / as soon / until* you get home.
4 Gillian has never played tennis before. *Nevertheless / Although / Despite* she is determined to have a go.
5 *Notwithstanding / No matter how / So much* tired he is, he won't stop till he's finished.
6 *Seeing as / Therefore / In case* it hadn't rained all week, I watered the garden.

5 **PAPER 3, PART 5** For questions 1–8, complete the second sentence so that it has a similar meaning to the first sentence, using the word given. Do not change the word given. You must use between three and six words, including the word given.

1 No sooner had the plane stopped than everyone started to get up.
when
Hardly _____ everyone started to get up.

2 I got wet because I forgot to take an umbrella with me.
consequently
I forgot to take an umbrella with me _____ _____ wet.

3 To ensure he'd get the job, John researched the background of the company.
order
John researched the background of the company _____ sure he'd get the job.

4 It's such a beautiful afternoon, so why don't we go out?
seeing
Let's go out _____ a beautiful afternoon.

5 I was the only person with any money, so I paid for everyone.
being
I paid for everyone _____ with any money.

6 If you don't put that back I will tell Mrs Jenkins you took it.
otherwise
Put that back _____ Mrs Jenkins you took it.

7 Even though he hated thrillers he decided to go to see the film.
spite
He decided to go to see the film _____ _____ he hated thrillers.

8 I wanted to get fit, so I took up cycling.
why
The _____ cycling was because I wanted to get fit.

Use of English: open cloze text

1   PAPER 3, PART 2 For questions 1–15, read the text below and think of the word which best fits each gap. Use only one word in each gap.

Body Language and Gestures

When travelling, it is important to take the time to learn about your host's customs (1) _____ that you do not seem ignorant or offensive. Often, something that we (2) _____ for granted as meaning one thing can mean something completely different elsewhere. For (3) _____, in Thailand, as the foot is the lowest part of the body it is held in the lowest esteem, and (4) _____ point a foot at someone is extremely insulting. Likewise, (5) _____ the head is the highest part of the body, it is never touched directly by others. For this (6) _____, a pat on the head in Thailand is an insult of the worst kind.

Greetings in Asia usually take the form of a bow. In Japan, your hands (7) _____ be at your side. The inferior person will bow longer and lower. In Mediterranean countries on the (8) _____ hand, it is customary to greet a friend or family member with a kiss on each cheek. In Latin America, one might greet someone of either sex (9) _____ a hug and a kiss. In Muslim nations, sexes generally do not mix at all (10) _____ they are family. Something as common as clasping hands may (11) _____ impending death to a Guatemalan.

Some simple gestures that are common in the States, (12) _____ as the 'thumbs-up' sign are vulgar to those in Middle Eastern countries, Nigeria, Australia and Afghanistan. Some gestures have widely different meanings almost everywhere they are used. For example, in Japan crooking a finger in a 'come here' gesture is obscene. In Yugoslavia, Vietnam and Malaysia (13) _____ is used to call animals, and (14) _____ insulting to people. Even something such as a smile, (15) _____ seems an instinctive reaction to happiness, can mean sadness or anger.

---

2   Read the text again and underline any adverbial clauses. Say what type they are.

3   PAPER 3 PART 4 For questions 1–5, think of one word only which can be used appropriately in all three sentences.

1   Malcolm believes that if something is out of _____, it's out of mind.
   As they rounded the corner, the mountains came into _____.
   After fifteen days in the desert, the green English fields were a most pleasing _____.

2   I hope Maggie didn't _____ the heater on.
   I wish you would go away and _____ me in peace!
   Has everyone got something to do or did we_____ anyone out?

3   The search _____ was called back last night when the children turned up unharmed.
   The new policy was attacked by the opposition _____.
   She sees herself as the innocent _____ in this dispute.

4   If the pain should _____ you'd better go and see a doctor.
   He promised that one day he would _____ the favour to me.
   The jury resolved to _____ a verdict of guilty.

5   I wish that dog would stop _____ whenever there's a full moon.
   Peter and James were _____ with laughter when I walked in the room.
   The wind was _____ round the building, and battering the windows.

Listening (2): short extracts

1   🎧 15.2 PAPER 4, PART 4 You will hear five short extracts in which people of different cultures talk about living in Britain.

Task One: For questions **1–5** choose from the list (A–H) the person who is speaking.

A   Someone who has never been to their parents' homeland.
B   Someone who was deported for political reasons.
C   Someone who left their country to study in England.
D   Someone who never intends to go home.
E   Someone who feels equally at home in two cultures.
F   Someone who left their country as a teenager.
G   Someone who despises the country they live in.
H   Someone who left their country because of social pressure.

Speaker 1	1
Speaker 2	2
Speaker 3	3
Speaker 4	4
Speaker 5	5

Task Two: For questions **6–10** choose from the list (A–H) what each person is expressing

A   An extended family brings you together collectively.
B   Our religion is more important than our culture.
C   In a cosmopolitan city we do not feel out of place.
D   My identity is who I am, not where I am.
E   Knowledge of the past need not restrict our liberty in the future.
F   I do not want my children following British traditions.
G   Using the language correctly is important in our culture.
H   My children have no interest in their heritage.

Speaker 1	6
Speaker 2	7
Speaker 3	8
Speaker 4	9
Speaker 5	10

Writing: an article (2)

1 Discuss. Which of the following have you ever witnessed or attended?

- baby shower or pre-natal baby party
- baptism or naming ceremony
- birthday celebration
- name's day celebration
- coming of age ceremony
- engagement party
- wedding
- anniversary
- retirement party
- funeral, memorial or wake

Are there any other significant milestone ceremonies in your country? If so, describe them. If not, how are any of the above events different or unusual in your country?

2 A travel magazine has invited readers to send in articles about customs and traditions in different cultures. Look at the advertisement below. What are you being asked to do?

Births / Birthdays / 'Coming of Age' Ceremonies / Engagements / Weddings / Funerals / Memorials

Every culture has a different way of celebrating these important events in their societies. Write an article that describes one of these events. Emphasis should especially be placed on unique and unusual customs to encourage readers to visit the countries where these events take place. We would prefer to receive first hand narrative descriptions of an event you have witnessed or taken part in. The best article will be published in next month's issue and the winner will receive an all expenses paid trip for two to Hawaii.

---

3 Read the extract from an article that was sent in below. What is wrong with it?

Coming of Age Ceremonies

Coming of age is a young person's transition from childhood or adolescence to adulthood. The age at which this transition takes place varies in society, as does the nature of the transition. It can be a simple legal convention or can be part of a ritualistic cycle, similar to those once practised by many societies. In the past, and in some societies today, such a change is associated with the age of sexual maturity (mid-adolescence); in others, it is associated with an age of religious responsibility.

In western societies, modern legal conventions tend to stipulate points in late adolescence or early adulthood, most commonly ages 18 and 21, at which time adolescents are generally no longer considered minors and are granted the full rights of an adult.

In either case, many cultures retain ceremonies, or 'rites of passage' to confirm the coming of age, and significant benefits come with the change. For instance ...

SPOTLIGHT ON WRITING

Using description and anecdote

Most articles in magazines do not just contain information but will most probably contain some descriptive details as well. In order to make them interesting to the reader they may possibly also contain an anecdote or two – a short and amusing account of something that has happened. This may be something funny that happened to other people, or to yourself. For example an anecdote may be something like:

'I was embarrassed to discover that when my turn came to pin some money on the bride's dress, I only had coins in my pocket!'

4 Read the article *Seijin Shiki* on the next page and underline

a descriptions of the event or custom.
b any examples of anecdote you can find.

HAPPY RETIREMENT!

Seijin Shiki

A person officially becomes an adult in Japan at the age of 20, and this is celebrated by 'coming-of-age' ceremonies, known as *seijin shiki*, which are held on the second Monday of January. The ceremony is held for all those who will reach this age during the current school year, which runs between April and the following March.

At the ceremony, all of the men and women participating are brought to a government building where they listen to many speakers, similar to a graduation ceremony. At the conclusion of the ceremony, small presents and money are handed out to the new adults.

Many women celebrate this day by wearing *furisode* – a special kind of traditional dress like the *kimono*. A full set of formal clothing is expensive, so it is usually either inherited or rented. While men sometimes also wear traditional dress (dark kimono or *hakama*), most men now wear business suits instead.

I remember my own *seijin shiki*, ceremony. Afterwards, my friends and I gathered together to continue celebrating. Not used to wearing the zori slippers, most of the girls, including myself, could be seen limping from one party to the next, as the evening wore on. Later in the evening, the town was full of wobbly young adults staggering on to the trains, heading home after a day of celebration.

In other words

Not knowing the right words ...

Sometimes you may have to describe something that is unique to a particular language or culture. In these cases it is OK to use the word in its own language – put it in italics or between 'quotation marks' to identify it, and then give a short description or explanation of what it means.

5 Find four Japanese words in the text above and explain what they mean in your own words.

Descriptive writing

6 Find three words in the last paragraph of the article about *Seijin Shiki* which describe how the young adults 'walked' home after the ceremony. Why does the writer use these words?

7 Plan an article in answer to the topic in exercise 2 on page 154. Try to think of an event that you know well, and that is unique to your culture. Make notes on the event itself under the following headings if appropriate, or make up your own headings.

1 Preparations for the event
2 During the event
3 After the main event
4 Costumes and clothes
5 Participants

8 Think of at least one anecdotal incident that you can relate that would make the piece more interesting.

9 Write the article you planned. (180–220 words).

Vocabulary organiser 15

15.1 Getting started, page 147 Match the words in the box with the traditions or countries they are associated with below.

| dyed eggs | henna | jack o' lantern |
| lobola | pinata | sado |

a Easter/spring time – Europe/Asia
b tea ceremony – Japan
c bride price – Africa
d children's parties – Mexico/Spain
e Halloween – Europe/USA
f hand/feet painting – India

15.2 Make a note of the following words.

a English words that are used in your language
b Foreign words that are used in the English language.

15.3 Reading, page 148 Scan the text, 'Morris dancing', to find words or phrases that mean the following definitions.

1 _____ [phr. verb] teach to children or younger people
2 _____ [adj] belonging to the country, not the towns
3 _____ [verb] carry or hold something in a particular way
4 _____ [adj] not sharp
5 _____ [adj] clear, easy to recognise
6 _____ [adverb] high, in the air

SPOTLIGHT ON VOCABULARY

Gauging the meaning of words in a text

15.4 Locate the following words in the reading texts on page 149 and try to explain their meanings or paraphrase them in your own words.

Text A
1 violate [verb] _____
2 transgress [verb] _____
3 ostracise [verb] _____

Text B
4 abducted [verb] _____
5 take stock of [adj] _____
6 grumble [adj] _____

Text C
7 spouse [noun] _____
8 patrilineal [adj] _____
9 exclusively [adv] _____

15.5 Language development, page 150 Write the phrasal verb or expression with *pass* that means the following.

1 die
2 give something to someone so they can give it to someone else
3 lose consciousness
4 fail to take advantage of an offer or opportunity
5 convince others that someone or something is someone or something else entirely
6 achieve very high marks in an exam or test
7 to not make a big deal out of a situation but to decide to forget about it
8 to cast blame or responsibility on someone else

15.6 Use of English, page 153 Look back at the text, 'Body Language and Gestures', and find words which match the following definitions.

1 A word that means 'unaware' or 'not knowledgeable' about something. _____
2 Four adjectives that mean 'rude'. _____
3 A word for a person who is lower in rank than his superiors.
   _____
4 Four verbs of movement using a part or parts of the body.
   _____

BANK OF ENGLISH

Culture

culture [noun] 1: activities such as the arts and philosophy, literature and music which are considered important for the development of civilisation., 2: a particular society or civilisation that exists or existed in history; 3: the habits, attitudes and beliefs that are shared by a particular society or civilisation; 4: bacteria or cells that are grown in a laboratory for scientific purposes.

cultural [adj] 1: belonging to a particular society and its ideas, behaviour and customs. 2: relating to art, literature, music etc; **culturally** [adv]

cultured [adj] intelligent, educated and sophisticated, with an interest in the arts.

cultural awareness [n phr] someone's understanding of the differences between themselves and people from other societies or backgrounds.

culture shock [n phr] a feeling of anxiety or discomfort that people experience when they visit a foreign country with very different customs.

Use your dictionary. Find an example sentence for each of the definitions above.

MAIN MENU

Topics:	saying goodbye
Language development:	collocations; key word: *end*
Grammar:	comparison

EXAM MENU

Reading:	specific information
Listening:	agreement and disagreement
Speaking:	redecorating talk
Use of English:	multiple-choice cloze; gapped sentences
Writing:	letter of reference

Getting started

1 Discuss. How do each of the pictures on this page reflect the idea of something coming to an end, and a new beginning?

2 In pairs. The word web below contains verbs that mean 'to end'. Complete the word web by adding a phrase from box 1, as shown in the example (*conclude*).

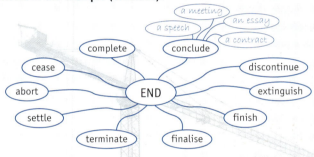

Word web:

- complete
- cease
- abort
- settle
- terminate
- finalise
- **END**
- conclude — a meeting, a speech, an essay, a contract
- discontinue
- extinguish
- finish

3 Complete the following sentences with a suitable verb from the word web above. In some sentences, more than one verb is possible. Use a different verb for each.

1 Our company _____ production of this model last year.
2 The two parties agreed to _____ the dispute out of court.
3 After battling with the flames for three hours, the firemen managed to _____ the fire.
4 The chairman _____ his speech by thanking the sales team for all their hard work over the last year.
5 As a result of your failure to submit the work on time, we have decided to _____ your contract.
6 Juanita has just _____ a four-year course in English, passing the FCE with a B.
7 The architects are _____ plans for the new shopping mall to be built on the outskirts of the town.
8 'Have you _____ writing that letter to the Principal yet?'
9 The coastguard had to _____ the rescue operation due to high winds.
10 The Prime Minister has asked both sides to _____ fire for a while, so that peace talks may begin.

4 In pairs. Which of the verbs in exercise 3 can be replaced by one of the phrasal verbs in box 2?

Box 1:
- a course
- a business deal
- a dispute
- a fire
- a form
- a lawsuit
- a contract
- an argument
- a plan
- a pregnancy
- a questionnaire
- a race
- a rescue operation
- differences
- fire
- hope
- manufacturing a product
- operations
- production
- school
- trading

Box 2:
- break off
- call off
- give up
- hand over
- lay off
- nail down
- pull out
- push off
- put out
- round off
- wind up
- wrap up

Reading: multiple matching texts

1 Discuss. If you had to say goodbye to your home, what things would you miss? What would you be happy to say goodbye to?

2 In pairs. Look at the comic strip above. The final picture is missing. Create a story to match the pictures, and give it a suitable ending, with a picture to match.

➡ Information File 16.1, page 203

EXAM SPOTLIGHT

PAPER 1, PART 4 Looking for specific information

The last part of the Reading Paper asks you to identify specific information in various parts of the text. You may be presented with extracts from different people writing about a general theme. The questions usually require you to identify differences in attitude and experience between those writers. In some cases, a question may apply to more than one extract.

3 Read the five extracts on page 159 about something ending and making a new start, and find a person for whom …

1 the decision to change was upsetting.
2 the decision to change was a moral one.
3 the decision to change was made despite criticism from others.
4 the decision to change was made on health grounds.

4 Underline the key information in each extract which helped you make your choice.

5 Which extract does the comic strip story reflect most closely?

6 **PAPER 1, PART 4** For questions 1–15, choose from the extracts on the next page (A–E). The extracts may be chosen more than once.

Which person(s) …

- felt they were stuck in a rut before they made their change? 1 _____
- found the process of change surprisingly easy? 2 _____
- received valuable support when making their decision? 3 _____
- were forced by circumstances to make their decision? 4 _____
- were accused of being extreme in their treatment of the situation? 5 _____
- received unexpected benefits from making the change? 6 _____ 7 _____
- miss certain elements of their previous situation? 8 _____
- gave the matter a lot of thought before making their decision? 9 _____
- have learned to take pleasure in small things? 10 _____
- made a decision which affected others? 11 _____ 12 _____
- initially chose to ignore an obvious fact about the way they lived? 13 _____
- have changed their priorities in life? 14 _____ 15 _____

7 Find words or phrases in the extracts which mean the following.

a heavily overweight [A] _____
b reduced in importance by sending away [A] _____
c inactive, hidden [A] _____
d television [A] _____
e monotonous routine [B] _____
f feeling of sadness when parting from something [C] _____
g settled the outcome of something decisively [C] _____
h claiming to be [D] _____
i given up [D] _____
j place where animals are killed for their meat and by-products [D] _____
k spent time worrying [E] _____
l listened and accepted [E] _____

8 Which of the words and phrases in exercise 7 are used metaphorically?

Saying Goodbye To ...

Have you ever made a decision to change your way of life? Hannah Wright talked to five people about some life-changing decisions they made ...

A

Homework was done as quickly as possible, to be finished in time for their favourite soap, and family conversation would be limited to comments on what was happening in *EastEnders*, or *Friends*.

The last straw, however, came when my son was diagnosed as obese. We decided drastic action was needed, so the TV was relegated to the back of the garage, and the children were signed up for swimming three times a week. Friends accused us of going too far, the kids blamed us for cutting them off from the rest of the world, but this was countered by the fact that my son lost ten pounds within a month, and my daughter suddenly found an interest in music that had so far been lying dormant. What's more, dinnertime conversation now centred on the children's real lives. So, saying goodbye to the "box" was the best thing for our family, for in so doing, we learned to concentrate on actually living.'

B

'I simply decided I'd reached the end of my tether. I'd been on the treadmill for too long, and the daily battle of travelling to work each day had begun to wear me down. Having to listen to so-called experts expounding their theories all day had become sheer torture, and I realised I just wasn't enjoying life.

So, I left, and have never looked back. Making my home in a tiny village in rural France, I now wake up each morning to the sound of birds singing. My staple diet is salad grown mainly in my own garden, goat's cheese made by the lady down the lane, and eggs provided by another neighbour's hens. The pace of my life has slowed almost to a standstill, but nothing can compare to the peace in my mind. I may not have as much money, or a fast car, but I've now got far more time to appreciate the simple fact of living.'

C

'Saying goodbye to the place that had been our home for 35 years was a huge wrench. After we retired, however, we realised that managing such a large house was becoming too difficult. Then my wife fell and broke her hip, and that clinched it.

By far the hardest thing about downsizing was deciding what to part with. Heartbreaking though it was, we had to be ruthless, both with ourselves and each other. It was a very emotional time, and we didn't always see eye to eye, but we got through it. We told ourselves it wasn't the end of the world, merely the end of one phase of our life and the beginning of a new one. I won't say we don't miss the old place, and some of our things, but life is both a lot easier and less stressful than it was before we moved.'

D

'A professed animal lover, I nevertheless remained a confirmed meat eater, not allowing the glaring ethical dilemma to cloud my conscience. I blandly dismissed the arguments of morally superior friends who had already forsaken animal products for a life eating lettuce as exaggerated and extreme. Until, that is, a documentary about the horrors of battery farming and the slaughterhouse shocked me out of my ignorance. The hamburger I'd been tucking into went straight into the bin, and I made a vow that my consumption of animal products was a thing of the past.

I'd always thought it would be difficult to maintain a healthy diet without meat, but some well-chosen books on nutrition soon dispelled that myth, and I can honestly say, one year down the line, I've never felt better. My skin has improved, and I find I've got a lot more energy and enthusiasm for daily life.'

E

'By the time of my daughter's fourth birthday, I was deep in the process of procrastination. Should I homeschool her or send her to kindergarten? I agonised over the decision, as I doubted my capacity to teach her. Then I asked my neighbour Peter, a dad who homeschooled his five children, for advice. He told me, 'You've made it through the sleepless nights of infancy and the tantrums of the two-year old. You've taught your daughter to speak, feed herself, dress herself and behave correctly. Now you're finally dealing with a rational little human being! This is when the real fun of being a parent is about to begin ... but suddenly you think you're no longer qualified?' My daughter never made it to kindergarten, and now, almost a decade later, I'm very glad I heeded Peter's advice.'

Language development: word partners

1 Choose the option which does not normally follow the words in bold.

a It **shocked me out of** my ignorance / knowledge / complacency / daydream

b **Drastic** action / measures / talk / changes

c **Expound** a theory / enthusiasm / a view / an idea

d **Confirmed** meat eater / bachelor / atheist / man

e **Staple** diet / excuses / mind / ingredient

f **Cloud** my conscience / temper / mood / mind

g **Dispel** the myth / the freedom / the rumours / the fears

h **Be cut off from** the rest of the world / civilisation / the road / society

Key word: *end*

2 Choose the correct phrase to complete the sentences below.

1 'Ellen's lost interest in school. She stays out late, doesn't do her homework ... I'm at _____! I don't know what to do with her!'
  a the end of the road
  b my wits' end

2 'The first time I went babysitting, I was really thrown in at _____, because I had to look after a nine-month old baby and a two-year-old!'
  a the deep end
  b the receiving end

3 'Since he retired, George doesn't want to do anything. He sits in front of the TV for hours _____.'
  a on end
  b no end

4 'Our new neighbours are so noisy! Day and night, they're either moving furniture, or arguing! I'm at _____!'
  a the end of my tether
  b the end of the world

5 'I was at _____ last night, so I went to the cinema.'
  a a loose end
  b a sticky end

6 'Miles, I can't go on like this. We argue all the time. This is the _____ for us!'
  a tail end
  b end of the road

3 PAPER 3, PART 4 For questions **1–5**, think of **one** word only which can be used appropriately in all three sentences.

1 James is _____ to anxiety attacks around exam time.
  Organic waste can be _____ of by building a compost in your garden.
  'The Education Minister seems to be favourably _____ towards making cuts in education.'

2 'Tom arrived at the party dressed up as Dracula, and scared me to _____!'
  'Boys! It's freezing out here. Come and put your coats on, or you'll catch your _____ of cold!'
  'Oh no! The school are putting on 'A Christmas Carol' for the third time! It's a great play, but they've done it to _____!'

3 'Now, everybody. I'd like to _____ your attention to the small child in the picture.'
  'Before you _____ any conclusions, why don't you get a second opinion from another doctor?'
  As the day began to _____ to a close and evening set in, Laura became increasingly nervous.

4 'Phew! That was _____! I was nearly late for my job interview!'
  'It's very _____ in here! Can we open a window?'
  'My sister and I are very _____. We share all our problems.'

5 'Poor John was thrown in at the deep _____ on his first day at his new job, by being given a really tough project.'
  'I hate my job, but I need the money to pay off a loan, so it's a means to a(n) _____, really.'
  'You walk down to the _____ of this road and turn right. After about 100 metres you'll see the post office on your left.'

4 PAPER 3, PART 5 For questions **1–6**, complete the second sentence so that it has a similar meaning to the first sentence, using the word given. Do not change the word given. You must use between three and six words, including the word given.

1 'I'd become complacent, so losing the match to Steve Gerrard really taught me a lesson.'
  shocked
  'Losing the match to Steve Gerrard _____ complacency.'

2 'Sorry! I misunderstood you. I thought you wanted me to *throw* the papers away!'
  end
  'Sorry! I got the _____ the stick! I thought you wanted me to *throw* the papers away!'

3 William's announcement of his engagement to Kate surprised us, as we'd never expected him to get married.
  confirmed
  We'd all believed William to be _____ until he announced he was getting married to Kate.

4 'The new teacher has relaxed slightly now, but at first she was really strict!'
  law
  'The new teacher really laid _____ at first, but she's relaxed a little since then!'

5 'I'm not going to feel guilty that my parents are upset about my decision.'
  cloud
  'I'm not going to allow my parents' feelings to _____ about my decision.'

6 The President called a press conference to reassure the public that the rumours of an alien invasion were not true.
  dispel
  The President called a press conference _____ an alien invasion.

Grammar: making and intensifying comparisons

1 Underline the comparative forms in the sentences below.

a They find life far more enjoyable than ever before.
b Nothing compares to the joy of having your first child.
c Petrol is significantly more expensive than it was six months ago.
d The show wasn't as spectacular as we'd expected.
e The more fruit and vegetables you eat, the healthier you will be.
f This jam isn't nearly as tasty as the one my mother makes.

GRAMMAR SPOTLIGHT

Intensifying comparisons
April is better than Alison at Maths. To intensify this comparison (make it stronger), we can make the following changes:
1 April is **much** better than Alison at Maths.
2 April is **significantly cleverer** than Alison at Maths.
3 Of the two girls, April is **by far the best** at Maths.

➡ Grammar Reference 16.1, page 182

2 Intensify the following comparisons in different ways.

1 Brian is not as happy at this school as he was at his old one.
2 This is the best holiday I've ever had!
3 Shelley is not as calm as she used to be.
4 This film was more interesting than the last one he made.
5 Lyn works harder than Sue.
6 She's got more time for her family now that she's stopped working.
7 He goes to bed earlier, so he's got more energy during the day.
8 Renee takes longer to get ready in the morning than Shane.

3 Complete the following sentences which appeared in the Reading text on page 159 with one of the words in the box below. More than one word may be possible.

a lot	both	by far	far	much	never	than

a 'I may not have as _____ money, or a fast car, but I've now got _____ more time to appreciate the simple fact of living.'
b '_____ the hardest thing about downsizing was deciding what to part with.'
c 'Life is _____ a lot easier and less stressful _____ it was before we moved.'
d 'I've _____ felt better.'
e 'My skin has improved, and I find I've got _____ more energy and enthusiasm for daily life.'

4 Compare the two photographs below.

5 Look at text A on page 159. Use suitable words and phrases to make comparisons about the family's lifestyle before and after they dispensed with the TV.

6 🎧 16.1 **PAPER 4, PART 2** Listen to two friends comparing a new book with other novels by the same author. For questions 1–8, complete the sentences with a word or short phrase of comparison:

According to James, *'The Last Will'* was (1) _____ believable as the author's previous novels.
Sally feels that this book is (2) _____ the author's (3) _____ yet.
James thinks that the plot is rather unrealistic (4) _____ the author's first novel.
Sally particularly likes the fact that there is (5) _____ action in court in the latest novel.
James thinks the courtroom drama sections are (6) _____ ones in the book.
Sally believes that the protagonist is significantly (7) _____ richly drawn than in previous novels by the same author.
James feels the characters are (8) _____ well developed as they are in another book.

7 Make comparisons either between two books by the same author, or between a film and its sequel.

Use of English: multiple-choice cloze

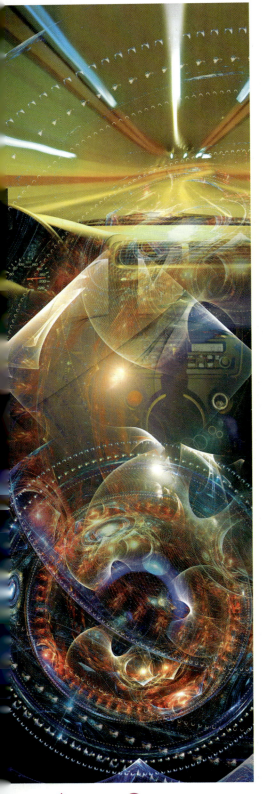

1 Tell the class about a film you have seen or a book you have read involving time travel.

2 Read the article below about time travel. Do you agree with the writer's view?

Say goodbye to the here and now: time travel possibilities

Today it's becoming increasingly well-known that time travel doesn't need to be confined to myths, science fiction, Hollywood blockbusters, or even the conjecture of physicists. Today – time travel is possible. For example, did you realise that an object travelling at high speed ages slower than a (1) _____ object? What this means is that if you travelled into outer space and back, moving at close to light speed, you could actually travel thousands of years into the Earth's future!

Albert Einstein's first significant input to the study of time occurred when he revolutionised physics with his 'special theory of relativity'. This eminent scientist showed us how time changes with motion. Nowadays, scientists don't see problems of time or motion as 'absolute' with (2) _____ correct answer. Time is (3) _____ to the speed one is travelling at; there can never be a clock at the centre of the universe to which everyone is able set their clock. Your entire life – from birth to death – is only the (4) _____ of an alien's eye, travelling at the speed of light. Einstein's relativity is destined to eventually become a subset of a brand new science more (5) _____ in its description of the fabric of our universe. Remember, the word 'relativity' (6) _____ from the known fact that the world's appearance depends purely on our state of motion; it is 'relative'.

Humanity is currently a mere moment in time. To put it bluntly, we're dinner guests at earth's table. Mysteries of space and time simply are not understood by our flimsy brains. If you think about it, these brains of ours (7) _____ to make us run from glittering-eyed lions in Africa, to hunt deer, and to collect our meals from the spoils of large carnivores. (8) _____, our mental limitations, we have come so remarkably far. Humankind has succeeded in (9) _____ the cosmic curtains a crack to let in the light. Questions raised by physicists, from Newton to Godel, to Einstein to Stephen Hawking, are among the most philosophical we can possibly ask.

Is time itself real? Does it (10) _____ in one direction only? Does it have a beginning or an end? And what is eternity? Infinity? None of these questions can be answered to the physicists' (11) _____. Yet the (12) _____ asking of these questions expands our minds ... and the endless search for answers supplies valuable insights along the way.

3 **PAPER 3, PART 1** For questions 1–12, read the text above and decide which answer (A, B, C or D) best fits each gap.

1	A stable	B standing	C stationary	D standard
2	A a lone	B a solitary	C a single	D a sole
3	A consistent	B relative	C relating	D consisting
4	A twitch	B blink	C wink	D flutter
5	A comprehensive	B compulsive	C comprehending	D confounding
6	A follows	B derives	C results	D evolves
7	A evolved	B emerged	C formed	D arose
8	A Although	B In spite	C But for	D Despite
9	A pulling to	B pulling out	C pulling back	D pulling down
10	A pass by	B flow	C run	D go by
11	A pleasure	B delight	C satisfaction	D standards
12	A mere	B just	C only	D slight

EXAM SPOTLIGHT

PAPER 3, PART 1 Consolidation of things to look for in this part
During this course, you have learned that when tackling part 1 of the Use of English, you need to look out for several things. This task tests your lexical knowledge, in terms of meaning and use. The options you are presented with in each question, therefore, may contain:
1 words which look similar, but have different meanings
2 parts of collocations, fixed phrases, and phrasal verbs
3 words which have similar meanings, but are used in different contexts
4 words which are followed by a different preposition, or have a different grammatical structure

4 Read through 'Say goodbye to the here and now' again, and find an example of each of the question types (1–4) mentioned above.

5 Discuss. If you could travel through time, would you like to go to the future or the past? Why?

Listening: three short extracts

Recognising agreement and disagreement

In Paper 4, part 1, you are sometimes required to recognise whether speakers agree or disagree.

1 ♫ **16.2** Listen to extract one, and decide whether the statements below are true or false.

   1   Neither speaker enjoys the peace and quiet.   T / F
   2   Both speakers miss their children.   T / F

2 ♫ **16.2 PAPER 4, PART 1** You will hear three different extracts. For questions 1–6, choose the answer (A, B or C) which fits best according to what you hear. There are two questions for each extract.

Extract One

You hear two people discussing how they felt when their children left home.

1 Which word best sums up the woman's feelings towards her son leaving home?
   A tension
   B relief
   C loneliness

2 Both the man and the woman agree that
   A they sometimes feel lonely without the children at home.
   B they sometimes dislike the responsibility of bringing up children.
   C it is not fair to make demands on children once they leave.

Extract Two

You will hear part of an interview with a man talking about taking early retirement.

3 According to the speaker, one of the initial problems he faced when he retired was
   A the fact that his wife expected him to do the shopping.
   B the fact that his wife expected him to do everything with her.
   C the difference between his wife's expectations and his own.

4 Which of the following does the speaker not think is important in order to enjoy one's retirement?
   A having help from your children
   B having sufficient funds
   C having your own interests

Extract Three
You hear two people talking about working at home.

5 The woman differs from the man in that
   A she anticipated problems of working at home.
   B she was mainly interested in the freedom of being self-employed.
   C struggled to maintain a balance between work and family.

6 Both speakers feel that
   A it is easy to be distracted by domestic issues when you work at home.
   B going to work in an office is preferable to working from home.
   C making your own decisions is the main advantage of being self-employed.

Speaking: individual long turn

1 Discuss. Have you ever dreamed of giving your bedroom a complete makeover? How would you change it?

In other words

In Paper 5, part 2, you are usually presented with four pictures, and have to talk about them. You may have to compare and contrast them. Use as much variety of language as possible.

2 In pairs. Make a list of different comparative forms that could be used to express the following sentences.

   a *'The second room is more cramped than the first one.'*
   b *'The first room is much lighter than the second one.'*

➡ Grammar Reference 16.1, page 182

3 Student A, look at your pictures below. They show different kinds of children's bedrooms. Compare and contrast them, and say what kind of child you think each one is suitable for, and why.

Castle room

Magic bedroom

Creativity room

Activity room

4 Student B, say which design you think would be most suitable for a girl aged four. Why?

5 Student B, turn to page 201, and look at your pictures. They show different designs for kitchens. Compare and contrast them, and say which one you would choose for your own house, and why?

6 Student A, say which design you like least. Why?

Writing: letter of reference

1 **Discuss.** When people apply for a job, they are usually required to supply two letters of reference from people they know or have worked with. Have you ever been asked to provide someone with a reference? What information did you include? If not, what do you think you would be expected to say in such a letter?

2 Read the question below, and underline the key points you would need to include in your answer.

> You are a teacher at an English language college in your home town. You have been asked to provide a reference for a student of yours who has applied for a job as a nanny for an English family. The person appointed will be good at dealing with small children, and have knowledge of first aid.
>
> You should include information about your student's character and personal qualities and skills, their previous relevant experience and reasons why they should be considered for this job.
>
> Write your **reference**.

SPOTLIGHT ON WRITING

A letter of reference

Providing a character reference for someone who has applied for a job or position of responsibility requires a fairly formal style. It usually takes the form of a letter, but begins in a standard way, with the following phrases:

- 'Dear Sir/Madam', or 'To whom it may concern' (for professional positions)
- 'Dear Mr Green; Ms Smith' (if you are given a name)

You should always end formally. Use the following phrases:

- 'Yours faithfully, … ' (if the person's name is unknown)
- 'Yours sincerely, … ' (if the person's name is known).

When answering a question of this kind, read the instructions carefully, to make sure you include all the necessary information in your character reference. Remember, your letter should persuade the prospective employer that your friend/former colleague is suitable for the job.

3 In pairs, complete the outline plan below for a letter of reference in answer to the question in exercise two.

Paragraph 1: Opening paragraph	*State the name of the person you are writing about, and your relationship with them, explaining why you feel qualified to discuss their suitability for the job.*
Paragraph 2	
Paragraph 3	

PAPER 2 Final reminder – check your work!

When you finish writing your answer in the Writing Paper, it's very important to check your work.

You can use the following checklist when you write:

- [ ] **Relevance**   Have you answered the question?
- [ ] **Register**   Have you used the correct style of formal/informal language?
- [ ] **Use of language**   Does it make sense, grammatically?
- [ ] **Range of vocabulary**   Is it varied enough and appropriate?
- [ ] **Spelling and punctuation**   Have you made any careless mistakes?
- [ ] **Organisation**   Is the development of points organised, with an introductory paragraph, a paragraph developing the main points, and a concluding paragraph?
- [ ] **Length**   Is your answer long enough, or too long? Remember, in part one, you should write 180–220 words, whereas in part two, your answer should be 220–260 words.

4   Read the following letter of reference that one examination candidate wrote in answer to exercise 2 on page 164. Underline any mistakes you notice, and use the checklist above to consider its merits. What mark do you think it deserves?

Dear Sir/Madam,

I was asked to provide this reference for Maria Fernandes, who I know since 2004. As a teacher and the Director of Studies at the Top Grade English Language College in Cuenca, I teach Maria for the last five years. During this time, she had proved herself both a competent student, and a popular member of the school.

She rapidly progressed to FCE level, achieving a B last December, and is presently studying for the CAE examination. She is a warm, outgoing girl, who is great fun and popular with her fellow students. As the eldest of four, Maria has to take care her younger brother and sisters after school, since her parents both work. She likes telling stories, and often relates us funny tales of her five-year-old brother's antics.

A skilful musician, she took up the responsibility of preparing our youngest students to sing in the school play at the end of last term, and entertained a wonderful rapport with them overall. When one of the boys fell and cut his head, she remained serene and administrated to him efficiently, while maintaining control of the other children until one of the teachers arrived.

For these reasons, I am confident that Maria has the right qualities for this job, and have no hesitation in recommending you her.

Yours,

Amanda

5   **PAPER 2, PART 2** Prepare and write an answer to the following question. Use the checklist in the Exam Spotlight above to check your work.

You have been asked to provide a reference for a friend of yours who has applied for a job as a group leader in an English-speaking summer camp. The person appointed will be good at dealing with a range of young people and will display excellent leadership skills.

You should include information about your friend's character and personal qualities and skills, their previous relevant experience and reasons why they should be considered for this job.

Write your **reference**.

Vocabulary organiser 16

Organise your vocabulary for examination revision!

16.1 Reading, page 159 Circle the odd one out in the following word groups.

a **obese** *chubby, stout, overweight, skinny, plump, well-built*
b **relegate** *demote, downgrade, promote, lower*
c **dormant** *inactive, sleeping, useless, undeveloped, hidden*
d **threshold** *door, doorway, doorstep, doorknob, entrance*
e **treadmill** *trial, daily grind, routine, slog, grindstone*
f **clinch (it)** *settle, confuse, seal, decide, determine*
g **accumulate** *build up, accrue, take up, gather, amass, collect*
h **cumbersome** *annoying, awkward, bulky, clumsy, unwieldy*
i **profess** *admit, confess, acknowledge, teach, recognise*
j **forsake** *abandon, provide, leave, disown, give up, sacrifice*
k **agonise** *worry, be in pain, dwell on, brood, torment yourself*
l **heed** *listen to, take note, involve, follow*

> **Final revision tip:** Group synonyms and words of similar meaning together, to help you create variety in your use of language in writing tasks.

16.2 Language development, page 160 Complete the sentences below with a suitable phrase.

a After his divorce, Paul felt the need to make some _____ in his life.
b Some scientists are now _____ about the possibility of time travel.
c In order to _____ that she was leaving the school, Mrs Scoones told the students of her decision to stay.
d 'Sorry, Mum!' said Ian, 'I'm a _____, so don't expect me to ever get married!'
e I thought I'd be working in that factory for the rest of my life, so the news of its closure really _____.
f Rice is a _____ in the Chinese diet.
g When I first moved to the island of Skye, I felt lonely and _____.
h 'Yes, I eat meat, and I simply don't allow the knowledge that animals are killed to feed me to _____.'

16.3 Language development, page 160 Match the first half of the following sentences to their endings.

1 'I made a mistake in my calculations, and found myself on
2 'Stephen cheated people all his life, but he came to
3 'I had no idea what they'd been talking about, because I came in on
4 'Heidi helped me
5 'So you didn't do well in your Geography test! It's hardly the

a *no end, by taking the kids out for the day so I could work.'*
b *end of the world!'*
c *a sticky end, when someone shot him.'*
d *the receiving end of my boss's anger.'*
e *the tail end of the conversation.'*

16.4 Language Development, page 160 For questions 1–5, think of **one** word only which can be used appropriately in all three sentences.

1 'Jennifer was going to become a lawyer, but now she's had a _____ of heart, and is thinking of accountancy.'
  'Today's rain is a welcome _____ from all the heat we've been having.'
  'John's leaving his office job and going to work on a farm, which I think will be a _____ for the better.'

2 'It's suddenly gone very quiet, which means that the kids are up to no _____!'
  'James has decided to move away from the city, for the _____ of his family.'
  'Why don't you go out tonight? It'll do you _____.'

3 'At one _____, there were buses every twenty minutes, but now there's only one every hour.'
  'Although Bryan is very busy, he always makes _____ for his family at weekends.'
  'If you have any _____ on your hands this weekend, come over for a meal.'

4 'There have been _____ sightings of a killer whale in the area.'
  'Frederic has declared himself a _____ bachelor, saying he will never marry.'
  'Fifteen _____ cases of the disease have been reported in this village alone.'

5 'Karen _____ a deep breath and dived into the water.'
  'The police searched the whole area for the missing boy yesterday, but _____ a blank.'
  'In yesterday's match, Liverpool _____ one all against Chelsea.'

16.5 Use of English, page 162 Complete the following sentences with a word or phrase.

a 'I don't want details; a _____ 'yes' or 'no' will do. Did you hit your brother?'
b Lisa _____ at Andy, to show him she was joking.
c 'My sister's a _____ shopper; she just can't stop herself!'
d Tom was late to work five times last month, and that _____ in him being given a warning.
e The _____ nature of fashion makes it hard to keep up with.
f She _____ from her room dressed in an elegant long red gown.
g '_____ we worked hard, we couldn't finish the project on time.'
h We were devastated when our biggest client decided to _____ of the deal.
i Henry was _____ in his gratitude for the gift.
j The road _____ alongside the railway line for about five miles.
k 'I take great _____ in welcoming Sir Paul McCartney on tonight's show!'

BANK OF ENGLISH

Word partnerships: re-
The prefix *re-* is used before many words to give the meaning of 'doing something again.' Write down whether each word is a noun (N), verb (V) or adjective (A), according to the part of speech.

rebuild	reconsider	reform	reformist
regain	regenerated	reintroduction	rejuvenate
relapse	remake	remix	renewal
reorganise	repeatable	replay	

Review 4 Units 13–16

1 Complete the sentences below with a suitable adjective from the box below. There are two extra words you do not need to use.

baffled	biodegradable	compulsive	compatible
contagious	cursory	incompatible	ludicrous
obscene	pristine	ruthless	vague

1 I've heard some lame excuses in my time, but your story is utterly _____.
2 If you want to cut this down to fewer than two hundred words you're going to have to be _____.
3 Sally had to stay in her room for an extra day in case her measles were still _____.
4 You can throw the banana skin in the compost – it's completely _____.
5 I wouldn't believe a word Mike says – he's a _____ liar you know!
6 I'm not surprised Tim and Sue didn't get on – they're such _____ types!
7 I was a bit _____ by the puzzle until John showed me there was a simple solution.
8 I asked Peter what he thought of the film, but his answer was a bit _____.
9 Roger asked his teacher to check his work, but she only gave it a _____ glance.
10 I'm not going to repeat the _____ word that boy said to me!

2 Complete the sentences below with a verb from the box below in its correct form, and one or more particles to form a phrasal verb that means the same as the word(s) in brackets.

die	drown	lay	pass
pass	stand	wind	wear

1 Miriam has been known to _____ _____ at the sight of a drop of blood. (faint)
2 If we don't do something soon, millions more species will soon _____ _____. (become extinct)
3 Over fifty workers were _____ _____ when the company started losing money. (made redundant)
4 I turned the music up but still couldn't _____ _____ the sound of the neighbours' arguing. (cover with sound)
5 Wilson, with his red hair and pale skin, always _____ _____ in a crowd. (is noticeable)
6 Lucy said she wanted to _____ _____ her diamonds to her great granddaughter. (leave in a will)
7 If you're not careful, you'll _____ _____ unemployed. (become as a result)
8 I told Jack I wasn't going to come, but he _____ me _____. (destroyed my resistance)

3 Replace the underlined part of the sentences that follow with an expression which uses the word in capitals.

1 When he was five, Bob nearly burnt the house. SET
2 He explained that he had become completely absorbed in the accounts. BOGGED
3 The party was supposed to be a surprise, but somehow Geoffrey heard about it. WIND
4 If you're not careful, both you and Martin are going to be in a lot of trouble! WATER
5 I couldn't cope any more – I had reached the limit of my patience! TETHER
6 It was supposed to be a joke but it failed to work as intended! FLAT
7 If you have nothing to do, I can give you a few chores. LOOSE
8 Will could have been really annoyed by what happened, but he decided to ignore it. PASS

4 Write down the word or phrase that completes the collocation in each of the sentences in the column on the left. Choose a further example of nouns that collocate with each group from the column on the right.

cloud	confirmed	(be) cut off	dispel
drastic	expound	shock	staple

1 _____ someone out of their *ignorance*   a a view / an idea
2 _____ *action*   b bachelor / atheist
3 _____ *a theory*   c mood / mind
4 _____ *meat eater*   d complacency / daydream
5 _____ *diet*   e the rumours / the fears
6 _____ my *conscience*   f civilisation / society
7 _____ *the myth*   g measures / changes
8 _____ from *the rest*   h excuses / ingredient
of the world

5 Complete the gaps in the sentences with a suitable word from the box below and one suitable particle.

ashamed	deficient	derived
eligible	immune	obsessed

1 Lucinda has been _____ _____ this particular rock band for the past three years!
2 Rupert's _____ _____ to criticism; you can say what you like, but he won't care at all.
3 If you're _____ _____ vitamin C, you'll suffer from all kinds of problems.
4 This shampoo is _____ _____ various plant oils.
5 My next door neighbours are _____ _____ a building grant from the council.
6 Laura was so _____ _____ her brother's behaviour that she told him to walk home alone.

6 Choose the best word from the options **A, B, C** or **D** to complete each of the sentences below.

1 The human ear is unable to hear the dolphins' signals, but we have developed machinery which can pick _____ up.
A these   C it
B them   D those

2 One area of study that scientists are particularly interested in is _____ of communication between mother dolphins and their offspring.
A such   C that
B what   D one

3 I'd rather you _____ the bus every day instead of driving.
A take   C were taking
B took   D will take

4 _____ you had the chance to do one selfless act. What would it be?
A As if   C Had
B Were   D Suppose

5 _____ the fire, many birds lost their nests.
A Because   C Due to
B Consequently   D As a result

6 _____ it hadn't rained all week, I watered the garden.
A Seeing as   C In case
B Therefore   D Notwithstanding

7 **PAPER 3, PART 1** For questions 1–15, read the text below and think of the word which best fits each gap. Use only one word in each gap.

Saturn runs rings round all the other planets

Why are Saturn's rings so astonishingly stunning? It could be that the planet managed to cling on to a moon (1) _____ all the other gas giants in our solar system had already lost (2) _____. Today's rings formed when the moon was shattered.

Astronomists at the university of Diderot, Paris, suggest (3) _____ was during the 'late heavy bombardment', 700 million years after Saturn formed, (4) _____ a fragment of debris collided (5) _____ one of the planet's moons. Because the moon was orbiting (6) _____ just the right distance from Saturn when it exploded – within what's known as the Roche limit – the tiny pieces created the rings (7) _____ of dispersing.

(8) _____ could explain (9) _____ other planets don't have rings like Saturn's. Even (10) _____ other planets had moons within their Roche limits at the birth of the solar system, the French astronomers' calculations show that the moons (11) _____ soon have been yanked down into the planet or unchained from (12) _____ orbits. Yet Saturn's rapid rotation meant it could hold a satellite within (13) _____ Roche limit until the bombardment.

Other astronomers around the world say the French way of showing Saturn's uniqueness among gas giants is interesting, (14) _____ that their hypothesis cannot be proved (15) _____ we have better ways of replicating in model-form the evolution of the solar system.

8 **PAPER 3, PART 5** For questions 1–8, complete the second sentence so that it has a similar meaning to the first sentence, using the word given. **Do not change the word given.** You must use between **three** and **six** words, including the word given.

1 Instead of finishing the leftovers, I'd prefer to cook something fresh.
rather
I _____ finish the leftovers.

2 Anthropologists have learned a lot about human behaviour by studying dolphins.
so
If anthropologists hadn't studied dolphins they _____ about human behaviour.

3 I'd sooner find out some things about their culture first.
better
It _____ out some things about their culture first.

4 Even though he hated cartoons, he agreed to watch it with the kids.
fact
He agreed to watch it with the kids _____ _____ he hated cartoons.

5 No sooner had the lightning struck than all the lights went off.
when
Hardly _____ all the lights went off.

6 Two months ago this dress was quite a lot cheaper.
significantly
This dress _____ was six months ago.

7 My Dad's pie is far tastier than this one.
nearly
This pie _____ the one my Dad makes.

8 He had to get off the bus because he didn't have a valid ticket.
consequently
He didn't have a valid ticket _____ to get off the bus.

Grammar Reference

Index

Unit 1 Beginnings

1.1 Revision of tenses

The present simple is used to talk about:	
• habits and routines • permanent situations • scientific or natural facts	I **always walk** the dog after breakfast. She **lives** in Sweden. Water **boils** at 100 degrees Celsius.

The present continuous is used to talk about:	
• actions happening now • temporary situations • annoying habits (with *always, forever* etc)	She's **talking** to someone. I'm **staying** with Jenny until I find a place of my own. He's **always** being mean to me.

The past simple is used for:	
• a sequence of actions that happened in the past • complete past actions • actions that happened in the past at a stated or definite time • past habits or general past states	First she **picked** up her umbrella, then she **opened** the door. She **walked** to the train station. Edward **went** on holiday last month. She **went** to bed at 8 o'clock. She always **had** porridge for breakfast.

The past continuous is used for:	
• an action in progress in the past that was interrupted by another action • parallel actions happening at the same time in the past	She **was getting** on the bus when someone stole her bag. While she **was having** a lesson, the children **were making** a noise.

The present perfect is used for:	
• actions that happened in the past but the time is unknown or not stated • actions which began or happened in the past but relate to the present • actions that have happened in a period of time that has not yet finished	I think I must **have been** here before. They **have lived** in this town for several years. They **have been woken** by the neighbours' shouting three times **this week**.

The present perfect continuous is used to:	
• focus on the duration of an action that started in the past and continues up to the present	The universe **has been expanding** for over 13 billion years.

The past perfect is used for:	
• an action that happened before another action or time in the past	When I arrived at the airport, the plane **had** already **landed**.

The past perfect continuous is used to:	
• focus on the duration of an action that started and finished before another action or time in the past	We **had** already **been waiting** for over an hour, when they informed us that the train to Brighton had been cancelled.

Unit 2 A child's world

2.1 Passive voice

The passive

The passive voice is *not* a tense. We form it by using a suitable tense of the verb **be** and a past participle.

	Active voice	Passive voice
Present simple	He writes a letter.	A letter is written.
Present continuous	He is writing a letter.	A letter is being written.
Simple past	He wrote a letter.	A letter was written.
Past continuous	He was writing a letter.	A letter was being written.
Present perfect	He has written a letter.	A letter has been written.
Past perfect	He had written a letter.	A letter had been written.
Going to future	He is going to write a letter.	A letter is going to be written.
Modals in present	He can/should/will write a letter.	A letter can/should/will be written.
Future perfect	He will have written a letter.	A letter will have been written.

> **Remember:** The present and past perfect continuous do not have a passive form (except in rare cases). The passive cannot be used for intransitive verbs, such as *appear*, *disappear* etc.

The passive voice is used:

- when we are more interested in the action than who or what did it or caused it (the agent)
- when the agent is obvious, unimportant, or unknown
- to avoid saying *they, someone* etc
- for formal situations and events

Helen was robbed last night.
Andy was made redundant yesterday.
Cars are not permitted in the centre of Zurich.
Our house was broken into last night.
You are kindly requested not to smoke.

The causative **have** and **get**:

- **have something done** usually describes an action or service that someone else does for us
- it can also be used to describe unfortunate incidents or accidents
- **get something done** can be used in a similar way to **have**
- **get** is sometimes more emphatic than **have**, and is used to create a sense of urgency or obligation in some cases

*We're **having** our living room decorated.*

*Officer, I've **had** my bag stolen!*

*I **got** the leak in the bathroom repaired.*
*'I must **get** this work finished by lunchtime.'*
*'**Get** your homework done!'*

As a passive:

- **get** can also replace **be** in a passive sense

After the party, the house was a mess, but it eventually got cleaned up.

Passive with auxiliary verbs: **can, will, may/might, should** are used to signify:

- certainty about the effect of an action
- possible effect of an action
- advice on how an action should be viewed or treated
- occasional reaction to an action or event

*The new law **will** be regarded as a restriction on freedom of speech.*
*Katie's marriage to Tom **may** be viewed unfavourably by some members of the family.*
*This new approach **should** be implemented with caution.*
*This new approach to teaching literature **can** be regarded as too radical.*

Need can be used:

- with a passive sense, to signify when something has to be done without saying who should do it

The plants need watering (passive sense: gerund).
The plants need to be watered (passive infinitive).

Impersonal passive with **say, consider, believe, think, assume, suppose, report**

Reporting verbs are often used in the passive in news broadcasts or newspaper articles to report widely held views, which may or may not have been proven. There are two forms.

It is thought that the victim knew her attacker.
It is said that Mr Cole's tomatoes are the largest ever recorded in the UK.

The victim is thought to have known her attacker.
Mr Cole's tomatoes are said to be the largest ever recorded in the UK.

Let and **make**

Let does not have a passive form, but needs to be replaced with **allow**:
'Mum won't let me go to the party.'
'I'm not allowed to go to the party.'
Make takes a passive infinitive form after it:
John's father made him wash the car and cut the grass before he could go out on Saturday.
John was made to wash the car and cut the grass before he could go out on Saturday.

Unit 3 Are you game?

3.1 Modals (1): auxiliaries in discussion

Form

The modal auxiliary verbs are generally followed by the bare infinitive of the main verb (with the exception of **ought to**):

'It must be ...'; 'It may be ...'; 'It might be ...'; 'It could be ...'; 'It can't be ...'

The past form takes the bare infinitive of **have** and the past participle of the main verb:

'It must have been ...'; 'It could have been ...'; 'It can't have been ...' etc

Speculation and suggestion

• We use **may be, could be** and **might be** to talk about possibility, speculate or suggest, when we are not sure of an answer, or a reaction. • We use **must be** when we are fairly certain that something is true. • We use **can't be** when we are fairly certain that something is not true. • We use **could have been, might have been, must have been** and **can't have been** to speculate about the past.	'Who's that talking to Mark?' – 'I'm not sure. It may be his new secretary.' 'When's your mum coming to visit?' – 'It could be Tuesday or Wednesday of next week.' 'That must be Anna's new car! She said she was getting an Audi.' 'Isn't that Tony over there?' – 'It can't be! He's in Tunisia this week.' 'It could have been young Henry who broke the kitchen window.' 'Fred's car's a write off! He must have been doing 100km when he drove off the road!' 'The concert can't have been last night! It says here that it's on the 25th!'

Deduction

• We use **must** to talk about deduction, when we are certain that something is true, based on the information we have. • We use **can't** and **couldn't** to talk about negative deduction, when we are certain that something is not true, based on the information we have.	'The murderer must have known that his victim went along that route every evening, as he knew exactly where to attack her.' 'This must be the right house as it's the only one with a red wooden gate.' 'The number nine can't go in that square, as there's one in the box directly above it.' 'You couldn't have done anything to stop him from leaving, as he'd made up his mind a long time ago.'

Assumption

• We use **will** or **would** to make an assumption, when we think something is true without having evidence.	'There's the doorbell! That will be John.' 'If you'd told him, he would have been angry. You know what he's like!'

Refuting a comment and qualifying criticism

• We use **may** or **might ... but** when we want to refute someone else's argument or comment, or qualify someone's criticism of us.	"I may not talk a lot, but I'm not stupid!"

Unit 4 Eureka!

4.1 The future

Future form	Use	Example
Present simple	programmed/scheduled events	The plane leaves at 4pm.
Will/shall + infinitive	statements of fact	The sun will rise tomorrow.
Will/shall + infinitive	predictions	You will win some money.
Will/shall + infinitive	promises	I will never leave you.
Present continuous	prearranged events	I'm going to the doctor tomorrow.
Going to + infinitive	intentions/plans	I'm going to make an appointment with the doctor tomorrow.
Going to + infinitive	statements based on present evidence	It looks as if it's going to snow.
Future continuous	actions in progress at a certain time in the future	He will be taking his French exam this time tomorrow.

Future perfect	actions which will be finished by a given future time	He will have retired by then.
Future perfect continuous	expresses the duration of an action or state at a given future time	On the 11th March, she will have been working here for thirty years.

Other ways of talking about the future
The following expressions can be used to introduce the future, or future ideas.

be about to do something	I'm about to put the kettle on. Do you want a cup?
be on the point of do*ing* something	Peter's on the point of resigning from his job.
be bound/certain/sure to do something	Lucile is bound to pass her French exam.
should + infinitive	You should be promoted!
it's (about) time somebody *did* something/something *happened*	It's about time you were promoted!
there's a good chance that	There's a good chance that Laurence will get the job.
I doubt whether/if/that	I doubt that Vicky will get the job.

4.2 Future time in subordinate clauses

With certain time reference words, a different tense is sometimes used in the subordinate clause to the one used in the main clause.

	Main clause	Example
While is used to link two clauses in which two actions are happening simultaneously.	subject + future *will/while* + [subordinate clause] subject + simple present	I'll open the wine while you find some glasses.
By the time is used to link two clauses in which one action happens after another action has happened.	*by the time* + subject + simple present + [subordinate clause] subject + future/ future perfect.	By the time the rest of the group arrive, it will have started to rain.
As soon as is used to link two clauses in which one action happens immediately after another.	*As soon as* + subject + simple present + [subordinate clause] subject + future.	As soon as the film starts, I'll sit down.
Until is used to link two clauses in which one action is completed before another one happens.	subject + future *will/won't* (usually negative) *until* + [subordinate clause] subject + simple present/present perfect	I won't leave the house until Martha calls.

Unit 5 Safe and sound?

5.1 Verbs followed by the infinitive or *-ing*

Please note: the list below is not exhaustive. These are simply among the most common examples.

1 Normally followed by infinitive with *to*:		2 Normally followed by infinitive without *to*:	3 Normally followed by *-ing*:
agree to do	dare to do	make somebody do	appreciate somebody doing
order somebody to do	threaten to do	let somebody do	contemplate doing
pretend to be	decide to do	watch somebody do	deny doing
persuade somebody to do	fail to do	see somebody do	enjoy doing
attempt to do	arrange to do	hear somebody do	like doing
expect to do	advise somebody to do		hate doing
choose to do	encourage somebody to do		consider doing
refuse to do	want to do		involve doing
ask (somebody) to do	need to do		avoid doing
			face doing

Problematic items
There are many verbs which can be followed by more than one structure. This can alter the meaning considerably, so be careful about which structure you use!

A	*like, love, hate, prefer*	
•	***Like doing*** refers to somebody's attitude towards something	*'I like swimming and playing basketball.'*
•	***Like to do*** refers to habitual preferences	*'We like to go to the cinema on Fridays.'*
•	***Not like to*** or ***hate to*** means to think something is wrong	*'I hate to disturb you at home, doctor, but it's rather urgent.'*

B	*remember, forget*	
•	***Remember doing*** and ***forget doing*** refer to past events	*'I remember putting my keys in my bag before I left the house.'*
•	With ***to*** both verbs refer to some kind of obligation	*'I don't remember telling you that at all.'*
		'I'll never forget dancing with Brad Pitt at that wedding last month!'
		'He was supposed to phone me but he forgot to do so.'
		'Will you remember to water the plants on Sunday?'

C	*go on*	
•	***Go on doing*** refers to the continuation of an action, sometimes for too long	*'He went on working until midnight.'*
•	***Go on to*** refers to the next thing someone does	*'She went on talking for an hour.'*
		'The Headmaster went on to praise the school football team for winning the southern counties cup.'

D	*mean*	
•	***Mean doing*** refers to what is involved in performing an action	*If we take that flight, it'll mean getting up at 5 in the morning!'*
•	***Mean to do*** refers to intend to do	*'I meant to tell you earlier, but we're having a meeting at 4 o'clock.'*

E	*stop*	
•	***Stop doing*** refers to the ending of an activity	*'Kevin stopped smoking a month ago.'*
•	***Stop to do*** refers to the interruption of one action in order to do something else	*'As she was walking along the High Street, Sara stopped to look in the shop windows.'*

F	*regret*	
•	***Regret to do*** is usually used in formal letters, when the writer is sorry about what he is going to say	*' We regret to inform you that your application to join the army has been unsuccessful.'*
•	***Regret doing*** refers to a regret about an action in the past	*'I regret arguing with him over such a silly matter.'*

G	*watch, see, hear*	
•	With ***-ing***, these verbs refer to an action that is still in progress when the speaker stops paying attention to it	*'I saw someone coming out of the bank, but then I turned away to talk to my friend.'*
•	With the bare infinitive, these verbs refer to an action that is complete	*'We watched David Beckham score that fabulous goal against Juventus.'*

H	*consider*	
•	***Consider doing*** means think about doing	*'I considered becoming a doctor for a while, but didn't want to have to study so hard.'*
•	***Consider*** + object + ***to*** refers to an opinion	*'This piece of music is considered to be one of Mozart's finest compositions.'*

Unit 6 Hale and hearty

6.1 Conditionals

Type	Use	Form	Example
Zero conditional	What is always true	Present + present	*If I **eat** sweets, I **feel** awful afterwards.*
1st conditional	What is likely or probable	Present + future	*If you **take up** Pilates, you**'ll soon lose** weight.*
2nd conditional	Hypothetical situations	Past + ***would***	*If I **found** the time, **I'd join** a gym.*
3rd conditional	Hypothetical past situations	Past perfect + ***would have***	*If I **hadn't eaten** so much, I **would have had** some cake.*
Conditionals with modals	Possible situations	Present, past or past perfect + ***should, could, can, may, might (have)***	*If you **don't feel** well, you **should see** a doctor.* *If you **hadn't woken** me, I **might have missed** the meeting.*
Mixed conditionals	Possible or hypothetical situations in the past, present or future (when the time reference in the conditional clause is different from that in the main clause).	Past perfect + ***would*** Past + ***would have*** Past + future	*If **I'd looked** after my health better, I **wouldn't feel** so sick now.* *If I **were** a different person, I **wouldn't have put** up with your behaviour for so long!* *If you **slept** well, **you'll do** well in the exam.*

False conditional	A sentence with **if** but the meaning is not a condition or a hypothesis.	Present + present Past + past	If you **hate** sailing, why **are you getting** on the boat? If we **ate** all our dinner we **had** dessert.

Other types of conditionals

Conditional phrase	Use	Example
unless	means **but not if** (and only if)	*I'll cook chicken, **unless** Jackie doesn't eat meat.*
on condition that/provided/ providing/as long as/so long as	can be used as alternative to **if**	*I'll cook **if/as long as/on condition that/ provided** you wash up afterwards.*
even if	emphasises the conditional clause	***Even if** you miss the wedding, you should still get them a present.*
but for	can be used to mean **if it hadn't been for**	***But for** Malcolm's insistence, I would never have applied for the job.*
supposing/suppose	can be used to introduce a hypothetical situation; can be used to mean: **if you were to …**	***Supposing** you saw a UFO, would you tell anyone?*
otherwise/or else	used to introduce an alternative situation	*You'd better not be late; **otherwise** you'll be in trouble.*
in case/lest	used as a conditional when the speaker does not know the future outcome	*I'll take an umbrella **in case** it rains.*

More formal or less likely conditionals

were to	used to make an event more formal or hypothetical	*If I were to apply for the position, do you think I would stand a chance?*
should	used when you do not expect something to happen	*If you should see my keys anywhere, do let me know.*
happen to	as above: used when something is unlikely or unexpected; sometimes used with **should**	*If you should happen to see my keys anywhere, do let me know.*

Inverted conditionals

If he were to eat all his dinner, he could have an ice cream.	***Were he to eat** all his dinner …*
If you had come when I told you, you'd have seen the eagle!	***Had you come** when I called you …*
If you should get a part in the film, I want to be the first to know.	***Should you get** a part in the film …*

Unit 7 Wish you were there …

7.1 Inversion

Function

We tend to use inversion in the following ways.

1	In formal situations	*'Not only is our guest speaker tonight an accomplished scientist, he is also a musician of considerable talent.'*
2	To emphasise a point, especially in official or political speeches	*'Never before has the community been in such desperate need for change!'*
3	To make a statement more convincing or interesting	*'No sooner had she walked in than the phone rang, and it was him!'*
4	To make a recommendation more persuasive	*'Not only can this new vacuum cleaner save you time, but also money, as it uses only 40% of the electricity that other cleaners use.'*
5	To make a narrative more dramatic	*'No sooner did she say his name, than he appeared.'*
6	To make conditional sentences more emphatic	*'If I had known it would cause so much trouble, I would never have told him the truth.'* *'Had I known it would cause so much trouble, I would never have told him the truth.'* *'If she contacts you, please call me.'* *'Should she contact you, please call me.'*

Structures taking inversion	
We can invert certain negative adverbs and adverbial phrases by placing them at the beginning of the sentence for emphasis, in the following ways:	
• We may invert a sentence by inserting **do/did** as in the question form	*Nicole hardly ever speaks to Tom.* *Hardly ever does Nicole speak to Tom.*
• When an auxiliary is present, we reverse the auxiliary and the subject	*You can use this mobile phone to access the Internet and also watch videos.* *Not only can you use this mobile phone to access the Internet, but also to watch videos.*
• It can be used with negative adverbs of frequency	*I've never been treated so badly before!* *Never before have I been treated so badly!* *Rarely have we seen such a magnificent performance of this play!* *Seldom has the President given such a moving speech.*
• With time expressions: **no sooner, hardly, scarcely, barely** (when one event quickly follows another in the past)	*No sooner had I shut the front door than I realised I had left the keys inside.* *Scarcely had he walked into the room when the lights went out.* *Hardly had she sat down, when a stone came flying through the window.* *Barely had she finished answering her emails, when more started coming in.*
• After **not**	*Not only did he forget to lock the door, but he left several windows open!* *Not until we got home did we realise we had forgotten to pay the bill!*
• After certain phrases with **no**	*Under no circumstances are you to touch that wire!* *On no condition must you contact me while I'm away.* *On no account will you open my briefcase!* *At no time did I imagine he would jump.*
• After **only**	*Only when I saw him did I realise how much we had both changed.*
• After **little,** to express a lack of awareness of something	*Little did she realise how much he cared for her.*
• After **so** and **such,** used to emphasise the strong effect of something	*So catastrophic was the earthquake that it will take years to rebuild the town.*
• **Such** followed by **be**	*Such was the force of the wind that the fire quickly swept across the forest.*

Unit 8 Making our mark

8.1 Relative pronouns

Relative pronouns		
To talk about people	• **who/that/whom/whose** • **all/some/many/both/neither/none + of whom** • **to/for/about + whom** • **someone/anyone/everyone + who**	*Ali and Mike, **neither of whom** had been abroad before, thought it was great.* ***Who** were you talking to just now?*
To talk about things, animals, etc	• **which/that/whose** • **all/some/many/both/neither/none + of which** • **something/anything/everything + that**	*The play **which/that** I saw.* *He examined the reports, **some of which** had quite shocking results*
To talk about places	• **where** • **in/at/on** etc **+ which**	*That was the hospital **where/in which** my mother was born.*
To talk about time	• **when** • **by which time, at which point** etc • **by/since/until + when**	*He got there after 6 o'clock, **by which time** the doors had been closed.*
To talk about situations	• **in which case** • **as a result of which**	*She said she might bring a friend, **in which case**, I'd better cook a bit extra.*
To talk about reasons	• **why/that** • **which was why**	*Her car broke down, **which is why** she was late for the lecture.*

8.2 Defining and non-defining relative clauses

Relative clauses	
A defining relative clause: • contains essential information that must be included. • is not surrounded by commas.	*The people **who/that had insulated their houses** had much lower fuel bills that winter.* → *Only the people who had insulated their houses had lower fuel bills.*

> **Remember:** We can omit the defining relative pronoun if it is an object.
> *She's the woman (who/that) I gave my money to!*

A non-defining relative clause: • adds extra information which is not essential to the main clause. • is surrounded by commas.	*The people,* **who had insulated their houses,** *had much lower fuel bills that winter.* → All the people had insulated their houses and had lower fuel bills.	**Remember:** We cannot omit the relative pronoun. ***That*** cannot be used in non-defining relative clauses.
Reduced relative clauses:		
A relative clause in the present or past continuous can be 'reduced' to just the present participle clause *(-ing)*.	*The men* **who are building** *that house over there are friends of mine.* *The men* **building that house** *over there are …*	
A passive relative clause can be 'reduced' to a past participle.	*The film,* **which was written** *and directed by an Asian woman, was a box-office hit.* *The film,* **written and directed** *by an Asian woman, was …*	
Some relative clauses can also be reduced by using the infinitive with **to**.	*The last person* **who crossed** *the line was given a consolation prize.* *The last person* **to cross** *the line was given a consolation prize.*	

Unit 9 Brushstrokes and blueprints

9.1 Changing sentence structure: change in emphasis or meaning?

Altering emphasis and meaning

Inverting the word order generally alters the emphasis	*It was Bryan who broke the kitchen window.* *It was the kitchen window that Bryan broke.* [See also Unit 7, Inversion]
Changing the position of the comma, or adding and omitting words in a sentence can alter the meaning.	*John admired that photograph of Heidi.* → Heidi is the subject of the photograph. *John admired that photograph of Heidi's.* → Heidi *took* the photograph (of a landscape). *We went to the taverna which was owned by a Greek couple.* → We went to that particular one because it was owned by a Greek couple. *We went to the taverna, which was owned by a Greek couple.* → The fact that the taverna was owned by a Greek couple is extra information.

Position of the comma	
Relative clauses a Defining relative clause: *We bought the house in Boston which was close to a school.*	The reason we bought it was because it was close to a school.
b Non-defining relative clause: *We bought the house in Boston, which was close to a school.*	We bought the house in Boston, not New York. The fact that it was close to a school is simply extra information, and not important.
Numbers of people mentioned a *The boys, Will and Harry, had a great time together.*	There are two boys, and their names are Will and Harry.
b *The boys, Will, and Harry had a great time together.*	There are four boys or more. 'The boys' refers to boys who are well known to the speaker, possibly family, and Will and Harry are two extra boys who have joined them. The extra comma makes it clear that Will and Harry are not 'the boys'.
It or what	
Sarah crashed into my car last night. *It was Sarah who crashed into my car last night.*	I'm making a simple statement. I'm emphasising the fact that Sarah, not Diana or Elizabeth, crashed into my car.
I was surprised that Charles didn't call to say that he wouldn't be coming. *What surprised me was that Charles didn't call to say he wouldn't be coming.*	I'm surprised that Charles didn't come. I might not have been surprised that he didn't come, but I was surprised that he didn't *call*.
The position of a clause	
As I'd expected, George didn't pass his driving test. *George didn't pass his driving test as I'd expected.*	I knew he would fail. I believed he would pass.

Unit 10 The good life

10.1 Reported speech, reporting verbs

1 Tense changes: to report something said in the past using a past tense reporting verb, we use a tense one step back in the past (backshift).

Words spoken	Reported speech with backshift
*'I **like** sport.'* *'He **is reading** a book.'* *'I **have been** to Spain twice.'* *'I**'ve been running**.'* *'Angela **went** home.'* *'I **was listening to music**.'*	*She said (that) she **liked** sport.* *She said (that) he **was reading** a book.* *He said (that) he **had been** to Spain twice.* *He said (that) he **had been running**.* *I said (that) Angela **had gone** home.* *She said (that) she **had been listening** to music.*

We do not backshift:

• when the reporting verb is in the present tense • when the reporter sees the past events from the same point of view as the speaker • with the past perfect simple and past perfect continuous • when we report modals: **would, should, might, could, ought to**	*'I**'m going to** quit my job.'* → She **says** she**'s going to** quit her job. *'We **are** very happy about your engagement.'* → They said they **are** very happy about my engagement. *'The show **had** already **started**.'* → He said the show **had** already **started**. *'You **ought to** study harder.'* → She said I **ought to** study harder.

> **Remember:** when **shall** refers to the future we use **would**; when it is a suggestion, we use **should**. For example, *'We **shall** have to leave soon,'* means that they said they **would** have to leave soon – but *'**Shall** I pick you up at seven?'* means that he asked if he **should** pick me up at seven.

We can choose whether to backshift or not:

• when present and future events are still true	*'The moon **orbits** the earth.'* → He said the moon **orbits** the earth.

2 Changes of pronouns and adverbs: these change only if the person, place or time of reporting is significantly different from the words in the direct speech.

*'I'm meeting **your** sister **here tomorrow**.'*	Reported the same day in the same place: *He said he's meeting **my** sister **here tomorrow**.* Reported three days later somewhere else: *He said **he** was meeting **my** sister **there the next day**.*

3 Word order in reported questions: to report questions, we use the same order as in statements.

*'**Where is** the supermarket?'* *'**Would you** like a lift home?'*	*He asked **where** the supermarket was.* *He asked me if **I would** like a lift home.*
*'**Which is** your first choice?'*	*She wanted to know **which was** my first choice/ **which** my first choice was.*

> With **what/who/which** questions + **be** + complement, **be** can go before the complement.

10.2 Patterns after reporting verbs

Verb + *that* clause	
verb + that *add, admit, agree, announce, answer, argue, claim, complain, confess, decide, deny, expect, explain, hope, promise, realise, remember, repeat, reply, swear, suggest, think, threaten, warn*	She **confessed** (**that**) she had got on the wrong bus without noticing it.
verb + that clause (+ should) *advise, beg, demand, insist, prefer, propose, recommend, request, suggest*	I **propose** (**that**) we should all listen to what Garry has to say.

> **Remember:** in more formal contexts we can omit **should**. For example, *He demanded that he be released from prison.*

> In less formal contexts, we use an ordinary tense. For example, *He demanded that he was released from prison.*

Verb + *to-* infinitive	
agree, ask, claim, decide, demand, expect, hope, intend, offer, promise, refuse, swear, threaten	She **swore to leave** if he ever did it again.

verb + object + *to-* infinitive	
advise, ask, beg, command, encourage, expect, forbid, intend, invite, order, persuade, recommend, remind, tell, urge, warn	He **begged her not to break** off their relationship.

verb + *-ing* form	
admit, deny, mention, propose, recommend, regret, report, suggest	She **suggested going** for a walk.

Verb + (object) + preposition (+ object or genitive) + -*ing* form	
accuse (somebody) of, apologise (to somebody) about/for, blame somebody for, complain (to somebody) about, comment on, confess to, insist on, object to	She **apologised to** him **for crashing** the car.

Unit 11 Making ends meet

11.1 Modals (2): plans, prediction, criticism, annoyance, resignation

Making plans	*will* and *would* can be used for making decisions about future plans	*'I think I* **will go** *for a swim later.'* *'He decided he* **would take** *his girlfriend out for a romantic meal.'*
Making predictions	*will* and *would* can also be used to make predictions:	*'Mr Bond* **won't be** *available today, as his wife's having a baby. '* *'Jennifer thought it* **would be** *a great party.'*
Criticism	*might* and *could* can be used to express criticism or annoyance	*'You must be careful! You* **might have cut yourself** *with that knife!'* *'You* **could at least** *explain to me why you didn't turn up last night!'*
	should have and *ought to have*	*'You* **should have** *told her you were getting married.'* *'They* **ought to** *have gone to see the doctor.'*
Annoyance	*will* and *would* can also be used to express annoyance	*'She* **will keep** *talking to me while I'm trying to work!'* *'He* **would call now**, *just when we've sat down to eat!'*
Resignation	*may as well* and *might as well* can be used to express acceptance of a situation when there is no better alternative	*'You* **may as well** *go home, because Angelina Jolie's not coming.'* *'It's getting dark, so we* **might as well** *go inside.'*

Unit 12 Behind the silver screen

12.1 Participles

The present participle can be used:	
• as an adjective • to form continuous tenses • after verbs of sensation • after **catch** or **find** + object • after **have** + object • **spend** or **waste** • after **be busy** • to introduce a statement in indirect speech	*boring, exciting* He is **watching** you. I heard him **moving**. I saw him **talking** … She **caught** him **stealing**. I'll **have** you **dancing** again in no time. She **spends** two hours **commuting** every day. He **was busy working** in the garden. **Apologising** for his lateness …

A present participle can replace a sentence or main clause:	
• when two actions by the same subject occur simultaneously • when one action is immediately followed by another and is performed by the same subject • when the second action is caused by, or is a result of, the first action	**Holding** the dogs in one hand, he tried to unlock the door with the other. **Hanging** up the phone she turned and faced us. He pushed past me, **knocking** over a priceless vase.

A present participle can replace:			
• a subordinate clause with as/since/ because + subject + verb	**Remember:** it is possible to use two or more participles one after the other. For example, *Being* interested in music, and not *wanting* to change anyone's plans, I agreed to go to the concert.	**Realising** that he would be late, he decided to call a taxi.	**Note** – the subject of the participle clause can be different from the subject in the main/subordinate clause. For example, *The weather being lousy, we decided to stay at home.*

• a relative clause (reduced relative clauses)	Anyone **needing** assistance should call the supervisor.
The perfect participle (active) can be used:	
• to more clearly show that one action had finished before another began	**Having failed** his driving test twice before, he lacked confidence. (not always necessary)
The perfect participle (passive) can be used:	
• to emphasise that an action expressed by the participle happened before the action expressed by the next verb	**Having been laughed** at before, he decided not to make the same mistake again.
The past participle can be used:	
• as an adjective • to form the perfect tenses/infinitives/passive voice • to replace a subject + passive verb	a **broken** bottle, the **scared** cat he had **fallen**, to have **slept**, it had been **stolen** **Made** by the finest Italian shoemakers …

Unit 13 Getting the message across

13.1 Text references: *this, that, it, such, these, those*

Reference words

Reference words may:	
1 refer to something that has already been mentioned	'There is now a new method of extraction. **This** method is called …'
2 point forward to something about to be mentioned	The point is **this:** you must work harder.

Text references

We generally use them to avoid repetition when explaining or describing something.	Janet decided to leave her job and go to live in Kenya. **This** was to change her life dramatically. Paul wrote his first novel at school, with encouragement from his English teacher. **That's** how he became a writer. Laura had a bad accident when she was 10, and **it** affected her for the rest of her life. John said that the local council were irresponsible in their attitude towards energy conservation. **Such** open criticism will cost him his seat in the next election. 'I have with me today two very special people, Mary and Peter. **These** two are responsible for setting up a charity organisation to help old people in the local area.' I realised that I couldn't fit any more clothes in my wardrobe. So, I decided to throw out **those** that I didn't wear any more.'
We can also avoid repetition in a number of other ways.	He liked the film, and **so did I**. Sally doesn't want to go to Paris, and **neither does** Jenny. She asked me to finish the report, but I'd already **done so**. 'Are you ready?' 'I **think so**.' 'Do you think he'll break down on the stage?' 'I **hope not**. 'I'm hoping Ian will be able to come on Saturday. **If not**, we'll arrange it for another date.' 'They say it's going to be hot at the weekend. **If so**, let's go to the beach.'

Unit 14 Gaia's legacy

14.1 Unreal tenses

> **Remember:** The unreal past is also sometimes called the past subjunctive.

The unreal past is used to express:	
Unfulfilled or impossible conditions (**If …**) Present and past	If you **were** to listen you'd know what I mean. **Were** I to go back in time, I would probably visit the Jurassic era. If I **had passed** the exam … / **Had** I **passed** …
Wishes and regrets (**wish/if only**) Present and past	I wish I **were** rich enough to buy my own house. If only we **had been** more careful. I wish I **had paid** more attention in class.

Unreal comparisons (*as if/as though*)	The earth looked *as if* it **were** a single living being. It looked *as though* the whole forest **had been** destroyed.
Advice, suggestions and complaints (*it's time*)	*It's time* we **did** something about global warming. *It's high time* the polluters **were held** accountable. *It's about time* you **took** responsibility for your actions.
Preference (*would + rather/sooner/prefer*)*	I'd rather/sooner you **left/didn't leave/hadn't left**. I'd prefer it if you **left/didn't go/hadn't left**.

> *** Remember:** With ***would + rather / sooner***, when the subject is the same in both clauses, we use the bare infinitive. For example, I *would rather / sooner **live** in the country*. With ***would + prefer***, when the subject is the same in both clauses, we use the full infinitive. For example, *I would prefer **to go** out*.

Suppose and *imagine*	*Imagine* you **won** the lottery! *Suppose* you **met** someone you really liked! *Imagine* **I'd never met** you.

Unit 15 Our global village

15.1 Adverbial clauses

Types of adverbial clauses

Adverbial clauses give information about the circumstances of the event described by the verb in the main clause. There are many different types of adverbial clause: clauses of time, clauses of place, clauses of manner, clauses of comparison, clauses of cause or reason, clauses of purpose, clauses of result, clauses of condition and clauses of concession.

Time	I'll meet you **when** I've finished.	Purpose	She smiled **so that** I'd feel welcome.
Place	She wanted to know **where** I'd been.	Result	It got **so** hot **that** I couldn't concentrate.
Manner	She asked me **how** I had done it.	Condition	**If** I'd known you'd be late, I'd have started without you.
Comparison	It was as bad **as** I'd feared.	Concession	She won the game **although** she'd never played before.
Cause/reason	I walked fast **because** it was late.		

Clauses of time

after, since, ever since, once, before, now	**After** leaving the house she went straight to the station. **Once** she got on the train she relaxed. **Before** the train left, she looked out of the window.
while/whilst, as	**While** the train was moving she felt safe.
immediately, as soon as, on, the minute, the moment	**As soon as** the train arrived at the station, the detective got on.
until/till	He searched the carriages **until** he spotted her.
when, whenever, by which time	**When** she noticed him it was too late.
hardly ... when, no sooner ... than	**Hardly** had he moved towards her **when** the train screeched to a halt.

> **Remember:** The future perfect becomes present perfect in a time clause. ***By the time I have found** her it may be too late.* (not *by the time I will have found her ...*)

Note on tenses: Future forms and conditionals are not used in time clauses. We use the present simple when talking about the future, or the present continuous if we need to show that an action is continuous.
When I **get** on the train I will give her your message. (not *when I will get ...*)
While I **am travelling** I will be careful. (not *while I will be travelling ...*)

Clauses of result

Consequently, therefore, as a result, so	I overslept and **therefore/consequently/as a result/so** I missed the bus.
So that/such that (*so* and *such* can be used in very formal sentences with inverted forms to precede that clauses of result)	It is **so** hot **that** I'd rather stay at home. It was **such** a hot day that I preferred to stay at home. **Such** is the damage **that** I'll need a new car. **So** badly damaged was the car **that** I had to replace it.
Clauses of result are often preceded by the expressions **so much/little** + noun, or **so many/few** + noun.	He's got **so little** money (**that**) he can't come out. She's got **so many** children (**that**) I feel sorry for her.

otherwise/or else (used to mention a consequence or result that we wish to avoid)	You'd better clean that up; **otherwise** I'll tell Mum. Give me your money **or else** you'll be sorry!

Clauses of concession

Although, though, even though, even if, despite the fact that, in spite of the fact that, notwithstanding the fact that + clause	**Although** she knew how to swim perfectly well, she was still afraid of the water.
While/whilst + -ing/subject clause Remember: **whilst** is formal or old-fashioned.	**While** believing/I believed her story, I wasn't very interested in it.
In spite of/Despite/Notwithstanding (one's) + noun/**-ing**	**In spite of** his lack of interest/his not being interested in the subject, he decided to attend the lecture.
but, yet Remember: **Yet** is slightly more formal and is sometimes preceded by a semi-colon rather than a comma.	I have been listening to the radio, **but** I'd rather read a book. I have been reading the book all morning; **yet** I have failed to understand a word.
however, nevertheless	Sandra has been researching her novel for over a year; **however**, she still hasn't started writing.
No matter how, however	**No matter how** hard I work, I never seem to finish my chores.
Adjective/adverb + **as/though**	**Tall though** he is, he can't reach the top shelf.
even so, all the same, (but) still	Yves is very smart; **even so**, he must study if he wants to do well.

Clauses of reason

The reason (why) + clause **The reason for** (object) + **-ing**	**The reason why** I dropped out of college was that I wanted to see the world. **The reason for (my)** dropping…
Due to/because of (the fact that)	**Due to the fact that** it was raining, we cancelled the picnic.
As/since/for/because	He gave me a bonus **as/since/because** I'd worked/**for working** hard.
In that/insofar	I couldn't do any work **in that/insofar as** it was far too hot.
In case	I took some extra money **in case** I needed to catch the train home.
Present participle **(that)** + clause	**Realising** that it was almost nine o'clock, I ran all the way to the theatre. **Being** the only person who could speak French, I ordered the meal. **Seeing as** it's a lovely day, let's go out.

Clauses of purpose

Full infinitive (can't be used to express negative purpose)	He stayed up all night **to complete** his project.
In order (not) to, in order that, so as (not) to	He stayed up all night **in order to/so as to** complete his project. **In order not to/So as not to** fail, he worked extra hard.
so that (+ subject + **could/would**)	He stayed up all night **so that** he could complete his project.
to avoid + gerund, **to prevent** + noun/pronoun + gerund	I have set three alarm clocks **to avoid oversleeping**. The rabbits were placed in different boxes **to prevent fighting/their fighting/them (from) fighting**.
in case, for fear of, **for fear that, lest** (formal or rare)	He wore a disguise **in case** he was followed/**for fear of** being followed/**for fear that** he might be followed/**lest** he were/was/be followed.
For + gerund/**for** + noun	Aromatherapy is good **for strengthening** the immune system. We had a water-fight **for fun**.
with a view to, with the aim of	We decided to go to Paris **with a view to/with the aim of** visiting Le Louvre.

Unit 16 Endings — and new beginnings

16.1 Making and intensifying comparisons

Making comparisons
We can make comparisons in the following ways: *Life is **easier now than** it used to be.*
*It was **more difficult** saying goodbye to friends **than** to places. I try to be **less critical** of my son **than** I used to be.*

There are also other ways of making comparisons either more descriptive, or more emphatic.

Comparing past situations with the present	She **now** has **more** time to enjoy the simple things in life. **Instead of** parkland, there is **now** an ugly shopping centre. **Where once** she had to drive 50 miles to work, she **now** walks 10 metres from the kitchen to the computer in her study. They find life **far more** enjoyable **than ever before**.
Qualifying comparisons It is possible to qualify comparisons using various words and phrases.	Computer technology has made it **considerably** easier to work or study at home. Petrol is **significantly** more expensive than it was six months ago. Pollution levels in the town are **slightly** lower than they were last year. Life is a **lot more** stressful than it used to be. There are **far fewer** families living in the villages than before. There aren't **quite** as many cars on the road as before. **The more** fruit and vegetables you eat, **the healthier** you will be.
Emphatic comparisons	**By far the hardest** thing about changing jobs is fitting in with your new colleagues. **Nothing compares to/with** the joy of having your first child. The journey up the mountain was exciting enough, but **that was nothing compared to/with** skiing down it. Your mobile phone is **nowhere near** as impressive as mine. Fran's painting was the best in the class, **by a long way**.
So and such	I'd never seen **such a** big garden as that one. The show wasn't **so** spectacular **as** we'd expected. When choosing a place to live, it's **not so much** the position that's important **as** who your neighbours are going to be.

How is **so** used in the second sentence below?
Her house is **as** spacious **as** John's.
My new curtains are **not so** well made **as** the old ones.

Forms of comparison for adjectives and adverbs	
comparative + **than**	*Bob is **cleverer than** Jim.*
the + superlative + **in/of**	*... the most expensive in the shop.*
the superlative to mean **very**	*Her decision was **most** irregular!*
-**er** and -**er**/**more** and **more** + adj	*I wake up **earlier** and **earlier**.*
the + comparative, **the** + comparative	*... the longer you wait. the harder it will be.*
as ... **as**	*Sally is **as** spoilt **as** Matthew.*
less ... than, more ... than, not so/as ... as	*Paul is **not so** relaxed **as** his brother.*
any/no + comparative	*You aren't **any smarter** than me.*
prefer, would prefer, would rather, would sooner	[covered in unit 14]
Too/enough/very	
too + adjective/adverb	*This exercise is **too hard** for me to do on my own.*
much too + adj/adv	*You've been working **much too hard**! Have a rest!*
too much + noun	*The neighbours are making **too much** noise. I can't sleep!*
adjective/adverb + **enough**	*It isn't **warm enough** to go swimming in the sea today.*
enough + noun	*Is there **enough room** in the car for one more?*
very + noun	*He is the **very person** I want to talk to.*
Like/as	
like for similarities	*He swims **like** a fish.*
as	*He works **as** a nurse.*
as	*You should do **as** you're told.*
Qualifying/intensifying comparisons	
a bit/a little	*James is a **little** less shy than his sister.*
slightly	*This cake is **slightly** sweeter than the last one you made.*
much	*Katie's **much** friendlier than Karen.*
a lot	*It's **a lot** hotter in the Bahamas than here.*
far	*The owners of this hotel **are far** less welcoming than the last one I stayed in.*

Writing Guide

Informal letter or email

Narrative or descriptive writing

Part one: 180–220 words
Part two: 220–260 words

PART 2

> A friend of yours is looking for a summer job and has asked you to suggest a good job based on your experiences. Write a letter to your friend describing a temporary job you had and saying why you would recommend it.

Write your **letter**. You do not need to include postal addresses. (220–260 words)

Dear Jeanette,

Thanks for your email. I'm glad to hear that you've decided to take a year out between school and university to get some work experience. I found it was very useful and I started my university studies the following year feeling refreshed and enthusiastic!

If you remember I worked last year on a sailing yacht. I've always loved the sea, so it wasn't difficult for me to decide what I wanted to do. I didn't have much experience but it didn't matter. I completed a basic sailing course and learned how to be a useful member of a ship's crew. Then I got myself a job on a sailing yacht in the Caribbean!

I can't say the money was great, but I did benefit from the experience and made a lot of friends. I also got to see a part of the world I probably wouldn't have seen otherwise, and most of the time it was like a working holiday! We saw dolphins and once we even saw whales! On the whole it was an unforgettable experience. By the end of the summer I had learned so much about sailing that I did a course when I got home, got my skipper's certificate, and now I can charter a sailing yacht whenever I want, anywhere in the world!

So my recommendation to you would be to do something similar if you are looking for good experiences and plenty of laughs! But only if you don't get seasick!

Let me know how it goes. All the best,

Jimmy

ALTERNATIVE QUESTION (PART 1)

> An aunt of yours wants to buy a nice present for your parents, whose wedding anniversary is coming up soon. She has asked you to suggest a suitable present and to say why you think it would be appreciated by both of them. Write a letter to your aunt describing a possible gift and saying why you would recommend it.

Write your **letter**. You do not need to include postal addresses. (180–220 words)

Planning a letter / Descriptive or narrative writing

1 **Brainstorm ideas**: try to come up with several possible answers.

2 **Write an outline**: make sure you answer both parts of the question.

3 **Paragraph plan**: make sure you link ideas appropriately.

4 **Write your letter**: remember to include descriptive vocabulary.

5 **Check your work**: for spelling, punctuation and grammatical errors.

A letter or email in CAE involves answering according to a situation outlined in the question you are given. You must reply in a way which is appropriate for your (imagined) reader.

Review

Part two only: 220–260 words

> A tourist agency is updating its website, and has asked its customers to send in reviews of holidays they have had. You decide to write about a holiday you went on recently. Describe the place and type of holiday, what you really enjoyed about it, and if there was anything you disliked. Then say who you would recommend the holiday to, and why.

Write your **review.** (220-260 words)

Planning your review

1 Brainstorm ideas: Which holiday are you going to write about? What aspects of it did you particularly enjoy? Did anything unexpected or unpleasant happen? Who would you recommend it to and why?

2 Style and register: Check who the target reader is to decide whether your review should be formal or informal, and whether your style should be lively or remain fairly neutral.

3 Paragraphs: Use the points mentioned in the question to help you organise your answer into paragraphs.

4 Check your work.

A review in CAE is usually written for an English-language website, magazine or newspaper. You usually need to describe an experience or express a personal opinion about something. You need to give your reader a clear impression of what the item described is like.

One way of really relaxing and getting away from it all is to take a canal boat along the Canal du Midi, in the south of France. My family and I did just that this summer, and discovered how pleasant it can be to travel in the slow lane for a while.

Introduction. State what you're going to write about.

Being inexperienced boaters, my parents felt uncomfortable about trying to manoeuvre a large boat, and opted for a 30-foot canal cruiser. In fact, they needn't have worried, because the company provided us with excellent instruction before we set off, and it was a lot easier than we'd expected. Even my brother and I had a go!

We spent a wonderful week gliding along the beautiful waterways of Languedoc and the Camargue. The facilities on board were excellent, and any worries we'd had of getting bored were soon forgotten about, as every day proved to be an adventure. We'd spend three to four hours cruising each day, before stopping to explore places inland. We passed through pretty little villages, practised our appalling French on the amused locals, and saw some fascinating wildlife. The highlight of the holiday, however, was the nautical jousting tournament held in the seaside port of Sete. This was great fun, and the town was buzzing with excitement.

Use a range of descriptive vocabulary to convey your attitude.

Looking back, I think we'd all agree that we should have booked a bigger boat. Thirty feet for four people can be rather cramped. Nevertheless, I'd definitely recommend this trip to anyone who really needs to unwind for a while.

Remember to include a recommendation in your concluding paragraph.

ALTERNATIVE QUESTION

> Your local bookshop wants to run a special promotion of children's books. The manager has asked customers to send reviews of their favourite children's book, to appear on the shop's website. You decide to write a review of the book you most enjoyed reading as a child, saying why you enjoyed it so much and who you would recommend should read it.

Write your **review.** (220-260 words)

Formal letter: Letter of application

Part one: 180–220 words
Part two: 220–260 words

PART 1

Planning a formal letter

1 Analyse the question: Who is the target reader? What is your reason for writing? What information must you include?

2 Style and register: Make sure your language is appropriate for the specific question, and that your tone remains fairly neutral and polite.

3 Write your answer: Make sure you address all the points in the question.

4 Check your work: Remember the number of words required differs in part one and part two.

The advertisement below appeared in an English Language magazine. Read the advertisement, and the notes you have written on it, and, using the information given, write a letter of application.

Writers!

We are updating our popular 'Connections' website, and need writers to contribute regularly to our blog, presenting articles of interest to young people worldwide. Successful candidates will have some writing experience, and show an awareness of young people's interests and concerns.
Send us an application, electronically, or by post, explaining why you think you are suitable, and describing two or three subjects you would like to write about.

school magazine – bullying, safety on the Net, exam stress

students – more active role in addressing issues

problems in multi-cultural classroom; environmental feature?

Write your **letter of application**. You do not need to include postal addresses. (180–220 words)

Dear Sir/Madam,

I am writing in response to your advertisement in the 'English Today' magazine, asking for people to contribute to the blog on your website, 'Connections'.

I am a student in my final year at school, and have written various articles for our school magazine, on such subjects as child safety on the Internet, exam stress and bullying, samples of which you will find in the attachment I've included. I feel quite strongly that these issues need to be addressed, not only by teachers and parents, but by the student body as a whole. We need to take more active responsibility for our actions and those of our peers.

For this reason, I feel that your blog could offer young people the opportunity to reach out to people in other countries, and would welcome the opportunity to contribute to promoting a greater understanding between multi-national groups. One of the issues I would like to address on the blog is the problems which sometimes arise in the multi-cultural classroom, and I would also like to examine the possibility of setting up a regular environmental feature.

I would therefore be grateful if you could consider my application, and accept me as a contributing writer. I look forward to hearing from you.

Yours faithfully,
Razia Azad

USEFUL FORMAL LETTER WRITING PHRASES

Opening: Dear Sir/ Madam..., Dear Mrs Smith... To whom it may concern [usually for writing a reference]

Main paragraphs: I am writing in response to your advertisement / announcement etc ...
I am writing with regard to ...
I am interested in applying for the post of ...
I would like to enquire about / apply for etc ...
I feel strongly that not only is this ...

Ending: I would therefore be grateful if you could ...,
I would appreciate it if you could ...
I look forward to hearing from you.
Yours sincerely / Yours faithfully

ALTERNATIVE QUESTION (PART 2)

You have seen the following advertisement in a magazine:

Volunteers required!

We need young, enthusiastic people to help at our Recreational Centre for Children with Special Needs. Duties will involve organising and participating in games, dancing and painting classes. Previous experience is preferable, but not essential. It is more important that applicants love children, and enjoy being involved in lively, sometimes messy activities. Patience, and a willingness to work as part of a team are essential.
Applications should be sent to Mrs Trixie Anderson.

Write your **letter of application**. You do not need to include postal addresses. (220–260 words)

Article

Part one: 180–220 words
Part two: 220–260 words

> You read the following announcement in a family lifestyle magazine.

VIDEO and COMPUTER GAMES

A recent survey has shown us that video and computer games are very popular, especially with young people. We are interested to know why. We would like you, the readers, to submit articles explaining why you think these games are so popular in general and describing the best video or computer game you have ever played.
We will publish the most interesting articles.

Write your **article**. (180–220 words)

title

Who likes Video Games?

Everyone always goes on these days about how video games are ruining our health and intellectual development. But with the exception of some extreme cases, is there actually any evidence to support this?

introduction ; use a question?

answers first part of the question

I, like many young people, enjoy playing video games because they drop you into a story, give you control over events and let you interact with other characters. Video games allow you to stretch your imagination and exist for a while in a fantasy world – more immediately than a good book can. They also force you to utilise various skills simultaneously. Tests have shown that playing video games from an early age actually strengthens hand-eye coordination and stimulates brain development. Many video games require the player to make logical decisions, or emotional choices, which help to develop brain function in a way that watching TV never can.

The best video game I have ever played is 'Ratchet and Clank'. Ratchet is a weird rabbit-like creature from a far off world, who befriends a small robot with useful skills. Together they fly off in a space rocket to different planets, on each of which they are given a mission to complete. It's fast-paced, exciting, colourful and hugely imaginative!

Answers second part of the question.

conclusion / statement / message.

However, I'm not saying that all video games are good, or for everyone. Certainly we should draw the line at violent or unethical game scenarios and we should limit the hours spent playing to a reasonable number to avoid the consequences of sitting in front of a screen all day.

ALTERNATIVE QUESTION

You read the following announcement in a family lifestyle magazine.

EXOTIC PETS

A recent survey has shown us that exotic pets such as snakes, lizards and spiders are very popular with some people. We are interested to know why. We would like you, the readers, to submit articles explaining why you think these animals are so popular and describing the exotic animal that you think makes the best pet.
We will publish the most interesting articles.

Write your **article**. (220–260 words)

An article in CAE is usually written for an English-language newspaper or magazine. You should assume that the reader has similar interests to you. To keep it interesting, your article should express a personal opinion or comment which will engage your reader.

Planning an essay

1 **Brainstorm ideas:** What kind of essay is it: For and against? Opinion? or Development of an Argument? Make sure you brainstorm points to answer the question.

2 **Write an outline or paragraph plan:** What will you say in your main body paragraphs? Think about your introduction and conclusion also.

3 **Write your essay:** Use linking words and examples if necessary to make your argument stronger or your points clearer.

4 **Check your work.**

USEFUL LINKING PHRASES

To introduce: It is often said that ... Many people believe / claim that ... Everyone often says / mentions / claims / goes on ...

To add points: Also, Moreover, Furthermore, Secondly, On the one hand ...

To contrast points: However, Alternatively, Nevertheless, In contrast, On the other hand, whereas, while, Despite the fact that ...

To introduce a result: For which reason, Subsequently, which is why, As a result of this / which ...

To conclude: Therefore, To sum up, On balance, To Conclude, In conclusion, Consequently, Finally ...

A CAE essay is usually written for a teacher. It may follow up on a classroom activity. It should be well-organised, with an introduction, clear development and appropriate conclusion.

Essay

Part two only: 220–260 words

> You have recently had a lesson on environmental issues. One of the topics discussed was how life would be without cars. Your teacher has asked you to write a follow-up essay on the topic entitled: 'Should Cars Be Banned?' giving your reasons for and against.

Write your **essay.** (220–260 words)

Should cars be banned?

With an environmental crisis looming over us, and much of it caused by carbon dioxide emissions, many people have started asking what we can do about it. One of the most extreme questions to be asked is whether cars should be banned entirely from our towns and cities.

Unfortunately, we live in a vehicle-dependent society. We use cars to get to and from our work, our schools, our friends and all basic amenities. We often don't think twice about taking our car one mile down the road instead of cycling or walking. More than that, to many, the car is a status symbol that defines our position in society. To ban the car completely from our society would be a huge shock and many people wouldn't like it.

On the other hand, think of the benefits. If there were no cars we would live free of air and noise pollution, traffic congestion, parking problems and dangerous accidents. Naturally, we would be forced to live and work in a more local environment, but this would be good for communities. Let's not forget this is how people always lived before the car was invented. We would walk, cycle or use public transport more – perhaps we may even return to using horses – and the potential benefits to our health and the environment are obvious.

So maybe it's time we bit the bullet and answered (with the exception of ambulances and the emergency services): Yes, let's ban cars and look forward to a brighter future for us all.

ALTERNATIVE QUESTION

> You have recently had a lesson on social issues. One of the topics discussed was how dangerous smoking is to our health. Your teacher has asked you to write a follow-up essay on the topic entitled: 'Should Smoking be Banned?' giving your reasons for and against.

Write your **essay.** (220–260 words)

Report

Part one: 180–220 words
Part two: 220–260 words

PART 2

You are an independent business consultant. The owner of a bookshop has asked you to investigate why sales are falling. You have examined various aspects of the business, including the interior design of the premises and the threat of competition in the area. Write a report to the owner based on your findings, and make recommendations for improvements.

Write your **report**. (220–260 words)

Introduction

This report presents the findings of my research into why business in the Tawny Owl bookshop is declining, and makes some recommendations for improvement.

The competition

Although the shop is ideally located in the centre of the town, it has suffered losses as a result of the opening of a large discount bookstore almost directly opposite. To combat this, one solution would be to create a series of promotions involving special-interest authors, aimed at attracting a particular section of the market each time. Book signing sessions by well-known authors are also an effective way to attract customers.

The shop premises

The shop is housed in an old building, and decorated in an old-fashioned, rather plain style. Although the shop has a wide range of books on offer, these are placed in rows of tightly packed bookshelves throughout, creating a rather dark atmosphere, and making it difficult to browse. A solution to this problem would be to remove some of the bookshelves, and open up space to create a reading area, where customers could examine books at leisure. A children's corner would also encourage busy mothers to enter the shop. The interior could be redecorated, and the shop front redesigned to create a brighter atmosphere.

Conclusion

With some investment and careful planning, the Tawny Owl could attract more customers, by offering them something different to its competitors. The key lies in offering them quality, and creating a pleasant, welcoming atmosphere.

Proposal

Part one: 180–220 words
Part two: 220–260 words

PART 1

You are a school teacher. You have received the email below from the school principal, regarding the question of raising funds to build a new science laboratory. Read the email, and the notes you have made on it, and, using the information given, write a proposal for a fundraising event.

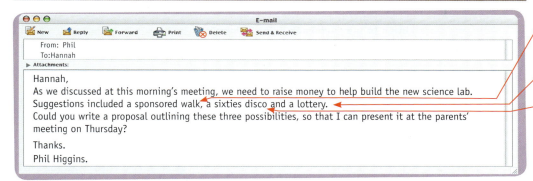

E-mail

From: Phil
To: Hannah

Attachments:

Hannah,
As we discussed at this morning's meeting, we need to raise money to help build the new science lab.
Suggestions included a sponsored walk, a sixties disco and a lottery.
Could you write a proposal outlining these three possibilities, so that I can present it at the parents' meeting on Thursday?

Thanks.
Phil Higgins.

ten miles far enough for younger students to walk – fancy dress?

local company to donate prize?

fun for some – but will shy students dance?

Write your **proposal.** (180–220 words)

Introduction
The aim of this proposal is to present the Parents and Teachers Association with suggestions to raise money for the school's new science laboratory.

A sponsored walk
One idea put forward is to organise a sponsored walk. A ten-mile route would be sufficient for younger students, and could be clearly marked out around the town. Also, to make the walk more fun, students could be dressed in fancy dress. Under careful supervision, this could be a very enjoyable fundraising event.

A sixties disco
Another suggestion is to hold a sixties disco. This has certain advantages over the walk, in that it is held indoors, so would not be affected by bad weather, and would be easier to both organise and monitor. One possible drawback, however, is that shy students may feel too inhibited to participate.

A lottery
Possibly the easiest way to raise money would be to hold a lottery. Several local businesses have kindly offered prizes to support our efforts, and so this would need little input on the part of the students.

Conclusion
One solution could be to organise all three fundraising events, to ensure that all students in the school can be involved in the scheme in some way. With careful planning and organisation, this could prove rewarding for everyone.

Planning your proposal

1 **Analyse the question: consider what it's asking you.**

2 **Plan your answer: Decide on suitable headings and points for each paragraph.**

3 **Write your answer: Remember to make, support and summarise suggestions.**

4 **Check your work.**

In a CAE proposal, you're expected to give factual information and make suggestions which will be followed by your readers.

ALTERNATIVE QUESTION

You are a representative of your school council. You have received the email below from the school principal, regarding the forthcoming visit of a group of foreign students. Read the email and the notes you have written on it, and, using the information given, write a proposal for offering the visitors a warm welcome.

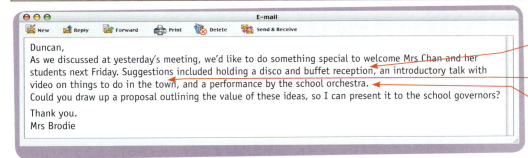

E-mail

Duncan,
As we discussed at yesterday's meeting, we'd like to do something special to welcome Mrs Chan and her students next Friday. Suggestions included holding a disco and buffet reception, an introductory talk with video on things to do in the town, and a performance by the school orchestra.
Could you draw up a proposal outlining the value of these ideas, so I can present it to the school governors?

Thank you.
Mrs Brodie

will young people talk to each other?

video of activities suitable for age level.

15-year-olds will be bored!

Write your **proposal.** (180–220 words)

Contribution to a longer piece

Part two only: 220–260 words

Write your **contribution to the guidebook.** (220–260 words)

THE TOWNS AND CITIES OF GREECE

VOLOS

LOCATION

Volos is a city of approximately 100,000 people that lies on the east coast mainland of Greece, in the Gulf of Volos (Pagasitikos Kolpos). It is approximately 325 kilometres north of Athens and 215 kilometres south of Thessaloniki.

HISTORY

Historically Volos is an interesting city because it is believed to be the place from where the legendary Jason set off in his ship, the Argo, on his quest for the Golden Fleece. As it also provides access to the central Aegean islands it has always been an important port.

VOLOS TODAY

Today Volos is a bustling modern city that sits against the backdrop of the great Pelion mountain. The main architecture consists of blocks of flats but there are some interesting older houses that date back to the time of the last major earthquake that all but flattened the city in the 1950s.

PLACES TO SEE

Visitors should pay a trip to the museum which contains artefacts from the nearby Neolithic settlement of Dimini. It is also nice to stroll along the main seafront, where there are restaurants and cafeterias, and a bronze statue of the Argo herself. The main shopping centre is also worth a visit and in the evening most locals eat at one of the many 'tsipouradika' – a type of specialised seafood restaurant that sells its own home-brewed version of an ouzo-like drink.

PLACES TO VISIT

Visitors should not pass up the chance to go beyond Volos and visit any of the beautiful mountain villages or the beautiful islands of the Sporades.

ALTERNATIVE QUESTION

Write your **contribution to the guidebook.** (220–260 words)

Competition entry

Part two only: 220–260 words

You have seen the following announcement in a sports magazine, and have decided to enter the competition:

> ## Competition to find the weirdest sport in the country!
> We want to run a feature on unusual sports. Readers are invited to nominate a sport, or sporting event, giving a brief description of how it is played, and explaining why they think it deserves to be chosen.

Write your **competition entry**. (220–260 words)

One of the strangest sports I've come across has got to be Octopush. When I heard the name, I thought it must have something to do with fishing! In fact, Octopush is a kind of underwater game of hockey.

To play, you need a mask, snorkel, a protective glove to stop your hands getting scratched on the bottom of the pool, a small, specially designed stick and a puck, which is a lead disc, rather like those used in ice hockey. There's an underwater goal at each end of the pool, and the object of the game is to flick the puck into the opposition's goal. There are six players per team, and each team is allowed four substitutes. The game must look funny to people outside the pool, due to the number of bodies splashing around under water! It's often impossible to tell who your opponents and teammates are, so to combat this, the sticks are black for one team, and white for the other.

The game is fast and physically demanding, as players have to learn to rise to the surface for air quickly before diving back down to play. It provides excellent training for your lungs, though, since you have a strong incentive to hold your breath for longer, and you learn to use your lungs more effectively.

I have no hesitation in nominating Octopush for the competition, however, as the look of disbelief on people's faces when I tell them about my new pastime is ample proof of just how weird a sport it is!

state your nomination

description of nomination

supporting example or reason to emphasise the value of your choice

concluding paragraph should reiterate your nomination, with a final good reason to support it.

Planning your competition entry

1 Brainstorm ideas: Think carefully about who or what you wish to nominate, and two or three reasons for doing so.

2 Organisation: Make a plan to organise your points into paragraphs.

3 Persuasion: The aim of this task is to persuade judges to choose your nomination, so think of examples to make your points convincing. Aim for a lively, natural style that is appropriate for the target reader.

4 Write your entry: Remember to conclude with a powerful argument in support of your nomination.

5 Check your work.

ALTERNATIVE QUESTION

You have seen the following announcement in your local newspaper, and have decided to enter the competition.

> ## Best film of the year competition!
> We are going to run a feature at the end of the year on the best films of the last twelve months. Readers are invited to nominate their favourite film, giving a brief description of its plot, and explain why they think it deserves to be chosen.

Write your **competition entry**. (220–260 words)

A competition entry is written for a judge. You will usually be expected to persuasively nominate somebody for an award or propose yourself for selection for something.

An information sheet

Part two only: 220–260 words

Planning your information sheet

1   Analyse the question: Make sure you understand what you are being asked for. What are the functions: describing, explaining, giving advice etc?

2   Headings and paragraphs: Decide if you want to use headings and brainstorm suitable ideas that answer the points outlined in the question.

3   Style and register: Pay attention to your register. How formal, neutral or informal your information sheet is will depend on who you are writing it for and the intended audience.

4   Write your information sheet: Keep your sentences short, sharp and to the point. Use appropriate vocabulary wherever possible.

5   Check your work: Have you done what you were asked to do? Have you written enough? If you have written under 220 words you will be penalised so make sure you are between the indicated word counts.

An information sheet for CAE is written for readers who need instruction, information or help in an area. You should write clearly and factually. Usually you'll also be expected to offer some advice on the topic as well.

> The local council has set up a youth centre in your town and you have been asked to write an information sheet to distribute. You should explain what the youth centre is for, who can go there, its facilities, what activities will be on offer and mention its location, opening times and cost.

Write your **information sheet**. (220–260 words)

LOCAL YOUTH CENTRE OPENS

WHAT IT IS
The youth centre is a non-profit-making facility that has been established with the aim of offering a place for young people to go outside of school hours, where they will be able to engage in various social and leisure activities.

WHO IT'S FOR
The youth centre is available to anyone between the ages of 10 and 17. Children under 10 can join the Play Centre but must be accompanied by an adult.

FACILITIES
The youth centre has a sports room, reading room, a cafeteria and a lounge. There are separate washroom facilities for boys and girls and a cloakroom. There is also access for the disabled.

ACTIVITIES
Youth club members can engage in any of the following activities: ping pong (table tennis), snooker, pool, cards, board-games and darts. They can also read in the reading room although books cannot be taken home. Outdoor activities include tennis and basketball. Timetabled events such as debate meetings and dance classes will also be arranged and information about these will be posted on the central notice board.

FURTHER INFORMATION
Three attendants will be on full-time duty. The price for admission is 1.50 euro. The cafeteria charges at cost-only prices. Extra activities may be charged separately. All visitors must sign in and out of the youth centre and all equipment must be returned after use.

OPENING TIMES AND LOCATION
The youth centre is located on Wirral Street opposite the park. Opening hours are Monday – Friday (4pm–9pm) and Saturdays and Sundays (9am–5pm)

ALTERNATIVE QUESTION

> A local environmental group has arranged a 'Rubbish Clear Up Day' in your area, and you have been asked to write an information sheet to distribute. You should explain why it is important to clear up certain areas (such as countryside, rivers or beaches), who can volunteer, and what they can expect to do. Mention the date, time and meeting point for the day in question also.

Write your **information sheet**. (220-260 words)

Speaking Reference Files

Unit 2

- Are these activities suitable for small children?
- How might the children be feeling?

- At what age are these activities legal in your country?
- How might the people in the pictures be feeling?

193

- Which of these suggestions would make good improvements for the sports centre?
- Which suggestion would attract more people to the sports centre?

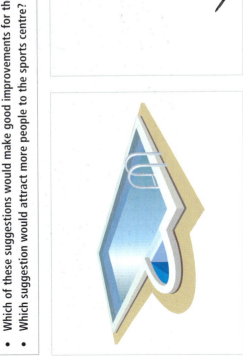

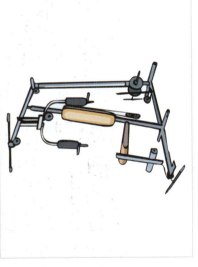

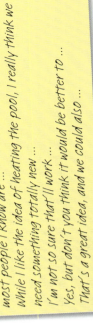

USEFUL LANGUAGE

Making suggestions and responding to ideas
Try to vary your language when discussing ideas. Avoid repeating phrases your partner uses. Use the following to help you:

Suggestions
It might be a good idea to …
One solution is to …
Another possibility is to install …
What about building …

Responding
The new cafe may be popular, but I'm not sure about …
The climbing wall might be attractive to some people, but most people I know are …
While I like the idea of heating the pool, I really think we need something totally new …
I'm not so sure that I'll work …
Yes, but don't you think it would be better to …
That's a great idea, and we could also …

- Can food affect our mood?
- How might these people be feeling?

- How can exercise help people to stay healthy?
- How might the people be feeling?

- How might these monuments have been important?
- Which is the most interesting to visit?

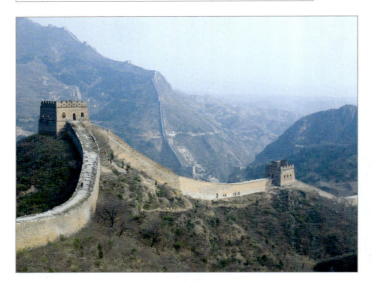

Unit 10

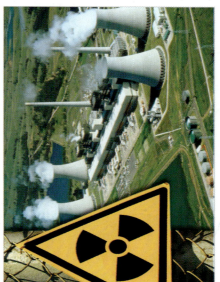

A How might these forms of food production affect your health / the environment?

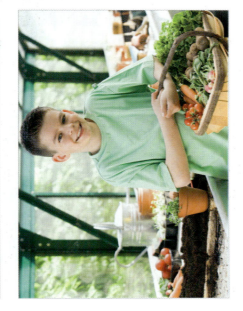

B How might these forms of energy production affect your health or the environment?

197

- Which different aspects of the film industry are depicted?
- Which picture best depicts the film industry?

Ethically Chic – clothes you won't feel ashamed to wear

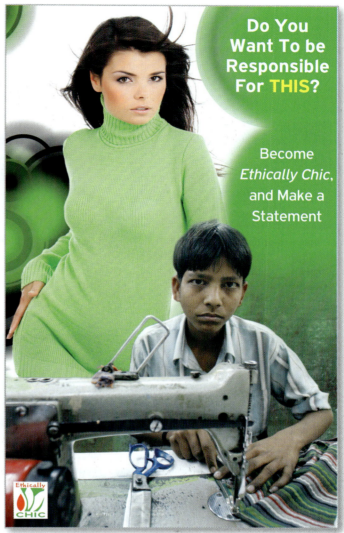

Do You Want To be Responsible For THIS?

Become *Ethically Chic*, and Make a Statement

You can dress ETHICALLY and still be CHIC

- How do these animals reflect what is happening to animal species?
- Which of these animals would you prefer to try to save from extinction?

Status: Critically endangered

Yangtze river dolphin: the most endangered cetacean, probably already extinct; population: between one and ten individuals, although none have been seen for several years.

Long-beaked echidna: one of the most primitive egg-laying mammals; population: 30,000 individuals. One species already thought to be extinct.

Sumatran rhinoceros: smallest and most endangered of all rhino species; population: around 300 individuals are thought to remain.

Bactrian camel: probably the ancestor of all domestic two-humped camels; population: fewer than 1000 individuals live in the world's most hostile desert.

Mediterranean monk seal: considered the world's most endangered marine mammal; population: 400-500 individuals.

California condor: classified as a member of the order *Falconiformes* (*eagles, hawks, and vultures*), the condor is classified as a critically endangered species due to an estimated population of fewer than 50 mature individuals.

Yellow tailed woolly monkey: thought to be extinct until its rediscovery in 1974; population: fewer than 250 individuals are thought to survive today.

Blue whale: the largest mammal ever known to have lived; population: approximately 5000 individuals.

USEFUL LANGUAGE: THINKING OUT LOUD

Well, it's not exactly my favourite animal but ...
While it may not be the cutest looking animal, I think ...
At first glance I would have to say that ...
We shouldn't ignore the fact that ...
If we don't do something now ...
Personally, I think the greater cause is ...
I think we have to consider various aspects ...
I know I said... but on second thoughts ...
Forget what I said before ... I now think ...
Taking everything into consideration ...

- B Which kitchen would you choose for your own house, and why?
- A Which design do you like least? Why?

Information Files

Unit 1
Getting started (page 1)

File 1.1 Answers to General knowledge quiz, exercise 2

1 **b** protest against nuclear testing. Motivated by a vision of a peaceful and environmentally-secure world, a small team of activists set sail in 1971 to Amchitka, a tiny island off the coast of Alaska. There, the United States were conducting underground nuclear tests. These protestors were the founders of Greenpeace.

2 **c** Germany. This was the eighteenth World Cup, the quadrennial international football world championship tournament. It was held from 9 June to 9 July 2006 in Germany.

3 Christopher Columbus set off on his voyage of discovery to …
b find another trade. Although Europe had long enjoyed a safe passage to China and India (for goods such as spices and silks), the land route was becoming increasingly perilous.

4 **a** 1911. The ship was launched on 31st May 1911 from Queen's Island, Belfast. She began her maiden voyage on 10th April 1912 from Southampton. She sank at 2.20 am on April 15th off the coast of Newfoundland.

5 **a** South Africa. In the first multi-racial democratic elections in South Africa's history, Mr. Mandela was elected President in 1994.

6 **c** ancient Greece. The concept of democracy first appeared in Ancient Greek political and philosophical thought. The philosopher Plato contrasted democracy, the system of 'rule by the governed', with the alternative systems of monarchy, oligarchy and timarchy.

Unit 4
Getting started (page 31)

File 4.1 Answers to General science quiz

1c The Milky Way has four spiral arms radiating out from a central cluster of stars or 'nucleus'. Our solar system is located on one of the spiral arms, quite far from the centre.

2a A shark's skeleton is made of cartilage – a material somewhat softer and more flexible than bone.

3b Mercury (or quicksilver) forms a liquid at room temperature. It is poisonous.

4c The process occurs in the Earth's crust and produces natural diamonds.

5c A large meteorite is now believed to have collided with the earth at the end of the Cretaceous period, some 65 million years ago. It probably struck near Mexico's Yucatan peninsula. The climate change which resulted from the collision caused the extinction of the dinosaurs.

6b Darwin was extremely curious about the many unusual flora and fauna that he observed in the Galapagos Islands.

7c So far, androids exist only in science fiction; engineers cannot yet build a robot that comes anywhere near human appearance or behaviour.

8a Sirius belongs to the constellation Canis Major (the Big Dog).

Unit 3
Getting started (page 21)

File 3.1 How game are you?

Quiz

Answer the following questions as truthfully as possible.

1 What would you do if you saw someone stealing an old lady's purse?
   A Ignore it and carry on with what you were doing.
   B Shout 'stop, thief!' and chase after him.
   C Telephone the police.

2 You are offered a free lesson in kite land-boarding. Do you …
   A say 'Thanks, but no thanks'?
   B immediately accept?
   C find out a little more about it before accepting?

3 You see some boys bullying a smaller boy. Do you …
   A do nothing, and walk away?
   B go to help him?
   C go and get someone to stop them?

4 You are offered a place on an expedition to the South Pole. Do you …
   A politely decline?
   B start packing your bags?
   C ask for some time to think about it?

Answers to *How game are you?*

If you answered all B, you are very daring, and a little reckless!

If you answered all C, you are game, but more cautious, thinking about safety.

If you answered all A, you are not daring at all, and try to avoid trouble at all costs.

If you answered with a combination of B and C, you are daring, but consider safety occasionally.

If you answered with a combination of A and C, you only take risks in certain situations.

Unit 11

Getting started (page 105)

File 11.1 Answers to Money management quiz

If you chose mainly A as your answer, you are very cautious about money. You like to be in control of it.

If you chose mainly B as your answer, you are fairly careful. However, you do want to enjoy yourself as well!

If you chose mainly C as your answer, you are careless with money, so watch out!

Unit 15

Getting started (page 147)

File 15.1 Answers to the General knowledge quiz

1a A *piñata* is a brightly-coloured paper container, usually in the shape of an animal, and it is filled with sweets, fruit or toys, and suspended on a rope from a tree or somewhere high. Then the children, who are wearing blindfolds and holding a stick, try to break them open and collect the reward.

2c At *Hallowe'en* it's customary to have pumpkins that have been hollowed out and carved with a face – usually bearing a simple crooked toothy grin. A candle is then placed inside them so that in the dark you see this orange glowing face, a jack o'lantern.

3b *Sado*, the tea ceremony, is a ritual way of preparing and drinking tea, a custom that has been strongly influenced by Zen Buddhism. Nowadays, the tea ceremony is a relatively popular kind of hobby and many people take tea ceremony lessons with a teacher.

4a *Lobola* (sometimes translated as *Bride-price*) is a traditional southern African dowry custom whereby the man pays the family of his fiancée for her hand in marriage. The custom is supposed to bring the two families together, to foster mutual respect, and show that the man can support his wife financially and emotionally.

5c *Henna* has been used to adorn young women's bodies as part of social and holiday celebrations since the late Bronze Age in the eastern Mediterranean. Many statuettes of young women dating between 1500 and 500 BCE along the Mediterranean coastline have raised hands with markings consistent with henna.

6a *The tradition of painting or decorating eggs* has existed for at least 2,500 years. The egg is widely used as a symbol of the start of new life, just as new life emerges from an egg when the chick hatches out. The egg is seen as symbolic of the grave and life renewed or resurrected by breaking out of it.

7b *Chinese New Year* or Spring Festival is the most important of the traditional Chinese holidays. It is sometimes called the Lunar New Year, especially by people outside China. The festival traditionally begins on the first day of the first lunar month in the Chinese calendar and ends on the 15th. In the Gregorian calendar, Chinese New Year falls on different dates each year, a date between January 21 and February 20.

Unit 16

Reading (page 158)

File 16.1

Where did she actually end up? Here! In a water-lily pool in Bali.

Tapescript

Unit 1

Listening 1.1

Husband: Mandy! This one sounds good for Joey.

Mandy: Go on, then. What have you found?

Husband: 'A Child's First Clock ... Most children don't learn how to tell the time until they are in first grade, or beyond, but with this lovely 'no-numbers-needed' clock, even toddlers can learn the basics of timekeeping.'

Mandy: Mm. Sounds interesting. Tell me more...

Husband: 'Developed by two mothers – a children's television presenter Noni Anderson and artist Alison Perrin – the woodland clock features a slow painted turtle for the hour hand, a faster grey rabbit for the minute hand, and a speedy red-breasted robin on the second hand' ... Blah, blah, blah. 'You can assemble a clock much like ours by printing out the art materials attached, and applying them to a clock from a do-it-yourself kit.' So, Mandy, what do you think? Shall we download the attachment?

Listening 1.2

Woman 1: So, what's brought this on, then?

Woman 2: Yeah, well, Bill's just had enough of living in the city. It's all the stress, you know. Not only at the office itself, but when he's to-in' and fro-in' in all that traffic! He's just sick of it. So, he suddenly decided to pack it all in, and make a fresh start. So, we're off to the Isle of Man, in the middle of the Irish Sea. Middle of nowhere, if you ask me! Still, at least it's not like moving abroad. He's taking up sheep farming, of all things! God knows if it'll work. But you know Bill, when he sets his mind to something, there's no stopping him.

Woman 1: Well, I never! It seems a bit drastic, though.

Woman 2: He reckons it'll be good for us, like starting over. All I can think of is sitting alone, with the wind howling outside. I mean, how many people stay there in the winter? We're used to the noise of the traffic. But, I've told 'im I'll give it a go. Who knows, it may be the making of us!

Listening 1.3

Oliver: So, what do you think of our ideas, Jane?

Jane: Well, overall, quite acceptable, Oliver, but I'm not happy about some of the omissions. I mean, ignoring the details in the first two chapters means that members of the audience who haven't read the book will be left in the dark. They won't understand the reasons behind the protagonist's actions in the film.

Oliver: Yeah, but most people have read the book! It was a blockbuster, after all!

Jane: We shouldn't take that for granted, though. I feel that, as it stands, your proposal threatens to focus too much on action and special effects, leaving little room for character development.

Oliver: Huh! Yeah, well, you know, this is only a rough outline of the scenes, as yet...

Jane: OK. But, personally, I would prefer the opening scene to include some sense of Jim's confusion and fear about what he's about to do.

Oliver: OooKaay!... But don't you think hitting the audience with the murder straight away creates suspense?

Jane: Perhaps. But it also looks like a cold-blooded, calculated murder rather than ... Look, I don't know what you got out of the book, but I wrote a psychological thriller, Oliver, and I'd like some element of the psychology to come through in the film, and not just the thriller aspect! Jim's character is a complex one, and your plans for him threaten to reduce it to a wooden stereotype!

Listening 1.4

Teacher: OK, let's brainstorm some ideas. What new experiences have you had that you clearly remember?

Student A: I tried bungee jumping once. I'll never forget that!

Student B: Really? That must have been terrifying. I don't even like heights. But I did travel to America – a totally new experience for me.

Teacher: Good – don't forget you also need to tell us why it was memorable or significant for you.

Student B: I was very impressed by the lifestyle there and I decided I wanted to improve my English enough to go and study over there.

Teacher: Excellent! What about you Vasilis?

Student C: I've been swimming with dolphins in the water. It was amazing. I would love to write about that, because it made me respect animals and nature.

Teacher: How wonderful! I can't wait to read about it. Massimo, what about you?

Student D: I, er, haven't had any new or exciting experiences that I can think of.

Teacher: Well ... maybe you could make one up?

Student D: Mm, well I suppose I could say I have been to a rock concert.

Teacher: Yes, and why would that have been memorable or significant to you?

Student D: Er – I could say that it changed my life and made me want to become a rock star.

Student A: Oh, I almost forgot. I have flown in a helicopter too.

Teacher: Well, we've certainly got a few ideas there.

Listening 1.5

Teacher: OK, so you've brainstormed some ideas for your writing and chosen one. Now we need to outline the structure. What's the best way of doing that?

Student D: With paragraphs?

Teacher: That's right, Massimo. But you need to have an idea about what to say in each paragraph, and they should link together well. What's an easy way to do that?

Student D: You need to decide what the main purpose is of each paragraph.

Teacher: Good. Claudine, what would be the main purpose of the first paragraph?

Student A: Um, I think I would have to write about what made me decide to go bungee jumping in the first place.

Teacher: OK, so for planning purposes, we could say: 'What led to the experience.' What else could you call that ... Svetlana?

Student B: I would talk about how I prepared for my journey to America, and the hopes and fears I had.

Teacher: Good, so you could write about the preparations and the background to the experience then. Right, now, what about the main body of our piece? What would we need to focus on?

Student C: It would have to be about the experience itself. Describing it, our feelings, what happened.

Teacher: Very good Vasilis, and very important too. And what mustn't we forget?

Student B: An ending? And the reason why it was significant.

Student D: I would say what happened afterwards, and how I felt about it later, and why it changed my life.

Teacher: Excellent – so a good, strong concluding paragraph. Now we're getting somewhere.

Unit 2

Listening 2.1

Man: I remember the time we went to the seaside for the day. Er, I must have been about eight. We had to clamber over rocks to get to the beach, with Father heaving this huge picnic basket all the way. Mother was worried he would fall, slide down into the sea and get the sandwiches wet, so she kept shouting instructions to him. The funny thing was that when we eventually sat down to eat, a huge, wet dog bounded up to us and sprayed sand and water all over the sandwiches, so they were spoiled anyway!

We kids didn't care, though, and had a great time. My brother and I wrestled with each other on the sand, and played football with Father, while the girls went skipping off down to the water's edge to look for shells. Mother – not much of a swimmer – paddled in the shallows, while Father boldly waded out into deep water and showed off his swimming skills. Then both of them returned to our spot on the beach, and lay down for a peaceful nap. Not for long with my brother around! He couldn't resist such a golden opportunity. So, filling a bucket with water, he tiptoed over to our dozing parents, and poured ice-cold sea water all over them! He paid for it, though, because, as he ran away, he trod on a piece of broken glass, and cut his foot! So he was forced to hop on one leg all the way back to the car, and, not only face Father's anger, but his brother and sisters' too, at having their glorious day cut short!

Listening 2.2

Anthropologist: We still don't fully understand how or why human language came about, although there are certainly a good number of theories. One main theory suggests that when men became hunters, they needed to develop a language in order to share hunting tactics with one another during the chase, despite the fact that most carnivorous animals – even those that hunt in packs – find silence to be a distinct advantage. And yet historians are agreed that the first spoken languages must have been very crude. How then could they have been of any practical use?

There is, however, one theory that proposes that it wasn't men who first used language. It wasn't even women. It was in fact children who invented it, and taught it to their parents. The truth is that fully grown adults actually lack the ability to learn to speak. Only children can do it. People that have never been exposed to any kind of spoken language before the age of five (and there are a handful of documented cases) have never been able to learn to speak at all, despite concerted efforts to teach them. Similarly, children that are born deaf may have difficulty learning to make verbal sounds because they've never heard them.

Children's natural propensity for learning languages is taken as read. They don't have to be taught their first language – they only have to hear it spoken around them. During the first four or five years of life a child can learn several languages simultaneously, without being taught, without any apparent effort.

Newborn babies all over the world have their own repertoire of involuntary sounds which are useful for communicating to the mother their most basic needs – hunger, pain or the need for attention. This is true of the young of most mammals. However, between three and four months of age the human baby begins to emit new sounds and before long, will start to 'babble'. This baby talk varies from country to country, suggesting that the baby is responding to, and trying to imitate, the sounds around him. Before long, he learns to control the sounds. He gets a response. He says 'ma' and mother responds. This could be the reason why the word for mother is so similar in almost every language. It's one of the first syllables a human child can voluntarily produce. Can we be sure that baby is really imitating mum or could it be the other way round? Next, he is inventing his own words for objects and his mother is using them too. Language is born. Perhaps this is why girls often learn to speak sooner and more fluently than boys, because at one time the ability to develop language was essential to the mother-infant relationship?

Listening 2.3

Interlocutor: Student one, here are your pictures. They show children doing different activities. I'd like you to compare two of them, and say whether you think these activities are suitable for young children, and how they might be feeling about doing them.

Interlocutor: Thank you.

Interlocutor: Student two, at what age do you think children should be allowed to do these activities?

Interlocutor: Thank you.

Listening 2.4

Interlocutor: Student one, here are your pictures. They show children doing different activities. I'd like you to compare two of them, and say how the children might be feeling.

Interlocutor: Student two, when do you think a young person is mature enough to do these activities?

Unit 3

Listening 3.1

Speaker 1: So, I said, well, I'm game, if you are. But I wish I hadn't. It was terrifying! The water flows so fast, with rocks appearing out of nowhere ... There's no time to think. I was petrified! Never again!

Speaker 2: Well, the long hours without sleep were exhausting, and the loneliness got me down occasionally, but I was determined not to give up, and would keep myself busy, by repairing sails and ropes, or sending faxes to folks back on dry land. Also, listening to music had a way of relaxing me, and was quite reassuring.

Speaker 3: That was awesome! Absolutely incredible! A real adrenalin rush! Everything happens so fast, you've got to be on your toes, and, like, keep control of both the board and the kite, otherwise you'll overturn ... and ... Man, it was so exhilarating!

Listening 3.2

Man: ... Right! That's everything. Are we ready to go?
Woman: Jane still hasn't arrived. It's not like her to be so late.
Man: She might have missed the bus.
Woman: I don't think so. She would have phoned to say she'd be late.
Man: She may have forgotten to take her mobile phone with her. You do that all the time!
Woman: Yeah, much to your annoyance! No, Jane's so organised. She wouldn't have forgotten her mobile, and even if she had, she would still be able to use a payphone! No. Something must have happened.
Man: Oh, come on, love. Don't worry so much. There's always a first time for forgetting things, you know. I'm sure it's ... [phone rings] ...There! That'll be her now!
Woman: Hello, Jane, is that you? ... Oh, sorry ... Yes ... Oh no! When? How did it happen? Yes, I'm on my way.

Listening 3.3

Speaker 1: Well, naturally, I was disappointed, but ... nothing I could do about it. Just one of those things, I suppose.

Speaker 2: Honestly, you could have told me about it beforehand. Then I wouldn't have gone to all that trouble, not to mention the expense!

Speaker 3: Who? James? Well, I wouldn't like to say, really. I mean, I don't know him all that well ... Why are you asking?

Speaker 4: Oh, don't let him worry you! He's just a nobody. Don't take any notice of him, dear.

Listening 3.4

Interviewer: ... Right! My next guest is someone who I personally admire very much. Nikos Magitsis has done it all! Whether it be climbing the highest peaks, such as Everest, trekking to the South Pole or kayaking along the coast from Alexandroupolis, on the Greek-Turkish border, to his home town of Agria in Central Greece ... a mere 505 kilometres ... You name it, he's probably done it! Niko, welcome. Tell me, how did all this start?
Nikos: Well, Tracy ... um ... I started rock climbing in nineteen eighty four, near my home town. Agria is at the foot of Pelion mountain, so there are lots of places to climb there. I trained as a .... how do you say ... P.E. teacher, and I'm not only a climbing instructor for the town council, but I also teach handball, skiing, and watersports such as kayaking and swimming in the summer months. Two summers ago, we took a group of nine teenagers and kayaked down the coast from Alexandroupolis to Agria. That was an amazing experience for all of us.
Interviewer: Wasn't it a little dangerous, being on the open sea in a canoe?
Nikos: Well, um, I suppose it was a little risky, but we were all experienced, and the kids did really well.
Interviewer: Did you see any interesting sea life on your voyage?
Nikos: We saw lots of dolphins. They liked swimming alongside us, but from a distance. Then one day, the leader thought he saw what looked like a sunken ship floating under the surface, but as we approached for a closer look, we realised it was a huge sea turtle. The guys in front were so surprised by the size of it they nearly overturned! It was an amazing feeling.
Interviewer: So, is the sea your true love?
Nikos: I enjoy being on the water, certainly ... but *climbing* is what I really love. The feeling when you're hanging from a rope, 300 metres from the ground ... There's nothing like it. It's the closest we can get to being a bird.
Interviewer: Is it easy being a member of an international team, Nikos?
Nikos: Not always. At Everest, I was the only Greek, together with an Indian woman, an American guy, two Belgians and two Japanese. That often caused misunderstandings, obviously, some amusing, some frustrating. But on the

whole, we got on well and became good friends. You're in close proximity with each other 24 hours a day, under extreme conditions ... There's going to be friction, but also you form strong bonds. Climbing is about teamwork – you have to rely on the next person holding the rope. Every mountaineer understands that, and everyone is working towards a common goal.

Interviewer: Did you experience any difficulties during the climb?

Nikos: Well, the worst thing that happened was that two of the team got very bad ... er, um ... in English it is called, er ... frostbite, and had to have the ends of two of their fingers chopped off. That meant returning to base camp for a while. But they recovered and carried on. It's one of the recognised hazards of mountaineering. Experienced climbers accept it as a risk they take.

Interviewer: I wouldn't like to have been in their shoes, though! Now, the trip to Everest was just part of a bigger project, wasn't it?

Nikos: Yes. We've just managed to complete the ascent of the 'Seven Summits', as it's known. These are the highest peaks in each continent – Everest, in Asia; Aconcagua, in South America; Denali, in North America; ... um ... Kilimanjaro, Africa; Elbros ... in Europe; Vinson, Antarctica; and Carstensz Pyramid, Papua New Guinea. The last of these proved the most difficult to climb, due to problems beyond our control, such as helicopter failure, and before that we were stopped by rebel activity in the area. However, we finally succeeded in March of this year, and it was a special achievement for me, as only eighty four people worldwide have ever climbed all seven, none of them Greek. This time, we had a tough climb in a snowstorm, but when myself and the Belgian climber, Robert Huygh, reached the top, it was a moment neither of us will ever forget. The culmination of a lifetime dream ...

Interviewer: The Seven Summits isn't the only 'first' you've achieved for your country, though, is it?

Nikos: I was the first Greek to reach the South Pole – on skis – and I had the honour of setting up my country's flag there. That felt really good!

Interviewer: Very impressive! And I believe you've written a book ...

Unit 4

Listening 4.1

Kate: Hi Sally. I wanted to tell you about what happened to me yesterday, but I don't want you to think I'm being a tell tale.

Sally: Tell you what, why don't you tell me about it and I promise I won't kiss and tell.

Kate: I'll try. But I don't want you to say 'I told you so'!

Sally: Well, you can never tell ...

Kate: I can't tell you how much it means to me that you're my friend.

Sally: As far as I can tell you're my friend too!

Kate: Yes, but only time will tell!

Listening 4.2

Interlocutor: In the future, do you think it will be essential to know how to use a computer to get a job in your country, Fernando?

Student A: No, I think there will always be a need for people who don't know how to use a computer. Computers cannot do everything – for example, we still need bus drivers, and shop assistants, farmers, erm ... craftsmen, and, although technology may help them, it's not an essential aspect of those jobs.

Interlocutor: What do you think, Maria?

Student B: I agree with that point. Er ...

Student A: And ... erm, I also think that at some point, technology will have given us all it has to offer, and after that, people will be looking for alternatives. I mean, even today, you see that more and more people actually want to cycle to work instead of driving, or go to the gym more instead of watching TV. Technology has taken over our lives so much, we are almost fed up with it. What do you think?

Student B: Yes, er ... that sounds like an interesting point. Erm ...

Interlocutor: Thank you. That is the end of the test.

Listening 4.3

Speaker 1: Well, I don't know where I'd be without it, to tell the truth. There's just no other way to get around these days, unless you want the stress and pollution brought on by driving in the city.

Speaker 2: At first, I hated them. Only the rich and pretentious seemed to have them – do you remember what they were like then? Uh, great big unwieldy things, almost the size of a briefcase. Now of course they fit in the palm of your hand and I'd be lost without one.

Speaker 3: It's probably the greatest invention of all time because just imagine where we'd be without it. I mean, there wouldn't be vehicles of any kind – except trains perhaps, but even they would have to be redesigned.

Speaker 4: It's amazing – and great fun too. First time I've actually enjoyed doing domestic chores. Marjory can get on with her writing and I just blaze round the house with my new toy!

Speaker 5: I would have to say it's the best invention till now because it offers so many opportunities for research, plus it's great for communication, and the kids can do their homework without having to go to the library.

Listening 4.4

Speaker 1: Well, I don't know where I'd be without it, to tell the truth. There's just no other way to get around these days, unless you want the stress and pollution brought on by driving in the city. I live out in the suburbs, so it's good exercise. And of course, ecologically speaking, I know I'm doing my bit to save the planet. I'm setting an example for the kids to follow as well although you do occasionally get some bright spark shouting out something clever as 'sir' goes by. Just because they're stuck on a double-decker bus in rush hour traffic.

Speaker 2: At first I hated them. Only the rich and pretentious seemed to have them – do you remember what they were like then? Uh, great big unwieldy things, almost the size of a briefcase. Now of course they fit in the palm of your hand and I'd be lost without one. I have to spend so much of my day visiting sites, negotiating with clients, co-ordinating workers and then back to the office to go over designs, or tweak a plan. I use it to check the time, do quick calculations, store reminders. And then of course wherever I am, Harry or the kids can find me if they need to tell me something or to find out what time I'll be home for dinner. In the old days they would just have to leave messages all over the place.

Speaker 3: It's probably the greatest invention of all time because just imagine where we'd be without it. I mean, there wouldn't be vehicles of any kind – except trains perhaps, but even they would have to be redesigned. Boats would be OK, but planes wouldn't be able to take off. We had to do a project on its role in world history and it's quite obvious that we'd still be stuck in the dark ages if some clever sod hadn't come up with it. I know most people would probably say the most important invention was television, or the computer, or something, but I don't think we would even have them if this hadn't come first.

Speaker 4: It's amazing – and great fun too. First time I've actually enjoyed doing domestic chores. Marjory can get on with her writing and I just blaze round the house with my new toy. Compared to our old one, this has loads of advantages. First, you don't have to carry a heavy load around the house with you; two: there are no bags to change – you just empty the bin every now and then; three: it doesn't smell out the house because the actual engine is down in the basement; and four: it's quieter too. There are several outlets in the house that automatically switch on when you plug in, but the hose is nine metres long anyway, so it reaches every corner.

Speaker 5: I would have to say it's the best invention till now because it offers so many opportunities for research, plus it's great for communication, and the kids can do their homework without having to go to the library. It provides entertainment as well as knowledge, and they enjoy it too. It keeps them off the streets, off the TV and I think they learn a lot. OK, granted, there is a downside because the doors are open to all kinds of dodgy places, but if you trust your children to know what's good for them, and they use it wisely, there's so much potential for their own development.

Unit 5

Listening 5.1

... The three main types of forensic DNA testing, then, are all extremely useful, but each has its own limitations. The first type, RFLP testing, requires large amounts of DNA from a recent sample. Therefore, old evidence from a crime scene is quite unlikely to be suitable for RFLP testing. Furthermore, warm and moist conditions usually cause DNA to become degraded quicker, so samples from crime scenes near water are unsuitable. The second type, STR testing, can be used on smaller amounts of DNA, but is still subject to the same limitations as the first type.

The third type, PCR-based testing, has certain advantages over the other two, in that it requires smaller amounts of DNA, and the sample may be partially degraded. However, it still has limitations which must not be ignored. PCR testing can easily become contaminated, both at the crime scene and in the lab. This can affect the test results, particularly if laboratory regulations are not strict.

Listening 5.2

Personally, I see the idea of a national DNA database with everyone's DNA on record as a necessary evil. Yes, it has its risks, and there would need to be strict legislation to protect people, but if it were universal, surely it would eliminate the possibility of suspects being picked out at will.

More importantly, the risk of almost certain detection would act as a powerful deterrent to first-time offenders, and so reduce the risk of innocent people becoming the victims of a violent crime.

Listening 5.3

Daniel: Since the mid-1980s, when Sir Alec Jeffreys first discovered that every human being has his or her own unique genetic makeup, DNA profiling has replaced fingerprinting as the chief forensic tool in criminal investigations. Technological advances enable new techniques for testing DNA to be developed all the time, and forensic scientists are now able to solve cases from years ago. The recent conviction of John Lloyd, who attacked a number of women between 1983 and 1986, is a case in point.

As a result of all the media attention, the discipline has come to be seen as glamorous, with forensic scientists now occupying centre stage in TV detective series, rather than detective inspectors. Many people assume that DNA testing provides unquestionable proof of a person's guilt or innocence, leaving no room for error. Yet the controversy now surrounding the case of Barry George, convicted in 2001 for the murder of TV presenter Jill Dando, brings to light a number of problems with this idealistic point of view. One of the jurors expressed doubt about the

living energy of plants. Enzymes are of vital importance to our health because without them we would get sick and many of our bodily systems wouldn't be able to function properly. We need enzymes to digest our food, to strengthen our immune systems, to flush out toxins and to regenerate our cells. In fact, clinical tests have shown that enzyme-rich diets can even help people suffering from some serious illnesses.

Interviewer: I think most people are aware that fresh fruit and vegetables are good for us. But in your book you mention that eating too much cooked food can actually be bad for us and this has caused some strong reactions. Can you tell us why you advocate reducing our intake of cooked food?

Maureen: I'm certainly not suggesting that anyone should suddenly switch to a strictly raw food diet, but most of us do rely far too heavily on cooked meals to fulfil most of our nutritional requirements, which it simply can't do because cooking destroys so many of the nutrients. Obviously, if we're always eating cooked food, then we can't be eating enough raw plant food.

Interviewer: In your book, you cite a famous experiment involving about 900 cats I think.

Maureen: Yes, that's right. Half of the cats, which were studied over four generations, were fed a diet of raw meat (which is of course the natural diet of cats), while the other half were fed cooked processed meat (tinned cat food). Within only one generation this second group had started to develop a variety of pathological problems, similar to the health problems that so often afflict even humans today. The second generation of cats suffered even more and with each subsequent generation, the problems increased so that by the fourth generation the cats were displaying all kinds of problems. Conversely the majority of cats in the first group lived healthy long lives in each generation, with very few of them developing serious illnesses.

Interviewer: But surely humans are not cats – and our bodies react differently to cooked foods?

Maureen: Yes, but we all need enzymes to digest our food, which unfortunately suffer complete and total destruction by cooking. This means we have to draw on our own limited reserve of enzymes, which puts enormous strain on our bodies. Similarly, as most people are aware, much of the vitamin content of foods is destroyed by cooking. But that's not all; a great deal of protein is damaged or destroyed when we cook our food, so that it becomes either completely useless or worse still, toxic to us.

Interviewer: Well, how are we supposed to get enough protein then?

Maureen: Well – fortunately most raw foods contain protein in easily digestible form. All nuts and beans are rich in protein, and in fact the richest source of protein is found in sprouted seeds and beans.

Interviewer: So does that mean that we don't need to worry about eating two square, home-cooked meals every day, as long as we eat a salad or some fruit?

Maureen: Well, basically, I would recommend eating plenty of raw food salads and vegetables with every meal. Further evidence is showing that the majority of our health problems are related to an ineffective immune system that has been weakened by a bad diet: too much junk food, not enough raw plant food. In fact, it is has been shown that the body's response to cooked food is to suddenly increase the number of white blood cells in our blood, something that usually happens when our bodies are attacked by alien invaders. By mixing our cooked food with at least 50 per cent raw, we can reverse this reaction and keep our immune system on standby for when it's needed.

Interviewer: So your advice to anyone who hates boiled carrots, as I do, would be ...?

Maureen: That's simple. Eat them raw!

Unit 7

Listening 7.1

Well, I think you're going to see airship hotels. You know, like cruise ships, but in the air. That's likely to be big business, because it'll be affordable for most people. Space hotels are a possibility, but they'll be pricey, so accessible only to the few. What's really taking off are eco-friendly holidays, as people are becoming more concerned about how they affect the environment. They're going to be really big, I reckon. Another thing in the offing is your holiday down under. Hydropolis is being designed for an area off the coast of Dubai, an underwater paradise, but again, this is not going to do your bank balance a lot of good. Also, we shouldn't forget that you're still going to get the traditionalist tourist who wants to see the world as it is at ground level, who still yearns to walk the streets of cities of old. You know what I mean? What I can't see happening is this so-called virtual tourism being popular. I mean, you like travel because you want to leave home for a while. That's the whole point, isn't it? I don't think computers will ever be able to really capture that feeling of excitement you get as you climb on board a plane or a ship to go somewhere new, do you?

Listening 7.2

Nick: ...You know, I think of all the places we've been to, Edinburgh was my favourite.

Fiona: Really? It's certainly one of my favourites, but compared to Prague, and Amsterdam ... I don't really think I've got one particular favourite.

Nick: No? Well, for me, Edinburgh's got it all. Amazing architecture, culture, great shops and this warm, friendly air about it.

Fiona: I have to agree with you on that point. You feel safe walking about. Perhaps because it's a small city, and everything's easy to get to. Personally though, I found the architecture rather intimidating. All those tall, stark buildings and dark stone. You can really believe all the ghost stories that come out of Scotland!

Nick: That's exactly what's so amazing about it! The setting and buildings make you feel you've walked onto a Charles Dickens film set, with their medieval and Georgian facades. Then you walk inside, and you're hit with vibrant colours and the innovative designs of modern life.

Fiona: Umm ... I think what I liked about the place most were the coffee shops and art cafes. As you say, they were colourful, but I was struck by the friendliness of the people. Did you notice how chatty everyone was? And the laughter ... I seem to remember lots of animated conversation and laughter. Fantastic!

Nick: Yes, they were very helpful, too, weren't they? And I remember the aroma of fresh coffee and bread in the shops, while outside, the crisp sea breeze left a faint taste of salt in my mouth.

Fiona: Yes ... Definitely worth a return visit, possibly around Festival time ...

Listening 7.3

Speaker 1: I've been fascinated by the universe and our place in it for as long as I can remember! As a property developer I built up a real empire here in sunny California, all the time keeping a close eye on developments in the space program. The current race to create spaceflights for tourists is particularly exciting, but no sooner had NASA announced plans for a space station than I decided I had to have a piece of that pie. Space tourism is just moments away, so why not be the first to build an orbiting space hotel? Wild, huh!? We're almost there, though!

Speaker 2: To be honest, studying the space science modules in my physics course here at university have put me right off the idea of going into orbit in a spacecraft in this day and age. Not only are there risks involved in launching, but there's also the danger of space debris ... surely that's more than enough to make me feel just fine looking at the stars with my feet placed firmly on the ground!

Speaker 3: Astronaut passengers will come to the spaceport three days prior to their flight for pre-flight training. This is to prepare them mentally and physically for the spaceflight experience, and enable astronauts to become acquainted with the spacecraft and their fellow passengers. As we speak, doctors and spaceflight specialists are developing the training programme, which will include g-force training.

Speaker 4: Space tourism, I ask you! No sooner have they made it to the moon than they start talking about commercialising space travel! Has anybody really stopped to consider the effects this is going to have on the environment? Not only on earth, but in space, too! I recently interviewed an astro-environmentalist for an article I was writing, who stressed the need to avoid making the same mistakes in space as we have on earth. What I want to know is, does anybody in authority really care about these issues, or are the potential profits to be made from commercial space travel too great?'

Speaker 5: It's been my dream since I was small, really. I used to look up at the night sky and think about what it must be like to be up there, among the stars ... And the money? Well, I know it's a lot, and I've heard all the ethical arguments about what better use it could be put to, and I agree with them all, but I think it'll be worth it. I've worked hard all my life, and it's my money! Rarely do people of my generation get the chance to fulfil such a dream. At my age, don't I have the right to have this once-in-a-lifetime experience?

Unit 8

Listening 8.1

Here are seven great reasons why you should consider building your next house with straw bales:

Reason number one: Energy efficiency. A well-built straw bale home can save you up to 75 per cent on heating and cooling costs. In fact, in most climates, we do not even install air conditioning units into our homes as the natural cooling cycles of the planet are enough to keep the house cool all summer long.

Reason number two: Sound proofing. Straw bale walls provide excellent sound insulation and are superior wall systems for home owners looking to block out the sounds of traffic or aircraft in urban environments.

Reason number three: Fire resistance. Straw bale homes have roughly three times the fire resistance of conventional homes. Thick, dense bales mean limited oxygen which, in turn, means no flames.

Reason number four: Environmental responsibility. Building with straw helps the planet in many ways. For example, straw is a waste product that is either burned or composted in standing water. By using the straw instead of eliminating it, we reduce either air pollution or water consumption, both of which impact the environment in general.

Reason number five: Natural materials. The use of straw as insulation means that the usual, standard insulation materials are removed from the home. Standard fibreglass insulation has formaldehyde in it, which is known to cause cancer. Bale walls also eliminate the use of plywood in the walls. Plywood contains unhealthy glues that can off-gas into the house over time.

Reason number six: Aesthetics. There is nothing as calming and beautiful as a straw bale wall in a home. Time and time again I walk people through homes and they are immediately struck by the beauty and the "feeling" of the walls. I really can't explain this one, you'll just have to walk through your own to see what I mean.

Reason number seven: Minimise wood consumption. If built as a 'load bearing assembly', which can support a roof, the wood in the walls can be completely eliminated, except for around the windows. The harvesting of forests is a global concern and any reduction in the use of wood material is a good thing for the long term health of the planet.

Listening 8.2

Interviewer: So what interests you most about your work?

Man: Well, being able to create something that has real value is the main thing. I mean, it's great to be an artist or a sculptor and I'm certainly not belittling the value of fine art in society, but it's a totally different feeling knowing that what you create will have real practical value. I mean, people actually live in your creations! And of course, egotistically speaking, it's a chance to make a real mark on the landscape, something that can probably be seen for miles around.

Interviewer: Sometimes that's not such a good thing though. There are some undeniable monstrosities in the landscape which somebody must have thought was beautiful.

Man: Well, that's the second main reason I love my work. My philosophy is to design structures that blend into the landscape, using natural materials and organic shapes. My clients come to me for that reason. I am confident that no-one would call any of my designs an eye-sore and that gives me a real feeling of satisfaction.

Listening 8.3

Extract 1

Woman 1: When I first saw it I didn't realise quite how important it would turn out to be, although my first thought was that I was probably looking at something very old indeed.

Woman 2: It must have been very exciting.

Woman 1: I suppose it was, but I didn't know then that it would be a turning point for the project, and for me. I mean, the dig had been turning up very little, and our sponsors were threatening to pull our funds, so it was significant in more ways than one.

Woman 2: When did you realise the significance of the find itself?

Woman 1: Well, more or less at once. I called over Professor Hargreaves, and we carefully brushed out the piece in order to define it more clearly. It appeared to be man-made, but of course we couldn't date it until we submitted it for radio carbon testing, but from the level of the dig, we knew we must have been looking at something pre-Egyptian, possibly ten thousand years old.

Extract 2

Interviewer: So it was ambition that drove you, from an early age?

Angel: Yeah, I suppose you could say that. I knew I wanted to be famous when I was little. I used to tell all my parents friends and say: 'I'm gonna be dead famous one day!'

Interviewer: And what did they say?

Angel: Well they laughed mostly. They thought I was being cute but that just made me more and more determined, see, so that's all I thought about all through school. I wrote my own songs and got a band together, even though my teachers kept telling me I'd never achieve anything the way I was going.

Interviewer: And do you think that your fame will last? Are you more concerned about being the flavour of the month, or creating a legacy in music that has your name on it?

Angel: Well, I've since realised that being famous isn't all roses. I mean, I love the media attention, and the money ain't bad either, but there comes a point where you think: 'OK, that's enough for today, can you leave me alone now!' and they don't. It just keeps going on and then you start

to cherish your privacy and you put dark glasses and hats on and try to achieve anonymity like you had before – well, some of the time anyway.

Interviewer: It must be a tough life!

Listening 8.4

Between 1200 and 1600 AD, the people of Easter Island built and erected around 400 enormous statues, or 'moai' as they are called, and another 400 were left unfinished in the quarries where they were made. Up to ten metres tall and weighing up to 75 tonnes, the enigmatic statues raise a host of questions – not least, why did the islanders build them, how did they move them and why were so many left unfinished? One theory is that different groups competed against each other, striving to build the most impressive moai.

Some researchers have suggested that this 'moai mania' was a disaster for the society. Yet others point to mounting evidence that prehistoric occupants made a success of life on the island and state that there is in fact painfully little archaeological evidence for the fundamental claims that underpin the self-destruction theory.

When the Dutch explorer Jacob Roggeveen 'discovered' the island on Easter day in 1722, he was stunned at the sight of monumental stone statues lined along the coast. He could see few trees, and he wondered how this apparently small, primitive society had transported and erected such monoliths without timber or ropes. Later on, pollen and soil analysis revealed that the island had once been home to flourishing palm forests with an estimated 16 million trees. Deforestation seems to have begun as soon as the settlers arrived around 1200, and was complete by about 1500. The reason why the islanders wiped out their forest has long nagged at researchers and is still open to dispute. Some palms may indeed have been cut down to assist in moving the statues, though, with their very soft interiors they would not have been ideal for the job. Other trees were used for firewood, and land was cleared for agriculture. Still, the blame for the disappearance of the palms might not rest entirely with people. Recent genetic research suggests rats, which love to eat palm nuts, were introduced to the island in the canoes of the original colonisers.

Most of the evidence for starvation and cannibalism comes from oral histories, which are extremely contradictory and unreliable. Some researchers suspect that stories of cannibalism, in particular, could have been invented by missionaries. Very few of the remains of prehistoric islanders show any signs of personal violence. True, the 17th and 18th centuries saw an increase in artefacts identified by some as spearheads, but many believe the artefacts are agricultural implements.

The story of ecocide may usefully confirm our darkest fears about humanity but, for every society that self-destructs there is another that does the right thing. It is far from clear that the Easter Islanders made their situation much worse for themselves, but only more evidence will resolve the issue.

Unit 9

Listening 9.1

Joe: Will ya look at this? The amount of work that's gone into it! It's amazing!

Clare: Ummm ... But seriously, Joe, would you really want that hanging on your wall?

Joe: Yeah, why not? So, OK, it's bulky, but it's powerful, and I love the symbolic effect of all those lyrics scrawled across the glass background. Set within the boat like that, it creates the effect of a window on the world as you travel on your voyage through life.

Clare: Wow, Joe! That's a bit deep for you! Personally, I find the colours rather garish for my tastes.

Joe: Well, ya see, Clare, I think they're meant to be. I mean, it's boat paint ... No, I really like it!

Listening 9.2

Interviewer: Good morning, and welcome to this week's Art Corner. On the show today, I'm delighted to have with me a particularly interesting guest. Few of you will have heard of him as yet, but this is not due to a lack of talent on his part. Vasilis Kapodistrias is in fact a man of many talents. An accomplished dentist by profession, he spends most of his spare time creating wonderful works of art. Vasilis, welcome.

Vasilis: Thank you, Judith.

Interviewer: Now, your kind of art is rather unusual, so, can you start by giving us a brief description of what you do?

Vasilis: Yes, well, I do a lot of different things, really, because I love experimenting with materials. I'm not just interested in the look of something, but in how it feels to the touch, if you know what I mean. So, I suppose my work is a combination of three-dimensional painting and sculpture. To give you an idea, I've been influenced by the work of Kostas Tsoklis, a well-known Greek 3-D artist, who I admire a great deal.

Interviewer: Would you say he was the reason you became interested in producing your own work?

Vasilis: He certainly influenced the direction in which my art developed ... But I think really I've always had an interest. My father painted for a hobby also. Landscapes, mainly, and as a boy I remember following him and sometimes drawing, too. Then, at university, it was photography for a while, and I gradually moved on to painting watercolours, and then acryllic. After that, in round about 1985, I started using other materials.

Interviewer: What kind of materials?

Vasilis: At first, I used cardboard, and then plaster ... Err ... Here, my professional work helped. As a dentist, I use plaster, glues and materials for making false plates, wire for braces, and so on. So, it seemed natural to experiment with such materials to develop my hobby. Then, about 15 years ago, I started using polystyrene and fibreglass – what they use to make boats: more durable materials, longer-lasting. A major theme in my art is the sea. I live by the sea, and I love boats ...

Interviewer: Isn't polystyrene a rather difficult substance to work with?

Vasilis: Yes, and not very healthy, either! I'm attracted to it because of its durability, but I make sure I've got the windows open when I'm working with it! It's so versatile, though, and easy to mix with other materials in order to create different textures. I love that, you see. I haven't followed any art course, so I don't know much about particular techniques. I just follow my heart in a painting. For this reason, I feel I'm a permanent student of art. To describe me as an artist ... well, I'm not sure I'm ready for that yet! There is no real beginning or end for me. When I start a new piece, I have no idea how it will turn out. I feel I participate in a painting, but the materials I am using gradually take on a life of their own, and seem to start moulding themselves! It's exciting!

Interviewer: You've produced a lot of work in the last few years. So, why haven't you held an exhibition yet?

Vasilis: My dental practice houses my permanent exhibition! No, really. Many people have asked me that, but it's a difficult question to answer. You see, my art is my hobby, my form of escape. As I get older, the symbolism in my work is increasingly reflective, and very personal. You will have noticed that many of my recent backgrounds contain the lyrics from songs or poems that have a special meaning for me. I don't see myself in a professional light. I've never sold anything. I'm not sure I could put a price on it, since it takes me months to finish one piece. Also, I'm rather shy of publicity, so reluctant to take that step. Perhaps I just don't feel mature enough yet! I don't know ...

Female interviewer: Well, you should seriously think about it! So, ladies and gentlemen, if you want to see any of Vasilis' work, you'll just have to book an appointment to have your teeth checked! For the time being, anyway. Vasilis, thank you very much for coming to talk to us today, and good luck ...

Listening 9.3

Female: I don't know where she finds the time to do all those activities.

Male: Where she finds the time to do all those activities, I don't know.

Female: Although this exercise may seem boring, it is useful.

Male: Boring though this exercise may seem, it is useful.

Male: You need a complete break from the office.

Female: What you need is a complete break from the office.

Male: They are creating unnecessary waste.

Female: What they are doing is creating unnecessary waste.

Male: Don't get upset. You just need to go and talk to your teacher about the problem.

Female: Don't get upset. All you need to do is talk to your teacher about the problem.

Listening 9.4

Vincent Van Gogh cut off his ear after a quarrel with his good friend Gauguin.

Vincent Van Gogh **cut off** his ear after a quarrel with his good friend Gauguin.

Vincent Van Gogh cut off his **ear** after a quarrel with his good friend Gauguin.

Vincent Van Gogh cut off his ear after **a quarrel** with his good friend Gauguin.

Vincent Van Gogh cut off his ear after a quarrel with his good friend **Gauguin.**

Listening 9.5

Michelle: So, who are you going to nominate, Maria?

Maria: Oh, I don't know. I like Paul Klee's work, because it has this childlike quality, but if we're talking about the most *popular* artists, I'd choose Marc Chagall.

Caitlin: Really? For myself, I prefer Klimt. I mean, the passion in 'The Kiss'. Think about how often you see that painting on people's walls, guys.

Alice: Yawn, yawn. C'mon, Caitlin! Most of us are bored of it! Now, a genuinely provocative artist of the twentieth century for me is Takashi Murakami ...

Caitlin: Come again?

Alice: Takashi Murakami. His work reflects what's happening in modern Japan, and shows just how far the Manga cartoon images have influenced contemporary art. You see his smiley flowers and Mr Dob figure all over the place.

Tony: You definitely do when you walk into your room, Alice! You've got Murakami posters all over your walls! Who would you choose, Michelle?

Michelle: Well, Tony, my choice would be Wassily Kandinsky, although I don't like all of his work. It's the precision of his shapes. Somehow, you can sense the music in them, as if he composed them in the same way you would compose a piece of music. The colours seem to be in perfect harmony, like a melody.

Maria: I feel like that about Chagall's work, though. His paintings seem to depict aspects of the subconscious mind. Just as Kandinsky speaks to you of music in his paintings, Chagall's paintings remind me of dreams I've had.

Caitlin: They're rather too abstract for me! I think Gustav Klimt's work speaks more directly to us as people – don't laugh, Tony! – certainly in the case of his portraits. It's not just 'The Kiss'. You take a look at some of his portraits of women. He manages to capture their strength and vitality, an inner beauty. It's amazing!

Alice: Well, Tony and I'll stick with the crazily happy images of Murakami ...

Tony: Speak for yourself! I like Murakami, but I wouldn't nominate him here ... No! My choice would be Miro. I just love those blues, greens and yellows in his landscapes. A particular favourite is 'Ciurana, The Path'.

Maria: And I thought we all had similar tastes in art! ... I wonder if any of our choices will be chosen.

Listening 10.1

Speaker 1: Nowadays, with the climate change crisis, everyone's suddenly jumping on the ecological band-wagon and trying to do their bit. But back in the forties, when the war was on, it was a way of life. We grew up with it. We used to get told off if we accidentally left a light on in another part of the house; it's something that's stuck with me for I always switch the light off when I leave the room – even if it's only for a minute. When my kids were young I even imposed a five pence fine on them if they left the lights on in their room! At night, I switch off all the appliances at the wall sockets because I remember reading somewhere that those little red lights from the TV and DVD left on standby, consume enough electricity in a year to power the whole of the UK for a week.

Speaker 2: We've all got used to the hose pipe bans these days but our family always did their bit to conserve water. My father always used the water from his hot water bottle to wash in the mornings as it was still nice and warm. My Mum always had a bowl in the bathroom sink and when it was full from washing our hands and face, we'd tip it into the toilet instead of flushing – did the job just as well. Kitchen water was saved for watering the pot plants, so long as it didn't have detergent in it. We also attached water-butts to the drainpipes around our house and we collected rainwater for watering the garden. The vegetable garden had an old bathtub that used to fill up and during hot summer hose-pipe bans we always had enough water, while everyone else had to watch their gardens dry out.

Speaker 3: Children these days don't know how privileged they are. I remember wearing itchy school uniforms that my mother made, and having to make do with them as long as we could. When our pullovers wore thin on the elbow, Mum simply unstitched the sleeves and reversed them, left sleeve to right armhole, and we wore them until the reversed elbows also began to wear out. Then it was time to unravel the wool and knit it again as part of a stripy jumper. My grandchildren turn their noses up at anything without a label on it – usually on the outside. I still find it hard to buy anything new, and almost impossible to throw anything away if it could be used by someone else.

Speaker 4: Absolutely everything organic that comes out of my kitchen gets composted. Potato peelings, egg shells, banana skins, melon rinds, coffee grounds – you name it. Even newspapers, cardboard egg-boxes, cat hairs. It all gets chucked into my garden compost bin and within a few months nature's done her work and you've got beautiful, crumbly, rich brown compost – the perfect fertiliser for your garden plants, so there's no need for artificial chemical fertilisers and the best thing is knowing that absolutely everything is getting recycled back into nature. I got it from my Mum – she's been composting for as long as I can remember and back in those days she must have been seen as an eccentric in our village. Now everyone wants advice. I hate seeing people throw their organic waste in the bin. I have been known to slip apple cores and tea bags into my bag while at work in order to bring it home for compost.

Speaker 5: Every time I go to the shops I grab a bundle of plastic bags and take them with me to use again – most of them can be used five or six times. Otherwise they need 50 years to decompose in the ground. I also save the paper bags from market stalls – they can be used to ripen avocados and tomatoes and when I'm done with them, I use them to soak up the fat from fried food. I also use ordinary plastic water bottles as cloches for young garden plants to protect my lettuces from slugs and frost. I just cut the bottoms off and push a thin cane through to stop them from falling over. Another tip that my father passed on was that instead of using expensive hand cream you should just rub sheep's fat into your hand. I know it sounds horrible but if you think about it, most lanolin-based creams are made from mutton fat anyway, only with perfume added to it.

Listening 10.2

Dave: We love *Freecycle*. My girlfriend Helen enforces a policy of household recycling as much as possible and it was her idea to join, because we were about to move in together and had a lot of stuff lying around that was doubled up. We've also used the site to help furnish our new flat. We had absolutely no furniture so it was a big challenge for us. But our *Freecycle* group seemed to offer everything we needed, from three-piece suites to the kitchen sink. After bagging some great stuff in the first few weeks, we were completely hooked. We managed to wangle a bathroom cabinet, a set of bookshelves, a laundry basket and loads of kitchen utensils and crockery. Helen seemed to have more success at claiming things than I did – maybe it was the female touch or maybe it was the sheer speed of her email responses, I don't know. I have shifted, among other things, an old chair, some speakers, and Helen's old curling tongs. It is so much more rewarding to have people pick up the goods from you than just putting things in the bin.

The pinnacle of our *Freecycle* success has got to be claiming a huge shelving unit and a lovely sofa. Helen then requested a sewing machine, which she used to make a cover for the new sofa. We have been able to put other people's unwanted (but perfectly good) furniture to new use. It has also made the cost of decorating an entire flat far easier to stomach. I am now offering a lot more stuff on the site. I'm well and truly converted, and use it more than Helen! I check the site all the time for new offers – come summer, I'd love a garden table and chairs.

Julia: I found out about *Freecycle* when my colleague posted up loads of our ancient office furniture that would have been dumped otherwise. I've been hooked since.

When I drive past the dump, the amount of wonderful stuff I see that's going to waste seems criminal. I'm tempted to give out flyers for *Freecycle* when I go past, to tell people they don't have to throw good things away. There are

three main benefits to *Freecycle*. First: people can get things for free. I've got a massive list of things I'm really happy with: shower doors, a sewing machine, a farm gate, a china umbrella stand. I've actually taken more than I've been able to give. Second: people usually post up stuff that they think isn't worth selling, which makes *Freecycle* good for avoiding landfill. Third: people come and collect what you've advertised, so it's very convenient for you. I once offered a broken lawnmower, which somebody snapped up!

Freecycle in Oxford has quite strict guidelines, because everything on the forum should be stuff that could end up on the dump otherwise. People accept the rules, but they also love the community feel of the group, so in order to avoid clogging up the *Freecycle* forum, a subgroup has been set up called the Oxford Freecycle Cafe. The cafe is more chatty and people offer all kinds of things on it, such as wind-fallen apples or spare firewood. It really shows the demand for free community networks.

Anna: My partner and I moved to a smallholding here just over a year ago with the aim of setting up a more sustainable lifestyle. We provide for ourselves by growing produce, raising and eating our own poultry and meat and using our own fuel. We found out about our local *Freecycle* group from an article in our daily newspaper (recycled for composting and firelighting), and its philosophy seemed to go hand-in-hand with our own, so we thought there would be no better way of offloading some of the excess chicks we had at the time. We instantly got involved with this wonderful system of free exchange, and have since taken many items that have been incredibly useful. Since we started out we have found homes for two cockerels, and we took someone's vacuum cleaner which is now in my son's flat, and we have given away some lovely 'eggs for sale' signs written on slate.

One of the great things about *Freecycle* is that you can choose whom to give things to. You are encouraged to give items to charities if they request it, but otherwise choosing a recipient is entirely up to you and no explanations are necessary. In our *Freecycle* group, there are the 'usual' postings for items like sofas, TVs, computers and cots, all of which are extremely useful to members, but there are also postings which probably would not be found in groups in cities; requests to re-house dogs, geese, a sow and her piglets and sheep. These latter items reflect the fact that here *Freecycle* has become a real aid to those of us who value the idea of sustainability while being part of the farming community.

Unit 11

Listening 11.1

Analyst: ... Well, the statistics for weekly spending among families in Britain are quite revealing, as they mirror a certain shift in certain social attitudes.

Consider tobacco, for example. In 1980, the average

household spent £8.60 a week on tobacco, whereas by 2003, this had gone down to only £5.40, reflecting a reduction in the number of smokers. Household goods and services, on the other hand, showed a considerable increase, with families spending approximately £33.80 on household goods in 2003, as opposed to only £22 in 1980. The largest increase by far was in the area of leisure services, which rose from £18.90 in 1980 to £53.60 by 2003. The reasons for this appear to vary. Motoring also saw a steep rise, from £35 in 1980 to £62.70 in 2003, almost twice as much. Here, though, the figures have been greatly influenced by the significant rise in prices. Interestingly enough, families spent less on fuel and power in 2003 than they had 23 years earlier, only £11.70 a week, instead of £15. This clearly represents a growing awareness of the energy crisis. However, other areas such as clothing and footwear and food and drink, showed little change, and I think this can be credited to the ...

Listening 11.2

Interviewer: Now, Rodney, credit card fraud has become a huge problem worldwide in recent years, with global losses reaching almost four billion US dollars, and rising ... Just how bad is the situation for Britain?

Rodney: Well, unfortunately, it's steadily worsening. According to a survey conducted by APACS in 2003 on card fraud, the total value of fraud committed on UK-issued credit cards rose from 406.3 million pounds in 2001 to 411.6 million in 2003, and the figures are still rising.

Interviewer: Incredible. Just how is this happening?

Rodney: I think one of the main problems is that consumers fail to realise how easy it is for a determined crook to steal their card details. Many are far too relaxed in their attitude towards keeping their card safe, or not revealing their bank details or personal identification number. There are several ways in which cards can be used fraudulently. The obvious one is actual theft of the card itself. Then there's counterfeiting, or 'skimming', as it's known in the trade. Employees in a shop, restaurant or petrol station may place your card into an electronic reading device, copy your details and then return your card without you noticing. The details can then be used for 'card-not-present' fraud.

Interviewer: What is that exactly?

Rodney: Credit card details are obtained from card theft, or skimming, as I've already mentioned, or going through someone's card receipts – some unscrupulous individuals even go through rubbish bins to obtain these. Then the details can be used fraudulently to buy goods or services online, over the phone, via mail order or by fax, without the card itself needing to be presented. The problem is that customers don't realise that some shop assistants will try to steal their details.

Interviewer: A frightening thought! So what should someone do if they realise their card's been stolen or copied?

Rodney: Call the card issuer right away. This will prevent you from being held liable for any large debts. The most you will have to pay is about £50, and you may not have to pay anything at all. The issuer will cancel your card, so remember not to use it again if you still have it.

Interviewer: But what can be done to prevent fraud from happening in the first place?

Rodney: People have to be more vigilant when using their cards. It always amazes me how relaxed many are about revealing personal card details, and PIN numbers, or lending their card to friends. Also, when paying by card, they shouldn't let the card out of their sight. In the UK, skimming and counterfeiting are the most common types of credit card fraud, whereas in the US, it's actual card theft that's the biggest offender. The implication here is that maybe Americans are more careful when paying by card.

Listening 11.3

Interlocutor: ... Some people say that having any job is better than no job at all. What do you think?

Fernando: Well, I think it depends on the kind of job we're talking about, and the kind of person you are. A university graduate, for instance, would not want to clean the streets for a living! I mean, he'd expect something better than that!

Katrina: Yes, but if there was no other job available, what then? Would you rather be unemployed?

Fernando: I think I would try to create a job for myself. Now, with the Internet, an imaginative person can find a way to earn a living.

Katrina: I'm afraid I don't agree with you. Perhaps you can do that, but it's not always so easy. For me, I would find it frustrating to be unemployed, so I think I would get a job cleaning rather than not work at all. I hate sitting around doing nothing.

Fernando: I think there are certain jobs I would find it embarrassing to do, so I cannot say the same for me. Also, if you are looking for a specific career, you need to be available for interviews, etc. So, remaining unemployed until you find what you are looking for is not always bad.

Katrina: Maybe, but that becomes a problem when you are out of work for ... six months! I think a potential employer will be more impressed by someone who shows a general willingness to work.

Fernando: Yes, but ...!

Interlocutor: Thank you. That is the end of the test.

Unit 12

Listening 12.1

a: I think it's time Roger retired.
Yes, well, *quite!*
b: Gillian is *quite* a little trouble maker isn't she!
c: I think it's *quite* a good idea to take her advice.
d: It's *quite* clear to me that you weren't listening.
e: After the accident, he was never *quite* the same.
f: I thought the script was *quite* ridiculous.

Listening 12.2

Extract 1

Interviewer: So Richard, tell us about what got you started as an independent filmmaker.

Richard: From an early age I was obsessive about film, about directing and cinematography but it never occurred to me that I could do it myself until one day I picked up my Dad's eight millimetre camera and started recording family life. I used to watch films all the time too. My local video shop had a section of 'unclassifiable' films that didn't belong in any section, and these were all my favourite films. They were totally unique, they made up their own rules and they always left me feeling as if something inside me had changed. These films proved that the medium of film had the power to change someone's perception of the world, and that just made me more determined.

Interviewer: And yet you claim that you don't make 'arty' films.

Richard: While I knew I wanted to work in this genre, I also knew how easy it was for experimental films to turn into pretentious rubbish. I wanted to express my message through film, using abstraction and music, but not some over the top art piece. I'm just not interested in art films where I watch ten minutes and know what is going to happen in the next hour.

Extract 2

Woman: Have you seen the latest Narnia film? It's got great special effects and everything, but it couldn't have been more different from my childhood memory of the book.

Man: No, and I don't think I will. I loved the Narnia books and I hate seeing film adaptations of children's books in general, especially if they're books I grew up with. It's almost like they belong to me, if you know what I mean.

Woman: True, but sometimes a bad adaptation can remind you of why you loved the original book in the first place. As soon as I saw the film I went and dug out my old copy and started reading it again.

Man: Yes, but have you noticed how they always make the films with the express intention of not offending any of the 'book fans'? That's why they can never live up to the original.

Woman: Maybe, but in some ways though it's interesting to see another take on the book. To see the characters come to life. And if they choose the right actors to bring out the characters, you might find your understanding of the book to be deepened by the film version.

Man: I just don't think I'll ever be satisfied by any adaptation. You read these children's books so much that you come to inhabit them – every scene in those books has a specific visual reality for me; one that's very difficult to relinquish.

Extract 3

Woman 1: I think it's depressing that women film directors are in such a tiny minority. Did you know that in Britain, only seven per cent of film directors are women? And apart from a couple of obvious commercial successes, like Jane Campion's film 'The Piano', or Gurinder Chadha's 'Bend it like Beckham', how many films can you actually think of that were directed by women? I can't help thinking that if this imbalance were to occur in any other profession, there would be some kind of major outcry. Why is it that film-making continues to be the most unbalanced career in the arts?

Woman 2: Well, obviously there are the difficulties of working in a male-dominated industry. Women need role-models – like the two women you just mentioned. They need self-confidence, and they need tips on how to raise children and commit themselves to their work at the same time. But the truth is that, whether you're female or male, it is really hard to make films. Creativity is stifled because film-makers have to spend far too much time fundraising. There is so much courage involved in being a film director because there is so much at stake, and women are not generally raised to gamble with other people's money – a thing that seems to come more easily to men.

Listening 12.3

Speaker 1: Well it's about a pirate, Jack Sparrow, played by Johnnie Depp, who used to be captain of a ship called 'The Black Pearl', but now that ship's been commandeered by a zombie pirate called Captain Barbosa. He has been cursed with living death until he can find the living heir of old 'Bootstrap' Bill Turner, who is actually played by Orlando Bloom and, to that end he has kidnapped the beautiful Elizabeth Swann ...

Speaker 2: It's an animated film about an ogre who lives in a swamp. Coming home one day he finds that all these fairy tale characters have moved in, which he is not very happy about, to say the least. Accompanied by a talking donkey that irritates him greatly, he sets off on a fairy tale adventure of his own, and comes face to face with dragons, princesses and even happy endings ...

Speaker 3: It's a musical actually, and it's about two brothers, Jake and Elwood, who are on a mission from God to save a convent orphanage from closure. In order to legitimately raise the money they need, they have to put their old blues band back together, no mean feat in itself, despite the fact that the police and all their old enemies are all in hot pursuit. What I love is the wonderful performances by John Lee Hooker, James Brown, Aretha Franklin, Ray Charles, to name but a few ...

Speaker 4: The film is based on an actual historical event of course, but the main story is a romance, told in flashback by the old woman, Rose, remembering Jack, whom she met on board the ship for the first time. He is a penniless artist who won his ticket to America in a game of cards; she is an attractive young lady engaged to marry a wealthy aristocrat to pay off her family's debts ...

Speaker 5: I love this film – even though it's quite spooky really. I think the actor who plays the scared little boy with psychic abilities is excellent, and Bruce Willis is great as the failed child psychologist who wants to make sure he gets it right second time around. You really need to see it twice because only then do you really appreciate all the details leading to the final twist ...

Unit 13

Listening 13.1

Interlocutor: Now, I'd like you to talk about something together for about three minutes. Here are some pictures showing different ways of advertising a product. First, talk to each other about the merits and limitations of using these forms of advertising. Then, decide which one would be the most effective to promote a new language school in your area. All right?

Carlos: Yes ... Well, I think the billboard is a very effective way of advertising, as it can be seen by everyone in the area. Also, people are not so angry at seeing billboards, whereas they get annoyed when people push leaflets under their door ... Do you agree, Magda?

Magda: Yes, you're right. They don't like leaflets ... Erm ... not at all ...

Carlos: Er ... I know I usually throw leaflets away without looking at them! But I think it depends on what product you want to advertise. Leaflets might be a good idea for a new language school, because you can include information on courses, and photos of the classrooms and facilities in the school ... and a bold advert in the local newspaper is a good idea, as most people read the newspaper, and so they will see it. But I still think the billboard is the best idea, don't you?

Magda: Yes, I agree with you. It will be seen by the largest number of people, and so will be most effective ... Erm ... That's all.

Listening 13.2

While observing gorillas at Zurich Zoo – one of my favourite places for study – I was witness to something very special. The Gorilla House was celebrating the recent birth of a baby gorilla, and so was chock-a-block with visitors. Next to where I was sitting quietly making notes, there was a couple with a nine-month-old baby in a pushchair. The woman sat down in front of the compound and took her baby out of the pushchair, presumably to show him the gorillas. Within seconds, the gorilla mother appeared in front of her, proudly sporting her own offspring, sat down and proceeded to play with it. It was as if she was saying, 'Look, I've got a baby, too! And isn't he adorable, just like yours?'

Listening 13.3

Speaker 1: Communication is one of the most complex skills we can learn, but it's frequently taken for granted by parents, childcare workers and policy makers. In consequence, the barriers, problems and exclusion experienced by children with poor communication skills are ignored along with the importance of speech and language development for all children.

'I CAN' is a non-profit-making organisation that encourages the development of communication skills for all children through UK-wide programmes with a special focus on those kids who find this hard: children with a communication disability.

Speaker 2: Getting it right with ad copy is a sensitive business. The worst kind of advertising exaggerates to grab your attention, while the best gets your interest without appearing to try. I believe the skill is in finding *exactly* the right words, and making every word count in getting your message across to the public. If you use long-winded, wordy copy – you've lost your audience, simple as that. Make your point quickly and effectively, to create an impression that lasts.

Speaker 3: English is peppered through and through with idiomatic phrases. You could ask someone 'What's cooking?', 'What's up?' or 'What's going on?' and expect the same response. Someone who asks 'What's the damage?' may want to know how much he's got to pay for something. The meaning of such phrases is apparent to native-born Americans, but can cause bewilderment in a multicultural setting, such as the area of health care. Nowadays, more and more health care providers are from multicultural backgrounds, making effective communication problematical. As managers, we're concerned that immigrant staff cannot understand guidelines or instructions, and nurse–patient communication is often adversely affected.

Speaker 4: We head on into the school with our mobile cell block, and give students an authentic taste of what it's like to be locked up. The kids follow the inmate's routine for the day, supervised by myself and two other professional officers. We usually discover that a few minutes spent stuck inside the cell is more than enough to dispel the myth created by TV of prison being like a hotel. The reality is *extremely* different, I can tell you! The message we're trying to put across is that you have choices in life, but what you need to think about is the consequences of those choices. Our workshops are very effective in showing the cost of making the wrong choices.

Speaker 5: The guy next door asked me how I would deal with an annoying colleague. I told him that, for example, if I was having trouble with a neighbour's children kicking their ball into my garden all the time, I would never go over and tell the neighbour to get control of their kids. I would go over casually, talk about the weather, gossip a bit, then say something like, 'I see you've got material over there to build that fence you were talking about. I've got some time today to help'.
'That seems so indirect', he said.

'Well, here's the thing', I replied. 'My way the children aren't a problem any more, and I'm still talking to my neighbour. Your way, you're at war with your neighbour, *and* his kids'.

Unit 14

Listening 14.1

Palaeontologist: The earliest multi-celled animals might have been sponges, which although they look like plants are actually animals. They most likely appeared around 700 million years ago. Invertebrates, which are the first animals that could get around, such as flatworms and jellyfish, are believed to have evolved around 570 million years ago. And then, about 500 million years ago, vertebrates, the group which includes fish and other animals with a backbone, suddenly appeared.

About 470 million years ago, the first plants began to grow out of the water, and this is when life on land established itself. Insects originally appeared on land about 380 million years ago and were followed, relatively soon after that, by the first amphibians, which surfaced from the water to become land animals approximately 350 million years ago. Essentially, they were fish that evolved lungs to breathe air. They employed their fins to crawl from one pond to another and these gradually became legs. The next group to emerge, about 300 million years ago, were the reptiles.

For the next 50 million years, life on earth prospered – but about 250 million years ago, the earth experienced a period of mass extinction, which meant that many species disappeared. Around this time, one group of reptiles, called 'dinosaurs', started to dominate all others. Their name means 'terrible lizard'. They were the commonest vertebrates and they controlled the earth for the next 150 million years.

Throughout this time, a new type of animal began to evolve. These animals were the mammals. They gave birth to live young, which they nourished with milk from their bodies, and they first appeared about 200 million years ago.

The closest living family to the dinosaurs is believed to be birds. The first known bird, 'Archaeopteryx', appeared about 150 million years ago. It existed for around 70 million years, before becoming extinct, and was replaced by the group which includes modern birds, believed to have appeared around 60 million years ago, at the same time that the dinosaurs became extinct.

The group of mammals to which humans belong – the primates – emerged from an ancestral group of animals that ate mainly insects, around 50 million years ago. But it wasn't until about three million years ago – about the time the last ice-age started – that intelligent apes, with the ability to walk on their back legs, appeared in southern Africa. Simultaneously, their brains evolved and they learnt to make and use tools. Although called *Homo habilis,* meaning 'handy man', these creatures were more like apes than men. About two million years ago, Homo habilis evolved into the first people called *Homo erectus.* Their bodies were like ours, but their faces were still ape-like. They evolved in Africa and spread as far as South East Asia. Modern people *(Homo sapiens)* appear to have evolved in Africa about 100 thousand years ago (although the date is far from certain).

Listening 14.2

Jeremy Sargon: One of the things we all take for granted is the air we breathe, and the oxygen essential for our survival. But you might be startled to hear that the Earth's atmosphere didn't always contain oxygen! In fact, for most of its history there wasn't really any oxygen in the air at all! It's only been during the last 600 million years that there's been enough to support life, which, as it happens, is how long there has been life on land. From that time then, the amount of oxygen in the atmosphere has swung wildly between tiny amounts – as little as 12 per cent compared to today's 21 per cent – to huge proportions – up to 30 per cent oxygen during one particular period. This variation has of course had a massive impact on the animals living on earth at any particular time. Animals have either taken advantage of the sudden increases in oxygen in order to evolve and colonise the land, or they have faced being made extinct during the periods when oxygen was scarce.

Palaeontologists have always had an interest in the occurrences that may have caused species to become extinct. The leading causes have been attributed to meteors, ice-ages, climate change, and so on, but fascinatingly enough, proof now exists which demonstrates that each mass extinction on earth coincides with times of reduced oxygen. These periods have usually been followed by bursts of much higher oxygen levels, which again have coincided with a time of incredibly fast evolution in animal species. In most cases it appears that the most successful animals to inhabit the land during these times were those that developed more advanced respiratory systems. For example, invertebrates appeared on land for the first time around 420 million years ago – at a time when oxygen levels were higher than today's. Yet soon after that, approximately 400 million years ago, oxygen levels suddenly fell dramatically and most of these animals disappeared: either becoming extinct or returning to the ocean. Oxygen levels did not increase again for another 50 million years or so, during which time only a small number of animals could survive on land. Then 350 million years ago, oxygen levels suddenly started to rise, reaching their highest ever levels around 280 to 300 million years ago. This is when reptiles appeared, for they thrived in this rich atmosphere, but as oxygen levels started to fall once more over the next 50 million years, they had to make some swift adjustments, or they were destined to suffocate for lack of air.

The animals that did this most efficiently were the dinosaurs ... and what they did was to add another pair of air sacs next to the lungs. This enabled them to extract even greater amounts of oxygen from the thinning air. Because of this evolutionary adaptation, it appears that they were the only animals that managed to do well during the late Triassic mass extinction of 200 million years ago. This was the time with the lowest recorded oxygen levels. We can still see these air-sac adaptations in their descendants left on our planet today – the birds – and it's actually this which then allows some birds to fly at altitudes with little oxygen.

Listening 14.3

Interlocutor: Now, I'd like you to talk about something together for about three minutes. I'd like you to imagine that you want to give your support to an important ecological campaign. Here are some of the ecological issues that need our immediate attention. First, talk to each other about how serious each of these issues is. Then decide which campaign you would most like to support. All right?

Elisabeth: OK ... well, at first glance I would say that 'deforestation' is probably the most important ecological issue. What do you think?

Giovanni: Yes, I agree. It is terrible that they are cutting down the rainforests so fast. These forests are important because they are the home to so many species of animals and plants. If they are all cut down there will be many problems.

Elisabeth: Yes, and the forests also control the weather and the Earth's temperature, I think, don't they? However, we shouldn't ignore the issue of 'pollution'. That is another very serious issue.

Giovanni: Yes, you're quite right. Pollution is dangerous for our health and it's also dangerous to wildlife. Some species may disappear for ever because their habitats have been destroyed by pollution. On the other hand, 'the extinction of species' is a very serious issue. It says here that if we don't do something now, over half the Earth's species could be extinct in the next one hundred years.

Elisabeth: Yes, and that is a frightening idea! But I believe that there's not much point in saving all these endangered species if there's nowhere for them to live. Personally I think 'habitat destruction' is the biggest issue facing wild animals at the moment and so I would probably choose to support the campaign for 'conservation of natural habitats'.

Giovanni: I agree it is a serious problem, but I would not choose that one because I think we have to tackle the issue of climate change before it's too late. All life on Earth is being threatened by this at the moment, and if the planet keeps getting hotter and all the ice melts, most of the land will be under water, and then what difference does it make if you have put all your money into 'habitat conservation'? So the issue of 'climate change' would be my first choice.

Interlocutor: Thank you.

Unit 15

Listening 15.1

Interviewer: Today we're here to discuss the subject of 'kissing' and its origins. With me in the studio are two anthropologists: Professor Rosemary O'Bryan and Dr Andrew Peters. Professor O'Bryan, is kissing learned or instinctive behaviour?

Rosemary: Affectionate kissing is a learned behaviour that most probably originated from a mother gently touching or nibbling her child's body with her lips, to cement the bond between them, or it may have arisen from premasticating food to make it easier for her child to swallow. From there it developed into a way of showing affection towards family members, close friends or other members of society and as a sign of respect to older, senior group members.

Interviewer: And yet, according to some anthropologists, kissing is an echo of an ancient form of communication that was necessary for the healthy and successful continuation of the species. Dr Peters ...

Andrew: Yes, kissing in humans is an instinctive behaviour which most likely evolved from grooming behaviour common in mammals. However, recent research has indicated that this kind of behaviour had a much more serious biological function than just social bonding. Kissing, or rubbing noses, actually allows prospective mates to smell or taste each other's pheromones ...

Interviewer: ... You mean the chemicals which give off information about our biological make-up?

Andrew: ... Correct, and thus we get more information about our biological compatibility. Women are more attracted to men who are more genetically compatible to them, and a woman picks this up by breathing in his pheromones. Any resulting offspring will have better resistance to a greater number of diseases, and will consequently have a better chance of survival. That's why we still like to kiss – to maximise our chances of sampling each other's aroma.

Interviewer: So that's why couples are more likely to bond if they have the right 'chemistry'.

Andrew: Yes, and it's not just a mating tool. Chimpanzees, for instance, use it for reconciliation, by kissing and embracing after fights, providing good evidence that kissing in the higher primates has the function of repairing of social relationships.

Interviewer: So when did the romantic act of kissing one's sweetheart on the mouth as a form of affection actually develop?

Rosemary: Well ... not until comparatively late in the evolution of love in fact. In antiquity, kissing – especially on the eyes or cheek – was mainly a form of greeting, but there's no evidence of it being romantic. One of the earliest descriptions of kissing as a form of love and affection comes from the 6th century, in France. Around that time it seems to have become fashionable for a young man to give his betrothed a kiss on the lips as a seal of his affection.

Interviewer: But the rest of the world did not practice kissing as a sign of affection?

Rosemary: In the years before cinema the lovers' kiss was largely a Western habit – unknown in other parts of the world. By the end of the Second World War Western motion pictures had carried the image of romantic couples engaged in a kiss to many other parts of the world. Until quite recently, it was only in North America and Europe that kissing was an important aspect of courtship, which puts paid to the notion that kissing must be instinctive in all people. For instance, the Chinese and the Japanese never kissed on the lips.

Andrew: Yes, but in other cultures affection was expressed in a number of ways – for instance, in Samoa, lovers would express affection by sniffing the air beside each other's cheek; in Polynesia affection was shown by rubbing noses together. The same goes for Eskimos and Laplanders, as with many animals who smell each other or rub noses to smell each other's pheromones. This indicates that it's still instinctive ...

Rosemary: It's hardly the same thing ...

Andrew: ... What about monkeys? Bonobos? They'll kiss each other on the lips for just about any excuse at all. They do it to make up after fights, to comfort each other, to develop social bonds, and sometimes for no clear reason at all – just like us ...

Listening 15.2

Speaker 1: My identity is most certainly Nigerian. It's vital to establish that differentiation because in the United Kingdom, we are all described as either African or perhaps West Indian. What isn't taken into account is that black people are really quite territorial – and in Nigeria we even go slightly further because we have three tribes and take immense pride in our tribe. Since I'm an Ibo, I wouldn't like to be called a Yoruba or a Hausa. I was born in Nigeria and came to England when I was 13. I have a huge family here, but still the allure of Nigeria is very strong. The responsibilities of family need to be taken very seriously. There is no getting away from our background, no matter how much we want to belong in our new home and integrate well. We look and are different, but London is so ethnically mixed, especially where we live in West London which helps. I'm bringing up my daughters to value and recognise their roots ... but still to appreciate the culture they are growing up in.

Speaker 2: Being a Greek Cypriot isn't about religion, but a way of life. It's 100 per cent about the family – and that means the extended one, too. If you are some kind of blood relation, no matter how tenuous, you're considered part of the family. This can be a blessing and a curse, believe me! Being Greek means making decisions collectively, forever in a crowd: essentially, it's a community experience. Now, perhaps that might sound a little claustrophobic, but it has many advantages. There is always support and love. Even though the film *My Big Fat Greek Wedding* was a caricature of this lifestyle, it was also very true. When the girl tells her American boyfriend about her 27 first cousins, I had to laugh. I have 74! Our parents were first generation immigrants, and so were determined to preserve their culture because it was all they had. We are much more confident of who we are, but can also dip in and out of the British way of life and not be excluded. Our children likewise appreciate their background, but don't have a particularly close attachment to Cyprus, unlike their grandparents.

Speaker 3: You cannot escape from who you are culturally but, given the opportunity, you can create your own traditions and become a more improved person. We are Persian-Iranian. Our culture is very rich in so many areas, like in our history, our language, our literature and food and our music. These are all what we want to save and pass down to our next generation and then the generation after that. In our own country, our modern principles came under attack, so we left and have learned not to keep looking back. I am a person who likes to welcome the future and I am not afraid of change. As parents, we believe in giving our children the knowledge of their heritage. But we don't want to force our values on them; we have faith in their reasoning. I feel we are truly fortunate to be able to understand two cultures and it is beneficial not only to us as immigrants, but to our host country, too. This process – it is two-way.

Speaker 4: I'm a British Muslim and am very proud to call myself both. My parents came from Gujarat and settled in Batley where I was born. But although I've never been to India, as a young boy I always had a sense of who I was, where I was from. I was happy with this, even though growing up I endured a lot of racial jeering – many of the kids at school told me to go back to my country. There's a huge Gujarat community in Batley – we've more relatives here than in India! So, together with my parents, this community gave me my ethnic identity. Now that I too am a father I will do the same for my children. My wife is from the same background and we feel strongly that we must keep our customs and traditions because this is what gives us a sense of ourselves. Being Indian is not what our identity is about; I have a British passport, and if I go to India I need to have a visa. My ethnic identity is a religious one, not a geographic one. It's inevitable that our religion, language and customs will vanish if we don't pass them on to our children.

Speaker 5: My ethnic identity is of great importance to me, but I didn't realise the extent of this until my daughter was born. I came to England as a student and I always believed I would be returning home to Osaka. But then I ended up getting married to an English guy that I met here, and realised I'd be staying in this country – and raising my daughter here. I knew that I would always remember my roots and cultural heritage, but I also wanted Lily to know as well. I wanted to bring her up to be both English and Japanese. I realised how hard this task would be that I had set myself for, without effort on my part, she was bound to become more British than Japanese. Of grave importance to me was that she learnt the language so that she could converse with her grandparents and truly understand the culture, so I spoke to her only in Japanese, and left it to her father to speak English with her. The Japanese language is very poetic, there are several different words to describe the moon; just being able to use those words in the correct sense makes a huge difference and shows a true understanding of the language. The other day Lily looked out of the window. She told me that she could see a 'natsu no tsuki', which means a summer moon. I was so pleased.

Unit 16

Listening 16.1

James: Here you are, Sally. I've finished it.
Sally: Hmm? Oh, *The Last Will*! Thanks, James. What did you think of it? Great, wasn't it?
James: Actually, I found it rather disappointing in comparison with his other books. Not so believable, if you know what I mean.
Sally: Really? I find that hard to believe. I thought it was by far his best ever! Far superior to *Waiting to Die* and *A Just Cause,* for instance.

James: I feel just the opposite. Compared to his first novel, the plot in this one is far-fetched and unrealistic, to say the least …

Sally: You're joking! For a start, we see a lot more courtroom drama in this book, which is lacking from his others. They tend to focus purely on lawyers playing detective, which is not always very convincing.

James: It keeps things interesting, though, wouldn't you say?

Sally: Perhaps. But you have to admit that the courtroom drama in this novel lends weight to it, makes it even more believable.

James: Well, admittedly, the courtroom scenes are the most exciting in the book, quite gripping in places in fact, but the rest of the book is often slow and boring. I mean, all that description during the search in South Africa – I practically fell asleep!

Sally: But the protagonist is significantly more rounded and better developed here, wouldn't you say? The way we are led through his drug-induced self-pity to his struggle to redeem himself is cleverly created.

James: It was exactly this that I found just too good to be true! Our hero goes from being a total waster to becoming a knight in shining armour, against a background of support characters who are singularly wooden in their weakness and selfishness. They're nowhere near as realistic as the cast in *A Just Cause,* where good and bad qualities are more evenly shared out.

Sally: Funny! I didn't feel that way at all when I read it, and I thought you'd like it more than that. A pity …

Listening 16.2

Extract 1

Man: … For a while, it felt like we were on a second honeymoon. But then the quiet started getting to us.

Woman: Yes, well, I won't say I don't miss Mike, but quite frankly I was glad when he left to go to university. It was as if the house was no longer big enough for the both of us. We both like our independence, and I think the pressure of feeling responsible towards someone else was getting us both down.

Man: But don't you feel lonely in the house?

Woman: Well, that's just it. I like having the house to myself, but I can see Mike when we both feel like it. I also think it's good for him to know that I'm not waiting by the phone for his every call. That puts a hell of a lot of pressure on any child.

Man: Too right! Jan gets frantic if more than three days go by without a phone call from one of the boys, and I know that bugs Davy, in particular! I try to tell her to relax about it, that 'no news is good news', and all that.

Woman: Mmm, at their age, it can be restrictive to have to account for their movements all the time. They don't want to be thinking about us right now, but about enjoying themselves as much as possible …

Extract 2

Interviewer: So, how did you feel when you first retired?

Man: Guilty, basically.

Interviewer: Guilty? About what?

Man: The fact that I wasn't going to work. As the weeks went by, I became bored and irritable. The change was hard on my wife as well, because I started making demands on her time. I'd expected to do more things together, while she thought that she would go on as before, meeting up with her friends for coffee, going on shopping sprees, all without me. That was difficult for both of us. I had to find my own interests, and she had to make some room for me.

Interviewer: So how do you feel now?

Man: Well, I wonder how I ever had the time to go to work! I find I'm busy nearly all the time now. I think the secret to enjoying your retirement is firstly, health, and then having enough money to do the things you really want to do. Those two elements prevent you from being a burden on your children. Having a good circle of friends has helped. We see the kids when we can, of course, but we're not under their feet, and they're not under ours, either! So, life is fairly good now …

Extract 3

Woman: My decision to go out on my own was all about money. I was stuck in a poorly paid job, with virtually no prospects. I saw an opportunity and grabbed it. Being a Mum, however, I knew I'd need some kind of routine to my working day, and there'd be too many distractions at home! Difficult to ignore the pile of washing up in the sink, and the ironing waiting by the ironing board! So, I opened an office, and I think that was the key to making it work – keeping work and home separate.

Man: Yes, I can see that. Working at home just didn't work for me. I also found it stressful having to rely on myself for all the decision-making. Sometimes, I wanted to share ideas with someone, to get some feedback before putting things into operation, and there was no one. That began to get to me. Now, I'm back in an office, with other people around me, and I feel part of the team again.

Woman: That's it, I've never really been a team player. I like the independence of making my own decisions. I won't say it always works, but on the whole, we've got a better quality of life …

Wordlist

Unit 1 Beginnings

Nouns

institution
predecessor
protestor
revelation
speculation

Verbs

activate
coin
embark (on)
establish
found
generate
inaugurate
initiate
instigate
launch
originate
postulate
prompt
provoke
spawn
stimulate
trigger

Adjectives and adverbs

auspicious
elated
intriguing
invaluable
reluctant
vulnerable

Unit 2 A child's world

Nouns

childminder
conception
nursery
offspring
perception

Verbs

bound
clamber
heave
hop
infer

imply
jump
march
paddle
stroll
skip
stride
slide
thrive
tiptoe
wade
wander
wrestle

Adjectives and adverbs

altruistic
detrimental
innovative
sedentary

Unit 3 Are you game?

Nouns

adrenalin
bodyboarding
din
dissident
endurance
guts
hang gliding
kite landboarding
masochist
stake
triathlon
white water rafting

Verbs

culminate
extricate

Adjectives and adverbs

daft
dismissive
exhilarating
gruelling
nauseated
noncommittal
petrified
precariously
prostrate
reassuring

Unit 4 Eureka!

Nouns

android
aristocracy
device
diversity
duration
eclipse
genetics
geology
impact
inhabitant
intervention
legislation
palaeontology
phenomenon
predator

Verbs

advance
astound
detect
disintegrate
dissolve
emit
eradicate
erode
inscribe
salvage

Adjectives and adverbs

anatomical
concisely
efficient
rational
rigorous
visually

Unit 5 Safe and sound?

Nouns

anti-virus
arson
backup
broadband
crimeware
cyber-crime
drug trafficking
fraud
hacker

hitman
hoax
kidnapping
lawsuit
murder

Verbs

confess
confide
convict
crack
decode
incite
solicit

Adjectives and adverbs

benign
infamous
law-abiding
malicious
undercover

Unit 6 Hale and hearty

Nouns

component
confection
consumption
discretion
efficacy
immune system
impairment
medication
moderation
morality
nutrient
obesity
optimism
resistance

Verbs

boost
consume
derive
digest
duplicate
eliminate
endorse
enhance
prescribe
renovate
restore

Adjectives and adverbs

abundant

complementary
conventional
external
harmonious
invasive
nourishing
nutritive
organic
processed
raw
stimulating
subsequent

Unit 7 Wish you were there …

Nouns

autonomy
avatar
dome
essence
grandeur
persona
roadie
roadblock
roadhog
roadhouse
roadside
roadshow
roadworks
slum

Verbs

beckon
board up
overlook

Adjectives and adverbs

breathless
crumbling
distorted
eerie
extortionate
industrious
pragmatic
run down
shoddy
simulated
surreal
triumphal
virtual

Unit 8 Making our mark

Nouns

abode

construction
contaminant
durability
dwelling
flexibility
habitat
immigrant
installation
motivation
novice
precision
preconception
residence

Verbs

commemorate
erect
excavate
insulate
isolate
resume
topple
vanquish

Adjectives and adverbs

accessible
awe-inspiring
disarming
dominating
empowering
imposing
imprecise
invariably
painstakingly
pivotal
protruding
radically
remote
stunning

Unit 9 Brushstrokes and blueprints

Nouns

adornment
apprentice
composure
eyesore
perspective
reams
scrap
strip
stroke
synergy
transition

versatility
wordiness

Verbs

compile
convey
fiddle
gravitate
nominate
patent
squint

Adjectives and adverbs

absent-mindedly
adjacent
animated
banal
illuminating
indispensable
intricate
minimalist
modish
poignant
sheer
springy
ubiquitous

Unit 10 The good life

Nouns

chore
commodity
custody
discourse
penalty
scruples
spouse

Verbs

commute
conserve
constitute
demolish
infuriate
moderate
undermine

Adjectives and adverbs

adversely
intolerable
terminal
unsettling

Unit 11 Making ends meet

Nouns

fragment
garment
holdall
lint
middleman
piecework
weave
zip

Verbs

exorcise
tug
twiddle
venture

Adjectives and adverbs

fleetingly
lacy
negligible
pungent
rudimentary
tattered
unscrupulous

Unit 12 Behind the silver screen

Nouns

adaptation
ambivalence
blockbuster
cast
crew
deficiency
farce
glamour
interpretation
paparazzi
perseverance
plot
portrayal
protagonist
satire
slapstick
suspense
thriller
trailer
villain
wit

Verbs

diverge

embellish
enamour
entrance
intensify
jest
mock
offend
render
resemble
restore
tweak

Adjectives and adverbs

adept
anonymous
commercially
convincingly
cynical
disjointed
elegant
enigmatic
hilarious
implausible
inspired
intrepid
irresistible
mainstream
offensive
preposterous
staggering
subtle
succinct
tedious
uproarious
wooden

Unit 13 Getting the message across

Nouns

cluster
constellation
dignitary
echolocation
extraterrestrial
galaxy
kerosene
observatory

Verbs

ascertain
broadcast
chirp
clarify

convene
decipher
explain
impart
instil
ponder
publish
publicise
squawk
transmit

Adjectives and adverbs

random
transparent

Unit 14 Gaia's legacy

Nouns

abundance
biodiversity
brink
conservation
ecosystem
equilibrium
imbalance
legacy
refuge
resource

Verbs

accelerate
adapt
colonise
conquer
deplete
diminish
evolve
exacerbate
flourish
inherit
regulate

Adjectives and adverbs

biodegradable
drastic
ignorant
incompatible
inconstant
optimum
pristine
vague

Unit 15 Our global village

Nouns

adolescence
anecdote
compatibility
convention
esteem
etiquette
gesture
heritage
idiosyncrasy
irreverence
liberty
rite of passage
taboo
transition

Verbs

abolish
attend
bond
cement
clash
deport
despise
misinterpret
ostracise
prohibit
restrict
stipulate
transgress
violate

Adjectives and adverbs

conflicting
endearing
ethnic
impending
improper
instinctive
ludicrous
obscene
prospective
ritualistic
rural
vulgar

Unit 16 Endings – and new beginnings ...

Nouns

grindstone

relapse
relativity
slaughterhouse
slog
treadmill
threshold
wrench

Verbs

abort
cease
complete
conclude
demote
discontinue
downgrade
extinguish
finalise
finish
forsake
heed
reform
regenerate
rejuvenate
relegate
scavenge
settle
terminate

Adjectives and adverbs

cursory
comprehensive
compulsive
confounding
cumbersome
dormant
forsaken
professed
ruthless
transient
unwieldy
wrinkled

Credits

The publishers would like to thank the following sources for permission to reproduce their copyright protected texts:

Page 3: From 'Drawing on the Right Side of the Brain' by Betty Edwards Copyright © J.P. Tarcher, Inc. Harper Collins. Pages 12–13: 'Pioneer nursery stays open in all weather' by Severin Carroll. Copyright © The Guardian at http://education.guardian.co.uk/earlyyears/story/0,,1934990,00 ,html. Page 23: 'Close To The Wind' by Pete Goss (pages 220–223) Copyright © Headline book publishing. Page 26: Nikos Magitsis Copyright © www.magitsis.gr. Page 32: 'Growing Up With Lucy' by Steve Grand reviewed by Elizabeth Sourbut. Copyright © New Scientist magazine issue 2436; 'Understanding Intelligence' by Rolf Pfeifer and Christian Scheier reviewed by Inman Harvey. Copyright © New Scientist magazine issue 2233. Page 33: 'Dinosaurs of Italy by Cristiano Dal Sasso and Mammals from the Age of Dinosaurs: Origins, evolution and structure' by Zofia Kielan-Jaworowska, Richard Cifelli and Zhe-Xi Luo reviewed by Douglas Palmer. Copyright © New Scientist magazine issue 2500; 'The Cretaceous World' edited by Peter Skelton reviewed by Douglas Palmer. Copyright © NewScientist.com news service; 'Dinosaurs of the Air' by Gregory Paul reviewed by Jeff Hecht. Copyright © New Scientist magazine issue 2349; 'Chasing monsters' by Michael Benton and 'The Dinosaur Hunters' by Deborah Cadbury. Copyright © New Scientist magazine issue 2259; 'There be dragons' by Christopher McGowan reviewed by Simon Knell. Copyright © New Scientist Magazine issue 2293; 'A Field Guide to Dinosaurs: The essential handbook for travelers in the Mesozoic' by Henry Gee and Luis V. Rey reviewed by Jeff Hecht. Copyright © New Scientist magazine issue 2387. Pages 44–45: 'Of worms and woodpecker, the changing world of the virus-busters fighting rise in internet crime' by Bobbie Johnson. Copyright © The Guardian http:// www. guardian.co.uk/russia/article/0,,1703160,00.html. Page 55: 'Living Food for Health' by Dr Gillian McKeith. Copyright © Piatkus, an imprint of Little, Brown Book Group 2000. Page 64: 'I lost my heart in Dublin' by Craig Doyle; 'St. Petersburg' by Katya Galitzine. Page 65: 'Calcutta' by Joe Roberts; 'Barcelona' by Luice Graves. Page 75: 'Straw Bale Futures, Introduction, Information guide to Straw Bale Building' Copyright © Amazon Nails, 2001. Page 79: 'Easter Island: A monumental collapse' by Emma Young. Copyright © New Scientist magazine issue 2562. Page 86: 'Classics of everyday Design no.3'. Copyright © http://blogs.guardian.co.uk/art/2006/11/classics_of_everyday_ design_no_1.html. Page 87: From 'The Dark Room' by Rachel Seiffert, published by William Heinemann. Copyright © Random House Group Ltd. Page 96: 'Nice week at the office, darling?' by Joanna Moorhead. Copyright © The Guardian http://lifeandhealth.guardian.co.uk/family/ story/0,,1989023,00.html. Page 107: From 'Brick Lane' by Monica Ali. pages 170–172 Copyright © Random House Group Ltd. UK and Commonwealth rights, excluding Canada. All other rights Abner Stein. Page 116: 'Happy Feet' review by Peter Bradshaw. Copyright © Peter Bradshaw. http://film.guardian.co.uk/News_Story/Critic_Review/Guardian_review/0,,1966585,00.html. Page 117: 'Casablanca' review by Peter Bradshaw. Copyright © Peter Bradshaw http://film. guardian.co.uk/News_Story/Critic_ Review/Guardian_review/0,,2013773,00.html ; 'The Truth About Love' review by Peter Bradshaw. Copyright © Peter Bradshaw. http://film.guardian.co.uk /Film_ Page/0,,2007893,00.html; 'Spiderman 3' review by Peter Bradshaw. Copyright © The Guardian http://film.guardian.co.uk/News_Story/Critic_Review/Guardian_Film_of_the_week/0,,2071555,00. html; 'Rocky Balboa' review by Peter Bradshaw. Copyright © Peter Bradshaw. http://film.guardian. co.uk/News_Story/Critic_Review/Guardian_review/0,,1993447,00.html; 'The Simpson's Movie' review by Peter Bradshaw. Copyright © The Guardian http://film.guardian.co.uk/News_Story/ Critic_Review/Guardian_review/0,,2133231,00.html; 'Casino Royale' review by Peter Bradshaw. Copyright © Peter Bradshaw http://film.guardian.co.uk/News_Story/Critic_Review/Guardian_ review/0,,1943415,00.html. Pages 128–129: 'How to talk to aliens' by David M. Ewait. Copyright © Forbes Magazine http://www.forbes.com/ 2005/10 /21/space- seti-aliens-comm05- cx_de_1024ewalt.html. Page 148: Morris dancing. Copyright © http://www.woodlandsjunior.kent. sch. uk/customs/maycustoms/index.html. Page 149: From 'Notes from a Small Island' by Bill Bryson. Copyright © Random House.

Photo credits

The publishers would like to thanks the following sources for permission to reproduce their copyright protected photographs:

Alamy pp 7 (l/Mary Evans Picture Library) (tr/ Pictorial Press Ltd) (trb/Allstar Picture Library), 92 tl–bl (Joe Sohn) (INTERFOTO / Fine Arts) (INTERFOTO / Fine Arts) (INTERFOTO / Fine Arts), 122 (tr/Pictorial Press Ltd) 122 & 123 (c/Photos 12) 123 (tl/Pictorial Press Ltd); Getty Images p 92 (bl/ Ethan Miller); Jupiterimages Corporation pp 7 (l) (c), 11(ct), 19 art gallery pamphlet (ct) (lt) (lb) (cb), 23 (r) (br) (bl), 26 (bg) (b), 47 (bc), 63 (tl), 74, 85 (t), 87 The Photographer's Apprentice (t) (c) (b) Art and poetic metaphor (l), 92 (tr) (cl), 98 (t) (b) (c), 99 (t) (c), 105 (t), 105 (c) (b), 117 (bg), 140 (t) (t), 147 (bc), 157 (cl) (c) (bl) (bc) (cl), 158 (tc) (bc) (bc), 194 (tl) (tc) (cl) (c) (cr) (bl) (bc), 203; Shutterstock pp 1 (t/ Dejan Novakov) (bl/Michael Svoboda) (br/Larry St. Pierre) (tcr/XYZ) (cl/Ivan Cholakov) (tr/Ronald Sumners) (bcr/Rui Alexandre Araujo), 4 (t/Gregor Kervina), 5 (t/Vallentin Vassileff) (b/MaxFX), 6 (l/ DeshaCAM) (l/Marten Czamanske) (c/Jose AS Reyes) (r/Sean Nel), 7 (r/iofoto), 9 (bl/BenC) (br/BenC), 11 (t/PhotoSky 4t com) (bg/CREATISTA) (l/Ian Wilson) (cb/Felix Mizioznikov) (r/J. Helgason) (bl/ wiredesign) (br/wiredesign), 12 (l/Heidi Brand) (c/Darren Baker) (r), 13 (Graeme Black), 14 (b/Beata Becla), 15 (r/Zastol`skiy Victor Leonidovich), 16 (Hakimata Photography), 17 (Maria Weidner), 18 (tl/ Dino) (tr/Hannah Gleghorn) (t/Michael Fuery) (c/anacarol) (c/SNEHIT) (b/Petronilo G. Dangoy Jr.) (b/ dragon_fang), 19 Dinosaur Pamphlet (tl/ Sakala) (tr/ Paunovic) Transport museum pamphlet (blr/ hfng) (bll/Steve Beer) (brt/Ralf Herschbach) (brl/Tonis Valing) (brc/Mark Yuill) (brr/David Burrows), 21 (t/Ilja Mašík) (ctl/Lisa Moon) (cbl/Simon-Krzic) (ctr/Drazen Vukelic) (cbr/Heather A. Craig) (bl/jarvis gray) (bl/Olga Besnard), 23 (br), 27 (tr/Joggie Botma) (l/afaizal) (br/Scott Leman), 29 (kristian sekulic), 31 (t/Paul B. Moore) (lc/PeterG) (lb/Amy Nichole Harris) (r/ArchMan), 32 (l/Linda Bucklin) (r/Kadak) 33 (t/Geoff Hardy) (bg/Andrejs Pidjass) (tl/Falk Kienas) (cl/fotoadamczyk) (bl/Ralf Juergen Kraft) (tr/ Sakala) (cr/Algol) (br/Mocart), 34 (Yuri Arcurs), 36 (Franck Boston), 37 (Ocean Image Photography), 38 (l/Andrea Danti) (r/Galushko Sergey), 38 & 39 (gudron), 43 (t/digitalife) (t/zimmytws) (t/Sean Gladwell) (cl/Perov Stanislav) (cr/Lisa F. Young) (b/apostol_8), 44 & 45 (Sean Gladwell), 46 (Antonio Jorge Nunes), 47 (Ofri Stern), 48 (t/Olga Rutko) (b/Benis Arapovic), 49 (AVAVA), 50 & 51 (t/ Radu Razvan) (c/Diego Cervo) (c/ 4525168) (b/Tony Sanchez-Espinosa), 53 (t/Dash) (bg/vgstudio) (c/t/Morgan Lane Photography) (ct/ajt) (c/Thomas M Perkins) (bl/Orange Line Media) (br/Elena Elisseeva) (bl/kristian sekulic) (br/franck camhi), 54 (l/ilker canikligil) (l/Brett Mulcahy) (c/Sandra Caldwell) (r/Radomir JIRSAK) (r/ostromec) (b/Petros Tsonis) (b/Filaphoto), 55 (l/Patrizia Tilly) (r/ Lepas), 56 (Andrey Armyagov), 57 (Zsolt Nyulaszi), 58 (Sean Nel), 59 (t/Sean Nel) (b/ZTS), 60 (Ingrid Balabanova), 61 (Ivan Josifovic), 63 (t/Galyna Andrushko) (br/Charles Shapiro) (cr//Raisa Kanareva) (bl/Eugene Buchko) (cl) (tr) (tr), 64 (l/Thierry Maffeis) (r/Serg Zastavkin), 65 (l/JeremyRichards) (r/ Regien Paassen), 66 (Dawn Hudson), 67 (Trevor Buttery), 68 (Vicente Barcelo Varona), 69 (zaharch), 70 (Mark Bonham), 71 (Ersler Dmitry), 73 (t/Markus Gann) (bl/gary718) (l/Alexey Stiop) (cb/Ant Clausen) (cb) (r/Luciano Mortula) (bl/Pedro Pinto) (c/José), 75 (t/Anna Kaminska) (r/Keo) (b/Elena Elisseeva), 76 (b/popo), 77 (l/Maksym Gorpenyuk) (r/Amy Nichole Harris), 78 (Alistair Scott), 79 (Happy Alex), 80 (t/Stephen Finn) (ct/Agb) (cb/ Brandus Dan Lucian) (b/Holger Mette) (r/rj lerich), 81 (t/Roman Sigaev) (ct/photooiasson) (cb/bhowe) (b/Xtuv Photography) (b/Petr Nad), 85 (tr/Yuran) (cr/Netfalls) (tl/Viktoriya) (br/Lauren Jade Goudie), 86 (r/Pavel K) (c/Stephen Aaron Rees) (l/ajt) (b/ Noam Armonn), 87 The Photographer's Apprentice (bg/argus) Art and poetic metaphor (r/Thomas M Perkins), 89 (Carina Lochner), 91 (tl/Galina Barskaya) (tr/llin Sergey) (bl/Caruntu) (br/Caruntu), 92 (tl/javarman) (cl)(bg/Ivana Rauski), 95 (t/Monkey Business Images) (lc/Ales Liska) (lc/paul Prescott) (rc/Dmitriy Shironosov) (r/Denis and Yulia Pogostins) (lb/Ragne Kabanova) (cb/Gladkova Svetlana) (rc/MaxFX), 96 (iofoto), 97 (iofoto), 99 (tc/Anne Kitzman) (bc//Copit) (b/Mariusz Szachowski), 102 (t/Mike McDonald) (b/David Arts), 103 (suravid), 105 (bg/sootra) (cl/Kristof Degreef) (cr/Semen Lixodeev) (bl/Saniphoto) (br/R. W. James Dennis), 106 (5078540), 109 (Dmitriy Shironosov), 112 (t/ Gabriel Openshaw) (b/Losevsky Pavel) (bg/Losevsky Pavel), 112 (t/Neale Cousland) (b/jamalludin) (bg/Racheal Grazias), 115 (t/egd) (bg/argus) (cl/Entertainment Press) (c/Entertainment Press) (cr/ Jose Gil) (c/Entertainment Press) (bl/Mayskyphoto) (bc/Graca Victoria) (c) (br/Entertainment Press), 116 (Jan Martin Will), 117 (b/sabri deniz kizil), 118 (XYZ), 119 (l/williammpark) (c/williammpark) (r/ Christos Georghiou), 120 (Stuart Elflett), 121 (b/Maisei Raman) (t/Tracy Whiteside), 122 (DCD), 123 (James Steidl), 127 (t/prism_68) (bg/dim stern) (cl/Bruce C. Murray) (bl/dim stern) (bc/Zsolt Nyulaszi) (br/Stephen Coburn) (cr/Steve Adamson), 128 (t/Israel Pabon) (c/MalibuBooks) (br/Andreas Meyer) (c/Paul B. Moore) (bc/Patrick Breig) (bl/3poD Animation) (bg/solos), 129 (bc/Shiva) (bl/Fernando Rodrigues) (t/Antonis Papantoniou) (bg/Sarah Harland), 130 (prism_68), 131 (t/Bobby Deal / RealDealPhoto) (c/Tom Hirtreiter) (b/Larry Westberg), 132 (c/Vladimir Melnik) (t/Eduard Titov) (bg/ Pres Panayotov) (b/Dmitriy Shironosov) (bg/Wallenrock) (bg/Vibrant Image Studio), 133 (t/Stephen Sweet) (c/Andresr) (b/Dino O), 135 (t/Viktor1) (c/Feng Yu) (b/Suzanne Tucker), 137 (t/Jiri Vaclavek) (bg/Pichugin Dmitry) (c/Paul Maguire) (c/Bob Ainsworth) (b/JJJ), 139 (bg/Sebastian Kaulitzki) (t/ Alex Staroseltsev), 140 (b/Erkki & Hanna), 142 (Gert Johannes Jacobus Very), 143 (l) (r/Trutta), 144 (Christophe Testi), 145 (Mark Atkins), 147 (t/Dallas Events Inc) (bg/Gordan Milic) (cr/Sergei Bachlakov) (cr/Sandra Cunningham) (br/Gordan Milic) (l/Steffen Foerster Photography), 148 (tl/Jose Gil) (tc/aga) (tc/vera bogaerts) (tr/Anyka) (c/ronfromyork) (b/ronfromyork), 149 (l/lbne Handel) (r/ Viacheslav Gorelik),150 (NEIL ROY JOHNSON), 151 (tl/Aga & Miko (arsat)) (cr/Supri Suharjoto) (cl/ Cristi Matei) (cr/Stanislav Popov) (b/Ismael Montero Verdu), 152 (vadim nardin), 153 (c/WizData, inc) (b/charles taylor), 154 (l/Alex Kotlov) (l/Dimitri) (ct/Olga Solovei) (cb/Yuri Arcurs) (r/Andresr), 155 (t/Hiroshi Ichikawa) (r/Brian Weed), 157 (t/Morgan Lane Photography) (bg/Racheal Grazias) (lb/ Orientaly), 158 (l/Christos Georghiou) (tc/Robert F. Balazik) (bl/solgas) (r//Triling Studio LTd.), 159 (c/Péter Gudella) (tr/Borislav Gnjidic) (bl/Soundsnaps) (br/Kiselev Andrey Valerevich) (bl/Lfoto), 161 (b/Michael Fuery) (cl/paparazzit) (cr/3185254), 162 (t/Ilja Mašík) (m/Pictoria) (b/manuela), 163 (t/ Cameramannz) (ct/Zastol`skiy Victor Leonidovich) (cb/Losevsky Pavel) (b/Losevsky Pavel), 164 (t/ Shmeliova Natalia) (b/Losevsky Pavel), 165 (t/Morgan Lane Photography) (b/Elena Elisseeva), 193 (tl/szefei) (tc/Elena Elisseeva) (tr/Cheryl Casey) (bl/Andresr) (bc/Waldemar Dabrowski) (br/Maciej Oleksy), 195 (tl/Wallenrock) (tc/dainis) (tr/Tomasz Trojanowski) (cl/Carme Balcells) (bc/Yuri Arcurs) (br/ prism_68), 196 (tl/Mikhail Nekrasov) (tr/Timo Kohlbacher) (clMaksym Gorpenyuk) (cr/David Peta) (bl/Andrey Grinyov) (br/ Amy Nichole Harris), 197 (tl/Monkey Business Images) (tc/Sascha Burkard) (tr/ Bruce Amos) (bl/ Christopher Scott) (bc/Postnikova Kristina) (bc/ Postnikova Kristina) (br/ TebNad), 199 (cl/Vladimir Melnik) (tl/Eduard Titov) (bl/Dmitriy Shironosov) (bg/Wallenrock) (cr/paul Prescott) (tr/Zoom Team), 200 (tl/Timothy Craig Lubcke) (tc/Joe Gough) (tr/Judy Worley) (lc/Brendan Howard) (c/Bonita R. Cheshier) (cr/Kim Worrell) (bl/Luis Louro) (bc/Sebastien Burel), 201 (tl/bhowe) (tr/Tomasz Markowski) (bl) (br/Melanie DeFazio); Provided by the authors pp 26 (t).

Cover photos by Erol Taskoparan.

Illustrations by Michael Perrin.

Every effort has been made to trace all the copyright holders but if any have been inadvertently overlooked, the publisher will be pleased to make the necessary arrangements at the first opportunity. Please contact the publisher directly.

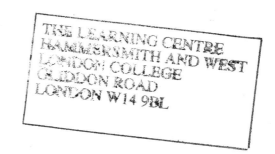